D1201390

To what extent, if at all, is language involved in thinking? Do we think in natural language? Or is language simply an input and output module for central cognition? Peter Carruthers here makes a fresh and provocative contribution to an ancient debate, and claims, in contrast to much recent work in philosophy and cognitive science, that the independence of thought from language is by no means clear-cut. He argues against the *communicative* conception of language put forward by thinkers such as Fodor and Pinker, and espouses the *cognitive* conception of language proposed by, for example, Wittgenstein and Dennett; but he refuses to take on board the Whorfian linguistic relativism so often seen as a natural corollary of this position. Instead he argues persuasively for the view that the cognitive conception of language can be deployed in combination with a modularist and nativist view of language and mind. The book defends a new theory of consciousness which is put to work in the final chapter to argue for the necessary involvement of natural language in human conscious thinking.

Language, thought and consciousness will be essential reading for all those interested in the nature and significance of natural language, whether they come from philosophy, psychology, or linguistics.

Language, thought and consciousness

Language, thought and consciousness

An essay in philosophical psychology

Peter Carruthers

Professor of Philosophy and Director, Hang Seng Centre for Cognitive Studies, University of Sheffield

CAMBRIDGE
UNIVERSITY PRESS

Published by the Press Syndicate of the University of Cambridge
The Pitt Building, Trumpington Street, Cambridge CB2 1RP
40 West 20th Street, New York, NY 10011-4211, USA
10 Stamford Road, Oakleigh, Melbourne 3166, Australia

First published 1996

Printed in Great Britain at the University Press, Cambridge

A catalogue record for this book is available from the British Library

Library of Congress cataloguing in publication data
Carruthers, Peter, 1952–
Language, thought and consciousness: an essay in philosophical
psychology / Peter Carruthers.
     p.   cm.
Includes bibliographical references and index.
ISBN 0 521 48158 9
1. Psycholinguistics. 2. Thought and thinking. 3. Philosophy
and cognitive science. 1. Title.
BF455.C275 1996
128'.2—dc20
                                             95–22782
                                                CIP

ISBN 0 521 48158 9 hardback

SE

for the staff at Endcliffe Children's Nursery
— and especially for Barbara and Penny —
whose love and wisdom made such a difference
in helping Daniel to enter the human world

Contents

Preface

This book began life as a series of lectures written for the third Sino-British summer school of philosophy, on philosophy of mind and cognitive science, held in Tianjin, China, between 27 July and 14 August 1992. I am grateful to the Chairman of the British Committee of the summer school, Dr Nicholas Bunnin, for extending me the invitation. This provided me with a valuable opportunity to develop, and commit to paper, my ideas on the interrelationships between language, thought, and consciousness. I am also grateful to our Chinese hosts from the Institute of Philosophy, Chinese Academy of Social Sciences, for making the experience such a pleasant and intellectually fruitful one. I hope that, partly as a result of my efforts, those who attended the summer school went away fired with enthusiasm for philosophical studies of the nature of human cognition.

Since then I have received help, of various sorts, from a great many people. I should especially like to thank my students at the University of Sheffield, both undergraduate and postgraduate, who have subjected my ideas to relentless and penetrating criticism over a number of years – mentioning particularly Chris Bowns, Gavin Boyce, Nick Creak, Duncan Cromarty, Kate Distin, Keith Frankish, Gillian Hind, Maxine Holdsworth, Tim Howe, James Kinch, Ewan McEachran, Stuart McWilliam, Simon Tomlinson, Mark Vale, and Clive Witcomb.

Thanks also go to the following individuals for their advice and/or comments on earlier drafts: David Archard, Judith Ayling, Alan Baddeley, David Bell, George Botterill, Jill Boucher, Jeremy Butterfield, David Chalmers, Jim Edwards, Rosanna Keefe, Bob Kirk, Stephen Laurence, Susan Levi, Bill Lyons, Stephen Makin, Adam Morton, Shaun Nichols, David Owens, Josef Perner, Tom Pink, Gabriel Segal, Barry Smith, Neil Smith, Peter Smith, Bob Stern, Julia Tanney, Ianthi-Maria Tsimpli, and Rosemary Varley.

I also benefited from the comments of an anonymous referee for Cambridge University Press, and from discussions with colleagues and students at seminars in Manchester, MIT, Oxford, Sheffield, and Cambridge.

What is philosophy? The main character and direction of my project are described in some detail in the Introduction and the opening chapter, and so do not need to be reiterated here. But I should like to say something very briefly about the way in which I understand the nature and methods of philosophy. Besides having some intrinsic interest, these remarks may help to orient the reader with respect to the arguments that follow.

It is often commented that there are two very different species of philosophy widely practised within the English-speaking world. (I ignore the small minority who attempt to do philosophy in Continental mode – they will not, in any case, be reading this.) One of these conceives of philosophy as broadly continuous with science, takes the goal of philosophy to be *truth* about a wide variety of subject-matters, and is prepared to make use of a posteriori inferences to the best explanation in pursuit of this goal. In contrast, the other species of philosophy sees itself as sharply distinct from science, takes the distinctive goal of philosophy to be *conceptual* truth, and insists that the methods of philosophy must be a priori conceptual analysis or argument. Let us label these the *substantive* and the *analytical* conceptions of philosophy respectively.

Substantive philosophy is more common in America, and appears to be heavily indebted to Quine, particularly his (1951) denial of the analytic/synthetic distinction. Analytical philosophy is more common in Britain, stemming partly from the influence of Wittgenstein (1953), who believed that the sole business of the philosopher is to gain a clear view of the inter-relations amongst our concepts. It might then seem that the kernel of the disagreement between the two conceptions concerns the legitimacy of a category of analytic truth. For substantive philosophy, in denying that there is any such category, must deny that there is any sharp distinction between philosophical and scientific truth. Whereas analytical philosophy, in accepting that category, can insist that the class of analytic truths constitutes the proper domain of the philosopher as opposed to the scientist. This way of viewing the disagreement between the two conceptions is mistaken, however, as I shall now try to explain.

The crucial point is that there is nothing to force a philosopher who accepts the existence of concepts and conceptual connections to believe that philosophy should be concerned *only* with such connections. Someone can accept the category of analytic truth, and so find a place for a priori conceptual analysis and discovery within philosophy, while maintaining that philosophers can also be concerned with substantive issues of fact, and can legitimately employ a posteriori inferences to the best explanation in attempting to resolve those issues. Indeed, I hold just such a combination of views myself. As will be seen in Chapter 4, I believe that the reasons for rejecting the existence of concepts and conceptual truths are not very powerful. But I also believe that philosophy can, and should, be substantive.

I think we can distinguish between two distinct strands within analytical philosophy, corresponding to two distinct sources of motivation. For what really pushes people towards a narrowly analytical conception of philosophy, I believe, is not merely the acceptance of the analytic/synthetic distinction, but either, or both, of the following: a certain kind of paranoia about the extent of the domain of philosophy, and a foundationalist position in the theory of knowledge. Let me take each of these sources of motivation in turn.

In the beginning, of course, philosophy was simply the pursuit of knowledge, and no distinction was drawn between philosophy and science. But with the passage of time the various special sciences – physics, chemistry, biology, and, now, psychology – grew up and became independent of their parent, leaving the subject-matter remaining to philosophy correspondingly diminished. This naturally gave rise to an anxiety, in the minds of some, that the domain of philosophy might one day shrink to zero, as science progressed still further. And it then seemed imperative to define a subject-matter proper to philosophy that would be forever safe from the encroachment of science. This was to be the domain of analytic, as opposed to synthetic, truth.

But in fact this anxiety was misplaced. For it should have been plain that there will always be substantive questions for philosophers to answer that are not scientific ones. This must be so, if only because those questions are *about* science, such as whether science is successful in obtaining real knowledge for us. Moreover there are, arguably, many domains of belief which are not, and do not purport to be, scientific, but which nevertheless give rise to philosophical problems. These include ethics, aesthetics, common-sense physics, and many others. One such body of beliefs, in my view, is that of common-sense beliefs about the mind (so called *folk-psychology*), as will be seen in the chapters that follow. And it should always have been obvious that the question of the relationship between these beliefs and those of science cannot itself be a scientific one.

The second reason why many have been tempted by a narrowly analytical conception of philosophy relates not so much to the latter's distinctive subject-matter, as to its methods. The line of thought goes something like this. We begin with the idea that the business of philosophy is to obtain for us genuine knowledge (or perhaps, on some conceptions of knowledge, to obtain the knowledge that we have such knowledge; see my 1992a, ch. 5). We then add to this a foundationalist conception of the architecture of knowledge, according to which all knowledge must be grounded in beliefs that are certainly true by means of principles of inference that are also certain. And then it follows that only *deduction* can be legitimate in primary philosophy. If other methods of inference – including inference to the best explanation – are to be employed at all, then they must first be vindicated by means of deductive argument from premises that are certainly true.

But the mistake in this argument, in my view, lies in the foundationalist premise. Rather, the best account of the architecture of our knowledge is *coherentist*. According to this view, a belief comes to be justified by forming part of an explanatory network of such beliefs, which collectively provide the simplest, most coherent, explanation for the course of our experience. From such a perspective, inference to the best explanation can play just as fundamental a role in the construction of appropriately coherent sets of belief as does deduction. There is then no reason why philosophers should not, at least tentatively, avail themselves of such modes of inference in advance of attempting to vindicate them. Indeed, there is some reason to think, contrariwise, that even deduction must rely, tacitly, upon an inference to the best explanation – if only on an inference from the fact that an argument *seems* valid to us to the conclusion that it *is* so – in which case there is *no* philosophy which can be done without employing explanatory inferences.

In the chapters that follow, then, I shall be concerned with questions that are substantive as well as with those that are more narrowly analytic. Indeed, many of these questions might equally be raised, from a somewhat different perspective, by scientific psychologists. There is a good reason for this. For it is particularly common in periods of scientific revolution (in Kuhn's sense; see his 1962) that scientists should need to consider the sorts of larger 'framework' questions distinctively raised by philosophers. (For example, Einstein engaged in extensive reflection on the nature of space and time, in the period when he was developing the theory of relativity, which might have seemed familiar to Locke, or to Leibniz, or to Kant.)

Arguably, psychology is in just such a state of revolution and self-analysis. For the basic nature and direction of psychological inquiry are currently topics of intense psychological debate; and one of the strands in this debate is – or should be – the role to be accorded to natural language in our best model of human cognition. Moreover, since the resolution of this latter issue is currently empirically undetermined (as I shall argue in Chapter 2), it is crucial to stake out and explore the implications of the different frameworks within which more detailed investigations may take place. That is what I have tried to do in this book, in connection with the presently unfashionable hypothesis that much of human thought is conducted in natural language. So my hope is that the ideas defended here will be of interest to psychologists and other cognitive scientists, just as much as to philosophers. But this must be for them to judge.

Introduction

The topic of this book is the subject of an ancient debate – whether thought is independent of language, or whether our thinking, on the contrary, necessarily requires or involves natural language. I shall be arguing for a version of the latter thesis. My view is that much of human conscious thinking is, necessarily (given the way in which human cognition is structured), conducted in the medium of natural-language sentences.

I do not make any claim to demonstrate the truth of this view beyond all reasonable doubt. For the arguments that I provide in its support are broadly empirical ones, involving inferences to the best explanation of a range of phenomena. They are therefore vulnerable to counter-attack from those who can provide further recalcitrant data, and may reasonably be rejected by anyone who can provide a better explanation of the phenomena in question. I do hope to show, however, that the case for the independence of thought from language is by no means as clear-cut as many philosophers and cognitive scientists have assumed. And I therefore hope to provide encouragement for further work to be conducted in the alternative, language-involving, paradigm. Roughly speaking, the overall message of the book has the form, 'Hey! Let's have a look over here! There's a view which hasn't been taken as seriously as it should be lately.'

One question at issue in this debate is our understanding of the nature and function of natural language. If thought is independent of such language, then language itself becomes only a medium for the communication of thoughts. I shall refer to this theory of the role and significance of natural language as *the communicative conception* of language. According to the communicative conception, the function and purpose of natural language is to facilitate communication and *not* (except indirectly, by enabling the acquisition of new beliefs) to facilitate thinking. Language thus functions wholly in the public – interpersonal – domain, rather than in the domain of individual cognition. Language will still have to be represented and processed within the cognition of each individual, of course. But such processing will exist only to support the public functions of language – namely, the exchange of information and the interpersonal co-ordination of action – rather than having a direct executive role in the thinking and practical reasoning of the individual subject.

The communicative conception of language has been widely endorsed in the history of philosophy, by figures such as John Locke (1690), Bertrand Russell (1921), Paul Grice (1957 and 1969) and David Lewis (1969). It is also the standard model for those now working in cognitive science, who view language as an isolable, and largely isolated, *module* of the mind, which is both innately structured and specialised for the interpretation and construction of natural-language sentences. See, for example, Jerry Fodor (1978, 1983, and 1987), Noam Chomsky (1988), Willem Levelt (1989), and Steven Pinker (1994).

If, on the other hand, natural language is constitutively involved in our conscious thinkings (as I shall argue), then language is itself the primary medium of such thought, and much such thinking is essentially linguistic. I shall refer to this as *the cognitive conception* of language, since it accords a central place to natural language within our cognition. On this account we often think *in* language, and the trains of reasoning which lead up to many of our decisions and actions will consist in sequences of natural-language sentences. Language thus has an *intra*-personal cognitive function, as well as having its obvious interpersonal uses. Here the picture of communication through language is quite different. When a speaker utters a sentence, on this view, their utterance expresses a thought by *constituting* it, not by encoding or signalling it. A hearer who is a competent user of the same language will then understand that utterance in virtue of it constitutively expressing, for them, the very same (or a sufficiently similar) thought.

The cognitive conception of language has been endorsed by such disparate figures as Ludwig Wittgenstein (1921 and 1953), Lev Vygotsky (1934), Benjamin Lee Whorf (1956), Daniel Dennett (1991), and also sometimes Noam Chomsky (1976 – at least, that is how I interpret Chapter 2 of that work; but Chomsky has since disavowed any such view in personal correspondence). Most often (but not in Chomsky's case) it has been associated with a radical empiricism about the mind, according to which many human concepts and ways of thinking, and indeed much of the very structure of the human mind itself, are acquired by the young child from adults when the child learns its native language – these concepts and structures differing widely depending upon the structure and conceptual resources of the natural language in question. This mind-structuring and social-relativist view of language is still dominant in the social sciences, following the writings early in this century of the amateur linguist Benjamin Lee Whorf (many of whose papers have been collected together in his 1956) – indeed, Steven Pinker (1994) refers to it disparagingly as 'the Standard Social Science Model'.

My own diagnosis of what has happened in the cognitive sciences in recent decades is this. Researchers have become increasingly convinced, by neuropsychological and other evidence, that the mind is more or less modular in structure, built up out of isolable, and largely isolated, components (see Fodor, 1983, Sachs, 1985, and Shallice, 1988). They have also become convinced that the structure and contents of the mind are substantially innate (see Fodor, 1981 and 1983, and Carey, 1985), and that *language* is one such isolable and largely innate module (see Fodor, 1983, and Chomsky, 1988). There has then been, amongst cognitive scientists, a near-universal reaction against the cognitive conception of language, by running it together with the Whorfian hypothesis. Most researchers have assumed, without argument, that if they were to accept any form of cognitive conception of language, then that would commit them to Whorfian linguistic relativism and radical empiricism, and would hence be inconsistent with their well-founded beliefs in modularity and nativism (see Pinker, 1994).

It is important to see, however, that someone endorsing the cognitive conception of language does not *have* to regard language and the mind as cultural constructs, either socially determined or culturally relative. In fact, the cognitive conception of language can equally well be deployed along with a modularist and nativist view of language and mind – or so, at least, it will be one of the main burdens of this book to argue. A large part of my task is to show that there is a position intermediate between the communicative conception of language on the one hand, and Whorfian relativism (the Standard Social Science Model) on the other, which deserves the attention of philosophers and cognitive scientists alike. I hope to show that there is a real possibility here which should be investigated further – one which is nativist as opposed to empiricist about language and much of the structure of the mind, but which nevertheless holds that language is constitutively employed in many of our conscious thoughts. More than this, of course, I hope to convince the reader that this combination of views is not only possible, but plausible.

In fact the issues before us are ones which have profound methodological implications for both philosophy and psychology, as we shall see in more detail in section 1.2 below. If thought is independent of language, then the philosophy of language has no right to claim the sort of foundational position within philosophy as a whole which it has been accorded through much of the twentieth century. On the contrary, it should be the philosophy of mind – more narrowly, the philosophy of thought – which is more basic. It will also follow that the study of the cognitive mechanisms involved in the acquisition and use of natural language should be accorded no more central position within psychology than the study of any other mental faculty, such as vision or memory. If thought requires or involves natural language, on the other hand, then many philosophical questions will be expressed most appropriately in linguistic mode, and it will follow that psychologists engaged in the study of natural language are examining one of the basic mechanisms of human cognition. It should hardly need saying, therefore, that our main question is an important one.

Much of this book has the form of an extended debate with Jerry Fodor. While I share many of my premises with him, as will be seen from the latter half of Chapter 1, I disagree in my conclusions, particularly in relation to the role of natural language in cognition. Fodor's view is that language is but an input and output module to central cognition (though perhaps drawing on a centrally stored lexicon and database), not implicated in the central processes of thinking and reasoning themselves (see his 1978 and 1983). These latter processes are held to involve sentence-like structures, to be sure, but these are not sentences of any natural language, but rather of an innate, universal, symbolic system, which Fodor calls 'Mentalese'. I shall begin to discuss Fodor's arguments for this view in the later sections of Chapter 2. Their further elaboration and critique is then distributed over many of the remaining chapters. I shall be arguing that the case for the communicative conception of language is not proven, and that one can share Fodor's nativism while endorsing the cognitive conception instead.

Plainly, the issues before us are ones that must straddle both the philosophy of mind and the philosophy of language. For one part of what is in question is the best account that can be given of the nature of thought, another being the best account that can be given of the character and semantics of natural language. If some version of the communicative conception of language is correct, then it must be possible to provide a semantics for the expressions of natural language in terms of prior notions of thought and intention. It must also be possible to provide a semantics for thought, in turn, without reintroducing natural language into the story. These possibilities will be considered in Chapter 3, where difficulties will be discovered for each.

If, on the other hand, any version of the cognitive conception of language is to be defensible, then it must either be possible to provide a semantics for language without presupposing thought, or it must at least be possible to provide a semantics for language which would leave language and thought on a par, without either being prior to the other. This will be investigated in Chapter 4, where two distinct options will be canvassed. I should emphasise that my main aim in these two chapters is not to establish any definite conclusions, but only to argue that options are left open. Their purpose is to show that no conclusive case has yet been made out, in the domain of semantic theory, for the independence of thought from language.

Almost the whole of the second half of this book is concerned, in one way or another, with the nature of consciousness. This may seem surprising in a book about the relations between language and thought, and requires some elucidation. In fact one of the main messages of the book is that questions to do with the interrelations of language and thought are, somewhat unexpectedly, closely interwoven with questions about the nature of human consciousness. Part of the explanation of the connection is that, for reasons which will begin to emerge in Chapter 1, my thesis is especially that it is our *conscious* thoughts which involve natural language, rather than that they all do. If any such thesis is to be made out, then enough has to be said about the nature of consciousness to make it seem plausible. But in the current climate, in order to say enough about consciousness one has to say quite a lot.

Chapters 5 through 7 are devoted to arguing for a particular version of higher-order thought theory, which I call 'the reflexive thinking theory' of consciousness, contrasting it with relevant alternatives. (Higher-order thoughts are thoughts which are *about* other mental states. For example, the thought *that I have just been thinking about Avignon* is a higher-order one.) This theory is then put to work, in Chapter 8, in the form of a proposed architecture for human cognition which links together conscious thinking with the deployment of natural-language sentences. The reflexive thinking theory also has, as one of its more surprising and controversial consequences, that the thoughts and experiences of most non-human animals and (probably) of human infants are non-conscious ones. But this is no mere accidental spin-off from the theory. On the contrary, it is a crucial component of the argument against Fodor, as will begin to emerge in the opening chapter.

Another reason for the extensive discussion of consciousness in the latter half of this book, is that the case for saying that conscious thinking involves natural language is partly grounded in introspection, as I explain in the early sections of Chapter 2. This introspective data will need to be explained, or explained away, by anyone who wishes to insist that all thinking takes place in Mentalese. To assess the prospects for providing such an explanation, some plausible candidates for the nature of introspective knowledge have to be laid on the table, as I do in Chapters 6 and 7. In fact, I shall go on to argue in Chapter 8 that it is a deep presupposition of our belief that we do sometimes entertain (propositional, as opposed to imagistic) thoughts which are conscious, that natural-language sentences are constitutive of those thoughts.

The minimal (because a-modal) thesis that I want to defend in Chapter 8, relates only to some *token* thoughts of ours (that is, to thoughts as particular occurrences, or mental events, such as me thinking to myself right now that grass is green), rather than to any of our thoughts considered as *types* (such as the thought *that grass is green*, which may be entertained on many different occasions, and by different people). The thesis is, that many human thought-tokens (specifically, those conscious human thoughts which are, in fact, tokened in the form of inner speech) are constituted by natural-language sentences. So there are at least some token thoughts of ours (specifically, conscious verbalised thoughts) which do, as a matter of fact, constitutively involve natural language. This is already enough to vindicate the cognitive conception of language, and to falsify the communicative conception.

Building on this, the stronger thesis to be defended in Chapter 8 is that there are some thought-types of ours (specifically, those thought-types tokens of which are, as a matter of fact, constituted by language in inner speech) which *can only be* tokened consciously, in us, in language. (This is the thesis I shall call 'NN_w' – a weak form of natural necessity thesis, establishing a modal version of the cognitive conception of language.) According to this thesis, many thought-types are such that their conscious tokenings in us are *necessarily* language-involving, even if thoughts of those types can also be tokened *non*-consciously *without* language. So human beings who lacked a language would be incapable of thinking thoughts of these types *consciously*.

The strongest thesis I will defend in Chapter 8, is then that many (though perhaps not all) of these conscious verbalised thoughts belong to types which *can only be entertained at all*, by us, (whether consciously or non-consciously) in virtue of their expression in language. So there are some thought-types which, for us at least, constitutively involve natural language. (This is the thesis I shall call 'NN_s' – a strong form of natural necessity thesis, establishing a version of the cognitive conception of language which is modal in relation to certain thought-types.) On this view, then, there would be many thought-types which could not be entertained *at all* by human beings who lacked a natural language.

In fact this last thesis will be left crucially vague, since I shall make little attempt to specify exactly which kinds of thought-types constitutively involve natural language, and which do not. Such vagueness is unavoidable, however, since I have neither the space nor the expertise to review and gather the vast extent of empirical data necessary to make it more precise. This would include a range of developmental evidence relating to the acquisition of language and the increasing sophistication of children's thought, including the evidence from a variety of language-related developmental disorders such as Williams' syndrome and autism. It would also include the evidence of thought of various kinds in the case of people who are profoundly deaf, but have not yet learned to sign properly. And, of course, there is also the evidence from cases of global aphasia following brain damage, relating to the kinds of thought which may still be possible for those who have lost their capacity to use and to understand language.

Note that a vague conclusion can still be an interesting one, however. If I tell you that the British prime minister will resign sometime next year, for example, then this is certainly vague in relation to the precise date on which a letter of resignation will be handed to the monarch; but it may still be well worth knowing. And often a vaguely formulated item of knowledge can be a crucial step in the search for a precise solution to a problem. It would be highly relevant to the police engaged in a murder-hunt to learn that the murderer resides in a particular town, or a particular street, for example. Similarly, then, in respect of thesis NN_s: if I am right, then cognitive scientists should now begin investigating a particular – vaguely circumscribed – region of logical space, hitherto largely ignored.

Although I am constitutionally inclined towards megalomania, I have tried to resist the impulse to announce that I have solved all of the outstanding problems of cognitive science in the space of just one book. In fact, all that I can really claim to have done is to have provided some non-conclusive reasons for taking seriously a particular, vaguely formulated, view of the relations that obtain between natural language, human thought, and human consciousness. But that, surely, is enough.

1 The geography of the issues

In this first chapter I shall outline the nature of my project, discuss its potential significance for both philosophy and psychology, and set out my background assumptions. Some of these assumptions I shall briefly defend, others I shall merely explain.

1.1 Conceptual versus natural modality

As philosophers so often do, I shall begin by making some distinctions. These are necessary to distinguish the project of this book from others which might travel under the same name. For if it is claimed that there can, or cannot, be thought without language, then much may depend upon the way in which the terms 'can' and 'cannot' are interpreted here. In fact, three distinct versions of independence and involvement thesis can be distinguished, corresponding to the distinctions philosophers have drawn between three different kinds of modality.

In the first place, a statement can be *conceptually* necessary, which means that it is true in virtue only of relations amongst the concepts involved in it. An example might be, 'Anything red is coloured.' A statement is conceptually necessary if its content cannot be conceived to be false without altering that content – it is a truth about all possible worlds in virtue only of what we *mean* by the terms involved. Taken in this conceptual sense, then, the claim that thought necessarily involves language can be true only if the *concept* of language is implicated in the *concept* of thought.

In the second place, as Saul Kripke (1980) has taught us, there are truths which are necessary, in the sense of being true about all possible worlds, without depending only on relations amongst our concepts. Such truths, which are logically necessary without being conceptually so, are said to be *metaphysically* necessary. The primary examples are true identity statements, such as, 'Ruth Rendell (the detective writer) is Barbara Vine (the author of psychological thrillers)', or true statements of the constitution of a natural kind, such as, 'Water is H_2O.' These express truths about all possible worlds, since there is no world in which Ruth Rendell fails to be Barbara Vine, or in which Rendell dies but Vine does not, or in which water – that very substance which we presently drink – has some other chemical constitution, and so on. But these necessary truths cannot be discovered to be so by thought alone, nor do they merely reflect connections amongst our concepts. Rather, they are necessary in virtue of the intentions with which we use the terms involved (for example, to refer to the real internal constitution of the substance in our rivers and oceans *whatever it may be*) together with the facts (for example, that water is composed of H_2O).

Finally, a statement can be *naturally* necessary, which means that it expresses a condition holding in virtue of the laws of nature. An example might be, 'All massive bodies attract.' This statement expresses a truth about all possible worlds in which the laws of nature obtain as they are. It is important to see, however, that true statements of natural modality are often premised upon some of the presumed actual initial conditions of the relevant law. That is to say, such statements are often confined to worlds in which the contingent initial conditions of some restricted sub-set of the laws of nature obtain.

Consider, for example, the statement, 'Bodies on earth must fall with an acceleration of 32 feet per second per second.' This restricted version of the law of gravity only obtains in virtue of the given mass of the earth, which could have been other than it is. The statement is a genuinely modal one for all that. It tells us what *has* to be the case given that the laws of nature are as they are, *and also* given some contingent fact embraced by those laws, in virtue of the obtaining of which a particular stable sub-system of laws holds. The claim to be defended in Chapter 8 – namely, that human conscious thinking necessarily involves natural language – is similar, in that it only obtains in virtue of the given architecture of human cognition, which could have evolved in ways other than it did.

In accordance with these distinctions, either one of thought or language might be said to be *conceptually*, or *metaphysically*, or *naturally* independent of, or involved in, the other. Most of the discussions amongst philosophers have related to an alleged conceptual independence or involvement. Thus, defenders of the independence of thought from language have generally claimed that it is possible to conceive of a creature with thoughts but no language, and that it is possible to state the identity conditions for thoughts without mention of language. Defenders of the involvement of language in thought have generally claimed, contrariwise, that it is inconceivable that languageless creatures should entertain thoughts, in the fullest sense, and that the very notion of 'thought' needs to be explained by recourse to concepts embedded in discourse about natural language.

In contrast with this tradition, I shall concentrate on the questions of *natural* independence and involvement in this book, for reasons which I shall shortly explain. I propose to argue, in fact, that it is naturally necessary that much of human conscious thinking should involve natural language. While this conclusion is weaker than more standard conceptual involvement claims, it has much the same significance for philosophical and psychological practice, as I shall argue in the next section. Then, in sections 1.3, 1.4, and 1.5, I shall argue against any conceptually necessary involvement of language in thought.

If we suppose, as I shall argue briefly in section 1.3, that some thoughts are actually independent of language (specifically, the thoughts of animals and infants), then it cannot be necessary (either conceptually, metaphysically, or naturally) that *all* thought should require or involve natural language. But it will remain open that *some* thoughts should necessarily involve such language. And if, as I shall argue briefly in section 1.4, all thoughts are conceptually independent of language, then it cannot be *conceptually* necessary that *any* thought should involve natural language. But it would remain open that it may be either naturally or metaphysically necessary that some thoughts should involve such language.

In particular, it would remain open that it may be naturally or metaphysically necessary that *conscious* thoughts should require or involve public language. So if we were prepared to endorse an account of consciousness which entails that neither the thoughts of animals nor infants are conscious ones, then we would be free to claim that, of natural or metaphysical necessity, all conscious thinking involves language – or, perhaps weaker again, that all *human* conscious thought involves language.

A thesis of natural necessity of just this kind would be established if it could be shown that the status of a thought as conscious somehow requires that the thinker be a language-user (this would give us a requirement-thesis), or if it could be shown that the given underlying architecture of human consciousness somehow requires thoughts to be linguistically expressed if they are to be conscious (this would give us an involvement-thesis; see section 1.3 below for more on the distinction between *requirement* and *involvement*). I shall set out arguments for the latter position in the final chapter of this book. Here I shall briefly discuss what more might be needed to establish a thesis of metaphysical necessity. Then in the next section I shall address the question of the significance of either form of thesis, if it could be established.

Metaphysical necessities, in general, result from true identities expressed by terms which are rigid designators – that is, terms which designate the same items in all possible worlds in which they exist. Thus,

'Ruth Rendell is Barbara Vine' is metaphysically necessary because we use the names 'Ruth Rendell' and 'Barbara Vine' with the intention of referring to the person who is their actual referent in all hypothetical and counterfactual circumstances. Then, since Ruth Rendell *is*, actually, Barbara Vine, any world which lacks Ruth Rendell must also lack Barbara Vine, and vice versa. Similarly, 'Water is H_2O' is metaphysically necessary because (and only because) we use the term 'water' with the intention of designating a particular natural kind – that is, because we use it with the intention of referring, rigidly, to the actual internal constitution of most of the stuff in our lakes and rivers, whatever it may turn out to be.

It follows, then, that if we are to show that it is metaphysically necessary that human conscious thinking involves language, it is not enough merely to claim that linguistic thinking is what conscious thinking *is*, for us, given the way in which our cognition is structured. We can only turn this conclusion into a statement of metaphysical necessity if we can show that we use the phrase 'human conscious thinking' with the intention of designating a natural kind – that is, with the intention of designating the inner functional structure of our conscious thinking, whatever it may turn out to be. For then (and only then) the statement that human conscious thinking involves natural language may turn out to be precisely analogous to the statement that water is H_2O – both may be metaphysically necessary in virtue of the inner structure of the kinds in question.

In fact, I doubt very much whether we *do* use the phrase 'human conscious thinking' with the intention of designating a natural kind. Although I am a realist about the mental, and hence believe that a good many of our folk-psychological words and phrases succeed in designating what are, in fact, natural kinds, I do not think they are used with that intention. Folk-psychology is not *intended as* scientific theory, even though it may actually be one, or forms an adequate basis for one. For it is not constructed by means of an inference to the best explanation, as scientific theories characteristically are, but is rather, in my view, innate, forming one of the given, and basic, components of human cognition. (See my 1992a, ch. 8, and section 1.7 below.)

All the same, there is nothing to stop someone turning the phrase 'human conscious thinking' into a natural kind term by fiat, simply by deciding to govern their use of the phrase by an intention to designate the real internal structure of the activity, whatever it may turn out to be. And so, for them, if it is naturally necessary that human conscious thinking involves language then it will also be metaphysically necessary. In general, wherever there are natural necessities to be found, there are also potential metaphysical necessities waiting in the wings. But it remains to be seen whether anything of any deep significance turns on this. Although claims of metaphysical necessity are stronger than claims of natural necessity, it may be that nothing much of extra philosophical or psychological significance will follow from the claim that it is metaphysically necessary that conscious thought involves language, which does not already follow from the parallel claim of natural necessity. To these questions I shall now turn.

1.2 Implications for philosophy and psychology

Supposing it were to turn out to be naturally necessary (and only naturally necessary) that human conscious thought involves language, what would be the significance of this fact? Part of the answer is immediately apparent: it would have profound effects on both theory and practice within contemporary cognitive psychology. For it is not just philosophers who are interested in the nature of the connections between language and thought. Indeed, one can distinguish between two broad research-programmes that are current within scientific psychology. One of these, whose most articulate spokesman is Jerry Fodor, regards language as nothing more than an input- and output-module for central cognition (albeit one that is of vital importance, and one which may have access to a centrally stored lexicon and database). On this view, the scientific study of language, like the study of vision, is an investigation into the structure of one of the peripheral modules of the mind, not an investigation into the nature of thought itself.

The alternative programme (much underrepresented in the cognitive sciences at present, but drawing its inspiration from some of the writings of Noam Chomsky) regards language as crucially implicated in the central functions of the mind, constituting one of the basic media in which our thoughts are formulated and expressed. On this view, it would be a gross exaggeration, but not radically mistaken, to say that the study of language *is* the study of the mind. Admittedly, Chomsky, too, believes that there is a distinct and innately structured language module, but the notion of modularity involved here is quite different from Fodor's (see Segal, 1996). Chomsky believes that there is an organised and largely innate body of knowledge which underlies our linguistic competence. But he has also sometimes subscribed to what I have called the cognitive conception of language (see his 1976 ch. 2), believing that natural language is used for thinking as well as for communicating. It is plain that the thesis of natural necessity sketched above would, if established, amount to a decisive vindication of this Chomskian position.

It may be granted as obvious that a thesis of natural necessity would have significance for empirical science. But what of its philosophical importance? Is there anything to be gained for philosophy if such a thesis could be established? These questions embody an assumption which I do not share – namely, that philosophy is an exclusively a priori and conceptual discipline. As I indicated in the Preface, I believe that philosophy can, and should, deal with issues which are substantive, and that there are many questions on which philosophers and scientists can seek a common understanding, albeit approached from different starting-points using somewhat different methodologies.

So I think that the question whether our cognition is so structured that we have to use language as our vehicle for thought is one which is of philosophical interest in its own right. Moreover, it is in fact not even clear that a thesis of natural necessity cannot have significance for more narrowly conceptual aspects of philosophy – indeed, perhaps much the same significance that a claim of the conceptually necessary involvement of language in thought would have had. But in order to see this we need to set out, first, what that significance was supposed to have been.

As I have already indicated (and will argue briefly in sections 1.4 and 1.5 below), I doubt whether it is conceptually necessary that thought should involve language. But if it *had* been so, then this would have justified the sort of foundational position which has been accorded to the philosophy of language throughout much of the twentieth century – the so-called 'linguistic turn' taken by analytic philosophy. On this view, exemplified, in particular, in the work of Michael Dummett (see his 1973 and 1991), many traditional philosophical questions concerning the nature of thought, the extent of knowledge, or the nature of truth and reality are best recast as semantic questions in the philosophy of language, and analyses of problematic concepts can proceed through an account of their linguistic expression.

Now, there are important distinctions which need to be drawn here. It is surely correct that if it had been conceptually necessary that all thought (or all conscious and sophisticated thought) involved language, then an account of the concept of thought itself could have focused on its linguistic expression, and similarly accounts of the component concepts involved in our thoughts, too, could have proceeded via an analysis of their mode of public expression. But what of the more radical claim, made by Dummett, that the philosophy of language would also have been shown to be prior to metaphysics and the theory of knowledge? This conclusion would have required a good deal of additional argument – and it is doubtful, in fact, whether it was ever really warranted. On the contrary, it is arguable that Dummett's case for his preferred style of anti-realist semantics for natural language itself makes epistemological assumptions (see Grayling, 1992). Moreover, most of those who have taken the 'linguistic turn' have not, in fact, endorsed anything so strong.

So the points to concentrate on, for our purposes, are the analysis of the notion of thought, and the analysis of particular philosophically problematic concepts.

Once it is granted that thought is conceptually independent of language, then it can no longer be guaranteed that an analysis of the concept of thought via an analysis of language will prove fruitful. Rather, that analysis will probably have to be direct, in terms that do not mention or presuppose natural language – for example, in terms of distinctive functional role (see Block, 1986, and section 4.7 below), or in terms of canonical acceptance conditions (see Peacocke, 1986 and 1992, and section 4.8 below). This conclusion would remain unaffected, moreover, by any demonstration that language is, of natural necessity, implicated in our thoughts. But the same is *not* the case with respect to the analysis of *particular* concepts.

Consider, for example, the class of moral concepts, such as *virtue, duty, right*, and so on. If thought is conceptually independent of language then it is conceivable that someone should entertain such thoughts without language, and the analysis of moral concepts cannot *require* mention of language. But if it is naturally necessary that our conscious thoughts should involve language, then it must be *legitimate* for us to analyse such thought-contents by analysing their characteristic mode of linguistic expression. For on this view there can be no significant difference between public and private thinking. Whether we think privately, to ourselves, or publicly, using spoken or written sentences, our thoughts will equally consist of deployments of natural-language words and sentences (perhaps supplemented by images) in accordance with certain rules or intentions.

Of course, we should have to be careful, in analysing public speech or writing, to distinguish between those properties of an utterance that it possesses in virtue of expressing a particular thought, and those properties that it might have in virtue of being an act, or potential act, of communication – such as the various conversational implicatures of the utterance. For it is only the former which would be relevant to the analysis of the particular concepts involved. But this is a distinction which we would need to have been careful to respect in any case, even had we been convinced of the conceptual necessity of language being involved in thought. So nothing need have changed in this respect.

It is plain, moreover, that the conclusions just defended would remain exactly the same, even if it were to turn out to be metaphysically, and not just naturally, necessary that language should be involved in thought. First, it is obvious that a thesis of metaphysical necessity would still not be strong enough to warrant the claim that the analysis of the concept of thought, itself, should proceed via analysis of language. Only a thesis of conceptual necessity would provide a sufficient guarantee of this. But second, a thesis of natural necessity is surely sufficient, by itself, to warrant the claim that the analysis of particular problematic concepts can legitimately proceed via an analysis of their linguistic expression. Since nothing more of philosophical significance would be entailed by a thesis of metaphysical necessity, it follows that we only need to focus on arguments for the weaker thesis of natural necessity.

I conclude that a demonstration of the naturally necessary involvement of language in thought would have much the same methodological significance for philosophy as could have been derived from a parallel demonstration of conceptually necessary involvement. While there would no longer be any guarantee that an analysis of the concept of thought, as such, could proceed via an analysis of language, analyses of all other philosophically problematic concepts could still proceed via consideration of their linguistic expression. So, given that there is little prospect of demonstrating any conceptual necessity, as I shall shortly begin to argue, much may depend on the question whether it is possible for us to establish the weaker thesis of natural necessity. That will be the main task of this book.

1.3   Of wolves and wolf-children

The most direct way of demonstrating that thought is independent of language (both naturally and conceptually) would be to show convincingly that there are creatures who have thoughts but lack any language. And it certainly does seem that there are such creatures. Most of us are inclined to believe that dogs, cats, wolves, and seals, as well as apes and pre-linguistic human infants, are capable of entertaining simple thoughts about their environment. Then, since none of these creatures has the use of a public language, it must follow that their thoughts are independent of such language. Of course, these claims about the thoughts of animals and infants are not entirely uncontroversial, and many have denied them. In my view the arguments for such denials are weak – though I shall not attempt to demonstrate this here (see my 1992c, ch. 6).

It is worth noticing, however, that those arguments all make, crucially, some anti-realist assumption about the nature of mental states. In particular, they move from difficulties in *attributing* determinate thoughts to animals and infants, or in *knowing* what those thoughts may be, to the conclusion that there can be no such thoughts in existence. It will follow, then, that anyone with broadly realist sympathies, such as myself, will lack any motive for denying that some thoughts, at least, can exist independently of any natural or public language. I shall briefly criticise anti-realist conceptions of the mental, and defend a contrasting realism, in sections 1.5 and 1.6 below. One conclusion, then, will be that no one who believes in realism about the mental has any good grounds for endorsing the conceptually necessary involvement of language in thought.

If I am proposing to allow that animals and infants have thoughts independently of language, then plainly I cannot, at the same time, insist that *all* thoughts require or involve public language. I shall then have to restrict myself to the weaker claim that *some* thoughts involve such language. This certainly fits with the common-sense intuition which many of us have, that it is hard to imagine a languageless creature entertaining thoughts about the sub-atomic particles of physics, say. But if such a position is to be tenable, then some non-arbitrary way of delimiting the relevant class of thoughts must be found.

One might, for example, mark the difference in terms of degree of conceptual sophistication. For it is surely true that the thoughts available to animals and pre-linguistic infants will be relatively simple ones – perhaps confined to perceptible aspects of the creature's immediate spatial and temporal environment. It might be possible to claim, then, that language is necessary for thoughts about remote times or places, about abstract objects, or more generally about objects that are imperceptible. This may be part of the truth. But another hypothesis is that it is *conscious* thoughts which require or involve natural language. This is the hypothesis that I shall pursue in some detail, at least when restricted further to the class of *human* conscious (and conceptually sophisticated) thoughts.

This is one reason why three of the eight chapters of this book – namely, Chapters 5 to 7 – are devoted to developing a theory of consciousness. I shall need to provide an account of consciousness which does two things: first, when instantiated in a plausible model of human cognitive architecture, it should deliver the conclusion that human conscious thought involves language; and second, it should underpin the claim that the thoughts of animals and pre-linguistic infants are *not* plausibly construed as conscious ones.

Now, if the claim to be considered in this book is only that *some* kinds of human thought involve language, then we may be tempted to appeal in justification to the immense cognitive deficits which can be observed in those rare cases where children grow up without exposure to natural language. Consider, for example, the cases of so-called 'wolf-children', who have survived in the wild in the company of animals, or of children sometimes kept by their parents locked away out of all human contact (see Malson, 1972, and Curtiss, 1977). Consider, also, the cognitive limitations of profoundly deaf children born of hearing parents, who have not yet learned to sign. (For some graphically described accounts, see Sachs, 1989, and Schaller, 1991.) These examples appear to show that human cognition is constructed in such a way as to require the presence of natural language if it is to function properly.

Now, it is obvious that these cases cannot be taken to show that language is necessary for thought as such, without begging questions. Granted that the cognitive deficits exhibited by the children in question were considerable. Yet their behaviour was still interpretable as displaying thought, in the same way and at least to the same degree that the behaviour of animals may be taken as displaying thought. So, unless we assume that animals cannot entertain genuine beliefs and desires, we cannot draw a parallel conclusion in the case of wolf-children or of pre-signing deaf children either. In fact, the very most that can legitimately be concluded from the data, is again that language may be involved in certain *types* or *levels* of thought, not that language is necessary for thinking as such.

Even this conclusion is too strong if left unqualified. For we can distinguish between two different senses in which it might be held that language is necessary for thought. In the first (stronger) sense, it may be claimed that language is actually implicated in the processes and mechanisms of thought, in such a way that thinking is conducted *in* natural language, or *involves* natural language (or, at least, that this is so for certain *kinds* of thinking). In the second (weaker) sense, it may be claimed only that language is a necessary *precondition* for entertaining certain kinds or levels of thought. Only the first of these senses entails that language is itself the *medium* of thought, or that we actually *think in* natural language.

It is the first, stronger, sense that mostly interests us. For it is only if language is implicated in the processes of thought itself that the study of language will, at the same time, be the study of an important aspect of general cognition. In fact it is plain that it would not be enough, in order to get us the conclusions that are of interest for psychology and philosophy, to establish that language is *required for* (as opposed to *involved in*) conscious thinking. For only if language is constitutively involved in the processes of thought itself will the cognitive conception of language be vindicated over the competing communicative picture. And, in the same way, only if language is constitutively involved in our thoughts will it be guaranteed that we can analyse philosophically problematic concepts by focusing on their mode of expression in language. For only then will our thoughts themselves use language for their very formulation.

Yet it is only the weaker thesis that appears, on the face of it, to be supported by the examples of wolf-children and pre-signing deaf children (I shall return to this question in section 2.1, and again in section 8.8). For it is plain that these children were deprived of the vast proportion of normal adult *belief*, since they were cut off from all normal channels of learning and communication. Their resulting cognitive deficits may then be easily explicable from within the standpoint of the communicative conception of language. It may be held that, through being deprived of natural language, they were deprived of the most important channel of human communication. And having been cut off from such communication, they were, in consequence, deprived of the belief-systems within which many fundamental human concepts are embedded.

In fact the important point to notice for our purposes is that someone who endorses the communicative conception of language, and who believes that thought itself is independent of language, can still allow – indeed, insist – that language is a vitally important channel for the acquisition of beliefs, at least in the case of human beings. Since humans are highly social creatures of limited lifespan and intelligence, they rely heavily on communication and testimony in constructing their belief-systems. In which case, any human incapable of understanding language will inevitably be deprived of the vast proportion of normal adult beliefs, including, of course, those relating to developed sciences like physics. This is immediately sufficient to explain many of the cognitive deficits experienced by children deprived of language, without having to allow that language is in any way implicated in the processes of thinking itself.

Indeed, since many adult and scientific concepts presuppose a rich background of theoretical belief, anyone deprived of those beliefs will be incapable of entertaining the corresponding thoughts, because lacking the component concepts. We can thus explain the common-sense intuition that anyone deprived of natural language would be incapable of thoughts about subatomic particles and suchlike, without having to allow that language is itself constitutively involved in those thoughts. What emerges, again, (to emphasise the point) is that we need to distinguish between the claim that natural language is *required for* – is a necessary condition of – thought, or some types of thought, and the claim that language is constitutively *involved in* those thoughts. (Note, however, that I shall, in fact, eventually argue that language is *involved in* all those types of thought for which it is also *required*; see section 8.8 below.)

There are two main points to emerge from the discussion of this section. First: if we allow that animals and pre-linguistic humans have thoughts, then any claim that language is essentially implicated in thought will have to be restricted to some particular *kind* of thought. My hypothesis is that the kind in question is *conscious* thought, which is one reason why so much of this book is devoted to the question of consciousness. Second: it should be clear that if we wish to argue that language is essentially implicated in some kinds of thinking, then it is not enough to show – what surely everyone will now grant – that language is *important for* cognition and thought (at least in humans). For this is consistent with the thesis that language itself is merely an input- and output-channel for central cognition. The thesis of naturally necessary involvement of language in (human conscious) thought will therefore have to be approached somewhat differently.

1.4   Stalnaker's intelligent Martians

As indicated above, I believe, and will assume throughout most of the discussion of this book, that all thought is *conceptually* independent of language (with the exception, trivially, of thoughts which are *about* language). In this and the following two sections I shall, very briefly, provide some defence for this stance. I begin with the question whether there are any powerful *intuitive* grounds for believing in a conceptual independence. And there do, indeed, seem to be such grounds. One way to develop the point would be to appeal to the common-sense belief that many non-linguistic animals – for example, most higher mammals – must be capable of thought, since they have beliefs and desires. Then, since they have thoughts but no language, it must be the case that thought is conceptually independent of language.

Such an argument is unlikely to carry much conviction in the present context, however, since those who maintain that language is conceptually involved in thought will claim that common sense is deluded on this matter, and that our attribution of beliefs and desires to non-linguistic animals is mere anthropomorphism. Moreover, this is not a line of argument that I can pursue myself, either, since in Chapter 7 I shall be developing a theory of the distinction between conscious and non-conscious mental states, according to which the beliefs and desires of most animals will turn out to be non-conscious ones. It would then remain an option for someone to concede that non-linguistic creatures can have non-conscious thoughts, but to insist that language is, nevertheless, conceptually necessary for *conscious* thought.

A more convincing way to develop the intuitive case that all thought – whether conscious or non-conscious – is conceptually independent of language is by imaginary example. (Since it is only a *conceptual* independence which is to be demonstrated, it does not matter that the example is only an imaginary one. Provided that we can successfully conceive of a case of sophisticated and conscious thought without language, then this will be sufficient to show that it cannot be *conceptually* necessary that any thought should involve language.) The following is a development of an example given by Robert Stalnaker (1984), which was itself anticipated more than fifteen years earlier in an example constructed by Robert Kirk (1967).

Suppose we arrive on Mars to discover that the planet is inhabited by a species of highly intelligent, but non-language-using, creature. These animals are extremely long-lived, having a lifespan of, say, one thousand years. They live in an environment that is by no means harsh, so each individual can, without difficulty, gather for itself the means necessary for subsistence. In these circumstances the species has evolved an a-social lifestyle, and consequently lacks any form of public language. We can suppose that the individual members of the species only meet once every few decades to mate, otherwise taking little interest in one another. Nevertheless, they seem to be a species of scientists and inventors. We can observe these creatures engaging in what look like scientific experiments, the results of which are that individuals are able to develop, in the course of their thousand-year lifespan, a number of items of sophisticated technology. Perhaps we find one creature building and using a microscope, another building and making successive improvements to a motor car (petroleum is a naturally occurring substance on Mars), and so on.

In the circumstances envisaged, it would surely be irresistible to suppose that the Martian creatures were engaging in conscious thinking. This is not to say that it would be easy, or indeed possible, to tell *what* they were thinking on any given occasion. But we would surely have the strongest possible grounds for saying that they must be thinking *something*, and something highly sophisticated.

I suppose it may be objected that ants and weaver-birds, too, engage in behaviours of remarkable complexity, without us being tempted to ascribe to them sophisticated (let alone conscious) thoughts. So why should these Martians be regarded any differently? Well for one thing, I am supposing that the behaviour which we observe in any given Martian (such as the construction of a microscope) is unique, not repeated in any other individual of the species. This is immediately sufficient to rule out an explanation in terms of instinct or habit. For another thing, the creativity and extreme sophistication of the Martian behaviours would suggest that they are capable, not only of thinking, but of thinking about their own previous thoughts and patterns of thinking – and this is sufficient for those thoughts to count as conscious ones, if the reflexive thinking account to be developed in Chapter 7 is correct. For the development of a Martian item of science or technology might parallel exactly what one would find in the case of human scientists, suggesting a complex combination of false starts, lucky guesses, rigorous testing, self-reflection, and creative insights.

It appears that we have been successful in conceiving of a case of (sophisticated and conscious) thinking without language, and it must follow that language is not conceptually necessary for any form of thought (with the exception, trivially, of thoughts *about* language). This is then one reason why I only propose to pursue, in this book, the question whether it is *naturally* necessary that language is involved in thought. Although a thesis of conceptually necessary involvement is, in my view, highly implausible, it seems well worth considering whether some (suitably restricted) thesis of naturally necessary involvement can be successfully defended.

1.5   Anti-realist arguments

The method of imaginary example is, of course, fallible. It is possible that it should *seem* to us that we have successfully conceived of a case of (conscious and sophisticated) thought without language, when in reality we have not. In a full discussion of this issue, then, we should also have to examine in detail the arguments for claiming that language is, despite appearances to the contrary, conceptually necessary for thought. But there is another reason why I do not propose to pursue the question of the conceptually necessary involvement of language in thought any further in this book, besides the intuitive implausibility of that thesis. It is, that all the arguments which I know of for supposing that language *is* conceptually necessary for thought involve a commitment to some kind of anti-realism, either in general, or about mental states and properties specifically. I shall mention arguments due to Wittgenstein (1953), Davidson (1975 and 1982), and Dummett (1981 and 1991).

Wittgenstein

Ludwig Wittgenstein is generally credited with having proposed a *criterial* theory of meaning in general, and of mental kind terms in particular (see Wright 1987, chs. 7 and 8, together with the references therein). On this view, certain types of behaviour are *criteria* for ascribing a given mental state, in the sense that they constitute, as a matter of conceptual necessity, *defeasibly good evidence* for the ascription of that state. It will thus be claimed that pain behaviour, such as screaming and grimacing, for example, is a criterion of pain, meaning that it is part of the concept of pain that such behaviour usually manifests pain. So it is supposed to be a conceptual truth that a grimace will warrant an ascription of pain, although such ascriptions may be defeated by further behavioural evidence (such as the person later saying, 'I was only pretending').

Now the important point to note is that there is, on this account, nothing *more* to possession of a given mental state than the undefeated satisfaction of its behavioural criteria. This sort of view may then be characterised as *quasi-behaviourist*. For although no attempt is made to analyse each mental kind term into a set of behavioural descriptions necessary and sufficient for its correct ascription, still it is behavioural evidence, and only behavioural evidence, which is held to be constitutive of their meaning.

Applied to the special case of ascriptions of thought, the criterial view will prioritise evidence which is linguistic. *Saying*, 'It will rain tomorrow', will be a criterion for possessing the *belief* that it will rain tomorrow, and *saying*, 'I want an apple', will be a criterion for having the *desire* to eat an apple. Although other sorts of (non-linguistic) behaviour may figure amongst the criteria for ascribing relatively simple thoughts, in the majority of cases linguistic behaviour will be the only criterion available. Thus, whatever one might think about the examples just given, it seems plain that there is nothing that could specifically manifest the belief *that life may be discovered on Mars in ten or twelve years time* apart from some appropriate written or spoken utterance. The claim will then be that it is conceptually impossible for a non-language-using creature to entertain any but the very simplest thoughts (and perhaps not even those), since language-behaviour is a centrally important (in many cases, the only) criterion for the ascription of thoughts.

This criterial view has little to recommend it, however. It is much more plausible to maintain that our concepts of the mental get their life and meaning from their role within a substantive theory of the mind, often referred to as 'folk-psychology', as I shall argue briefly in sections 1.6 and 1.7 below. Such an account preserves for us our common-sense realism about the mental, enabling us to maintain that mental states and events, such as thoughts and pains, are real internal states of the agent, which interact causally with one another in characteristic ways to produce behaviour.

On this theory-theory view, to understand a mental concept is to know (at least implicitly) sufficiently much of the corpus of folk-psychology, and to grasp the role of the concept within that theory. Also on this view, to ascribe a particular mental state to another person is an inference to the best explanation of their observed behaviour, warranted by the principles and implicit generalisations of folk-psychology. (And to ascribe a particular mental state to oneself, moreover, is generally to *recognise* that state *as* an item receiving a particular theoretical characterisation within folk-psychological theory; see my 1996a.) From this perspective, while we may have difficulty in ascribing precise thoughts to those who exhibit no linguistic behaviour, there will be no difficulty in the supposition that there are such thoughts, and there may be plenty of examples (such as is provided by the case of animals, or of the Stalnaker Martians) in which the best explanation is that there are *some* thoughts in play, although we do not know which.

Davidson

Donald Davidson has offered a variety of arguments for supposing that language is conceptually necessary for thought (see my 1992c, ch. 6, for some brief discussion). But the heart of his position may be characterised as *interpretationalist*. The very ideas of thought, and of belief and desire, are held to be constituted by the activity of interpretation. Faced with a subject's behaviour, we are to arrive at the best interpretation of it that we can, operating within certain general constraints, such as the principle of charity ('Try to make most of the subject's beliefs come out true') and the principle of rationality ('Assume that the subject will act so as to maximise expected utility'). In contrast with the criterial theory, the fit between behaviour and thought is by no means many-to-one, but is inevitably and totally holistic. It is the total set of thoughts ascribed which has to find a best fit with the subject's total behaviour.

Crucially, for Davidson, there is nothing *more* to possessing any given belief or desire than being interpretable in the light of a holistic scheme of thoughts containing it. It is a consequence of this, Davidson argues, that non-language-using creatures cannot possess fine-grained thoughts, since there is not, and cannot be, the requisite scheme of thoughts to ascribe to them on the basis of non-linguistic behaviour alone.

This view, too, although perhaps more plausible than Wittgenstein's in its recognition of the totally holistic character of interpretation, has little to recommend it. For epistemology is one thing, metaphysics is another. That our best *evidence* of thought should be holistic, is one thing, the conditions for thought *identity* may be quite another. That we lack sufficient evidence to ascribe any particular fine-grained beliefs and desires in the absence of linguistic behaviour is one thing, whether thought itself can exist in the absence of language may be quite another. Indeed, on the folk-theoretical view of the mental that I regard as most plausible, there will be just these sorts of gaps between the states ascribed by the theory, which are assumed to have real existence and real causal interactions of their own, and the evidence on which those ascriptions are based.

Dummett

Michael Dummett, too, is an anti-realist, though his views are driven by a global anti-realism, rather than by any considerations relating to the mental in particular. In Dummett's view, *all* truth is governed by relations of epistemic accessibility – crudely, there is no truth except verifiable truth. Then it cannot be that a creature possesses any given fine-grained thought, in particular, in the absence of any possible behavioural evidence of that thought. And in the absence of language, such evidence must be lacking. The arguments of Dummett and others (see also Wright, 1987) in support of global anti-realism cannot be considered in any detail here. For the most part, I shall simply help myself to the contrary realist assumption that some of our statements may have truth-conditions which transcend the possibility of verification. (For defence of semantic realism, see Appiah, 1986, Devitt, 1984, and my 1990, ch. 15.)

It is worth remarking, however, that at least one of the main arguments for global anti-realism – the so-called *manifestation argument* – itself presupposes some form of anti-realism about the mental. For the argument is, that anyone who grasps a concept (in this case the concept of verification-transcendent truth) must be capable of *fully manifesting* that understanding in their behaviour, specifically in their linguistic behaviour. This seems to involve a commitment to just the sort of quasi-behaviourism which is itself in need of support. For on any realist view of the mental, there may be mental states which cannot be directly and decisively manifested in behaviour.

1.6   Realism in mind

Having indicated what I take to be some of the weaknesses of anti-realist conceptions of the mental, in this section I shall sketch arguments in support of two different forms of contrasting realism, one stronger than the other.

Realism of intention about the mental

All three of the above authors seem committed to endorsing the *Turing Test* (see Turing, 1950). They must claim that if a computer could be successfully programmed to simulate normal human conversation, then it would have to count as possessing genuine intelligence and thought, irrespective of the details of its internal organisation. For such a computer would be interpretable as possessing thoughts, and it is held that there is nothing *more* to being a subject of thought than to be so interpretable. Yet this position is, I think, hugely counter-intuitive for most people. Most of us would maintain that evidence about the internal structure and functioning of the computer – for example, that it operates by consulting a vast look-up table – could be sufficient to establish that it is not a genuine thinker, irrespective of our success in so interpreting it.

Some people have claimed that the Turing Test has actually been passed, by computer-programs like *Eliza* and *Parry*, for example. But this is not so. In fact it is easy to ask questions of these programs which will trip them up, since they are based on fairly simple pattern-matching routines. But reflection on these examples leads Jack Copeland (1993, ch. 3) to construct the following imaginary example of a computer that *does* pass the Turing Test by pattern-matching. There are a finite number of possible English conversations consisting of less than, say, 10,000 sentences, each of which consists of less than 200 words. Then imagine a computer in which all of these conversations are listed in a look-up table. The computer operates by matching a given input against its lists, and selecting one possible continuation at random. Call this computer (which may well be dependent upon computer technology far in advance of ours!) *Superparry*. It seems plain that Superparry would pass the Turing Test in connection with any experimenter who does not actually know or suspect the details of its program. For we may suppose that no normal human conversation consists of more than 10,000 sentences, and that no normal human sentence consists of more than 200 words. But it is plain, is it not, that we would withhold mentality from Superparry as soon as we *do* learn that it operates by pattern-matching?

In fact, our reaction to the Turing Test is indicative of a belief that a computer should only be counted as a genuine thinker if sufficiently much of our common-sense psychology is actually *true of* it. Only if it is internally organised in ways sufficiently similar to ourselves – with real distinctions drawn between perception, memory, belief, and desire, for example, and with typically human patterns of causal interaction between them – would we be prepared to countenance the view that it has thoughts. In ascribing thoughts to a creature we are thus committing ourselves to a certain pattern of internal organisation.

Reactions to John Searle's famous *Chinese Room* example (1980) push in the same (realist) direction, I believe. Searle imagined a room containing a mono-lingual English operator, a stock of Chinese characters, and a rule-book correlating patterns of such characters. Sequences of Chinese characters are delivered into the room via a letter-box, on receipt of which the operator consults the rule-book and constructs the appropriate sequence of characters to be returned through the letter-box in reply. Unknown to the operator, the rule-book is so constructed that he is in fact engaging some native Chinese speakers outside the room in normal intelligent conversation. But we would not want to credit either the operator, or the room as a whole, with an understanding of Chinese, Searle thinks.

Most people share this reaction, without necessarily sharing Searle's diagnosis, that what is missing from the room is something with the *biological* properties of a Chinese-speaking human brain. I believe the correct diagnosis of the reaction is that there is nothing in the room corresponding to the *functional structure* of the human mind – that is, of distinctively human interactions between perception, belief, desire, intention, and action (to name but a few of the more salient mental categories). Indeed, I believe that the normal reactions to this example support the folk-psychological account of mental state terms. Such terms are embedded in a theory of the structure and functioning of the human mind, and only if a system instantiates that structure (as, manifestly, the Chinese Room does not) will we be prepared to ascribe mental states to it.

The moral of the Turing Test, and of the Chinese Room, is that possession of beliefs and desires is not constituted by the fact that the subject is *interpretable as* acting out of beliefs and desires. We also believe that the subject must possess a suitable *real internal structure* of interacting mental states and events. Evidence that this internal structure is lacking (as in the case of Superparry) undermines the claim that we are dealing with a genuine thinker. If this is correct, then we have established what I call *realism of intention* about mental states. The thesis is, that in ascribing thoughts to a creature we *intend* that our ascriptions will be true in virtue of a certain sort of inner structure, and are committed to the view that they will *only* be true given just such a pattern of organisation. In ascribing thoughts we *intend* to pick out real internal, causally effective, states of the agent, which might exist in the absence of behavioural evidence, or be absent in the presence of such evidence.

It may be objected that if the thesis of realism of intention were really correct, then we should be forced to withdraw attributions of thought *to ourselves*, if it were to turn out that we lack the requisite pattern of internal organisation. Suppose that it were demonstrated by some future scientific psychology that we ourselves are driven by some vast computational look-up table – a naturally occurring biological form of Superparry. Would we then withdraw our claims to be genuine subjects of thought? Intuition suggests not. In which case the thesis of realism of intention appears to be threatened.

There are two possible replies to this objection, I believe; both good ones. The first is simply that our habits of ascribing thoughts and other mental states to ourselves are too deeply entrenched – and, indeed, that the principles and generalisations grounding those ascriptions are too obviously true – for us to be able to set them aside in any mere thought-experiment. The second reply is that our common-sense psychology is very likely innate to the human species, as I shall argue briefly in the next section. So we may have no option but to think of ourselves as thinkers, just as we have no option (if we are native English speakers) but to hear an English sentence as imbued with meaning. If this is right, then the thesis of realism of intention can *only* be tested by our reactions to examples like Superparry, in respect of systems *other than ourselves*.

Realism of fact about the mental

I have been arguing that the best way of construing mental state concepts is realist, rather than interpretationalist or quasi-behaviourist. However this is, so far, only to argue that we are committed to realism of intention about mental states. It is it not yet to argue that we are *successful* in referring to such states – it is not yet to defend what I call *realism of fact* about mental states. Realism of fact has been denied by some (for example, Churchland, 1981, and Stich, 1983). But it has been defended most eloquently by Jerry Fodor (see his 1987, ch. 1; see also Horgan and Woodward, 1985).

Fodor's main argument is premised upon the immense *success* of folk-psychology (as well as its depth and indispensability, which I shall not discuss here). There are two elements of this success, one pertaining to success in *explanation*, and one to success in *prediction*. In respect of explanation, notice that there is almost no human behaviour which cannot be rendered intelligible by suitable attributions of belief and desire, except perhaps behaviour resulting from extreme forms of mental illness. In fact, we are intelligible to one another in a way that nothing else in the natural world is intelligible to us. To see the extent of our predictive success, reflect on the degree of successful co-operation and communication in human societies, even those that are as complex and technologically sophisticated as those of the West. For this is all underpinned by the predictions provided by common-sense psychology. In fact our predictive success is so ubiquitous that we may hardly notice it; and certainly our occasional failures have far greater salience for us.

How are we to explain this success, unless we suppose that the folk-psychological theory which generates it is largely *true*? It would seem to be a miracle that human beings should be so readily intelligible to one another, and that they should be capable of predicting each other's actions with such a high degree of accuracy (given enough accurate information relating to initial conditions, of course), unless the theory of the human mind through which they operate is a broadly correct one. The argument here is of exactly the same form as the argument for realism of fact about any scientific domain – namely, that the best explanation of substantive predictive and explanatory success is that the theory which generates it is very likely true, or close to the truth. Such an argument seems to me to be powerful enough to make the conclusion – realism of fact about the mental – a very plausible one indeed; at any rate, just *as* plausible as any other scientific realism. And it is a view that I propose to take for granted throughout the remainder of this book.

1.7   Innateness and theory of mind

In this section I shall briefly argue for the view that knowledge of folk-psychology is innate, making its appearance in young children as a result of cognitive maturation, rather than through any process of learning. (For more detailed development, see my 1992a, ch. 8, and Segal, 1996; see also Morton, 1979, and Fodor, 1992.) While this thesis is not strictly necessary to the main argument of the book, it does make it easier to develop an evolutionary perspective on consciousness, as we shall see in Chapters 7 and 8. And at various points it will serve as a useful ancillary premise – as it did in my response to an objection to realism of intention about the mental in the previous section, for example.

The basic argument for the innateness of folk-psychology parallels Chomsky's well-known argument for an innately structured language-faculty (see his 1988). In both cases the innateness hypothesis is reached by an inference to the best explanation, in response to what Chomsky calls 'Plato's Problem' (so-named after the slave-boy example in Plato's *Meno*). Plato's Problem, in any given domain, is this: *how does the child manage to learn so much, so fast, and on the basis of such meagre data?* In the case of natural language, children manage to master their native tongue within less than half-a-dozen years, attaining knowledge of an immense body of grammatical rules whose complexity is still such as to elude complete description by linguists. And they do this on the basis of only positive data (no one tells them what *can't* be said in their language, yet this is something they end up knowing), without any explicit teaching or training.

In my view the case for the parallel claim in connection with folk-psychology is impressive. Recent evidence from developmental psychology suggests that children have a good grasp of the basic principles of folk-psychology by the age of four or even younger (see, for example, Wellman, 1990). By this age they have developed a complex, deep, and highly sophisticated theory of the operation of the human mind, which they use to explain and predict the behaviour of themselves and others. Yet they are not taught that theory, and it is very hard to see how they could discover it for themselves.

In fact, there are only two real alternatives to the innateness hypothesis to explain our acquisition of common-sense psychology. One is the child-as-little-scientist view, developed for example by Gopnik and Wellman (1992), in which it is supposed that children do indeed reach adult folk-psychology just as a scientist might, by means of inference to the best explanation of the available data – though perhaps kick-started in this process by an innate capacity for imitation (see Gopnik and Melzoff, 1993). Yet it surely beggars belief that all children (save only those who are autistic – see below) should hit upon the same theory at the same age, irrespective of very wide differences in experience and general intelligence. We certainly would not expect this to happen in connection with any similarly diverse group of adult scientists!

The only other alternative (which is consistent with realism about the mental, at least) is to deny that children have to acquire a *theory* of the operation of the human mind at all. Rather, they just need to learn to use their knowledge of their own mental states as a model for the other, achieving knowledge of the mental states of other people through a process of *simulation*. (See Goldman, 1989, 1992, and 1993, and Harris, 1989.) But this view requires us to return to a quasi-Cartesian account of our knowledge of the mental, supposing that we have immediate non-theory-laden access to our own mental states. It is much more plausible to suppose that self-knowledge, like other-knowledge, is mediated by our implicit grasp of the theoretical principles of folk-psychology. (See my 1996a for further development of these arguments.) But these are points which we shall return to in the chapters that follow.

In addition to the argument from Plato's Problem sketched above, human beings would appear to exhibit exactly the pattern of biologically caused breakdown – namely, autism – which one would expect if folk-psychology *were* innate. (See Baron-Cohen, 1990, and my 1996b. Autistic subjects have great difficulty in interacting socially and emotionally with others, and also in reading the minds of other people; they are also inept at the pragmatic aspects of discourse, which require them to infer the intentions and expectations of their interlocutors.) Moreover, it would certainly make a good deal of sense that folk-psychology (like natural language, as almost every cognitive scientist now believes) should be largely innate, given its crucial position within the life of our species. For it is folk-psychology that underlies, in one way or another, almost all human communication and co-operative activity.

It is worth noting that Fodor uses the likely innateness of folk-psychology to provide a second, independent, argument for realism of fact about the mental, maintaining that the best explanation of this innateness is that the theory of mental functioning embodied in common-sense psychology is largely *true* (see his 1987, epilogue; see also my 1992a, ch. 8). The crucial claim in need of defence here is that, if folk-psychology is innate, then its basic principles are, very likely, true ones, or at least close to the truth. The case for believing that this is so is partly an induction, since wherever nature has conferred belief-forming mechanisms on complex practical-reasoning creatures such as ourselves it appears to have selected ones that are generally reliable (consider visual perception, for example). But it is also partly an inference to the best explanation, since the best explanation of the advantage that an innate belief in the principles of folk-psychology would confer on us, given the highly plastic and complex nature of human social life, requires that those principles should be broadly correct.

I do not pretend to have established an innateness-claim for folk-psychology here, of course; nor, indeed, to have established realism of fact about the mental. My intention has merely been to explain, and to give some of the background for, the realistic and nativistic assumptions within whose framework my investigations will be conducted. Those who disagree with those assumptions should read what follows as having the form of a conditional.

1.8   Thinking: images or sentences?

Given that thoughts are real internal states of the agent, which interact causally with one another to produce further thoughts and to produce behaviour, it is natural to ask how those thoughts are carried, and by what mechanisms they interact. In this section I shall discuss both *imagist* and *sententialist* proposals, before saying something more to distinguish the two hypotheses from one another, and to mark out the main topic of this book.

Imagism

One sort of answer to the questions just raised, is that thoughts consist entirely of mental (mostly visual) *images*, and that thoughts interact by means of associations (mostly learned) between those images. This view has been held very frequently throughout the history of philosophy, at least until quite recently, particularly amongst empiricists (see Locke, 1690, Hume, 1739, and Russell, 1921). Those who hold such a view will then endorse the communicative conception of language. They will argue that thought is independent of language on the grounds that possession and manipulation of mental images need not in any way involve or presuppose natural language.

In fact the imagist account is that all thinking consists in the manipulation of mental images, and that thoughts inherit their semantic properties from the representative powers of the images that constitute them. There may be something importantly correct in the first part of this claim, as I shall argue in the chapter that follows. It may be that all of our conscious thinking presupposes imagination, and that mental images are, in one way or another, implicated in all of our conscious thoughts. But the second – semantic – part of the claim is definitely incorrect, as I shall now briefly argue.

Images, of themselves, unsupplemented by much prior knowledge (and hence thought) on the part of the thinker, are confined to representations of appearance. To have a visual mental image is to represent to oneself how something would look; to have an auditory mental image is to represent to oneself how something would sound; and so on. This gives rise to an immediate problem for the imagist theory of thought, since many of our words and concepts do not stand for the kinds of thing that *have* an appearance. For example, and more or less at random, consider logical concepts like *and, or, not;* temporal concepts like *tomorrow, yesterday, year;* concepts for abstract properties like *inflation* (of money), *prime* (of numbers); and number-terms like *sixteen,* or *sixty-four.* In none of these cases is there any mental image that seems even remotely appropriate to express what we mean.

Moreover, we have many concepts which represent things that do *have* an appearance, but which do not represent them *in virtue of* their appearance. Consider, for example, the concept *bus-stop.* Bus-stops do, of course, have a characteristic appearance (though different in different parts of the country, let alone in different parts of the globe). But if I steal a bus-stop sign and erect it in my garden as an ornament, that does not turn my garden into a bus-stop. Rather, a bus-stop is *a place where buses are supposed to stop.* How is this to be expressed in an image? Even if my image is of a bus stopping at a bus-stop sign, with people getting on and off, this does not attain to the generality of the idea of a place where buses (in general) stop; nor does it touch the normativity implicit in the idea *supposed to stop.*

In the light of points such as these, it seems plain that no image, or sequence of images, can, of itself, carry the content of even a simple thought such as [that all grass is green], let alone of a complex proposition such as [that life may be discovered on Mars in the next ten or twelve years]. Yet it may be replied that there can be nothing to stop someone using images as *signs* to express their thoughts, somewhat as words are used. However, it will not, then, be the representational content of the image, as such, which determines the content of the thought. Of course it is true that someone may employ images of objects with conventionally determined conditions of application, somewhat like a hieroglyphic or ideographic script. But then this is not really distinct from the claim that thought involves natural language, since such an image-language would presumably mirror the rules and conventions of spoken natural language, if it is to approximate to the latter's expressive power, and would presumably need to be learned through the use of the latter.

There is a further argument against imagism which will serve to introduce some of the ideas I shall be developing in the following chapter, as well as driving one further nail into the coffin of the theory. This is the argument, due to Wittgenstein (1953, section 332), that one cannot, in most cases of normal meaningful speech, 'peel away' the utterance to leave the process of meaning exposed and intact. For example, say aloud, and mean, 'It is windy today', just as you would in a normal conversation. Then do what you did again, only just with the meaning remaining, without effecting any utterance. If the meaning attaching to the utterance (the thought expressed) were an image or sequence of images, then this certainly ought to be possible. But plainly, in most cases, it is not. Even if we sometimes have private thoughts and images illustrative of what we mean by a public utterance, this is not at all essential. In many real cases of public speech, if you imagine away the act of saying, retaining everything else as it was, then at the same time you have imagined away the thinking as well.

Sententialism

How, then, are thoughts to be carried in cognition, if not by mental images? Recall that the realist's view is that propositional attitudes – beliefs, desires, and the like – interact with one another causally to produce behaviour in ways which respect their semantic contents. The belief that it will shortly rain combines with the desire to stay dry, not randomly, but in such a way as to produce the intention to find some form of shelter. This in turn may combine with the belief that an umbrella is easily available, so as to cause me to carry an umbrella with me when I go out. How is this possible? How can propositional attitudes have causal powers which reflect their *relatedness to the world*, as well as their logical relations with one another, that are distinctive of their possessing a semantic content? There are really three different, but closely related, problems in need of solution here.

First, propositional attitudes are *systematic*, having contents that are systematically related to one another, in such a way that anyone capable of believing (or otherwise thinking) a given content must be capable of believing or thinking a number of closely related contents. Anyone capable of believing *that Jane loves John* must also be capable of the thought *that John loves Jane*. Why should this be so? How is this fact about propositional attitudes to be explained?

Second, propositional attitudes are *productive*, in the sense that anyone capable of thinking at all must be capable of entertaining unlimitedly many thoughts. If you can think that Jane has a mother, then you can think that Jane's mother has a mother, and that Jane's mother's mother has a mother, and so on (subject, of course, to limitations of memory and other cognitive space). There is no end to the new thoughts that thinkers must be capable of entertaining. This fact, too, is in need of explanation.

Third, propositional attitudes interact causally with one another in ways which respect their semantic contents. This was the point which was closest to the surface in my initial statement of the problem three paragraphs back. Beliefs and desires interact to cause intentions, and beliefs interact with other beliefs to generate new beliefs, in ways which are closely responsive to the *contents* of those states, and by means of transitions which are generally rational ones. How can this happen? How can patterns of causality respect semantic relations of entailment and evidential support?

The most plausible solution to these three problems is that beliefs are, not images, but relations to internal sentences, as Fodor argues in his 1978 (see also Field, 1978; for further powerful arguments in support of a sententialist position, see Davies, 1991). For sentences have contents that are systematically determined from the contents of their component words, together with rules of combination. If you understand the words, and know the rules of syntax, then you must be capable of understanding new combinations of those words, never before encountered. And by the same token, of course, sentences are productive, in virtue of the fact that rules of syntax are recursive. So the sententialist hypothesis provides us with solutions to the problems of systematicity and productivity.

Moreover (and providing us with a solution to the third problem also) sentence tokens can have causal powers, by virtue of being physical particulars. If beliefs and desires consist of sentences, or sentence-like structures, encoded in some distinctive way in the brain, then there will be no difficulty in explaining how beliefs and desires can be causes. (By way of analogy, think of the manner in which sentences can be stored in magnetic patterns on an audio-tape. These sentence tokens then *cause* the sound-waves which result when the tape is played.) And if we suppose, in addition, that the mind is arranged so as to effect computations on these sentences in ways which respect their syntax, then the causal roles of the sentences will respect their semantic properties. For semantics is, in part, a reflection of syntax. And then we shall have explained successfully how beliefs and desires can have causal roles which depend upon their semantic contents.

Looking back, now, to the problems which arose for the imagist theory of thinking, it is easy to see how this sententialist position may fare a great deal better. For a logical concept like *and* or *not* can be carried by a lexical item of some sort, distinguished by its capacity to enter into certain characteristic patterns of inference. Roughly, '&' means *and* provided that the computational system within which it belongs ensures that it is governed by the following forms of inference: $(P \& Q) \rightarrow P; (P \& Q) \rightarrow Q;$ and $P, Q \rightarrow (P \& Q)$. And the concept *bus-stop*, too, can be constituted by some lexical item ('bus-stop', as it might be) characterised both by its causal connections with worldly objects (bus-stops), and by the way in which it figures in distinctive patterns of inference (such as *bus-stop* $\rightarrow$ *buses should stop*) involving yet other lexical items from other parts of the language.

I propose to take this sententialist position for granted in what follows. It provides easily the most plausible picture of how realism about the mental can possibly be true. In fact the only real alternative to sententialism (since imagism is plainly not a viable option), is that propositional attitudes are relations to *propositions*, in each case the one picked out by the that-clause used in the description of the attitude. (The alternative provided by so called 'connectionist' approaches to cognition, while promising as an account of some sub-personal mental processes, is not, I think, viable as an account of propositional-attitude psychology, with the features outlined above. In this I follow Fodor, 1987, Appendix, Fodor and Pylyshyn, 1988, and Davies, 1991. For some further discussion see section 2.8 below.) But propositions are abstract entities, concerning which it is possible to take one of two contrasting metaphysical views.

The Platonist position on abstract entities is that they are objective, existing necessarily, and independently of the human mind. But then it is very hard indeed to see how the human mind or brain could be related to a proposition. What would an unmediated relation to a necessarily existing abstract object be like? The alternative, constructivist, position on abstract entities is that they have mind-dependent existence, supervening on, and abstracted out of similarities between, patterns of mental activity. (Compare the way in which *directions* supervene on, and can be abstracted out of, relations of parallelism between lines. For further discussion, see my 1992a, chs. 2 and 3.) Either way, the relationship to an abstract entity is most plausibly seen as a *mediated* one, and the only plausible candidate for a mediating relation to a proposition is to reintroduce sentences. This is Field's (1978) proposal: Person A believes that P = A believes some sentence S & S means that P.

It might seem that in accepting sententialism we have already done enough to establish that thought, in us at least, essentially involves some natural or public language. For what would these sentences be, whose inscription in the brain constitutes possession of a particular propositional attitude, but sentences from the native language of the subject whose attitudes they are? But this assumption, though easy, would be too swift. For as Fodor (1978) forcefully argues, the sentences may belong, not to a natural language, but to an innate, universal, language of thought, which he calls *Mentalese*. This language would consist of an innate lexicon, or vocabulary, and an innate set of combinatorial rules for the production of completed sentences, held in common by all human beings, and perhaps by all creatures sharing the basic features of our psychology. Fodor's arguments for these views will be considered and criticised at some length in Chapters 2 to 4.

Two kinds of thinking

Despite the points made above, I certainly do not want to claim that mental images can never play a part in anything which might properly be called 'thinking'. Sometimes, surely, our thoughts can consist in a mixture of sentences and mental images. Thus, when reasoning about some practical problem, I might entertain a mixed thought like the following: 'If I put this stool on the table *like so* [insert image], then by climbing on top of it I shall be able to reach up *like that* [insert image].' (Note that I do not mean to beg any questions here about the *language in which* such a thought is partly entertained. The non-imagistic components of the thought might very well be expressed in Mentalese, for all that I mean to imply here.)

Moreover, sometimes our conscious thoughts can consist *entirely* of images of objects (and not of images used as conventional symbols). The thoughts of composers may sometimes consist entirely of auditory images, as they manipulate images of melodies and chord patterns, trying out different possibilities until hitting upon something which satisfies them. The thoughts of an engineer, or of someone trying to pack a set of suitcases into the luggage compartment of a car, may consist entirely of visual images of arrangements of objects. And my thoughts as I try to find my way round a room in the dark might consist simply in an image of its layout in egocentric space.

If the thesis to be pursued in this book is that conscious thinking is conducted in natural language, then something had better be done to demarcate the *kind* of thinking in question. For it seems obvious that some kinds of thinking are *not* conducted in language. (This point is independent of the dispute within psychology between *pictorial* and *descriptivist* theories of the nature of mental images, by the way – see Tye, 1991. For that dispute is about the cognitive, sub-personal underpinnings of imagery, not the person-level phenomena themselves. Even the descriptivist does not intend to deny the difference between mental images and sententially based thoughts.) I suggest that the kind in question is: *propositional thinking* – the kind of thought whose content may properly and correctly be described by means of a propositional that-clause. I therefore need to argue that no imagistic thought can have such a content.

I think many of us feel intuitively that our imagistic thoughts are not properly described in the that-clauses which we are forced to use if we want to express them in language. For example, if I have been planning my route from my home to the railway station by mapping it out in my head, using an image of the layout of the city, then I would feel pretty lame to have to describe that thought by saying, 'I was thinking that I should start towards the city centre, and then turn right.' For this does not begin to approximate to the richness of what I had actually thought. But it is possible to do better than just appeal to intuition here.

I have already made the point that there are many propositional thoughts whose contents cannot be expressed imagistically. Some of these may be relatively simple ones, such as the thought, [that all grass is green]. So wherever such a thought is tokened in a sentence, we can at least conclude that a thought of that type could not be entertained in an image alone. Now the same point can be made, I believe, in connection with thoughts whose contents do not go beyond what can be perceptually manifest, where one might think that there was a strong case for their content to be thinkable in the form of an image.

Consider the thought, [that a cat is sitting on a mat]. Suppose that this thought is tokened in the form of the English sentence, 'A cat is sitting on a mat.' According to the view to be defended in this book, this token of that thought is then constituted by the sentence in question. But might one not also entertain a token of that very thought in the form of a visual image of a cat sitting on a mat? And would this not then be an alternative manner in which the thought could be entertained? I believe the answer to these questions is, 'No'. In entertaining such an image one would not really be entertaining a thought of the very same type, even though it might concern the same subject matter, and might on occasion play a somewhat similar role in cognition.

As I shall be arguing in Chapter 4, thought-contents are likely to be individuated, in part, in terms of their functional or conceptual role. One thought will be distinct from another provided that the two are apt to enter into different patterns of inferences, or provided that they are apt to interact with yet other thoughts in characteristically distinct ways, *even if* those thoughts otherwise share the same worldly truth-conditions. Applying this condition then suggests that imagistic and sentential thoughts (whether the latter are expressed in public language or in Mentalese) must always be distinct. For surely the *way in which* my sentential thought, 'A cat is on a mat', might give rise to the further thought that a mammal is on a mat, will differ from the manner in which an image of a cat on a mat might give rise to the same further thought.

The way to bring out this point is to notice that an image will always carry with it *excess content*, beyond mere entailment relations. The sentence, 'A cat is on a mat' carries no more, and no less, content than the proposition, [that a cat is on a mat]. So it will contain the content, [that a mammal is on a mat], since this is entailed; but it will not contain the content, [that a tabby cat is on a mat], nor the content, [that a cat is sitting on a mat]. Not so with an image. Although an image can be in various respects indeterminate or vague, it must always be *more* determinate than a proposition. My image of a cat on a mat must always be an image of some particular kind of cat (fluffy or short-haired, tabby or black) in some particular position (sitting or standing, facing or turned away) on some particular sort of mat. This certainly suggests that the process by which an image might give rise to a given effect in cognition will be highly context-sensitive, and will certainly differ from the manner in which a proposition (tokened by a sentence of some sort) might give rise to the same effect.

The topic of this book, then, is the nature of *propositional* thinking, rather than the nature of thought in general (yet further qualifications will be noted in section 2.3). I shall be assuming that propositional thinking consists in the tokening and mental manipulation of sentences of some kind, and will be developing the case for saying that these sentences are those of natural language, rather than sentences of Mentalese.

It is important to note, however, that for some purposes thought-contents may be individuated purely by subject-matter, or by worldly truth-conditions, rather than by conceptual or functional role. If we individuate their contents in this way, then we can ask which types of thought (if any) involve natural language, meaning: *thoughts about which kinds of subject-matter involve language?* We have already seen good reason, above, for saying that the range of subject-matters that we can think about purely imagistically is highly restricted. Employing visual images alone, we probably cannot think about anything other than the spatial distributions and layouts of perceptible objects. So if we could show that all propositional (non-imagistic) thoughts must involve natural language, it would follow that such language is implicated in our thoughts about any but the very simplest subject-matters. I shall not be able to demonstrate anything this strong, in fact. But the question of the range of subject-matters which might require us to employ natural language in order to think about them, is the one that is ultimately of greatest interest. I shall return to it again in the next chapter, and then again in the latter half of Chapter 8.

Summary

In this opening chapter I have explained the nature of my project, which is to investigate whether or not it is naturally necessary that human conscious thinking should constitutively involve public language. I have argued that this result, if established, would have much the same importance as could have been derived from more traditional philosophical claims of conceptually necessary involvement. Since all the arguments in support of such conceptually necessary involvement depend in one way or another upon anti-realism about the mental, I have pointed out that those who embrace a contrasting realism would be well-advised to concentrate on the weaker thesis of natural necessity. I have also set out the realist and nativist assumptions about the mind against whose background the investigations in this book will be carried out.

In the remainder of this book, then, I shall assume that there are such things as beliefs, desires, and other mental states, which have real existence and real causal roles which can be independent of our best evidence of them. I shall also assume that beliefs and desires, in particular, are best understood as relations to internal sentences. The main focus for debate will concern *which* sentences are constitutive of our (conscious propositional) thoughts – those of Mentalese, or those of natural language. I shall be arguing for the latter, beginning in the chapter that follows.

2   Which language do we think with?

I have accepted Fodor's view that propositional attitudes (beliefs, desires, and so on) are best understood as relations to sentences. The question then is: which sentences? In this chapter, after first considering the evidence from psychology (which is equivocal), I shall present an intuitive, introspection-based, argument for the view that human conscious thinking involves sentences of natural language. This is an initial presentation of the view that I shall wish to defend in this book. I shall then begin to consider Fodor's arguments for claiming that the sentences in question belong to an innate, universal, language of thought (Mentalese). Some of these arguments are easily responded to, but some will require extensive discussion in later chapters.

2.1   The evidence from scientific psychology

What does cognitive psychology tell us about the relationship between language and thought? I shall consider the developmental evidence first, and then briefly present and discuss the evidence from neuropsychology, particularly aphasia. I shall argue, in summary, that the scientific evidence is inconclusive, remaining open to a variety of interpretations.

The evidence from normal development

It is an oft-remarked fact that the linguistic and cognitive abilities of young children will normally develop together. If a child's language is advanced, then so will be its abilities across a range of tasks; and if a child's language is delayed, then so will be its cognitive abilities. To cite just one item from a wealth of empirical evidence: Janet Astington (1996) reports finding a high correlation between language-ability and children's capacity to pass false-belief tasks, whose solution requires them to attribute, and reason from, the false belief of another person. (A standard false-belief task has the form: Maxi places some chocolate in a cupboard and leaves the room; in his absence we move the chocolate to another location; question: where will Maxi look for the chocolate when he returns? Most three-year-old and autistic children fail this task, saying that Maxi will go to where the chocolate actually is. Almost all four-year-olds pass, saying that Maxi will look in the cupboard; see Wellman, 1990, and Perner, 1991.) Does this and similar data show that language is constitutively involved in children's thinking? By no means.

As we pointed out in section 1.3, the most that such data can reveal is that language is a necessary condition for certain kinds of thinking, not that it is constitutively involved in those kinds. And this is easily explicable from the standpoint of someone who endorses the communicative – as opposed to the cognitive – conception of language. For language, in human beings, is a necessary condition of normal enculturation. Without language, there are many things that the child cannot learn; and with delayed language, there are many things that the child will only learn later. It is only to be expected, then, that cognitive and linguistic development should proceed in parallel. It does not follow that language is itself actually *used in* the child's cognition.

But what of the fact that a child's language-development will often lag *behind* its conceptual and cognitive development? Does this serve to show, on the contrary, that thought is independent of language? For example, when observed (and video-taped) in context, a two-year-old who can only use two-word sentences like, 'Mummy shoes', may sometimes mean, 'Those are Mummy's shoes', (a possessive statement), and may sometimes mean, 'Mummy, put my shoes on', (a request to an actor to perform an action on an object – see Gregory, 1987, p. 427). Then since the child's capacities for thought go beyond what it is capable of expressing in language, does this show that thought is independent of language? In fact not, for two distinct reasons.

First, the argument would move too swiftly from the child's deficiency in language *production* to the more general conclusion that it is deficient in language-*ability*. But this inference is not warranted. For it may be that the language faculty divides into two distinct sub-systems, one concerned with production and one concerned with comprehension. (Indeed, the evidence from aphasia suggests that this is the case. Some aphasics are very poor at producing intelligible discourse themselves, but have quite good comprehension abilities.) And if language is implicated in thought, then it may be that it is (or can be) the comprehension system which is so implicated. So if the child is capable of *understanding* the difference between the two utterances, 'Those are Mummy's shoes', and 'Mummy, put my shoes on' (said by a sibling, say), then it may be that it *thinks to itself*, 'Those are Mummy's shoes', in circumstances in which it only has the ability to say aloud, 'Mummy shoes'.

Second (and even if the above point is waived), it does not follow from the data that language is not directly implicated in the child's thought. From the fact that the child makes use of one-and-the-same (two-word) sentence, now to mean, 'Those are Mummy's shoes', and now to mean, 'Mummy, put my shoes on', it does not follow that it can think those thoughts independently of the use of that (or an equivalent) sentence. It is possible that the child's ability to *make use of* signs outstrips its ability to *mark* those different uses by different signs – but that its thoughts are partly constituted by the signs so used.

The evidence from abnormal development

If the evidence from normal development is equivocal, then what of the evidence from cases where language development is wholly absent, such as the examples of 'wolf-children', or pre-signing deaf children? When these were discussed in section 1.3, it appeared that they, too, presented no real evidence either way. For we may grant that the cognitive development of these children is severely impaired; but this datum is consistent with either the cognitive or communicative conceptions of language. From the standpoint of the cognitive conception, the reason why their cognition is so impaired is because more complex forms of human thinking actually involve the use of language; so where language is absent, so must these forms of thinking be. But from the standpoint of the communicative conception of language, the reason why these children are cognitively impaired is that they lack many normal human concepts and beliefs, which can only be acquired through enculturation and linguistic communication.

But what of the fact that the isolated child Genie, when she was first discovered at age 13, had a mental age of between 1 and 2 – despite then going on to display intelligence in the normal range when she later acquired language? (see Curtiss, 1977). Is this *immense* cognitive deficit wholly explicable in terms of the absence of communication, and so in terms of Genie's lack of enculturated beliefs? Perhaps not. But then there are many other features of Genie's case which might explain the differential, consistent with the communicative conception of language. For it was not just communication that she was deprived of.

Genie was also deprived of all normal emotional contact with others, and of opportunities to explore her environment (which was in any case very impoverished). Almost her only contact with other people, between the ages of 1 and 13, were occasional visits from her father and brother, neither of whom spoke to her, the former of whom beat her regularly (especially if she made any sound), and both of whom tormented her and barked at her like a dog. She was also kept immobile for much of her life, almost all of which was spent in a dim, largely unfurnished room, either strapped to a commode, or zipped into a specially adapted sleeping bag, which effectively functioned as a strait-jacket. It would hardly be surprising if, in the circumstances, Genie's cognitive development was very severely delayed, way beyond what one might predict from her lack of opportunities to receive information from others. And, indeed, the pre-signing deaf man described by Schaller (1991) displayed deficits which were not nearly so severe.

Schaller describes the case of a profoundly deaf man, Ildefonso, who reached the age of 27 without acquiring any conventional language. He had been brought up in a community of migrant labourers, without any schooling, and without any contact with natural sign languages. He was balanced, alert, and normally affectionate, and capable of using and understanding simple gestures and uses of mime. He was capable of performing everyday tasks, and of earning a wage as a labourer. When introduced to ASL (American Sign Language) he learned it extremely fast, sucking in each new word hungrily. Schaller herself describes Ildefonso's predicament as one in which the absence of language had deprived him of a great deal of *information*, thus committing herself to the communicative conception of language. But actually, hardly any formal testing of Ildefonso's cognitive abilities was undertaken, either before and after language acquisition.

Moreover, it is doubtful whether Ildefonso was genuinely languageless. Evidence from elsewhere suggests that he would have developed for himself a gesture system having all of the properties of a simple language. (Indeed, this interpretation seems confirmed by Schaller's description of him engaging in animated 'conversations' with other non-signing deaf adults, using what she describes as a rich repertoire of gesture and mime.) Susan Goldin-Meadow and colleagues have studied deaf children born of hearing parents over a number of years, whose parents then took a decision that the children should not be taught any form of Sign (see Goldin-Meadow and Mylander, 1990, Butcher *et al.*, 1991, and Goldin-Meadow *et al.*, 1994). They found that without exception the children spontaneously developed a gesture language, initially taking over the gestures of their parents, but then systematising and regularising them into a genuine language, with all the properties of morphology and syntax which one would expect of simple three-year-old language. So it seems that it may actually be impossible to find any genuinely languageless humans, unless, like Genie, they are deprived of human contact altogether!

Does the fact that congenitally deaf children spontaneously develop a gesture language show that they are already capable (in advance of possessing *any* language) of entertaining complex thoughts? For certainly the invention of an entire language (albeit a simple one) can be no simple matter! But this is almost certainly not the right way to understand what takes place. For in fact the languages of these children pass through exactly the stages of development and spontaneous restructuring as do those of children acquiring ASL; and surely no one wants to say that in the normal case children have to invent their own language! (But see section 2.8 below.) Rather, it seems that the human language-forming faculty not only contains a powerful set of innate constraints (as Chomsky and others have argued; see Chomsky, 1988, Curtiss, 1989, and Pinker, 1994), but that it requires only minimal linguistic exposure to be triggered into growth and activity. This same interpretation is also strongly suggested by the way in which children brought up of pidgin-speaking parents will spontaneously elaborate them into Creoles in the space of a single generation (see Holm, 1988). So there is no real reason to believe that young children are capable of complex thought prior to the development of natural language – for languages are, in fact, *grown* rather than learned or invented.

Of course, the fact that Ildefonso probably already had some language does not show that he had nothing more to learn. And interestingly, Schaller reports that when she began to teach him to sign, he had particular problems in understanding and learning to use signs for temporal concepts. It took months of intensive training for him to begin to use tenses, for example. This certainly suggests that the process of learning to sign was not merely a matter of acquiring labels for a set of pre-existing concepts. Yet it is difficult to see, either, how temporal concepts might presuppose a set of beliefs which can only be acquired through the use of language after extensive enculturation. Acquiring the capacity to think about the past and the future is not a matter of acquiring a whole body of *beliefs* about the past and future, within which temporal concepts are embedded. On the contrary, it is, surely, inseparable from acquiring competence with some system of temporal markers, or symbols.

So does it then follow that temporal concepts, and the thoughts containing them, constitutively involve the use of public signs? Not necessarily, in fact. For it may be that there are concepts which can only be *acquired through the use of* language, but where the concepts so acquired are thereafter independent of language. That is, it may be that Ildefonso's initial temporal thoughts (considered as tokens, not types) were inseparable from the natural language signs which constitutively expressed them. But it may be that, once competence was acquired, he was thereafter capable of thinking thoughts of the same type *without* the use of those public signs. For example, competence in the use of public-language temporal signs, once attained, may be mapped across on to an equivalent system of Mentalese symbols, enabling temporal thoughts to be entertained independently of public language thereafter. So once again there is nothing in the data to force us to embrace the cognitive conception of language (at least in its strongest form). It would appear that the evidence from abnormal, as from normal, development is equivocal.

The crucial evidence which would seem to be needed here is this. What happens to a congenitally deaf child who is developmentally ready to acquire full-blown language (at age 5 or 6, say), but who has had no previous exposure to conventional sign-language, if they are then immersed in a signing community? One would predict that they would learn to sign extremely fast. If they were immediately to display evidence of dramatic changes in the creativity and flexibility of their thinking, across a range of cognitive domains, then this would count strongly in favour of the cognitive conception of language. For it would surely be implausible that at this stage the children could have had the opportunity to acquire many new beliefs through enculturation. Indeed, much of the early use of language involves comment upon items that are already perceptually present to both adult and child, and so the child cannot be acquiring any new (non-meta-linguistic) beliefs. The best explanation would be that these items of vocabulary, and the linguistic system of which they form part, would make it possible for the child to engage in a new kind of thinking – namely (as I shall argue), conscious thinking.

The only evidence bearing on the above proposal that I know of, arose out of the experiment conducted by Luria and Yudovich (1956). They took a pair of five-year-old twins who had, through neglect and lack of motivation resulting from the self-sufficiency of the 'twin situation', acquired barely any language. They separated the twins and placed them in environments where they would have the motivation to learn to communicate, and, in addition, subjected just one of them to a course of language-training. They reported marked improvements in cognitive ability with the beginnings of acquisition of language (after just three months, in fact). When first discovered, the twins appeared incapable of even rudimentary forms of play. They would move objects about and line them up, say, but would make no attempts at construction or planning, let alone at symbolic play. They also appeared incapable of classifying heterogeneous collections of objects into kinds. But as their language improved, so their play became more ordered, thoughtful, and creative; and similarly their classification abilities became more normal.

The results of this experiment are extremely suggestive for the thesis that some kinds of thinking actually involve natural language, but by no means conclusive. One initial source of worry is that the experiment was conducted within a theoretical framework which *assumes* the involvement of language in thought (following Vygotsky, 1934). Luria and Yudovich's interest was not so much in testing this framework, as in elaborating some of its details. This meant that alternative explanations of their data were neither proposed nor tested. It is therefore hard, now (especially at this distance in time), to have full confidence in the reliability of their results. And so far as I am aware the experiment has never been repeated.

It might also be objected that the twins' acquisition of language was not the only factor which may have increased the sophistication of their play. For their separation meant that they were no longer self-sufficient, and had to seek to interact with, and join in the play of, the other children in the kindergarten. Their improved play-performance may then be attributable to observational learning from the play of normal children, rather than to increased language ability. But this objection can be met, in fact, by appealing to the differential performance of the two twins after their initial separation. After three months, the language-abilities of the twin who had undergone special training were markedly better than that of his sibling, as were both the creativity of his play and his classification abilities. And this differential cannot be put down to increased opportunities for observational learning, of course.

There remains, however, the possible rejoinder which parallels the one we recently made in the case of Ildefonso – namely, that language may be necessary for the *acquisition of* certain concepts and modes of thinking, without necessarily thereafter being implicated *in* those thinkings. This proposal is hard to refute from the developmental evidence alone. For almost everyone accepts that language-acquisition is instrumental in the child's acquisition of new concepts (the notable exception being Fodor, 1981, who maintains that all concepts are innate). But it is quite another matter to maintain that the concepts so acquired are thereafter tied to the deployment of language.

So, much of the twins' dramatic cognitive development could be put down to their acquiring new conceptual structures resulting from their acquisition of language, without us necessarily having to allow that natural language was actually implicated in the use thereafter made of those conceptual structures – that is to say, in their thinking. It could be, in particular, that the twins' growing competence in the use of natural-language logical operators (particularly the conditional) was responsible for their increased creativity and improved planning abilities. In which case natural language may have been constitutively involved in their early *token* conditional thoughts. But it is another matter to claim that it remained constitutive of those thoughts as a type. It may be that once competence was attained it was transferred to some Mentalese equivalent of the conditional, enabling the twins to entertain conditional thoughts thereafter in the absence of natural language.

The evidence from aphasia

I turn, now, to consider the evidence from aphasia. This is a condition in which people who were previously normal have lost their capacity for language, resulting either from a head injury or from a stroke. The first point to be made is that there are many different forms of aphasia, each of which may admit of various degrees of severity. There are aphasias which only affect speech output, either removing it altogether, or reducing it to strings of meaningless jargon. There are aphasias which affect comprehension, aphasias which affect word-recall, aphasias which affect grammatical ability, and so on. The most interesting population for our purposes consists of so-called 'global aphasics', in whom both production and comprehension are severely affected.

Unfortunately, many investigations of intelligence in aphasia have been population-studies making little attempt to distinguish different types of aphasia (see Zangwill, 1964, and Wyke, 1988, for reviews). Moreover, severity of aphasia has often been measured by degree of impairment of language *output*, rather than by impairment of comprehension. Such aphasics are, for obvious reasons, more convenient test subjects, since they can understand and respond to instructions. And many researchers may still have been influenced by the account of inner speech due to the behaviourist John Watson, who analysed it in terms of *action inhibition* (see ch. 10 of his 1924, reproduced in Lycan, 1990). For on this account, any disruption in the capacity to *generate* speech would at the same time disrupt inner speech, hence also disrupting thought, on the hypothesis that thinking is conducted in language. But there seems no good theoretical reason for assuming that inner speech cannot be conducted in auditory imagination; and, indeed, there is a good deal of empirical evidence that it actually is (see Gathercole and Baddeley, 1993). Even Steven Pinker (who should know better) is to be found arguing from the spared cognitive abilities of a patient with production-aphasia, to the conclusion that thought is independent of language (see his 1994, ch. 2). Needless to say, no such conclusion is warranted.

It must therefore be cases of severe global aphasia which are of most direct relevance to the question of the involvement of language in thought. Unfortunately, however, it is by no means easy to devise non-linguistic tests of cognitive ability. (Witness the difficulties experienced by primatologists in devising a non-linguistic version of the false-belief tasks; see Gomez, 1996.) However, Raven's Matrices, some of which are rather like jigsaw puzzles, have been widely used. Andrew Kertesz (1988) summarises the data by remarking that aphasic performance in these and other non-verbal tasks is generally impaired, with the degree of impairment correlating significantly with the degree of comprehension deficit. But he also notes the existence of severe global aphasics in whom a variety of non-verbal abilities are quite well preserved.

Even if there is some cognitive ability which is *never* found to be left intact in cases of global aphasia, however, it would not necessarily follow that the normal operation of that ability actually involves the use of language. For it may be that the basis of the ability in question is sited in the same region of the brain as the language system, without either of them being functionally implicated in the operation of the other. It might then be that any brain-injury which damages the one will necessarily damage the other, without the one actually involving the other.

For example, many studies report some form of disorder of conceptual thinking associated with aphasia – that is, disorders which involve failures to classify objects appropriately, or to notice semantic connections between pictures, say (for reviews see Lebrun and Hoops, 1974, and Wyke, 1988). Does this support the view that deployment of concepts is tied to the use of lexical items of natural language? Not necessarily, for the reason just given. It would certainly make sense, after all, that conceptual structures (of Mentalese, by hypothesis) should be stored and processed in an area of the brain very close, at least, to the language centres, given that so much of their normal deployment is *through* language, by engagement in language production or language comprehension. If the essential function of natural language is the communication of thought, as the communicative conception of language maintains, then it is perhaps only to be expected that language should be represented in the brain very close to the thought-components (concepts, lexical items of Mentalese) which it has the function of communicating.

Conversely, even if there are clear cases of dissociation between global aphasia and some cognitive ability (such as spatial reasoning abilities), it does not follow that the ability in question is *not* language-involving. For it may well be that the language faculty consists of three distinct subsystems, and not just two. (This is Chomsky's view; see his 1995. He believes that in addition to the production and comprehension systems, there is a distinct knowledge-base which underpins both.) It may well therefore be that, besides a production system and a comprehension system, there is also what might be called a linguistic *inference system*. This would have the function of manipulating sentences, inferring other sentences from them, and so on. And it may be that this – thinking – system can be left intact when both production and comprehension systems are destroyed. (Note that Chomsky appears to commit himself to the possibility of such an inference system, when he postulates a level of representation in the language faculty which operates upon *logical form*, independently of phonological encoding; see Chomsky, 1995, and May, 1985.)

The issue of the extent of the involvement of language in thought has been much debated amongst aphasiologists, with expert opinion on the question being divided. (The terminology employed is striking: those who maintain that language is involved in thinking are known as 'sensualists', while those who maintain the independence of thought from language are 'spiritualists'. It pleases me that the thesis being defended in this book makes me a sensualist who is opposed to spiritualism!) As I understand it there is, even now, no emerging consensus on the issue, with many aphasiologists turning to investigate other, more tractable, matters.

While evidence from scientific psychology may eventually prove decisive in resolving the question of the involvement of natural language in thought, and would certainly be necessary to plot out in any detail precisely *which* kinds of thinking constitutively involve such language (as we shall see in Chapter 8), it is too early, as yet, for any firm conclusions to be drawn from the available scientific data. I shall therefore turn to consider whether we might fare better by contemplating a very different set of data, namely that delivered by ordinary introspection. It may be that, in looking to the evidence from science, we have been conducting our search too far from home, and that the case for the involvement of language in thought is actually right under our noses, available to consciousness.

2.2   The evidence of introspection – images and imaged sentences

If introspection is to be used to support the involvement of language in thought, then it is important that the question we direct to ourselves should be properly framed. Otherwise it can easily seem that introspection lends support to the sort of imagist theory of thinking which we discredited in section 1.8. For if the question I ask myself is, 'What do I mean by the word "car"?' (for example), and if I then say the word to myself while I introspect, what I find, almost inevitably, is that I have formed a visual image of a car. But the mistake here consists in asking for the meaning of a word in isolation – as Gottlob Frege pointed out long ago (see his 1884). Rather, the meaning of a word consists in its contribution to the meanings of whole sentences containing it, and a word only properly *has* its meaning within the context of a sentence.

So what one needs to do is, firstly, to introspect while (or shortly after) *using* some sentence of natural language in the course of one's daily life; and secondly, while (or shortly after) one has been entertaining privately some completed thought, or sequence of such thoughts. In the first sort of case what one discovers (as I have already indicated in the points made in section 1.8 above, following Wittgenstein) is that there is often *no* separable mental process accompanying the utterance of the sentence itself; or, at least, not one that is available to consciousness. In the second sort of case what one discovers, I believe, is that our private thoughts consist chiefly of deployments of natural language sentences in imagination – inner thinking is mostly done in inner speech.

In this second sort of case there is a limited body of systematically gathered introspective evidence available. Russ Hurlburt has devised a method for sampling people's inner experience (see Hurlburt, 1990 and 1993). Subjects wear headphones during the course of the day, through which they hear, at various intervals, a randomly generated series of bleeps. When they hear a bleep, they are instructed to immediately 'freeze', then record and elaborate, what was passing through their consciousness at the time. Although frequency varies widely, all normal subjects report experiencing inner speech on some occasions (with the minimum being 7% of occasions sampled, and the maximum being 80%; most subjects reported inner speech on more than half of the occasions sampled). Most subjects also sometimes report the occurrence of visual images, and the occurrence of emotional feelings (between 0% and 50% of occasions sampled in each case). (Moreover, most people also report entertaining some *wordless*, or purely propositional, thoughts. This is a finding I shall return to in section 2.4 below, and then again at some length in section 8.3.)

Introspection informs us, in fact, that many of our thoughts are expressed entirely in natural language – for example, my thoughts as I write this, and, no doubt, yours as you read it. When I sit and draft a letter to someone in my head, for example, what figures in my consciousness is a sequence of English sentences in auditory (and perhaps kinaesthetic) imagination, rather as if I were dictating that letter aloud. Or, if this is considered too easy for me (since the task is itself a linguistic one), take as an example any case where I sit and try to think through some abstract problem – comparing competing explanations of autism, say. In such cases I find that my thoughts will consist almost entirely of inner dialogue. Consider another point, too – learners of a second language will characteristically report that there is a watershed in the learning process at which they begin to be able to *think in* (and even dream in!) the language under study. Then such people, at least, must be under the impression that they do their thinking in one natural language or another.

Many others of our thoughts consist of combinations of natural-language sentences and mental images. For example, while driving home I might be considering how to re-arrange the furniture in my office, and I might think to myself, 'I shall put the desk *there*', where *there* relates to a visual image of a particular location by the window. Even in those rarer cases where the *only* introspective vehicle of thought is a mental image, it seems that there is, almost always, an implicit sentential embedding to endow the image with a determinate content. For example, when faced with a particular practical problem, such as how to reach an object on top of a tall wardrobe, the solution may come to me simply in the form of a visual image, such as myself standing on top of a stool. In such a case the image may get its significance from my *disposition* to entertain in thought a sentence such as, 'If I place the stool like *that*, then I shall be able to reach.'

Introspection informs us of a good deal more than all this, indeed. Some people report that their thoughts occur to them in the form of images of different heard voices, as if a number of different people were speaking to them, or as if they were hearing themselves speak (see Hurlburt, 1990 and 1993). For example, without prior teaching or prompting I asked my son Isaac (then aged 4½) how he did his thinking. He replied, 'I think in English.' I asked him how he knew this, and he replied, 'I can *hear* myself think.' As for myself, I can report that most of my thoughts occur in the form of imaged conversations, in which I imagine myself saying things, often, though by no means always, to a determinate audience.

In fact this is the grain of truth, it seems to me, in the imagist theory of thinking. It is images *of natural language sentences* which are the primary vehicles of our conscious thoughts, and we think and reason primarily by manipulating such images. So, while it may be true that we could not think consciously at all unless we had imagination, studying the nature of mental imagery will be a good deal less useful in investigating the nature of thought than will studying the nature of natural language. For it is not the image, as such, which carries the content of the thought, but rather *what is imaged* – namely, a natural-language sentence.

We often do our thinking aloud, or on paper. (Indeed, this fact causes particular problems for the communicative conception of language, with its special emphasis on the role of natural language in communication, as we shall see in Chapter 3.) It is common for young children to accompany their games and activities with spoken monologues, and many adults, too, will chat to themselves when alone, or to their babies and pets. Even more frequently, those of us whose work involves the written word – whether academics, or bureaucrats, or business executives – will do much of our thinking on paper, or at the keyboard. In many such cases one does not *first* entertain a private thought and *then* write it down; rather, the thinking *is* the writing.

Even many overtly communicative uses of language can equally be characterised as a kind of public thinking. For example, consider cases where one *reasons with* someone, trying to convince them of the truth of some proposition, or of something that they should do. Here, again, the activities of thinking and speaking seem inseparable. All this is provided, of course, that introspection is correct in telling us that we *think in* the public medium, rather than that we translate our prior thought *into* that medium.

According to introspection, then, private and public thought are alike in that they both involve sentences of natural language. Just as a good deal of private thinking consists in the imaging of spoken or heard sentences, and in the manipulation of such images; so, too, many overt uses of language would seem to constitute a sort of *public thinking*. And both sorts of thinking operate in an essentially similar manner – namely, in the one case in the imaging of, and in the other case in the utterance or writing of, sequences of natural language sentences.

These similarities may be further confirmed by our impression of what happens when we make the transition from private thought to public utterance, or vice versa. For example, I may be thinking, privately, about where to go on holiday next year, entertaining such thoughts as, 'It would be nice to go somewhere hot.' Then, realising that my wife has entered the room, I may say aloud, 'We could go to Avignon this time.' In such cases there is no introspective impression of *hiatus*, or of transition between radically distinct symbolic systems. It is quite unlike even those cases where one makes a spoken transition between different natural languages – as when, while in France, I negotiate a purchase for my son, and have to switch backwards and forwards between English and French. Indeed, it seems much *more* like those instances which often occur when I lecture, where I utter one sentence aloud and then write the next on the blackboard. In both cases the sentences follow one another smoothly, as part of the same unbroken chain of thought.

2.3   The scope and strength of the introspective thesis

The arguments sketched above seem to show that at least *some* human thought does in fact involve natural language – though I shall shortly begin to consider some possible replies from the lovers of Mentalese. But the scope of the thesis is, so far, quite severely restricted. In the first place, of course, the thesis defended above extends only to thoughts that are *conscious*, since it was based on the deliverances of introspection. If there are thoughts that are *non*-conscious, as I shall suggest in Chapter 5 that there are, then nothing has as yet been said to suggest that they, too, will involve natural language. Perhaps less obviously, but more importantly, the introspective thesis so far defended only extends to occurrent, or episodic, acts of thinking, not to thoughts that are standing states, as are most beliefs, desires, and intentions.

There is a general distinction to be drawn amongst mental states between those that are episodic events – occurring at particular times with particular, if not exactly measurable, durations – and those that are not. In the former category will fall bodily sensations, emotions, perceptions, imaginings, and after-images, as well as acts of thinking, wondering whether, supposing, deciding, remembering, and so on. When I feel a stab of pain in my ankle while running, or see a rabbit jump from my path into the bushes, or wonder whether it is time to turn for home, these are all mental events that occur at particular times in my life.

In the category of standing states, in contrast, will fall beliefs, desires, hopes, intentions, and memories, as well as character traits such as generosity and credulity. My belief that Sheffield is in England, and my memory of my fifth birthday-party, are states that I will retain throughout most of my life. The general term 'thought', in philosophical use, includes events and states from both categories, covering all those that take propositional objects, being canonically described by means of a that-clause. So perceptions, propositional thinkings, imaginings, and acts of remembering, as well as long-term beliefs, desires, and intentions (but not sensations or character traits) are all of them thoughts, in this sense.

Now it is only episodic thoughts that can be characterised as events in consciousness, or that are immediately available to introspection. For one can, for example, easily forget what one believes, or desires, or intends. Since we cannot directly introspect our beliefs, desires, or intentions, it has not yet been shown that they, too, involve natural language. So the most that has been established by the introspective argument given above, is that our *episodic* acts of thinking involve natural language, not that all thoughts do.

Even this is too strong, indeed. For in philosopher's usage, not only would acts of judging-that, wondering whether, and such like, be described as '(occurrent) thoughts', so too would perceptual states of seeing-that, hearing-that, and so on, as also would states of imagining-that. Yet it is hardly very plausible to claim that we *see in* natural language, or entertain visual or auditory images in natural language! When I notice a car approaching while I am crossing a road, and quicken my pace accordingly, it does not seem plausible to claim that my perception of the car is expressed in English, or constitutively involves any English sentence. Of course I *may* think consciously to myself, 'I had better get out of the way of that car'; but then I may not – I may just act appropriately, on the basis of my conscious perception. Equally, as we noted in section 1.8, when I entertain a visual image of the street-layout of the city of Sheffield, it is plain that I need not be entertaining any English description.

So the most that I should wish to claim on the basis of introspection, is that it is episodic, properly propositional, *thinkings* (in the narrow sense, to include acts of judging-that, wondering whether, supposing-that, and so on, but not including perceptual or quasi-perceptual states of seeing-that, or hearing-that, or imagining-that) which constitutively involve natural language. It is one thing to *notice* a car approaching, or to *imagine* the wind on my face, and another thing to *think to myself* that there is a car coming, or that it is windy today. And it is only the latter events which are language-involving, if introspection is to be believed – although, as we shall see in Chapters 7 and 8, it may well be the case that conscious perceivings and imaginings only achieve their status *as* conscious by virtue of being made available to a kind of thinking which *does* involve natural language.

I have suggested that the scope of the introspective thesis should be restricted to occurrent propositional thinkings. However, there may be a way in which it could be extended to include standing-state propositional attitudes as well. For we can draw a further distinction between beliefs and desires which are *dormant* and those which are *active*. Most of our beliefs and desires lie dormant for most of the time, continuing to exist, but without having any effect on current mental processes. My belief that Sheffield is in England is something that I retain throughout my life, but only rarely does it make any difference to what I think or do. Sometimes, however, those beliefs and desires become active, as when one forms new beliefs on the basis of old, or acts so as to satisfy a desire.

Now, it is highly plausible that *one* way in which a standing state can become active is by emerging as, or causing, an appropriately related episodic event. Thus, one way for my belief that roses are powerfully scented to become activated, is for it to cause me to think, in assertoric mode, 'Roses are powerfully scented.' And one way for my desire for fame to become activated, is for me to think to myself, 'Would that I were famous!', or something sufficiently similar. (These points will prove to be of some importance in Chapter 6.) Then if these latter episodic events involve natural language, as the argument from introspection suggests, it will follow that the standing states must also involve such language, at least to this extent – that they are partly constituted by their disposition to give rise to episodic events which involve natural language.

(It does not yet follow, of course, that one's beliefs and desires are *stored as*, or in the form of, natural-language sentences. But considerations of simplicity would certainly suggest it. If a large part of the way in which beliefs and desires function actively in cognition is through natural language, then it would certainly make sense that they should also be stored in that form.)

It begins to seem plausible that a good deal of conscious human thinking, at least, might involve natural language. But this claim is still relatively weak, for our purposes. For no modal conclusions are yet warranted. That our conscious thinkings *do* occur in, or involve, natural language does not yet show that they *must*, not even out of mere natural necessity. It will be the task of Chapter 8 to try to establish this stronger conclusion. But what does already follow from the considerations above – at least if they stand unchallenged – is that our conscious thinkings *do not* occur in Mentalese.

If my conscious thinkings take place in English, as I have claimed on the basis of introspection that they do, then of course they do not take place in any other natural language, let alone in a supposedly innate, universal, symbolic system such as Mentalese. So if the argument from introspection is allowed to stand, we have already done enough to show that Fodor and others are wrong to claim that all thoughts are expressed in Mentalese. It may turn out to be the case that *non*-conscious episodic thinkings occur in Mentalese, and it might remain possible, though unlikely, that standing state thoughts should be stored in that form. But conscious episodic thinkings would definitely seem, at this point, to involve natural language. I shall return to consider Fodor's possible avenues of reply in section 2.5 below.

2.4   Objections and elucidations

The introspective thesis that we do much of our conscious thinking in natural language sentences faces a number of intuitive objections. In this section I shall address as many of them as I can, taken in no particular order. Some of these objections will be returned to in much more detail in later chapters.

(1) 'A thought can surely occur to us in a flash, fully-formed and apparently determinate in content, without there being time for any sentence expressing that thought to be formulated, and without any such sentence being introspectively accessible.'

But the reply to this is relatively easy, and is the one given by

Wittgenstein (1953, sections 318–20). Lightning-like thought can occur in the same way and for the same reason that it is possible to make a note of a thought in a few pencilled dashes – namely, what makes those dashes into the expression of a complete thought is my ability to expand them *into* such a thought, together with my present disposition to make use of them as if they *already* expressed such a thought. The phenomenon of lightning-like thought is one which is, in fact, equally characteristic of public speech or writing as of private thinking, and so cannot serve to undermine the claim that we think in natural-language sentences.

(2) 'But surely we are often aware of a thought, or of entertaining a conscious thought, without any sentence figuring amongst the data available to introspection. For example, when choosing amongst a number of garments from a display I can surely judge that the right-hand one has the more attractive colour without the form of words, 'The right-hand one has the nicest colour', – or indeed *any* form of words – figuring in my consciousness. And this is confirmed in the experience-sampling data gathered by Hurlburt (1990 and 1993), since many subjects reported having wordless, purely propositional, thoughts on occasion.'

My response to this point is to grant that we often have thoughts which may not involve images, either of objects or of public-language sentences, but to deny that those thoughts are conscious ones. In part this reply will have to wait on the discussion of consciousness in later chapters. But very roughly, what I mean by a conscious thought is one that we are aware of ourselves having, when we have it, *non-inferentially* (in a way which is different from our awareness of the thoughts of other people). But what happens in cases of languageless (and imageless) apparently conscious thinking, in my view, is that the thought is, in fact, *not* so available. Rather, it is self-ascribed on the basis of a swift retrospective self-interpretation, much as it might be ascribed to a third party. I shall return to defend this way of looking at the issue in section 7.3, and then again more fully in section 8.3.

(3) 'But what of various forms of tip-of-the-tongue phenomena? It is a familiar occurrence that people find themselves knowing (or at least believing that they know) what they want to say, but being unable, for the moment, to find quite the right words to express it – often with the sense that there is a word or phrase which exactly fits what they mean, if only they could recall it. Here, it seems, there is a thought which is both conscious and determinate prior to any natural-language sentence being found for its expression, which would suggest that the thought itself is independent of such language.'

But there are a variety of different kinds of phenomena involved here, in fact (as Wittgenstein again points out, 1953, section 335), none of which raises a real problem for the introspective thesis defended above. One sort of case is where there is, indeed, a determinate thought present, which is expressed, at least in part, in some other form of representation. Asked for directions to the City Hall I may find myself floundering, trying to express my determinate (imagistic) knowledge in terms of names of streets, and right and left turns. But since I have already allowed that some thinking – particularly spatial thinking – can involve visual and other images, there is no particular problem here.

In other sorts of case I believe it can plausibly be denied that there is any determinate thought in existence prior to its linguistic formulation. Rather, what happens is that I know (or believe) that there is thought there to be had, and am confident that I would recognise it if I found it. In fact, I am struggling to *find* – or to *have* – a thought of a certain sort, not struggling to *express* a thought which I have already entertained. The situation is rather like one in which, looking at some sort of visual puzzle or maze, I can be entirely confident that the puzzle does have a solution, and a solution of a certain sort, prior to the actual discovery of that solution. Evidence supporting this reading of the phenomena come from those not-infrequent cases where, on pressing further for the thought which I took to be there, I find that I was really just confused, and that there exists *no* thought of the kind that I wanted.

(4) 'Consider examples where one makes a choice between alternative words in expressing a thought. Does this not show that the thought itself must already exist in consciousness independently of the words used to express it?'

In fact not. And once again, there are really two sorts of case here. One of them parallels the phenomenon just discussed. Sometimes choosing between alternative words is choosing between alternative, slightly different, thoughts – one of which may be more appropriate to the context, or each of which may be appropriate in different ways.

The other sort of case just requires – what I have anyway allowed – that some of our *non*-conscious thoughts may fail to involve natural language. In cases where I choose between alternative ways of expressing a thought, I am prepared to allow that there is, sometimes, a thought already there to be expressed; but I deny that it is a *conscious* thought. Similar points apply to the processes which constrain and guide the way in which we fit together words and phrases to form sentences – either aloud or in imagination. I can allow that such processes are thoughtful, but deny that the thoughts in question are conscious ones. My hypothesis – to be pursued in later chapters – is that thoughts only become conscious when they emerge into episodic *imagings*, either of public sentences alone, or of mixtures of sentences and of objects or places.

(5) 'But many sentences of natural language are ambiguous. To take a hackneyed example, the sentence, "John is at the bank", can mean either "bank-of-a-river" or "banking-institution". Yet my thoughts are, surely, not similarly ambiguous. When I think, "I shall go to the bank in the lunch-hour", there is normally no indeterminacy in my meaning. In which case my thoughts cannot be identified with the sentences used to express them.'

I have two replies. One is that it may not be the sentence, as such, which constitutes a given thought, according to the introspective thesis; it is, rather, the sentence *in use*. An occurrent thought will consist in an imaged sentence *taken together with my dispositions to reason and act on that sentence in one set of ways rather than another*. So it is not just the imaged sentence, 'I shall go to the bank', which constitutes my decision to attend a banking-institution; it is that together with a background of dispositions and abilities. (On the idea of 'the background' to thought, see Searle, 1983, ch. 5.) And it may well be the case that these in turn do not similarly involve natural language. But then neither are they conscious. So the thesis that it is our *conscious* thinkings which consist in deployments of imaged natural language sentences can remain intact.

The second reply is that an imaged sentence is not, in any case, a merely phonological representation; rather, the content is represented in the image too. The imaged sentence, 'I shall go to the bank', carries with it one or other possible interpretation, just as the heard sentence would do. When we hear people speak, we do not just hear phonology, and then have to figure out an interpretation. Rather, what we hear is already interpreted. If someone says to me, 'I shall go to the bank', then I will immediately *hear* this as meaning one thing or another (depending on the context) – though I may have to think again if the meaning I hear is sufficiently incongruous. So it is, too, with inner speech. Ambiguous sentences always carry with them some particular interpretation when imaged. Putting the point in terms of the reply of the previous paragraph: the background dispositions which constitute my meaning the sentence in one way or the other may be realised in some sort of representational structure (of Chomsky's logical form, or LF, as it might be) which is already attached to the phonological representation. So the image is actually an interpreted object – it is not ambiguous.

(6) 'But do not creative thinkers like Einstein often insist that their thinking is done without words, but rather through fleeting images and feelings which seem to bear no relation to words? (see Ghiselin, 1952). And do not the solutions to problems often just come to us, already formulated? In such cases one must have been thinking, in order to have reached a solution; but the thinking was not done in introspectively accessible words.'

These points are good ones. But to say that creative thinking is done wordlessly may only mean that it is done non-consciously. Not for nothing have poets traditionally prayed to the Muses for inspiration; for we often have no idea where our genuinely novel ideas come from, nor is there much that we can do intentionally in order to get them. Sometimes a relaxing environment can help – a hot bath, a daydream, or a good night's sleep. But when ideas do come, they seem to us to come of their own accord, often with no discernible history.

As has often been remarked, indeed, it may be that intelligence divides into two separate components – a creative, non-discursive, non-conscious idea-*generator* on the one hand, and a judgemental, logical, discursive, conscious planner and idea-*assessor* on the other. In which case, it may very well be the case that when engaged in creative thinking, all that will pass through my consciousness may be irrelevant and fleeting images and feelings. For the thinking itself is non-conscious. This is perfectly consistent with the claim to be defended in this book, that *conscious* thinking involves language. (It is also consistent with the claim, note, that the non-conscious creative thinking is *also* language-involving. It is hard to see any reason why language could *only* figure in thought in conscious mode. I shall return to this point in section 8.7.)

(7) 'But what are you to say about conversational implicatures, and about pragmatics? Consider metaphor, for example. Suppose that an irritated teacher remarks of a pupil, "That fat slug is just waiting for his lunch". Here what is *meant* – the thought expressed – is something like: that the pupil is fat and slow and indolent, and thinks about food instead of working. But what is *said* is something quite different – something which either fails to refer at all, since there is no appropriately salient slug, or which says, absurdly, that the pupil in question *is* a slug. Then, since there is a mismatch between what is thought and what is literally said, must not the two be wholly separate? The thought might be formulated in one way – in Mentalese, as it may be – but then given its public expression quite differently.'

This way of looking at the matter is by no means mandatory, however. The fact that a particular sentence-token of natural language only obtains its intended content, in a particular context, when taken together with a good many surrounding beliefs and intentions, does not mean that the occurrence of that content is independent of the sentence-token in question. Rather, we can say that *this* token occurrence of that thought is inseparably bound up with its (non-literal) linguistic expression, but also depends for its existence on a variety of other thoughts which make it the case that the latter is constitutive of the former.

2.5   Fallible introspection and Fodor

Recall from section 1.8 that I am accepting, with Fodor, that thoughts *are* sentences which are tokened, stored, and processed in characteristic ways. And recall, too, that Fodor's claim is that *all* thought is conducted in sentences of Mentalese. But now the introspection-based argument developed above maintains that our conscious thoughts (at least when episodic and properly propositional) are sentences of *natural* language. So there is an inconsistency: one or other of this trio of claims must be false. How should Fodor respond?

One way in which he *could* respond, would be by denying that introspection is reliable on such matters. If Fodor is to maintain that all thoughts, including conscious episodic ones, are expressed in Mentalese, in the face of an argument from introspection to the contrary, then he could try to find some way of rejecting the deliverances of introspection. This need not necessarily be as difficult as it sounds. For hardly anyone, nowadays, maintains that introspection is strictly infallible, in true Cartesian tradition. Most hold that there is scope for error in our awareness of our own mental states, just as there is in our awareness of objects outside us. So if Fodor claims that introspection misleads us into thinking that our conscious thoughts involve natural language when they do not, this cannot plausibly be refuted by an appeal to introspective infallibility.

However, most people today also think that introspection, like external perception, is generally reliable. True enough, there are some people who deny that mental states really exist at all (see Churchland, 1981). In which case introspective awareness could hardly be claimed to deliver us with truths about our mental lives. But almost everyone who believes that there are truths about mental states available to be had – whether realists, like myself and Fodor, or interpretationalists, like Davidson and Dummett – maintains that introspection will generally be reliable in getting us those truths. If I think that I feel pain, then I generally do; if I think that I am thirsty, then I generally am; if I think that I am fantasising, or reasoning, or deciding, then that is generally what I am doing; and so on. It is, therefore, not enough for Fodor merely to appeal to the possibility of introspective error. Some reason needs to be given why the error should be systematic and persistent. For if Fodor is correct, then we are all of us systematically misled into believing, on the basis of introspection, that we think in natural language.

But Fodor does not need to deny the phenomenon of inner speech *as such*, in fact, nor the reliability of introspection in relation to it. That is, he need not reject the introspective datum that images of natural language sentences figure prominently in consciousness *when* we think. But what he must deny is that such sentences *constitute* our thoughts. My claim is that when, in the course of trying to solve a practical problem, I am aware of imaging the sentence, 'I will get it by climbing on the box', then what I am aware of *is* the thought. My claim is that it is the imaged sentence itself, in context, which is the occurrent intention, and which then sets in train the motor routines which cause my body to climb up on the box. And this is the way in which I would naturally report my introspection – I was *aware of deciding* to climb on the box (and not just aware of something *caused by* my decision), and it is *because* I so decided that I did it. Our common-sense construal of the introspective datum, is that the imaged sentences which we are aware of occupy the causal roles in our cognition distinctive of thinking.

Fodor must claim that both I, and common sense, are mistaken. What I am aware of here is not the occurrent intention itself (which is, he will say, expressed in Mentalese), but some mere concomitant of it. My dispute with Fodor can thus concern the causal roles of imaged natural-language sentences, rather than their existence. The dispute can be about whether natural-language sentences occupy the causal roles within our cognition of thinkings, decidings, and wonderings whether; not about whether such sentences figure in cognition at all. My claim is that it is the imaged sentence itself – 'I shall get it by climbing on the box' – which occupies the causal role of the thought (the thought, namely, *that I will get it by climbing on the box*). Fodor's claim must rather be that the thought itself, expressed in Mentalese, somehow *causes* the imaging of the natural-language sentence (as well as causing me to climb on the box).

If Fodor's views on the nature of thinking are to be vindicated, then what he needs is either a full-blown theory of consciousness (a theory of introspective self-awareness), or at least a plausible account of the role of inner verbalisation within our cognition (if that role is not the one distinctive of thinking). He therefore needs at least enough of an account of introspection which will not only be plausible and convincing in its own right, but will at the same time explain how we come to be under the systematic illusion that our conscious thoughts involve natural language. This is not something that he actually provides anywhere in his writings. So we shall need to consider what can be done on his behalf.

We shall need to canvass a variety of theories of consciousness, and a variety of accounts of the causal role of inner speech, to see whether a thesis of systematic illusion can be made out. If the most plausible of these theories turns out to have the consequence that Fodor requires, then he will face no problem from the introspective argument presented in this chapter. He can reply that our best theory of consciousness, and/or our best account of inner speech, implies that we shall all easily become deluded on this matter. So here is one reason why the question of the extent to which thought involves natural language should lead us to investigate theories of consciousness, as we shall do in Chapters 5 to 7. (Another reason will be given shortly, in section 2.7.)

Suppose, however, (and as I shall argue, in fact) that our best available theory of consciousness, and our best account of the function of inner speech, do *not* provide us with any grounds for believing that we might be systematically deluded about the nature of conscious thinking. Would this mean that Fodor's position – that all thinking is conducted in Mentalese – could not be rationally believed? Not necessarily. That would depend upon the strength of his arguments in support of his thesis. For suppose that those arguments were very powerful. Then provided that there were *some* theory of consciousness, or *some* theory of the function of inner speech, which would support the idea of systematic introspective illusion, then the most rational course might be to endorse that theory, even though it is, on other grounds, somewhat weaker. Indeed, even if *none* of the available theories were to support the idea of systematic illusion, this need not mean that Fodor's position could not be rationally believed. For if his arguments are strong enough, the best course might be to insist that introspection must be mistaken on this issue, and to maintain, in consequence, that no one has yet managed to propose an acceptable theory of introspective awareness, or an acceptable account of the role of inner speech.

This means that we shall have to spend some time considering the strength of Fodor's arguments for the thesis that all thought occurs in Mentalese. This task will be begun in the next section, and will occupy us through to Chapter 4. In the present chapter I shall confine myself to three of Fodor's more explicit arguments, as developed in his 1978 (see also his 1987, Appendix).

2.6   Individuating propositional attitudes

The first of Fodor's arguments that I shall consider here, proceeds by attacking the contrary claim that beliefs and desires are relations to sentences in the natural language which is native to the believer or desirer in question. The argument is, that claiming propositional attitudes to be relations to natural language sentences will *slice them too thin*. That is, if beliefs and desires are individuated in terms of the natural-language sentences which are claimed to constitute them, then the resulting identity conditions will lead us to distinguish beliefs and desires which are, in reality, the same.

It will then turn out, for example, that the belief *that the dog bit the man* is distinct from the belief *that the man was bitten by the dog*, because the natural-language sentences, 'The dog bit the man', and, 'The man was bitten by the dog', are different from one another. Whereas we would surely want to claim that those beliefs were one and the same. Similarly, it will turn out that Oedipus' desire *to marry Jocasta* is distinct from his desire *that Jocasta be his wife*, since the sentences, 'I am married to Jocasta', and, 'Jocasta is my wife', are different. But again, we would surely want to insist that these desires are identical.

The principle of propositional-attitude individuation appealed to here derives from Frege (1892), and is often known as *the intuitive criterion of difference*. On this account, thoughts are distinct in content if, and only if, it is possible for a thinker to take differing epistemic attitudes towards them at one and the same time. So the belief *that Venus has set* is distinct from the belief *that the evening star has set*, since it is possible for someone, not knowing that Venus and the evening star are one and the same, to believe that Venus has set while doubting that the evening star has. By the same token, Oedipus' desire *to marry Jocasta* is distinct from any desire *to marry his mother*, since it is plainly possible to have the one desire but not the other – as, in fact, he did. In contrast, it does not seem possible that someone should believe *that the dog bit the man* while doubting whether *the man was bitten by the dog*, except out of momentary confusion or madness. Nor does it seem intelligible that Oedipus should want to marry Jocasta while having an aversion to the thought that Jocasta should be his wife.

It is worth noting that while the intuitive criterion of difference slices thicker than natural-language sentences, it still cuts propositional attitudes pretty finely – in particular, more finely than logical equivalence. Thus, by the criterion, the belief *that there are 9 planets* will come out as distinct from the belief *that the number of planets is two larger than the smallest prime number larger than 5*. This is so for two distinct reasons. First, it seems plain that someone could believe the first while being inclined to doubt the second, because of errors in calculating the result. Second, the latter belief contains concepts – for example, the concept *prime number* – not contained in the former. So someone could believe the former while failing to believe the latter because they lacked the concept of a prime number.

Fodor's claim, then, is that once we have accepted that propositional attitudes are relations to sentences, the only theory consistent with the principle of individuation contained in the intuitive criterion of difference is that the sentences in question are sentences of Mentalese. The hypothesis can then be, that the sentences, 'The dog bit the man', and, 'The man was bitten by the dog', will both translate into the very same sentence of

Mentalese, as will each of the sentences, 'I am married to Jocasta', and, 'Jocasta is my wife.' So the reason why someone must assent to each of these pairs of sentences if they assent to either, is that they are both equally acceptable public translations of the Mentalese sentence which really constitutes their propositional attitude.

In reply to this argument, it is only necessary to introduce the distinction between *core* and *dispositional* propositional attitudes, deployed by Field, 1978, following Dennett, 1975. A core belief, for example, is one which has been explicitly computed and stored in memory – in the form of some sort of sentence, if the sentential account of propositional attitudes is correct. A dispositional belief, in contrast, will be any *obvious consequence of* a core belief, apt to be explicitly computed as soon as circumstances demand. Now, before I put this distinction to work in answering Fodor's argument, I shall show how it is independently motivated – that is, I shall show how the distinction is one which needs to be drawn anyway, whether we believe that propositional attitudes are relations to sentences of natural language, or of Mentalese.

The distinction between core and dispositional beliefs is required to explain how we may correctly attribute an unlimited set of beliefs to creatures, such as ourselves, with finite cognitive space. I surely say something true of you when I say that you believe that 61 is larger than 60; that 62 is larger than 61; that 63 is larger than 62; that 64 is larger than 63; . . . that 73,000,001 is larger than 73,000,000; and so on without limit. Equally (to use Dennett's more colourful example), I surely say something true of you when I say that you believe that zebras in the wild do not wear overcoats; that they do not hold barbecues; that they do not read Shakespeare; and so on, again without limit. But it is highly implausible to suggest that each of these beliefs corresponds to a distinct state of your brain (a stored sentence). For there are, to put it mildly, too many of them. Rather, each is an obvious consequence of some body of explicitly stored beliefs, in such a way that you will, for example, immediately answer 'Yes' if asked whether 73,000,001 is larger than 73,000,000. And note that something like this will need to be said whether beliefs are stored in natural language, or Mentalese, or some other system of representation altogether.

Now, with the distinction between core and dispositional beliefs in place, we can say that the belief *that P* is none other than (is the very same as) the belief *that Q* whenever the sentence 'P' is *obviously equivalent to* the sentence 'Q'. For then it will not matter, for purposes of psychological explanation, *which* sentence we use to characterise the subject's belief. For if either belief is core, then the other will be dispositional. No matter whether it is the sentence 'P' or the sentence 'Q' which is stored in memory, the person will be disposed immediately to compute the other sentence if required. So if they assent to the question, 'Do you believe that P?', then they will also assent to the question, 'Do you believe that Q?', and vice versa.

We can now reply to Fodor's argument against the thesis that beliefs are relations to sentences of natural language, by saying that, more strictly, beliefs are relations to sets of obviously equivalent natural-language sentences; and that a core belief will consist in the storage of any one of a set of obviously equivalent natural-language sentences. Indeed, it is an additional virtue of the natural-language account that it can provide a substantive *explanation* of the condition for thought-identity captured in the intuitive criterion of difference. It is *because* it makes no apparent psychological difference whether it is the sentence 'P' or the sentence 'Q' which is stored, if 'P' and 'Q' are obviously equivalent, that it will make no difference whether the thinker is described as believing *that P* or as believing *that Q*.

('Obvious equivalence to whom?', you might ask. Obvious to the subject to whom the beliefs are being attributed, in the first instance. It is because the subject in question will immediately assent to 'P' if they are already inclined to assent to 'Q', and will similarly assent to 'Q' if they are already inclined to assent to 'P', that it makes no significant difference whether we describe them, in either case, as believing *that P* or as believing *that Q*. But it is, on the present hypothesis, a presupposition of our practice of ascribing beliefs in accordance with the intuitive criterion of difference, that such patterns of obviousness should be widely shared. I rely on the fact that *I* find 'P' and 'Q' to be obviously equivalent when I judge that these two sentences should be counted as expressing the same belief. And generally such judgements are borne out in psychological practice.)

2.7   Animals and infants

Another of Fodor's major arguments for the thesis that the language in which we think is Mentalese, is that animals and pre-linguistic human infants have thoughts – beliefs, desires, intentions, and the rest – but no natural language. In which case the sentences constitutive of their thoughts cannot be natural-language ones. Now, it is not very plausible to deny the premise of this argument. While some have denied that animals and infants have beliefs and desires, their grounds for doing so have either been weak, or have depended upon some anti-realist conception of the mind. At any rate, their position is not one that I propose to take seriously in this book. (For further discussion, see my 1992c, ch. 6.) It is much more plausible to respond by denying that the conclusion follows from the premise – not even non-demonstratively, by means of an inference to the best explanation.

In the first place, the most that follows from the claim that non-human animals have propositional attitudes, of course, is that *they* entertain their thoughts in some form of Mentalese, whose sentences perhaps have the same meanings as some of the simpler sentences of human natural language. There seems no particular reason to believe, as yet, that human thoughts will employ the very same medium of representation, especially given the manifest differences that exist between human and animal modes of cognition.

The case of pre-linguistic human infants might seem more problematic, however. For if we concede that their thoughts occur in Mentalese, then the simplest hypothesis would appear to be that all human thoughts are similarly expressed. For it is simpler to suppose that human cognition employs just one system of representation rather than two. Not that this conclusion is by any means forced on us. For there remains the counter-suggestion put forward by Field (1978), that natural-language propositional attitudes get grafted onto a more primitive system of Mentalese employed by pre-linguistic children. Indeed, when put together with the evidence from introspection, presented earlier in this chapter, this might seem to be the most plausible proposal overall.

Field's counter-suggestion can be strengthened still further, however – even to the point of being able to stand independently of the evidence of introspection – if we can identify some major *functional* difference between the thoughts of adults and those of pre-linguistic infants and animals. For otherwise, why should it be supposed that there are two quite different systems of representation in operation, especially within the cognition of a single organism? This will occupy us extensively in the latter half of this book, where I shall argue that the difference in question corresponds to the distinction between *conscious* and *non*-conscious propositional attitudes. In fact this argument of Fodor's will only finally be answered in section 7.8, at the conclusion of my discussion of the nature of consciousness. I shall then go on to claim that conscious thinkings are relations to natural-language sentences, whereas non-conscious ones are – or may be – relations to sentences of Mentalese.

(In fact I shall remain agnostic on the question whether the non-conscious thoughts of animals and pre-linguistic infants are best understood on the sentential model, or whether they should be thought of as imagistic, or whether, indeed, they might be better approached from the standpoint of so-called *connectionist* cognitive architectures. I shall also remain agnostic about whether or not the central-process propositional attitudes of animals and pre-linguistic infants employ the same systems of representation as figure in the various sub-personal mental modules to be discussed in the second part of the next section.)

2.8   Language-learning and sub-personal thought

Yet another of Fodor's main arguments for the thesis that propositional attitudes are relations to sentences of Mentalese, turns on the question of how natural languages are learned. I shall first present and criticise this argument, before introducing some relevant considerations to do with the *modularity* of the mind.

The argument

Fodor claims that the only theory of learning which we have, is that learning always involves an inference to the best explanation. On this view, learning, of whatever kind, always involves the stages familiar to students of scientific method, of data-collection, hypothesis formation, testing, and confirmation. So when an infant learns the meaning of the word 'cat', for example, it must first gather some data about adult usage, then formulate a hypothesis, such as that 'cat' means 'furry animal', and then confirm or refute (and subsequently modify) that hypothesis in the light of further observation.

All of this presupposes, of course, that the infant has some symbolic system in which it can describe and record the initial data, and in which it can express and modify its hypotheses. It is hard to see how anything could serve, here, except an articulate language – indeed, a language with the full expressive power of human natural language. But, plainly, this symbolic system cannot *be* a natural language, on pain of vicious circularity. Since the symbolic system in question is the medium of representation through which natural languages are supposed to be learned, it must be a universal, presumably innate, language of thought – that is to say, Mentalese.

There is an obvious initial reply to this argument, which appears to have at least some independent motivation. It is, that knowledge of natural language is not so much a matter of knowledge *that* – that is, of propositional knowledge – as of knowledge *how*, the kind of knowledge which is involved in possessing a *skill*, or practical capacity. On this view, learning your first natural language is not like learning a body of facts, such as quantum physics, but is more like acquiring a practical skill, such as the ability to ride a bicycle. For we do say that the child is learning *how* to speak, and knowledge of the meaning of a word is quite naturally assimilated to an *ability* to use it correctly. And presumably no one thinks that, in order to learn to ride a bicycle, the child must formulate and test hypotheses about such matters as the correct angle at which to lean into a corner that is taken with a given angular velocity. So why should we think that the child learning its first language must be formulating hypotheses about the meanings of words, either?

Fodor has available to him a twofold rejoinder. First, he can point out that if knowledge of a natural language is a practical capacity, it must be a special sort of capacity, whose categorical basis in the brain somehow reflects the semantic and syntactic structures of the language in question. For no one who is not a behaviourist thinks that learning a natural language is a mere matter of behavioural training, or of developing the right conditioned responses. This is because of the unlimited creativity of language. Anyone who masters a natural language has the capacity to understand, to use, and to recognise the well-formedness of unlimitedly many distinct sentences. The basis of their capacity must, then, at least be structured into distinct recombinable components, rather as sentences are composed of distinct recombinable words. It is another matter, however, to claim that the basis of the capacity to use a natural language is properly characterised in terms of propositional knowledge, as Fodor does. In fact, we can continue to maintain against him that knowledge of a natural language is a practical capacity, albeit one whose categorical basis is appropriately structured. (For further discussion of this issue, see my 1992a, ch. 6.)

The second rejoinder available to Fodor, and the one he actually pursues (at least implicitly), is more radical. It is to claim that knowledge *how* is, at a deeper level, to be assimilated to knowledge *that*. For he claims that all cognitive processing, at all levels of cognition, involves computations on language-like representations. His argument for this is an argument from the presuppositions of much cognitive science, of which David Marr's 1982 might serve as a suitable example. Marr and others in the study of sub-personal systems of vision, language-acquisition, face recognition, and so on, postulate rich hierarchies of computation and inference between the incoming data and the output of those systems. So it may turn out, it appears, that even learning how to ride a bicycle is to be explained in terms of postulated processes of hypothesis formation and testing in some non-conscious, sub-personal, symbolic system. In which case, the claim that language-learning is a matter of learning *how* will have gained us nothing against Fodor.

How convincing should we find Fodor's second rejoinder? That depends on how plausible we find the alternative – *connectionist* – approach to cognitive science. Those working within this alternative tradition have attempted to construct models of cognitive processes (including various forms of learning) which involve, not computations on sentence-like representations, but rather distributed activations between connected neuron-like units (see, for example, Rumelhart and McClelland, 1986; see also Clark, 1989).

Now, it is not necessary that we should commit ourselves wholeheartedly to connectionist approaches to cognition in order to be able to reply to Fodor's second rejoinder. It is possible to be convinced, as I am, by Fodor's arguments in support of more traditional representational theories of mind (see his 1987, Appendix, and Fodor and Pylyshyn, 1988), but *only* in so far as they apply to central processes of thinking and reasoning. We could therefore continue to insist that beliefs, desires, and other propositional attitudes involve relations to sentences, while allowing that connectionist approaches may be able to account for many sub-personal cognitive processes, including those involved in language-acquisition. And even if language-acquisition, in general, is not adequately accounted for in connectionist terms (as Steven Pinker agues, 1988), it may be that vocabulary acquisition is different. It may well be that those aspects of language which are very definitely learned and not innate, such as vocabulary, can be adequately accounted for using connectionist models, leaving rule-based systems, of the sort postulated by Chomsky's innate universal grammar, to explain the rest. At any rate, this possibility has not yet been ruled out.

There is available, however, a much simpler and swifter response to Fodor's argument from language-learning. For we could allow that language-learning requires thought, but deny that the thoughts in question are *conscious* ones. Since the thesis to be pursued in this book is only that *conscious* thinking involves language, I need not be troubled by an argument whose only real upshot is that conscious thinking presupposes various forms of non-conscious thought. For such a claim is independently very plausible.

Yet in order for this reply to be convincing, enough needs to be said about the nature of consciousness for it to be apparent that the kinds of thought entered into by pre-linguistic, language-learning, children would be of the non-conscious variety. That, obviously, must be a task for later chapters. But, very roughly, I shall claim that conscious thoughts are those that are reflexively available for the subject to think about in turn – see sections 7.1 and 7.3 below. What makes an occurrent thought of mine conscious, on this account, is that it occurs in such a way that I can then go on to think, not only about *what* I have just thought, but also about *the fact that* I have just thought it. And I do believe that it is immensely implausible that pre-linguistic children should be capable of such thinking – see section 7.8.

Modularity of mind

The argument from language-learning appears less than convincing, then. We can, in addition, turn Fodor against himself, appealing to the thesis of modular mental organisation which he has himself defended elsewhere (see his 1983 and 1989). Fodor argues that the mind is organised into input and output systems – or modules – on the one hand, and central processes on the other. Modules would include vision, audition, language processing, and motor control. Central processes would include belief, desire, and practical reasoning. The distinctive features of mental modules are that they are *isolated, innately specified,* and *fast.* I shall say a few words about each of these features in turn.

Mental modules are held to be isolated from the rest of cognition, being largely impervious to changes in central belief. Thus, for example, people continue to be subject to the Mueller-Lyer illusion, continuing to see the arrow-tailed line as longer than the arrow-headed one, even when they know that the lines are of equal length. At *some* level of perception what you see will depend upon background belief, of course – thus, whether you see something as a car, or as a cup, will depend upon a whole battery of beliefs about cars and cups. But whether you see a particular three-dimensional solid shape against an immobile background is not similarly a function of belief, and will arguably remain the same no matter how your beliefs may change.

Mental modules have this isolation because they are dedicated processors, assigned a specialised role in cognition, much of whose operation is innately specified, or 'hard wired'. As a result of this specialisation, mental modules are *extremely fast* in relation to central processes. For example, subjects are capable of shadowing speech with a latency of 250 microseconds, thus allowing about 125 microseconds – or one eighth of a second – for the analysis of speech input. Since the speed of neural transmission is only 10 microseconds, this means that analysis of a heard sentence (or, indeed, of a visual scene) takes place within the space of 12 neural firings. This is, by any measure, fast.

Now, given the isolation of input systems from the rest of cognition, there is no particular reason to think that they function in the same way as central processes of thought, or that they employ the same system of representations. They merely have to deliver their *results* to central processes, or, in the case of output systems, take input from those processes. Moreover, given the speed of input and output systems in relation to conscious thought, there is some reason to think that mental modules do *not* operate in the same way, or employ the same system of representation.

These points seem to me to undermine the *unity* of the language of thought, leaving us free to maintain that propositional attitudes are relations to natural-language sentences, whereas input and output modules operate in some other medium – sentences of Mentalese, or connectionist nets, as it may be. So, granted that the mechanisms for language-acquisition may employ some sub-personal system of representation, it does not follow that personal thoughts must also employ that same system of representation. Indeed, as we saw earlier in this chapter, there is some reason to think that they do not.

It is worth noting, moreover, that although the states attributed by cognitive scientists to sub-personal systems dealing with vision or language can *sound like* propositional attitudes – for example, *formulating a hypothesis*, or *addressing a question to a sub-processor* – they do not have the essential functional characteristics of genuine propositional attitudes. In particular, these states play no role in anything genuinely analogous to practical reasoning. Thus, real (central process) hypotheses function in the fixation of beliefs, which in turn interact with desires in characteristic patterns of inference to produce intentions, which interact further with other beliefs and perceptions so as to produce actions. In sub-personal cognitive systems, in contrast, it does not seem plausible that there is any real place for desire, for intention, or for action. So the moral is, again, that there is no particular reason to think that sub-personal modules will employ representations of the same general kind as central thinking processes.

Suppose that the thesis of modular mental organisation is correct; and, in particular, that there is a dedicated language module which is isolated from central processes of thought and belief. This might then seem to cause a problem for the claim to be defended in this book, that human conscious thought involves natural language. For how can natural language be implicated in thought, if the language module is isolated from thought? The answer is that isolation need not be reciprocal. While the functioning of the language module may be largely isolated from changes in background belief, it may be that thought and belief can have access to some of the structures and information inherent in the language module.

This point will be expanded upon in Chapter 8, where I shall postulate the mechanisms subserving human consciousness. Here I merely note that just such an asymmetric relation seems to obtain between the visual system and central processes involving imagination, for example. There is evidence that while the visual module may be isolated (up to a certain level of visual output) from central belief, visual imagination itself accesses and employs some of the cognitive resources involved in visual perception. Thus, a task requiring visual imagery, such as counting the right-hand corners in an imaged F, will be interfered with if the responses have to be given visually (for example, by pointing to 'Yes' and 'No' buttons), but not if they may be spoken. In contrast, a task requiring auditory imagination, such as counting the nouns in a recently heard sentence, will be interfered with by a spoken, but not by a visual response (see Fodor, 1975, and Tye, 1991). It seems that imagination requires, and has access to, some of the cognitive resources of the appropriate sense modality.

Summary

In this chapter I have raised the question whether it is natural language, or rather Mentalese, which is constitutively involved in our thinking. I began by considering the evidence from developmental psychology, and from aphasia, which was found to be equivocal. I then presented an intuitive, introspection-based, argument for the view that human conscious thinking constitutively involves natural language. But this conclusion has, at best, the status of a bare matter of fact, with no necessity of any sort attached. And in any case, it could easily be overturned by a sufficiently powerful argument for the thesis that all thinking occurs in Mentalese. I have also discussed three of Fodor's arguments for this latter thesis (the arguments from propositional-attitude individuation, from the thoughts of animals and infants, and from language-learning) which were shown to be definitely unsound. But there remain a variety of further arguments to be discussed over the next two chapters, many of which have to do, roughly speaking, with questions of semantics.

3   Thought-based semantics

If Fodor is to maintain that the language of all thinking is Mentalese, then he must do two things. First, he must give some account of the way in which the semantics of natural language is inherited from the semantic properties of our thoughts. Then second, he must provide a semantic theory for the expressions of Mentalese in turn. In this chapter I shall begin by considering another of Fodor's arguments for the view that we think in Mentalese. This will lead us into discussion of the plausibility of Gricean attempts to provide a semantics for natural language in terms of a prior notion of thought, to some version of which Fodor is committed. I shall then consider Fodor's proposed causal co-variance semantics for the terms of Mentalese.

3.1   The argument from foreign believers

One of Fodor's more challenging arguments for the claim that the language of all thinking is Mentalese, starts from the obvious fact that speakers of many different natural languages can entertain one and the same thought. In particular, many who are incapable of speaking English can believe that grass is green. In which case, plainly, their belief cannot consist in a relation to the English sentence, 'Grass is green.' Rather, if beliefs are relations to natural-language sentences, then each person's belief must be encoded in some sentence of their own language, which bears a suitable similarity-relation to the sentence, 'Grass is green.' The relation in question is presumably that of *meaning the same*. Our view must be that anyone who believes that grass is green will entertain some sentence from their native language which means the same as, or which has the same content as, the sentence *I* use to express my belief that grass is green – that is, the English-language sentence, 'Grass is green.'

But now the troubles start. For what account are we to give of the relation, *means the same*? Fodor claims that two natural-language sentences will mean the same, in general, when they are standardly used to communicate the same beliefs. That is, for the English sentence, 'Snow is white', to mean the same as the German sentence, 'Schnee ist weiss', is for those sentences to be standardly used, by English and German speakers respectively, to communicate one and the same belief – the belief, namely, that snow is white. But now we cannot, without circularity, maintain that the belief that snow is white will consist in a relation to some natural-language sentence. For on the above account, the only way of picking out *which* natural-language sentences are in question, is by saying that they are those sentences which are alike in expressing the belief that snow is white.

The only option, Fodor thinks, is to drop the claim that beliefs are relations to natural-language sentences, and to accept that they are relations to sentences of Mentalese instead. In that case, what is common to the English and German speakers who believe that snow is white, will be a relation to the very same sentence of Mentalese, which the one set of believers are disposed to express in public by using the sentence, 'Snow is white', and which the other set of believers are disposed to express by using the sentence, 'Schnee ist weiss.'

Fodor here presupposes a Gricean approach to natural-language semantics, according to which sentence-meaning is to be explained in terms of the communication of belief (see Grice, 1957 and 1969). Roughly, on this account, to utter the sentence, 'Grass is green', and mean it, is to intend your audience to acquire the belief that grass is green as a result of recognising your intention in speaking. It is obvious that this approach takes thought to be prior to, and independent of, natural language. It takes the notions of belief and intention for granted, and uses them in explaining the idea of natural-language meaning. In which case we cannot, of course, maintain that beliefs and intentions are relations to natural-language sentences. Gricean semantics for natural language, and the idea that propositional attitudes are relations to sentences of Mentalese, would seem to be made for one another.

In fact, the argument from foreign believers is something of a red herring. The real work is being done by an argument premised simply on the adequacy of some or other version of Gricean semantics. The argument goes like this:

1. Gricean semantics explains the semantic properties of natural-language expressions in terms of the prior thoughts (beliefs and intentions) of language-users.
2. But thoughts in turn are relations to sentences or sentence-like structures.
3. Given the correctness of the Gricean approach we cannot, without circularity, maintain that these inner sentences, too, are natural language ones.

    4. So the language of thought is not a natural-language, but rather some form of Mentalese.

I have already agreed with premise 2 of this argument, in section 1.8 above. And the remainder of the argument seems to me to be sound. (See section 4.6 below, however, for a possible restriction on its scope). So the only option, if the conclusion is to be avoided, is to reject the Gricean approach to natural language semantics.

It is worth noting that Gricean semantics is, in fact, but one form of what I have called *the communicative conception* of language, which embraces a spectrum of views. At one extreme lies what is sometimes called *the code-breaking conception* of language, familiar from the classical empiricists (for example, Locke, 1690). What happens in normal speech, on this view, is that a speaker encodes their thought into the medium of a public utterance, and a hearer then has to decode that utterance into a thought of their own – the exchange proving successful if the thoughts at either end of this process are the same or sufficiently similar. At the other extreme are *inferential conceptions* of language, of the sort pioneered by Paul Grice. On these accounts, what a speaker does is produce a signal (which may be more or less arbitrary) from which the hearer must figure out, together with assumptions about the context and the speaker's beliefs, what the latter is attempting to communicate. In between these two there are various mixed accounts, such as the theory of relevance developed by Dan Sperber and Deirdre Wilson (1986). According to this conception there are, standardly, elements of both decoding and inference in the understanding of speech.

The problems with code-breaking conceptions are now well known. One is that the account of the nature of thought generally offered by those who endorse such conceptions – namely, mental images – is hopelessly inadequate, as we saw in section 1.8. Another problem is to explain how individual subjects come to know one another's codes, given that they have no access to one another's mental processes. It is obvious, in fact, that inference must play *some* role in all forms of communicative conception of language. For inference to someone's beliefs and intentions in effecting an utterance would be a crucial step in learning their code, at the very least. I shall therefore concentrate on inferential conceptions in their pure form in what follows. For the criticisms levelled at such accounts would in fact prove equally devastating of any decoding/inference hybrid.

We shall consequently need to spend some time, over this chapter and the chapter that follows, investigating the strengths and weaknesses of Gricean approaches to natural-language semantics, and contrasting them with relevant alternatives. For if it should turn out that some version of the Gricean approach is overwhelmingly the most plausible, then Fodor will have a powerful argument that the medium of thought is Mentalese – perhaps powerful enough to overcome the argument from introspection, even in the absence of an explanation of our systematic introspective illusion. If, on the other hand, there are alternative approaches to natural-language semantics which are equally plausible, then there will be nothing to stop us embracing one of them instead, and the Gricean argument for Mentalese will fail to get a grip on us. Moreover, we shall be able to deploy one of those theories to provide an alternative account of the *means the same* relation, and the argument from foreign believers will also have been undermined.

We shall need to consider, too, what account should be given of the semantics of Mentalese itself. For there is no real gain in explaining the meanings of natural-language sentences in terms of those of Mentalese, unless we are prepared to say what confers meaning on the latter in turn. If it should emerge that we can construct a plausible semantics for Mentalese, then Fodor's position would be strengthened still further – especially if there are general arguments for the conclusion that the semantics in question is of a kind that *any* adequate semantic theory, of whatever sort, should adopt. These will not, however, be my conclusions. I shall argue that Gricean approaches to the meaning of natural language face internal problems, as well as stiff competition from viable rivals. And I shall argue that there are powerful objections to Fodor's proposed semantics for Mentalese, and that the argument he offers for claiming that something along those lines *must* be correct is unsound.

3.2   Grice's thought-based semantics

Paul Grice (1957 and 1969) attempts to explain what it is for a speaker to mean something by an action or utterance in terms of the speaker's communicative intentions – more specifically, the intention to induce a belief in an audience. He starts by analysing the notion of *one-off* meaning, where an action is performed with meaning, but where the meaning does not result from any prior agreement or convention. For example, while walking in a forest, having got some way ahead of the rest of my party, I might draw an arrow, thus: ⇑, at a fork in the path, meaning that those who are following should go straight on. A first attempt at characterising what gives my action its meaning, would be to say that it is *intended to induce the belief* that those following me should go straight ahead. Generalising, we could define the notion of meaning as follows:

> Person A, by doing x, means that P = A intends x to induce the belief that P. (This is what Blackburn, 1984, calls 'an Action Intended to Induce a Belief', or AIIB for short.)

But it quickly emerges that this account is inadequate.

Suppose that while walking in front I had come upon some quicksand, and, knowing that the others were following behind, I had thrown in a log with the intention that they should see it sinking, and know not to go there. My action of throwing in the log is intended to induce them to believe that there is quicksand, but it is not, intuitively, an act of *meaning*, or *telling that*, there is quicksand. But there is an obvious way of emending the account, as Grice points out. For consider what would be likely to happen in the case where I draw an arrow on the path. Those following me would see the arrow, and wonder why I had drawn it. They would then realise that I had intended them to go straight on, and so would arrive at their belief about what to do as a result of recognising my intention. Generalising, we can give our account of meaning as follows:

> Person A, by doing x, means that P = A intends x to induce the audience to believe that P as a result of their recognition of A's intention. (This is what Blackburn calls 'a Gricean Action Intended to Induce a Belief', or GAIIB.)

Since Grice wrote, there has been a rich literature of counter-examples to this account (particularly relating to cases of deception), and of higher-order complexities introduced by Griceans to accommodate them. Blackburn helpfully suggests that we can cut through much of this complexity by introducing the idea of an *open GAIIB*, adding to the account just sketched the phrase, *and A wants that all their intentions in doing x should be recognised.*

The above account is intended to capture the notion of one-off meaning. So, applied to the case of language, it can also be regarded as an account of *speaker's meaning* – of what a speaker means by a sentence on a particular occasion of utterance. But what of regular, or conventional, meaning, such as is possessed by the sentence-types of a natural language? This is the idea of *sentence meaning* – of what a sentence means, quite apart from the question of what anyone may mean by uttering it on a particular occasion. Grice suggests that this latter notion is a matter of meaningful actions becoming *fossilised* – that is, of their being used regularly, or habitually, to induce the same belief. We can then say the following:

> x is an act of a type which means that P = x is a fossilised open GAIIB.

However, as Blackburn points out, once we have habits or conventions in the picture, then we no longer need the structure of intention and recognition of intention. Rather, we can say the following:

> x is an act of a type which means that P = x may conventionally be regarded as an attempt to induce the belief that P. (Call this a CAIIB.)

The notion of a convention can then be analysed, following David Lewis (1969), in terms of beliefs and desires. Roughly, an act is governed by a convention provided that most people obey it, most expect the others to obey it, and most prefer to obey it provided that the others do too.

It is important to note, however, that the idea of convention, and of a *CAIIB*, cannot do all the work needed of a theory of meaning – so we cannot simply drop the notion of an *open GAIIB* altogether. For consider someone who often confuses the names for their right and their left hands. Such a person may say, 'The book is in the right-hand drawer', *meaning* that it is in the left. They can, of course, conventionally be regarded as having tried to induce the belief that the book is on the right, which is why we may remonstrate with them when it turns out that they knew it to be on the left. ('But you *said* that it was on the right!') Yet in order to capture the idea of what they *meant* (of speaker's meaning) we need to appeal to the belief that the speaker *intended* to induce (namely, that the book is on the left).

3.3   Two objections

So far, all this looks promising. We have sketched accounts of both speaker's meaning and sentence meaning in terms of prior notions of belief, desire, and intention. If these accounts were successful, then they would amount to a forceful defence of the priority of thought over natural language. Rather than quibble about details, or raise technical difficulties, I shall present two powerful objections to the whole approach.

The objection from theory of mind

One difficulty for Grice concerns the complexity of the intentions attributed to speakers (especially young speakers) on his account. More specifically, it is presupposed that any speaker who can effect a meaningful utterance must have mastered the concepts of *belief* and *intention*, since these are embedded in the content of the intention which is supposed to confer meaning on that utterance. So Grice must claim that one- and two-year-olds who are just beginning to use language communicatively must already have mastered enough common-sense psychology to be capable of the right sorts of meaning-conferring intentions. But, in fact, developmental psychologists are agreed that children do not acquire the concept of *belief*, in particular, until some time in their fourth year (see Wellman, 1990, and Perner, 1991).

It can be replied that, while this objection might possibly be effective against Grice himself, it cannot touch Fodor, if the latter chooses to make use of Gricean ideas. For Fodor is a nativist about common-sense psychology – and not just in the sense of maintaining that the core of common-sense psychology is not learned but genetically determined, making its appearance in the individual as a result of normal biological maturation (which I accept: see section 1.7 above). Fodor maintains, in addition, that the core principles of common-sense psychology will already be present in the child at birth, or shortly thereafter; and the young child's failures in various sorts of theory-of-mind task are put down to constraints on processing, rather than to the absence of any core psychological concept (see Fodor, 1992).

But whether or not the objection can be effective against Fodor himself, the point remains that those of us who do *not* believe that common-sense psychology is present at birth (or at any rate matures within the first year of life) have a powerful reason for rejecting Grice's account. And in any case, Fodor would still owe us some explanation of why processing constraints should prevent a two-year-old from passing the false-belief task, for example, if they do not prevent the same child from forming and processing intentions of Gricean complexity, within which the notion of belief is embedded.

The objection from thinking aloud

The second objection to Grice's semantics that I shall consider was, to my knowledge, first developed by Noam Chomsky. (See his 1976, pp. 55–77. It is worth noting that these passages also provide my ground for the claim that Chomsky was once committed to the cognitive conception of language. Similar objections may be found in Sperber and Wilson, 1986, and in Schiffer, 1987. See also my 1989, ch. 10, which was written independently.) It will be worth our while to spell out the objection in some detail.

The Gricean focus is entirely on the use of language to communicate. But surely we also use natural language in thinking and reasoning? Now, we do not need to beg any questions here about the medium in which private thinking takes place, since we can appeal to the phenomenon noted in Chapter 2, of *thinking aloud*. When I think aloud, or on paper, there may surely be no intention to induce a belief in another person, since I may know that there is no audience, or be indifferent to the presence of an audience. Thus I may comment aloud, while sitting alone watching a television programme about the Hérault region of France, 'It would be nice to go *there* for a holiday this summer.' And Chomsky reports having once spent two years writing a manuscript purely for his own purposes, to work out his own thoughts, with no intention that it should ever be read by another person. In these cases there is, plainly, no intention to induce a belief in an audience. Yet such public performances are surely not intended to induce beliefs in oneself, either, since they involve the expression of beliefs which one already has.

Some people might be tempted to try to discount the significance of the phenomenon of thinking aloud, by *peripheralising* it. But there are two things that this might mean. First, it might mean that it is *rare*, or statistically unusual. But it is hard to see how this can be to the point. For the fact that a phenomenon is relatively rare need not prevent it from being of central theoretical importance. Consider, for example, the fact that reading aloud to oneself is rare among adults, and yet that we all learned to read in precisely that way. Indeed, for just this reason we would expect that silent reading should be cognitively very similar to reading aloud – that they should be the same *sorts* of activity, conducted in different modes. In the same way, then, it may be that silent thinking is a kind of internalised thinking aloud, and that the public phenomenon is central to understanding the private. And certainly it is true that young children will commonly accompany their activities with spoken monologues, just as they will do their early reading out loud. But in any case, it is doubtful whether thinking aloud is really so very rare, even among adults.

As I noted in section 2.2, many of us talk to our pets and babies, where there is no real intention to induce belief. Rather, an affectionate audience provides us with a convenient focus for the expression of thought. And thinking on paper (or, nowadays, at the computer key-board) is really very common indeed. Moreover, as Chomsky emphasises, once the grip of the Gricean model has been broken, it becomes obvious that much normal conversation does not consist of attempts to induce belief. Many ordinary assertoric utterances are better seen as intended to pass the time, or as mere friendly exchanges, or as attempts to keep a conversation going, and so on.

The second thing which might be meant by claiming that the phenomenon of thinking aloud is peripheral, is that the phenomenon can be explained in terms of central cases to which the Gricean analysis applies directly. This is in fact the strategy adopted by Grice in his 1969, and seems also to be the one canvassed by Bennett in his 1991. But this must mean, either explaining the phenomenon of thinking aloud in terms of *speaker's* meaning, or in terms of *sentence* meaning. I shall shortly discuss how Grice himself attempts to do the former, arguing that it is unsuccessful. And it is obvious, surely, that we cannot do the latter.

It is evident that we cannot use the fact that an utterance may *conventionally be taken* by one's speech community as an action intended to induce a particular belief, in order to explain how a speaker may use that very same utterance in quite another way in the expression of thought, as often occurs when language is used in soliloquy. For example, the person who regularly transposes their 'left' and 'right' might say, in the course of thinking aloud about the furniture in their office, 'The desk is too big to go on the left of the window', *meaning* that it is too big to go on the right. It is just irrelevant to this that their utterance of this sentence may conventionally be taken as meaning that the desk is too big to go on the left. Yet they are, of course, not trying to induce a belief in anybody, either.

Inducing beliefs in a hypothetical audience

Grice himself claims, in his 1969, that when I think aloud my utterances are really made with the intention of inducing beliefs in a *hypothetical* audience. So when I say aloud, while alone, 'It would be nice to go to France for a holiday this summer', my intention is supposed to be that *if* an audience *were* to be present, *then* they should come to believe that I would like to go to France for my holiday as a result of recognising my intention to get them to believe just that. But there are two major problems with this account.

The first is that I certainly do not *seem* to have any such intention when thinking aloud. When I think aloud I frequently do not have in mind any particular audience, and if asked about it I should be inclined to claim that the question of an audience was irrelevant. So Grice must at least maintain that the intentions involved are somehow, and for some reason, not accessible to consciousness. Then it needs explaining why this should be so. And in the absence of such an explanation, it will be more reasonable to accept that many uses of language are not even conditionally communicative.

The second problem for Grice's account concerns the question of how the hypothetical audience is to be specified. For, plainly, my intention cannot be that if literally *anyone* (including monolingual speakers of Russian, or of Serbo-Croat?) were to be present, then they would form the belief that I wish to go to France for my holiday. I can think of only three possible suggestions, as follows.

First, it might be said that the hypothetical audience is the set of people *who actually live around me*. But this plainly will not do. For I may, while staying in France, do my thinking aloud in English. And then my intention obviously cannot be that the French people around me should form any particular belief if they were to be present.

Second, it might be said that the hypothetical audience consists of anyone *who speaks my language or dialect*. But this, too, obviously will not do. For I may, in soliloquy, use words in ways that I know to be wholly idiosyncratic, in the full knowledge that speakers of my language would *not* form the appropriate beliefs if they were to overhear me. Consider, again, the person who is regularly inclined to transpose their 'left' and 'right', and who knows that they have a tendency to do so. When communicating with other English speakers, this person will have to take care to use the correct word. But in soliloquy they do not have to bother. They can say aloud, 'I shall put my desk on the right of the window', *meaning*, and knowing that they mean, that they will put it on the left, without of course intending that if any English speaker were to hear them they should form the belief that the desk will be placed on the left.

Third, (and finally), it might possibly be suggested that the hypothetical audience should be anyone *who uses words as I do*. But the problem, now, is to cash this out in a way consistent with the Gricean programme in semantics. For the phrase, 'using words as I do', cannot here mean, 'using them with the same intention to induce a belief in an actual audience', since I have no such intention. And yet we plainly cannot resort to the idea of a hypothetical audience, at this point, without blatant circularity. But then, on the other hand, if *using words in the same way that I do* is cashed out in terms of using words to express the same thoughts, we no longer have a semantic theory which explains the meanings of utterances in terms of intentions to induce belief.

In fact, I suggest, the basic flaw in Grice's approach to the semantics of natural language is that he takes the fundamental purpose and use of language to be communication, rather than thought. Certainly we do seem to use language for thinking as well as for communicating. And even if it were true that our natural language faculty had, as a matter of fact, been selected for in evolution because of its survival-value in facilitating communication, this need not mean that communication is, fundamentally, what language is for. Provided that the language faculty is also used for thinking, and that it is true that it *would have been* selected for because of its usefulness in thinking (for example, in circumstances in which there would have been no advantage in communication), then thought can equally be what language is for.

In reality, I claim, the key feature of language lies in its use in the expression of thought, which may be for many different purposes – as part of practical or theoretical reasoning, as part of casual social intercourse, *as well as* to induce beliefs in an audience. However, this does not yet mean that thought is essentially linguistic, or necessarily involves natural language, as we shall see in the next section.

3.4   Searle's version of thought-based semantics

John Searle once used to be an orthodox Gricean (see his 1969). But, seemingly as a result of Chomsky's criticisms, he now accepts that language may be used for many purposes besides communication (see his 1983). Yet he continues to insist that the mind imposes meaning on language, via the intention to do just that. Roughly, his claim is this:

> Person A, by doing x, means that P = x is an act which A intends to express the belief that P.

Now this is, obviously, too simple as it stands. For I may meaningfully say that P without possessing, myself, any belief that P, as when I am telling a lie. Moreover, it would surely be implausible to claim that whenever I make an assertion I *refer to* some actual or possible belief of mine, as the above account would imply. In order to explain how Searle's actual theory can overcome these problems I shall have to introduce and explain some of his technical terminology.

Intention in action – by this Searle means the intention which causes and controls an intentional action that is not caused by a *prior* intention; it is the intention which governs and controls a spontaneous and undeliberated action. For example, anyone playing baseball or cricket, who is swinging a bat at a ball flying towards them, may make their movements intentionally, but without prior intention. The intention *in* the action is to swing the bat just *so*, hitting the ball over *there*.

Direction of fit – this is the manner in which a *match* between mind and world is *supposed* to be achieved. Assertions and beliefs are supposed to match the world, and so have mind-to-world direction of fit. If they fail to match the world, it is the mind that has gone wrong, not the world. Imperatives and desires, on the other hand, are supposed to get the world to match them, and so have world-to-mind direction of fit. If they fail to match the world, it is the world that is wrong, not the mind of the agent.

Conditions of satisfaction – this is roughly the idea corresponding to that of *truth-conditions* for assertions and beliefs, only generalised to cover all forms of contentful linguistic act and mental state. It is the condition of the world which is *represented by* a contentful act or mental state. The condition of satisfaction for the belief that the door is open, the desire that the door should be open, and the hope or wish that the door should be open, are all *that the door is open*.

Now, with these notions explained, Searle's theory of meaning can be stated. Suppose that in the course of deliberating about France as a venue for a summer holiday I say the words, 'Avignon is hot in August.' On Searle's account, this performance acquires its meaning from the following intention:

> *I intend:* that this intention in action causes me to say, 'Avignon is hot in August', and that the utterance, 'Avignon is hot in August', has as conditions of satisfaction with the mind-to-world direction of fit *that Avignon is hot in August.*

This need not presuppose, of course, that I do actually believe that Avignon is hot in August (I may be lying), and nor does it make reference to any such belief. But for all that, the meaning of the utterance is still inherited from the content of the intention with which that utterance is made, just as on Grice's account. Communicative speech can then be explained as a special case of meaningful utterance, by adding to the above account the following clause:

> *And I intend:* that my audience should recognise, both that I have uttered, 'Avignon is hot in August', and that my utterance has just those conditions of satisfaction and direction of fit.

Problems for Searle

The theory outlined above may seem to have all of the virtues and not many of the vices of Grice's account of meaning. For, while communicative uses of language are no longer prioritised, it is still the intentions of language-users which ultimately confer meaning on their utterances. And for Searle, in contrast with Grice, the intentions which confer meaning on our utterances (even our communicative ones) do not have to have the concept of *belief* already embedded in their contents. So there is no objection, here, from theory-of-mind.

But how plausible is it to maintain, all the same, that such complex and sophisticated thought-contents can be entertained independently of natural language? Is it really believable that someone could have an intention part of whose content should be *that Avignon is hot in August* (let alone whose content should include such concepts as *condition of satisfaction* and *direction of fit*) independently of some linguistic means of expressing it? And is it really believable that a two-year-old child should be capable of having intentions of this complexity?

Surprisingly, Searle seems to concede that these things are *not* believable, and maintains, indeed, that most adult forms of intentionality are essentially linguistic (see his 1991, p. 94). Yet he still maintains that the meaning of language can be explained in terms of the intentionality of the mind, because the intentionality of the mind is *broader* – for example, there are kinds of intentionality present in the minds of animals and young children that do not presuppose natural language.

What we are offered, in fact, is a kind of boot-strapping story, which begins with simple forms of mental content not involving language, moves on, on that basis, to simple forms of language, to more complex mental states, to more complex forms of language, and so on. Now it is certainly very plausible that many concepts and beliefs can only be acquired on the basis of some prior linguistic competence, as this story suggests. Indeed, we conceded as much in the discussion of the 'wolf-children' cases in section 1.3. And yet this is, so far, entirely consistent with the view of thought as independent of natural language, exemplified in Gricean approaches to semantics. For language is, as we noted in 1.3, an important avenue for the acquisition of new beliefs and concepts, on any account of the matter.

But this is not really to the point, however. Rather, we need to ask how plausible it is that any given thought-content (such as, *that Avignon is hot in August*) can exist in the absence of some linguistic means for *its* expression. And a powerful case can be made for saying that it cannot. For how are we to explain our ability to entertain unlimitedly many *new* thought-contents of this sort except *generatively*, in terms of the construction of new linguistic means for the expression of those thoughts, by putting together old parts in new ways? As we saw in section 1.8, the best theory that we have for explaining the unlimited creativity of thought, is that such creativity is inherited from the generative powers of language.

Searle appears to concede exactly this point, in fact, allowing that reference to appropriate natural-language expressions should be included in an account of the content of any given adult thought. For example, he insists that reference to the German word 'Schnee' ('snow') should properly be included in a full account of the content of the belief of a German native speaker who believes that snow is white (see his 1991, p. 230). But now the whole attempt to maintain that the mind imposes its prior intentional contents on linguistic expressions must collapse. For we cannot characterise the content of the German sentence, 'Schnee ist weiss', in terms of a prior given notion of intention, if an account of the content of the latter must involve reference to those very words. At this point the Gricean programme of semantics appears to have run out into the sand.

3.5   A marriage of Searle and Fodor?

There is just one way forward remaining to Searle. He can allow that some language-like means of expression is essential if one is to entertain thoughts with any degree of complexity, and he can allow that it is the generative structure of such expressions which allows us to entertain unlimitedly many thought-contents. But he can insist that these expressions should belong, not to any natural language, but to an innate language of thought – namely, Mentalese. This would allow him to insist without circularity that the meanings of natural-language utterances are inherited from speaker's intentions, while also allowing that those intentions presuppose some language-like means for their expression.

In fact, Searle himself is emphatic in rejecting the very idea of Mentalese, and the whole computational model of the mind that goes with it (see his 1980). Many of us believe that his reasons for doing so are not good ones. But in any case it would be possible to marry Searle's approach to the semantics of natural-language sentences with Fodor's view that beliefs and desires are relations to sentences of Mentalese. Then we can say, both that the meanings of natural-language utterances will be inherited from the prior contents of a speaker's intentions, and that the contents of those intentions, in turn, reflect the meanings of the sentences of Mentalese through which they are primarily, and constitutively, expressed. This may not be Searle's view, but it is a possible view, and it is one that is certainly available to Fodor. Moreover, it appears to be just the sort of view which might make it plausible to maintain that propositional attitudes are relations to sentences of Mentalese, if the account appeared successful in other respects.

There is no easy refutation of the above marriage of Searle's approach to the semantics of natural language with Fodor's thesis that the language in which our thoughts are expressed is Mentalese. But notice that the intentions in question, which are appealed to in accounting for the meanings of natural-language utterances, had better be non-conscious ones. For when I think aloud spontaneously I am surely not aware that my intention is both, to utter a sentence under a certain description, and to impose a particular meaning on it. When I say in soliloquy, 'Avignon is hot in August', I am certainly not *conscious* of intending that my intention in action should cause me to utter the words, 'Avignon is hot in August', and that those words should have as conditions of satisfaction with mind-to-world direction of fit *that Avignon is hot in August*. It is, then, something of a puzzle for this account, as it was for Grice's, why the intentions which are supposed to confer meaning on our utterances should not be accessible to consciousness.

More importantly, the above approach means giving up on the common-sense belief that I think aloud *in* natural language. For on this account it is not the sentence, 'Avignon is hot in August', as such, which constitutively expresses my thought. Rather, it would have to be claimed that the thinking is actually done in Mentalese, and what is called 'thinking aloud' is really just a use of natural language to give public expression to a private thought, providing some sort of public record of that thought. This may be done for a number of different purposes – perhaps as an aid to memory, or perhaps as an aid to criticism by oneself or others.

Now, I have no way of demonstrating that common sense is correct in this regard. That is, I have no way of *proving* that the correct description of what happens when I do what we call 'thinking aloud', and utter the sentence, 'Avignon is hot in August', is that this sentence is *constitutive of* the act of thinking. The natural-language sentence may be, rather, a mere public expression of a thought which was antecedently, and non-consciously, expressed in a sentence of Mentalese, and from which it inherits its content. For we can at least begin to understand why we might go in for such activities, nevertheless, since it is in many ways useful for thoughts to receive formulation in a public medium – it may then be easier to remember them, for example, and it will certainly be easier to criticise and evaluate them.

But how *plausible* would these explanations of public soliloquy be? Can they explain the *range* of cases in which people talk to themselves, or do what we call 'thinking aloud'? Arguably not. For if the purpose of public soliloquy were to aid memory (like when one writes shopping-lists or notes to oneself), then one would only expect it to occur when there is a particular *problem* of memory. Equally, if the purpose of 'thinking aloud' were to *objectify* one's thoughts with a view to assessing them more easily for truth and plausibility, then one would only expect public soliloquy to occur when the subject-matter of one's speech was serious, or where one was especially aiming for truth or plausibility. But these predictions do not appear to match up with the evidence (albeit anecdotal). People (especially children) chat to themselves about the most trivial matters, sometimes keeping up a running commentary which appears to serve no real purpose, of memory or otherwise. This gives us some reason to accept the common-sense position, maintaining that the public commentary *is* their thinking. For everyone accepts, of course, that *thinking* can be trivial and apparently purposeless.

In fact the common-sense account of thinking aloud is closely connected to the introspective argument of section 2.2 (that many of our conscious private thinkings involve natural language) – to the point where one might expect them to stand or fall together. For if our private thinkings do constitutively involve natural language sentences, then our common-sense belief that we often think aloud with such sentences can obviously be allowed to stand. Conversely, any explanation of the phenomenon we call 'thinking aloud' which is offered by a defender of the Fodor/Searle account can probably be equally well extended to explain the introspective phenomenon of inner speech. This question will be returned to in more detail in section 8.3, when the introspective argument is finally re-evaluated in the light of our discussion of theories of consciousness. In that section one of my arguments will be that the

Fodor/Searle account cannot explain the range or frequency of inner speech, just as I have here sketched an argument that it cannot explain the range of public soliloquy.

In any case, however, it is plain that the Fodor/Searle approach does cost us an ingredient of common-sense belief, which is certainly not negligible. And it should be recalled that the very realism about the mind within whose framework Fodor and I are both operating was adopted in order to vindicate common sense. Any proposed view, like this one, which requires us to give up a component of common-sense belief should then be regarded with a measure of suspicion. At any rate, other approaches will surely be preferable if they allow us to construct semantic theories which are at least as plausible, while avoiding the cost of this one. In the next chapter I shall show that there are, indeed, such approaches to the semantics of natural language.

3.6   Causal co-variance theories

We have just seen how those who believe that the language of all thinking is Mentalese, and not a natural language, may be able to give an account of the semantics of natural language by appropriating Searle's intention-based theory. Indeed, to the extent that the resulting semantic theory is plausible, to that extent we have an additional argument for the view that the language of all thought is Mentalese. But this was not, in fact, what I have concluded. I have claimed, on the contrary, that while the Searle/Fodor view cannot be definitely refuted, it does face problems, and forces us to give up an important ingredient of common-sense belief – namely, that we often think aloud *in* natural language.

I shall now take up the question of the semantics of Mentalese. For if propositional attitudes are relations to sentences of Mentalese, and if the semantics of natural language is to be given in terms of those attitudes, then it must be possible to provide a semantics for Mentalese expressions without presupposing or mentioning natural language. (I shall also take up the question whether the best available account of the semantic content of thought, in general, provides yet further support for the theory that the language in which thoughts are expressed is Mentalese. In Chapter 4 this question will be pursued in more detail.)

Fodor sets the search for a semantics for thought within a number of general constraints. (See his 1987, chs. 3 and 4, his 1990, chs. 3 and 4, and his 1994.) The first derives from his realism about propositional attitudes, which I discussed, and endorsed, in the opening chapter. This gives rise to a constraint of *naturalism*. Since one of the main reasons for scepticism about the reality of propositional attitudes consists in a worry about the

place of intentionality – of mental content – in the natural order, realists
should be able to say, in naturalistically acceptable terms, what it is for a
belief or intention to have a particular content or meaning. The second
constraint is that of *atomism*. Fodor maintains (roughly speaking – see
below) that we should be able to give an account of the meaning of each
Mentalese term without mentioning any other mental state. The account
should thus be atomistic, as opposed to holistic, delivering the meanings
of mental terms one by one. Fodor believes that this constraint, too, is
entailed by his realism. I shall consider his argument for this belief in
Chapter 4.

Fodor maintains – correctly, I believe – that the only semantic theory
which stands any chance of satisfying his constraints must be some or
other version of *informational* or *causal* theory (see Stampe, 1977, Dretske,
1981 and 1988, as well as the works by Fodor cited above). Such theories
claim that meaning is carried by the causal connections between the mind
and the world. In fact, Fodor attempts to provide such a semantics via a
species of causal co-variance theory, claiming that for a Mentalese term
'S' to mean *S*, is for tokenings of 'S' to causally co-vary with Ss – that is,
Ss, and only Ss, cause tokenings of 'S'. Roughly, the idea is that for the
Mentalese equivalent of 'mouse' (which I shall henceforward write as
MOUSE) to mean *mouse*, is for tokenings of the term MOUSE in belief to be
reliably caused by the presence of mice, and only by the presence of mice.
I shall discuss the adequacy of this theory in a moment. First, I shall say
something about its bearing on the question of the language that we think
with.

I shall argue that there are various problems with Fodor's account. But
supposing that it, or some variant of it, were successful, would the resulting theory of mental semantics support Mentalese as against natural language as the language of thought? The answer, I think, is that it would. For
causal co-variance would be wildly implausible as an account of the
semantics of spoken or written language – I will often see a mouse without
saying 'mouse', and will often say, 'There is a mouse', without a mouse
being present. I sometimes make mistakes, claiming that there is a mouse
when it is really a shrew, or failing to notice a mouse when one is present.
I also sometimes tell lies, asserting that there is a mouse when there is not.
And in any case, of course, there are many aspects of my environment
which I simply do not choose to remark upon. Even if I notice the presence of a mouse I may say nothing about it, if I take the event to be sufficiently unremarkable. So my utterances of 'mouse' certainly do not
reliably co-vary with the presence of mice.

In reply, it might be said that the causal co-variance account could be
adopted for natural language as it figures in private thinking, in the first

instance. Perhaps a token of the English predicate 'mouse' gets inserted into my faculty of occurrent belief when, and only when, there is a mouse in the immediate vicinity, exactly as Fodor claims for tokens of the Mentalese predicate MOUSE. I may not *say* the word 'mouse' whenever I see a mouse, but perhaps I nevertheless *think* it.

Anyone who is seriously attracted by the idea that propositional attitudes are relations to natural-language sentences, however, would surely want their semantics for the expressions of natural language to apply to those expressions equally whether they figure in private thinking or in public speech. For, as we saw in section 2.2, a large part of the attraction of the claim that we think in natural language, is that we can then treat public language and private thinking on a par, claiming that essentially the same sort of activity is undertaken whether one thinks aloud or in private. We ought, then, to resist any suggestion that the semantics for public (spoken or written) tokens of natural-language expressions should have to be routed through their private counterparts, as on the proposal above.

If it were to turn out, then, that some form of causal co-variance semantics provides much the best account of intentional content, then this would provide yet further reason for believing that the language in which we think is Mentalese. For such a semantic theory could not be applied equally to public and private uses of natural language. In which case, one of the crucial premises supporting the view that we think in natural language – the premise, namely, that public and private thinkings are on a par, being essentially similar activities – would have been undermined.

Now, the causal co-variance theory maintains that for a Mentalese term 'S' to mean S, is for Ss, and only Ss, to cause tokenings of 'S'. There are two obvious problems for such an account. One arises from the claim that *Ss cause tokenings of 'S'*. For this cannot mean that *all* Ss do, since no one will be in causal contact with every member of the extension of the predicate. Since I shall never be in the vicinity of all mice, it can hardly be true of me that *every* mouse causes in me a token of MOUSE. This is *the all Ss problem*, discussion of which I shall postpone to the final section of this chapter. The other major difficulty arises from the claim that *only Ss cause tokenings of 'S'*. Since I sometimes make mistakes, classifying as 'S' things that are not, this clause plainly needs some emendation. For example, I may often, mistakenly, classify shrews as mice. But then why, on the co-variance account, do I have a *mis*-representation of a mouse when this occurs, rather than a correct representation of *shrew-or-mouse*? For shrews, too, cause tokenings of MOUSE. This is *the misrepresentation problem*, which I shall discuss in the section that follows.

Note that even if it should turn out that the above problems for causal co-variance semantics cannot be overcome, this will not amount to any sort of *refutation* of the view that the language of all thought is Mentalese. It will just mean that we lose any semantically based *argument for* Mentalese. For if we are forced to move on to adopt some alternative approach to the semantics of thought, then this may well turn out to be one which could equally be applied to natural-language sentences as to sentences of Mentalese, and so would be an approach which is consistent with the view that some of our thoughts, at any rate, are constituted by natural-language sentences. Indeed, there are at least two such alternatives (functional-role semantics, and the theory of canonical acceptance conditions) for which this is demonstrably the case – see sections 4.7 and 4.8 below.

3.7 Misrepresentation, and asymmetric causal dependence

One obvious option, in attempting to solve the misrepresentation problem, would be to appeal to causal co-variance *in ideal circumstances*. We might try claiming, that is, that tokens of the term MOUSE mean *mouse*, and not *shrew-or-mouse*, because only mice will, in *ideal* circumstances, cause a token of the Mentalese symbol MOUSE to be inserted into the faculty of belief. The cases in which I mistakenly identify a shrew as a mouse are then ones in which the circumstances are not ideal. Fodor rejects this suggestion for a number of different reasons – see his 1990, ch. 3. But one that is worth noticing and developing here, is that such an account would involve a degree of semantic holism. The suggestion would then be inconsistent with Fodor's commitment to semantic atomism. I shall first discuss, and dismiss, two ways in which an appeal to ideal circumstances might *appear* to entail a commitment to holism, before presenting what I take to be the real objection.

It is now commonly accepted, since Hilary Putnam's 1975, that many terms of natural language are governed by principles of linguistic division of labour. Many of us make meaningful use of predicates, such as 'mouse', while having only the haziest idea of their application-conditions. Rather, in our use of those predicates we hold ourselves responsible to some body of experts, whose judgement on such matters we undertake to accept. While I cannot, personally, tell many types of mice from many types of shrew, I can still use 'mouse' to mean *mouse* because I defer to the word of experts who *can* tell the difference. Something similar will presumably hold for terms of Mentalese. For it is not just what I say, but also what I believe or think, which can successfully refer to mice while I lack the capacity to reliably discriminate mice from shrews. And then the point would be this: that if we explain how I succeed in referring to mice (and not to shrews-or-mice) in terms of ideal conditions for judgement, then we shall need to mention the mental states – specifically, the beliefs and theories – of some body of rodent experts. And this would appear to violate Fodor's atomism requirement.

In fact, however, the phenomenon of linguistic division of labour is entirely consistent with Fodor's atomism, in the sense in which he intends it. As we shall see more fully in the next section, and again in the next chapter, Fodor is *not* committed to the view that any given mental state or predicate must be able to exist, and possess its semantic properties, independently of the existence and semantic properties of literally *any* other mental term. Rather, what matters is that no other mental states *of the agent* should need to be mentioned in the course of individuating the semantic properties of the term in question (for yet further qualifications, see below). So the fact that we might have to mention some of the mental states of *other* agents (*viz.* the beliefs of the rodent experts) in the course of stating the semantics of my Mentalese term MOUSE (as linguistic division of labour implies) raises no particular problem for Fodor.

The second way in which an appeal to ideal circumstances might be thought to introduce an element of holism into the account is this. All current cognitive theories of perception, at least since David Marr's 1982, maintain that our perceptual mechanisms make default assumptions about the objects of perception. For example, it appears to be an assumption embodied in our visual faculty that most moving bodies are rigid, and that most changes in the visual field result from the motions of rigid bodies. These assumptions help to keep the computations which have to be performed by our perceptual faculties within manageable bounds, and so are crucial in ensuring that they operate speedily. They are also crucial to the explanation of perceptual illusions. Then the important point for our purposes would be that any specification of the ideal circumstances for a particular perceptual judgement – such as MOUSE – would have to contain mention of other contentful mental states. Specifically, it would have to mention the governing assumptions of our perceptual mechanisms, and so would appear, again, to fail Fodor's atomism requirement.

But here, as before, there is no real conflict with Fodor's atomism, in the sense in which he intends it. As we shall see in the next chapter, what particularly worries Fodor is that if holism is true, then the individuation-conditions for any given mental state might vary *from person to person* (or within an individual over time). So the fact that we may have to mention other contentful states in providing the semantics for the Mentalese term MOUSE is no problem, provided that they are states which *all* thinkers may be presumed to share. And since the computational assumptions made by the visual faculty are presumably universal (because innate), there is then no real problem in mentioning them in course of stating the semantics of MOUSE.

The real difficulty about appealing to *ideal circumstances* in order to solve the misrepresentation problem is as follows, in fact. As Fodor (1983) notes, the outputs from that part of the visual faculty which is innate and universal (the *visual module*, as he calls it) are *shallow*. What is invariant in perception is only that we are presented with a 3-D world of moveable objects and shapes. The rest is down to what you know or believe. Whether you see something as a bird, or an aeroplane, or as a chariot of the gods, will depend upon much else that you believe about the world. And this *will* vary from person to person, and within any given person over time. That perception is, *to some extent* (in its deeper, more theoretical aspects) imbued with belief, is not just a truism: it is actually true. In which case it is obvious, both that a statement of the ideal circumstances for any given perceptual judgement will have to specify a great deal of what the observer should know, and also that there will inevitably be wide variations in these background beliefs between and within individuals. And then this really would introduce holism, in a sense which Fodor must find unacceptable.

I suppose it might be replied that these wide variations in background belief are an irrelevance. For the proposal is not, that in saying what it is for my tokens of MOUSE to refer to *mice* and not to *shrews-or-mice*, we should have to mention *my* background beliefs. Rather, it is that we should mention those background beliefs which, if I *were* to possess them, would lead me *not* to judge MOUSE in the presence of any shrew. But the trouble, now, is that this may be true of anyone – even someone who *does* mean *shrew-or-mouse* by MOUSE. If we allow ourselves to depart too far from the *actual* background beliefs of the thinker, that is, then we shall lose all power to discriminate between error and deviant meaning. For it will equally be true of the person who does in fact mean *shrew-or-mouse*, that they *would* fail to think MOUSE in the presence of a shrew *if* they had all the background beliefs of the ideal recogniser of mice.

Asymmetric causal dependence

Fodor's actual preferred solution to the misrepresentation problem, is to formulate his theory in terms of *asymmetric* causal dependence. That is, he claims that a Mentalese term 'S' will refer to Ss, and only Ss, provided that the causal connections between 'S' and any other (non-S) objects which may happen to cause tokenings of 'S' are asymmetrically causally dependent upon the causal connection between tokenings of 'S' and Ss.

So if any other types of object besides Ss cause tokenings of 'S', they will only do so *because* Ss cause tokenings of 'S'. On this account, then, MOUSE will mean *mouse* (and so shrews will be *mis*-represented by MOUSE) if:

(i)   mice cause tokenings of MOUSE,

(ii) if mice had not caused tokenings of MOUSE, shrews would not have, and

(iii) if shrews had not caused tokenings of MOUSE, mice still would have.

Thus the fact that shrews cause tokenings of MOUSE is asymmetrically causally dependent upon the fact that mice cause tokenings of MOUSE.

Already this account has spawned a very considerable secondary literature. For example, Cummins (1989) discusses the theory at length, raising a number of objections; and many of the papers in Loewer and Rey (1991) are devoted to the issue, raising a whole variety of different problems, followed by Fodor's vigorous (and mostly successful) replies. I have no intention of trying to engage with the details of these debates. Instead, I shall raise a very general, but inconclusive, worry about the attractiveness of the asymmetric-dependence account of misrepresentation. Remember that my purpose here is not to refute, definitively, Fodor's account of the semantics of thought, but only to show that there are no good reasons for preferring it to viable (natural language based) alternatives.

The intuitive worry is this: how plausible is it that our judgements of representation, or of misrepresentation, are actually guided by thoughts about asymmetric causal dependence? When someone says 'Mouse' in the presence of a shrew (by hypothesis expressing, in English, a tokening of the Mentalese term MOUSE), how plausible is it that my judgements about what they mean will be driven by considerations of causal asymmetry? Certainly these do not appear to enter into my conscious practice at all. (Here I set aside worries about the possibility of linguistic division of labour – which would otherwise just cloud the issue – by supposing it as known that the person in question does *not* particularly intend their terms to refer to whatever is referred to by others in the linguistic community.)

If the suggestion is made that by MOUSE this person may mean *shrew-or-mouse* rather than *mouse* (and hence that they may have said something true rather than false), then what steps would I take to resolve the issue? I would *not* ask whether their tokens of MOUSE would still have been caused by shrews like that one, if tokens of it had not *also* been caused by mice; nor conversely whether tokens of MOUSE would still have been caused by mice if they had not also been caused by shrews like this one. (That is, I would not ask whether clauses (i) to (iii) above are satisfied.) Rather, what I would want to know is whether the person in question *also* believes that any mouse can interbreed with any other mouse of the opposite sex. If not, then by MOUSE they may well mean *shrew-or-mouse*, for they will then not be intending MOUSE to refer to any particular single species. If so, then presumably they also believe, falsely, that this (shrew) can interbreed with any mouse (and so will give up their belief that it is a mouse when shown that it cannot interbreed); and then by MOUSE they do *not* mean *shrew-or-mouse*.

Consider another example to make the same point. It is sometimes easy to mistake some types of acid for water, since both can be clear colourless liquids. Then consider someone who thinks WATER in the presence of a beaker of hydrochloric acid. And suppose the question is raised whether by WATER they mean *water* or rather *water-or-acid*. How would I go about resolving the issue? Again, I would *not* ask whether their tokens of WATER would still have been caused by acids if such tokens had not also been caused by water; nor would I ask whether, if tokens of WATER in this person had not been caused by water, they would still have thought WATER in the presence of this acid. Rather, I would want to know whether they *also* believe that water slakes thirst, is good for plants, boils at 100°C, and is good for doing your washing in. If not, then by WATER they may well mean *water-or-acid* (that will be a matter for further investigation). If so, then they presumably believe, falsely, that it would be good to drink the stuff in the beaker in front of them, and that their dirty socks will become clean (rather than disintegrating) if rubbed in it. And then they will presumably give up the judgement WATER when these false consequences are pointed out to them, and by WATER they do *not* mean *water-or-acid*.

Our actual practice in making judgements of meaning support some or other form of functional or conceptual role semantics, I think (of the sort to be considered in the next chapter), as against Fodor's asymmetric causal dependence condition. What we actually do is look at various of the subject's *other* judgements, and ask questions about what they would think or say if they were to be convinced of the truth of various other claims, and what further inferences they would be prepared to draw. We *don't* consider whether this present type of judgement would still have been caused by its actual worldly causes if certain other thoughts of the same type had not also been caused by other sorts of object, and vice versa.

This is not to say that Fodor can have no reply to the objection, of course. He can claim, in particular, that our actual practice in making judgements about meaning are but a poor reflection of the property we are making judgements *about* (namely *meaning*). And he can claim that his theory is a theory of the latter. But this does mean, I think, that the burden of proof is on him, to motivate his own account. For it is surely a

constraint on an adequate theory of meaning – other things being equal –
that it should have as a consequence that our ordinary judgements about,
and practices in establishing, meanings are *appropriate to* the phenomenon they concern: namely, meaning.

3.8   The *all Ss* problem

The other main problem with causal co-variance accounts of intentional
content is that, of course, not *all* Ss cause tokenings of 'S'. So it looks as if
we shall have to specify the circumstances in which any S *would* cause a
tokening of 'S' (naturalistically and atomistically, for Fodor). For otherwise we shall have to say that 'S' represents just that subset of Ss which
actually cause tokenings of 'S'. And, plainly, this would be absurd. When I
think MOUSE, I am surely thinking about *mice*, and not just the subset of
mice that I actually encounter.

Now the trouble, for Fodor, is this. He seems to have to say, in naturalistically acceptable and atomistic terms, under what circumstances the
presence of a mouse would cause me to think MOUSE. But whether or not I
think MOUSE in the presence of a mouse seems plainly dependent upon
both my desires and my other beliefs. For what I notice in my environment may depend upon my interests (and hence desires) at the time. And
if, for example, I somehow come to believe that mice are extinct, then I
shall only be disposed to think THAT *SEEMS* LIKE A MOUSE in the presence
of a mouse, not THAT *IS* A MOUSE. But this now violates Fodor's requirement of atomism. For in order to explain, in causal terms, how MOUSE
means *mouse* he would have had to specify the circumstances under which
the presence of any mouse would cause him to think MOUSE; but in order
to do this, he would have had to mention, not just other contentful mental
states, but states which can vary from individual to individual. Now
Fodor has, in fact, proposed two quite different solutions to the *all Ss*
problem in different publications. I shall outline and criticise them each
in turn.

Fodor 1987

Fodor thinks (or once thought) that we can at least give psycho-physical
(genuinely atomistic) specifications of the conditions under which the
presence of a sensory stimulus will guarantee the tokening of a sensory
concept – for example, the Mentalese concept SEEMS RED (see his 1987,
ch. 4). For the presence of red light impinging on the retina guarantees (in
certain physically specifiable circumstances) the belief that something
seems red. Such a stimulus will 'stuff a token of SEEMS RED into one's

belief-box', as Fodor graphically puts it. But, plainly, this will only help us to provide a naturalistic account of mental representation *in general* if we can reduce – by definition – all other concepts to such purely sensory ones.

This was precisely the reductive programme of phenomenalism. But Fodor argues (and I agree) that this programme cannot possibly succeed. In fact, no remotely plausible phenomenalist analysis has ever been provided, even for relatively simple statements dealing with middle-sized perceptible objects like tables and chairs, let alone for statements concerning theoretical entities such as electrons and neutrinos. So the attempt to provide a causal co-variance solution to the *all Ss* problem lands Fodor with a dilemma – either to become committed to phenomenalism, or to abandon semantic atomism.

When he wrote his 1987, Fodor thought that he could slip through the horns of this dilemma, without commitment to any pernicious form of semantic holism, by claiming the following:

> A Mentalese term 'S' represents Ss if there are circumstances in which any S *would* cause psycho-physical traces which in fact guarantee, by *some* mechanism, a tokening of the term 'S'.

So the Mentalese term MOUSE will mean *mouse*, not if *all* mice cause me to think MOUSE (this is the *all Ss* problem), but rather, provided that there are circumstances in which the presence of any given mouse in my line of vision would cause psycho-physical traces which guarantee, by some mechanism, that I think MOUSE. Fodor grants that the mechanisms in question will *in fact* involve inferences and computations on beliefs and other representational states. But he claims that this does not matter, provided that he has not *mentioned* such states in giving his account – and he has not. Since nothing besides physical causal connections needs to be explicitly mentioned, the resulting account can be both atomistic and naturalistically acceptable, Fodor thinks.

Robert Cummins objects that this attempted solution to the *all Ss* problem is a cheat, and it certainly appears, on the face of it, to be one (see Cummins, 1989, ch. 5). For the problem of providing an atomistic and naturalistically acceptable account of what it is for a Mentalese expression to have meaning is not just the problem of *saying* in natural and atomistic terms what it is for 'S' to mean *S*. The problem is rather to show that the phenomenon of meaning *itself* is both natural and atomic. This must be so, because the anti-realist, and sceptical, argument to which Fodor is responding is *not a conceptual* one.

The problem is not to show that our *concept* of meaning can be explicated in a way that is both naturalistically and atomistically acceptable. It is, rather, to show that the *property* of meaning is itself both natural and atomic. In fact, the problem is about whether intentional properties themselves really do exist as part of the natural order. And this worry is not responded to merely by *saying* what intentional properties are in wholly natural and atomistic terms. Rather, it has to be shown that the properties themselves are both natural and atomic. And not only has Fodor failed to do this, but he has apparently conceded that it cannot be done. For he has conceded that tokenings of any given non-sensory concept will require – metaphysically, if not conceptually – the presence of other mental contents. His response to the *all Ss* problem (however satisfactory it may seem at a conceptual level), concedes that intentional, representational, properties are metaphysically holistic. And this appears sufficient to undermine the account from his own point of view.

In fact, however, these objections can pass Fodor by. Here, as in the previous section, it proves to be important to keep in mind the reasons *why* he finds holism unacceptable. (These will be explicated in the next chapter.) For they can be taken as defining, implicitly, the sense of 'atomism' which is in question. Indeed, Fodor can set his opponents a dilemma here. For either the mechanisms which mediate between the psycho-physical traces of Ss and the judgement 'S' can vary, involving different beliefs for different people on different occasions, or they cannot. If the first, then there *would* be a problem for atomism if we had to *mention* those states; but we don't. If the second, then there is no conflict with atomism in the sense that matters. Let me elaborate.

Suppose, first, that there are a variety of distinct cognitive pathways which can mediate between Ss and 'S'. Since these mechanisms can vary, no *particular* such mechanism (and so no particular mental states) are necessary to *individuate* a tokening of 'S'. If there is variation in causal pathways, in fact, then no particular pathway need be part of the *identity* of the state in question. (And note that the identity, here, is metaphysical, and not merely conceptual.) Fodor is quite right that atomistic individuation-conditions need not be compromised by inferentially based beliefs, provided that those inferences are various.

Suppose, second, that there are some beliefs which *always* figure in the transition from psycho-physical traces of Ss to 'S'. In that case we *would* need to mention those beliefs in individuating the semantic properties of the latter. But then this would not give rise to any holism which Fodor need find objectionable, since it would not introduce *variation between* people. For example, suppose that the inference from SEEMS F to IS F is always mediated (in us, at least) by the belief PERCEPTUAL CONDITIONS ARE NORMAL FOR JUDGING WHETHER F. Then the latter *is* one of the individuation-conditions for the judgement IS F. But the consequent weakening of the atomism of the latter is not one which need concern Fodor (as we shall see in due course) provided that the situation is the same for all normal human thinkers.

The real problem with Fodor's 1987 account, is just that it commits him to a set of subjunctive and counterfactual conditionals with impossible antecedents. For in order to explain how any *particular* mouse gets to be in the extension of my Mentalese term MOUSE – say, a mouse scurrying beneath the table of Julius Caesar in 55 BC; call this mouse 'Jules' – then he has to say this: that if Jules *were* to be present to my sense-organs in the right kind of circumstances, then he *would* cause psycho-physical traces which would cause me to think MOUSE. But on most accounts of organism-identity, the antecedent, here, is impossible. That is, on most accounts of the matter, it is *essential* to Jules, as the individual mouse that he is, that he should exist *when* he does, and probably, also, that he should be born of the parents that he was. This is the doctrine of essentiality of origin (see Kripke, 1980). So it is actually *impossible* for *Jules* to cause psycho-physical traces which cause me to think MOUSE. The closest we can get, in fact, is to talk about what would happen if a mouse *exactly like* Jules were to be presented to my sense-organs. But once we are in the business of appealing to *similarities between* mice in explaining the semantics of MOUSE, then we no longer need to appeal to *exact* similarity. Rather, we can appeal to all those things which are alike in sharing the property *mousehood*. And this is, in effect, the way in which Fodor now attempts to circumvent the problem, as we shall see.

Fodor 1990

Fodor has proposed quite a different way of dealing with the *all Ss* problem in later writing, perhaps in response to some of the difficulties raised above. (See his 1990, ch. 4.) He now attempts to circumvent the problem by saying the following:

> MOUSE refers to that property in the world, some instances of which cause tokenings of MOUSE in a way that is not asymmetrically dependent upon any other property-to-predicate connection.

Very roughly, his idea is that the world itself is already divided up into properties, independently of our systems of classification, and that I can then refer to *all* instances of a given property provided that I have identified *some* of its instances correctly. So when I think MOUSE, I am thinking about *mice* (that is, all mice) because all mice are instances of the appropriate worldly property. And in particular, Jules gets to be in the extension of MOUSE because he is relevantly similar to (by sharing the property of mousehood with) some mice which *do* cause me to think MOUSE.

My view is that this suggestion cannot possibly work, in general – in fact it founders on the metaphysics of properties. Now, I do not mean to object to the existence of worldly properties altogether. On the contrary, I believe that the sort of case made out by David Armstrong (1978) for recognising the real, mind-independent, existence of what he calls 'immanent universals', is a powerful one. But according to such accounts, the only properties that there *really* are in the world, independently of our systems of classification, are those which would be picked out by the predicate terms in a completed science. So Fodor's new solution to the *all Ss* problem might possibly succeed for natural kind terms, like MOUSE, where there is, plausibly, some mind-independent worldly property to which the term refers. But it cannot possibly work for the majority of our terms, which neither purport to refer to any unitary worldly property, nor succeed in so doing.

Terms like SPICE and SPORT do not attempt to refer to any particular worldly property, but rather class things together in a way which suits various of our human purposes. So we cannot, then, insist that SPORT will refer to *sports*, and not just to the subset of sports that I actually encounter, on the grounds that the latter are all instances of the same worldly property – namely, *sports*. For SPORT-THAT-I-ENCOUNTER is no less of a legitimate predicate than SPORT, and there is no more or less reason to think that either of them succeeds in referring to a worldly property.

In reply it may be said that all terms must at least refer to some *disjunction* (perhaps very complex) of worldly properties. Then provided that tokens of the Mentalese term in question have been caused (without being asymmetrically dependent upon any other property-to-term connection) by at least one instance of each of the properties in the disjunction, it will turn out that the term refers to the set of all items satisfying any one of the disjunctive properties – and hence SPORT, for example, will after all refer to *sports*.

I foresee a number of problems with this proposal. One relatively technical difficulty concerns the application of the asymmetric-dependence condition to disjunctive properties. If instances of each of the properties in the disjunction are to fall within the extension of the predicate, then the causation of the predicate by each of those properties will have to be, either symmetrically dependent on, or symmetrically independent of, the others. Otherwise the term will come out as *mis*-representing one of the properties in question, by application of the causal asymmetric-dependence account of misrepresentation. Now symmetric *independence* looks highly implausible, if the properties in question are linked together by their relation to the structure of human sense-organs, or by their relation to some human interest or purpose. For in such cases it will almost certainly fail to be true that, if any of the properties had failed to cause instances of the term then the others still would have, and vice versa.

So Fodor will have to claim that causation of the term by any one property in the disjunction is symmetrically *dependent* on its causation by each of the others. He will have to say that if any one of the properties had not caused tokenings of the term in belief, then nor would the others, and vice versa. But this now looks highly problematic for terms which have *marginal cases*. If one of the properties in the disjunction does fall within the extension of the term, but only because it is *just* similar enough to the others to meet the human purpose which lies behind the use of that concept, then it is unlikely that any dependence will be symmetric. On the contrary, it looks likely that the marginal-property-to-term connection *could* be broken without breaking the others, but not vice versa.

Much more fundamental, however, is the problem that there will often be no way of closing off the disjunction of properties falling within the extension of a term *except* by reference to variable human needs and purposes – which would violate Fodor's atomicity requirement. New sports are being invented all the time, for example. And what determines whether or not a new item gets to be in the extension of the predicate SPORT is not whether it possesses one of a pre-specified list of properties in a disjunction, but rather whether it comes close enough to meeting the kind of *interest* that we take in sports to be classified alongside the others. (Here I follow Wittgenstein, 1953, sections 66–75 and 562–70.)

To put what is essentially the same point slightly differently: someone may correctly be said to be referring to *sports* in their tokenings of the term SPORT, at a stage when they have not yet encountered items from all the properties in the disjunction. Then the only way of explaining how it is that they do indeed refer to all sports, and not just to the subset of types of sport that they have actually encountered, is to mention the background interests in virtue of which it is true that they *will* apply the term SPORT to the other cases too. (Remember, I am leaving linguistic division of labour to one side, here, as an irrelevance.) And then this would violate atomicity.

So I conclude that neither Fodor's 1987 nor his 1990 attempts to overcome the *all Ss* problem for co-variance semantics (while remaining true to his naturalism and atomism) are successful. At the very least, there are major problems with each. One possible option to explore, then, might be that of giving up the constraint of atomism, and embracing some (weak) form of semantic holism instead. (Naturalism is non-negotiable, for a realist; and anyway, it wasn't the naturalism in particular which gave rise to the problems above.) Indeed, this is just what I shall urge in the chapter that follows. If adopted, this proposal would enable us to find a place for causal co-variance within semantic theory, but embedded in a form of account (functional-role semantics, in fact) which no longer favours Mentalese over natural language as the language of thought.

Summary

In this chapter I have discussed the plausibility of a number of Gricean, thought-based, approaches to the semantics of natural language. Grice's own theory, with its exclusive concentration on the use of natural language to communicate, is definitely incorrect. But there remains the possibility of marrying Searle's theory of natural-language semantics to Fodor's thesis that the language of thinking is Mentalese. I have also outlined Fodor's proposed causal co-variance semantics for the terms of Mentalese, and have argued that it faces a number of severe difficulties. At any rate, the resulting theory of mental semantics can hardly claim to be sufficiently plausible to provide us with an additional argument for the view that the language of all thought is Mentalese.

4   Holism and language

In this chapter I shall consider, and criticise, Fodor's argument from realism about the status of propositional attitude psychology to the conclusion that some version of causal co-variance semantics *must* be correct, and so to the conclusion that the language of thinking is Mentalese. I shall also consider how plausible it would be to develop a semantics for natural language directly, not via a prior account of the semantics of thought. It is important that some form of language-based semantics should be defensible, I shall argue, if it is to be possible to defend any robust version of the thesis that public language is implicated in conscious thinking.

4.1   From mental realism to Mentalese

In the last chapter I outlined a number of criticisms of Fodor's form of causal co-variance semantics. It is hard to be confident, however, that Fodor can have no adequate reply to those objections. It is even harder to be confident that there can be no *other* version of causal co-variance theory which might avoid the objections. So there is no sense in which Fodor's approach to the semantics of thought can be regarded as having been definitively refuted. Moreover, Fodor has available to him, in addition, a general argument for claiming that *some* version of causal co-variance semantics *must* be right, since it is the only kind of semantic theory which stands any chance of being genuinely atomistic (see his 1994, ch. 1). That is, it is the only theory which might provide a semantic value for each expression, one by one, without mention of the semantic values of the others. So a convincing argument for semantic atomism would at the same time be a convincing argument that the language of thought is Mentalese, since the theory of causal co-variance can only be successful for the latter.

In fact, Fodor has a seemingly powerful argument for the conclusion that the language with which we think must be Mentalese, and not a natural language, which starts from realism about the existence of propositional attitudes as its major premise. This argument is implicit in his 1987. It runs as follows:

1. The states and properties postulated by common-sense psychology (particularly beliefs, desires, and intentions) really do exist, and enter into real causal interactions.

2. If (1) is true, then our talk of propositional attitudes like belief and desire will need to be vindicated by a future scientific psychology.

3. But scientific psychology will not employ any notion of content which is holistic.

4. So (from 1, 2, and 3) we should reject semantic holism.

5. So (from 4) we should accept some form of semantic atomism in accounting for the intentional content of propositional attitudes.

6. Causal co-variance semantics is the only form of semantic theory which stands any chance of being genuinely atomistic.

7. So (from 5 and 6) we should accept some form of causal co-variance semantics.

8. So (from 7) we should accept that the language with which we think is Mentalese, and not a natural language.

There are a number of comments to be made about this argument. The first is that I fully accept the opening premise. So it is not open to me to block the whole argument at the outset, by opting for some form of anti-realism about the mental. If I am to avoid the conclusion in (8), then, I shall have to find some other weakness in the argument.

Now I have already indicated, in section 3.6 above, that I believe premise (6) to be true. That is, I have accepted that no other form of semantic theory besides causal co-variance is likely to be able to deliver a semantic value for each thought-component independently of the others. I have also indicated, in the same section, that the step from (7) to (8) is sound, since it would be highly implausible to attempt to apply causal co-variance theory directly to the expressions of natural language. If that theory is correct, then the basic items to which it applies will have to be lexical items of Mentalese. It is plain, moreover, that the step from (5) and (6) to (7) is valid.

So from my perspective, any weakness in the argument must lie somewhere between premises (2) and (5). I shall argue, in fact, that the step from (4) to (5) is crucially invalid. But first, I shall spend some time commenting on the truth or falsity of premises (2) and (3). (The move to (4) is plainly sound, in the absence of ambiguity.)

Why should the supposed need for vindication of common-sense psychology by scientific psychology lead us to reject semantic holism, as premises (2) and (3) imply? The short answer, is that common-sense psychology will only be *vindicated*, in the intended sense, if the basic entities with which it deals (particularly the various propositional attitude types) will also figure in the theories of a completed scientific psychology; and yet there is reason to think that such a scientific psychology would *not* find a use for the notion of intentional content if the latter should turn out to be holistic. This answer will take some explaining, however; in part because the notions of *vindication* and of *holism* require some comment.

4.2   The demand for scientific vindication

To what extent is it true that realism about common-sense psychology requires a commitment to scientific vindication? The intended sense of premise (2) is very strong. It entails this: that realism about the entities postulated by any folk-theory requires that those entities will *continue* to be postulated by future scientific theory. According to premise (2), (or rather its generalisation) to be realistic about a folk-theory, T, is to believe that the basic terms and theoretical commitments of T will be incorporated into the future theories of a successful science. So to be realistic about folk-psychology is to believe that future scientific psychology will continue to find a place for notions such as *belief* and *desire*, in particular.

This may well be what is *intended* by premise (2), but is it actually the case that realism about common-sense psychology entails its eventual incorporation into a content-based scientific psychology? Surely, it may be objected, there are more real things in the world than would find mention in scientific laws. We continue to believe that there are tables and chairs, shrubs and hedges, and spices and sports, despite the fact that none of the terms for any of these things will figure in the laws of any scientific theory. It would surely be scientism of the most crass sort to insist that *only* those items which figure in scientific laws have real existence.

There are issues here which require careful handling, however, returning us to some of the questions touched upon in section 3.8 above, to do with the metaphysics of properties. It is true that we have many concepts – such as those of *table, chair, shrub, hedge, spice,* and *sport* – which are not scientific ones, and which have been constructed to subserve other human purposes besides that of scientific explanation. These concepts find their place in human practical activities, or in human social life. (For general discussion of the relationship between human concepts and human purposes, see my 1987.) Such concepts can have determinate conditions of application, nevertheless, and so can figure in truths which are genuinely objective. It is, in fact, true of me that I am sitting at a table as I write this, and that there are six chairs in my office. So individual tables and chairs certainly exist, as do the states of affairs which might make it the case that propositions such as, [that I am sitting at a table], are true.

It is arguable, then, that the real existence of individuals, and of states of affairs, does not require their eventual vindication by science. But the metaphysic of properties which is probably the most plausible (see Armstrong, 1978) maintains that the only real properties that there are in the world – the real 'divisions in nature', in Plato's famous phrase – are those which would find a place in a completed science. For suppose we ask whether every meaningful human concept – including concepts like *table*, *chair*, *shrub*, *hedge*, *spice*, and *sport* – picks out, or refers to, some real property in the world. If we say, 'Yes', then we face an embarrassing proliferation of properties, since there is literally no limit to the number of possible human concepts. It is better to say, 'No', allowing that many human concepts impose divisions upon nature that are artificial, which find no reflection in the mechanisms and principles by which nature itself operates.

The *real* divisions in nature are the business of science to discover. The only real properties that there are, are those which would figure in the laws of a completed science. So while individual tables really exist, and while there are true propositions involving the concept *table*, the *difference between* tables and other sorts of thing is not objectively there in the world, independently of the human mind. It is, rather, a human social construction. And similarly, while it is determinately true that there are no hedges in my garden, and while the particular hedge in my neighbour's garden really exists, the *difference between* hedges and other things is a humanly imposed distinction.

What emerges is this. If the truth of semantic holism were to mean that our concepts of *belief*, *desire*, and *intention* (among others) would be unlikely to figure in the laws and explanatory generalisations of a completed science of psychology, then it would not necessarily follow that there are no individual (token) propositional attitudes. Nor would it follow that there exist no states of affairs to make it true that I *believe* this or *desire* that. So to this extent realism about common-sense psychology requires no vindication from science. However, what *would* follow, is that there exist no real properties picked out by such terms as 'belief that P' and 'desire that Q'. It would follow that common-sense classifications fail to pick out real divisions in nature, just as the common-sense distinctions between 'table' and 'chair', or between 'bush' and 'shrub', fail to – failing, in this case, to pick out real divisions amongst states of the human mind.

Premise (2) of Fodor's argument is thus only strictly true if the realism expressed in premise (1) is a realism about *properties*. It that were waived, and the realism of (1) were weakened in such a way as to claim only that *token* attitudes, and the states of affairs in which they figure, have real existence and causal roles, then all that would be required is that common-sense psychology should not actually be *inconsistent with* a future scientific psychology. But there is little comfort to be derived from this, by any genuine realist about the mental, such as myself. For many of the considerations used in support of a realist view of propositional-attitude psychology – as against quasi-behaviourism, or interpretationalism – will *also* support the idea that the terms of such a psychology should pick out real *properties* of the human mind. In fact, the sort of realism which we defended briefly in Chapter 1 *was* a realism about mental properties.

The argument which arose out of our discussions of the Turing Test and the Chinese Room in section 1.6, for example, was that we are committed to a certain general – and hence property-involving – *structure and organisation* of the mind. In the same way, we argued in section 1.7 that the explanatory and predictive success of common-sense psychology gives us reason to think that the central core, at least, of its principles and generalisations is very likely to be true or close to the truth. But then this is an argument for saying that common-sense psychology should constitute a secure basis for science – which means that its basic terms should succeed in picking out what are, in fact, natural kinds (real properties). So the considerations which we advanced in Chapter 1 make me want to endorse premise (1) of the argument above in its strongest (property-involving) sense. In which case I am obliged to look for some other weakness in Fodor's argument for atomistic semantics if I can.

4.3   The problem of holism

Let me now turn to consider premise (3) of Fodor's argument, which claims that scientific psychology can have no use for a holistic notion of content. This requires us to elucidate the concept of *holism*. According to Fodor, content holism may be defined in terms of the notion of an *epistemic liaison*, as follows (see his 1987, ch. 3; see also Fodor and Lepore, 1992):

(1) Content holism = the doctrine that the content of any particular belief is determined by the totality of its epistemic liaisons.

(2) An epistemic liaison of a belief that P = any belief which the thinker takes to be relevant to deciding whether or not it is true that P.

For example, suppose I believe that the *Guardian* is generally reliable on politics and current affairs, whereas I believe that *The New York Times* is not. Then, 'the *Guardian* said so', will be, for me, an epistemic liaison of any of my beliefs on such matters; whereas, '*The New York Times* said so', will not be an epistemic liaison of those beliefs. Note that the notion of an *epistemic liaison* is relative to a thinker and a time. It is the beliefs which *I* take to be relevant to the evaluation of others which determine their epistemic liaisons, for me; and if my assessments of such relevance change over time, then so do the epistemic liaisons.

Now the thesis of content holism implies that my belief in the reliability of the *Guardian* will be partly determinative of the contents of all of my beliefs on current affairs, since it is an epistemic liaison of each one of them. So if, for example, the experience of being interviewed by a *Guardian* reporter were to cause me to lose my trust in the paper's reliability, then the contents of every one of those beliefs would change. In which case, the belief that I would express by saying, before my loss of faith, 'Mrs Thatcher was the longest serving UK Prime Minister of the twentieth century', and the belief that I would express by those words afterwards, are not really one and the same. Similarly, it will be impossible for any two people who differ over the *Guardian's* reliability to entertain the very same belief on any topic of current affairs.

This is an extremely strong version of content holism, and probably entails that no two people *ever* entertain beliefs with the very same content. For there will always be enough differences of belief between any two people to ramify through the whole network of their beliefs determining, according to the holistic thesis, differences of content. That is, for any candidate belief *P*, supposedly held in common by each of person A and person B, it will almost always turn out that *P* differs in some of its epistemic liaisons between A and B, and so will not be the same belief after all.

What would be wrong with that? One apparent problem turns out to be a red herring, although it has attracted a good deal of attention. It is, that if no two people ever entertain thoughts with the same content, then it is impossible for them ever to communicate, and equally impossible that they should ever genuinely disagree. When I attempt to communicate a belief to you by asserting the sentence, 'Communism is dead', then even if you accept what I have said, what you end up believing is not what I asserted, if holism is true. Equally, if you assert, 'Racism is ineliminable', and I deny it, asserting, 'No, racism is eliminable', then we are not really contradicting one another, because the content asserted by you is not the same as the content denied by me.

This difficulty for holism can be dealt with quite easily by distinguishing between two different notions of content, subserving distinct theoretical purposes. The notion of content we need in order to describe and explain communication and disagreement between people is *semantic* content, individuated by worldly truth-condition. Provided that the sentence, 'Racism is ineliminable', in each of our mouths, concerns the same worldly referents, and picks out the same putative state of affairs, then we can communicate or disagree with one another in its use, irrespective of our other differences of belief. For what matters in communication are (generally) the states of affairs (the states of the world) which our thoughts concern, not the manner in which we conceptualise or think about them.

The notion of content for which holism arises as an issue, in contrast, is *cognitive* content, the sort of content which we appeal to in psychological explanation. In general it will be crucial, if we are to explain the precise way in which someone acts or thinks as they do, to individuate their thoughts in a manner that respects their own mode of conceptualisation of the worldly states of affairs which their thoughts concern. It makes all the difference in explaining Oedipus' behaviour, for example, whether we describe him as believing *that he is married to Jocasta* or as believing *that he is married to his mother*. Now, it is only in connection with cognitive content that there is any suggestion that content should be individuated holistically. Holism about cognitive content would leave the notion of semantic (or 'communicative') content untouched, leaving us well able to explain how people can communicate or disagree.

(In the light of the above distinction, it is important that we should speak of 'content holism' rather than 'semantic holism', since the latter suggests that holism might arise for notions of content individuated for purposes of inter-personal semantics. The distinction between *semantic* content and *cognitive* content is developed at some length in my 1989. It also forms a central plank in Block's 1993 defence of functional-role semantics against Fodor's allegation of holism. But the way in which Block develops his defence does not touch Fodor's main argument, set out below.)

The real problem

In fact the real problem arising from the implication of content-holism noted above – that no two people will ever entertain beliefs with the same content – is that the notion of *belief content* would then be useless for the purposes of scientific psychology, as Fodor points out. For science, in general, seeks explanatory laws relating states of one kind to states of another kind. And the terms used in the expression of the laws have to be applicable across the whole domain of the science. So a scientific content-based psychology would seek to find laws and generalisations applicable to everyone, describing the causal roles of the various propositional-attitude contents. But if no two people ever entertain the *same* content, as holism implies, then there will be no psychological laws applicable to more than one individual thinker.

If holism were true then there would, at best, be some rough, approximate, generalisations involving the notion of content. For holism can allow that belief-contents can more or less *resemble* one another. But there will be no way of making these generalisations precise while retaining the notion of content. It would follow, indeed, if holism were true, that scientific psychology should head off in some new direction, not involving propositional attitudes with their holistic principles of individuation. And it would follow that our common-sense psychology is not a secure or appropriate basis for science.

It might be objected that this conclusion is, at least, too strong – on the grounds that many psychological generalisations *quantify over* content, in a way which does not require it to be true that any two thinkers ever entertain the *same* content (see Senor, 1992). Thus the practical reasoning syllogism tells us that anyone who desires that Q, and who believes that if P then Q, and who believes that P is within their power, will (other things being equal) try to bring it about that P. This generalisation can remain true, and can retain its predictive and explanatory power, even if no two thinkers ever instantiate the *same* instance of it (with particular contents substituted for *P* and for *Q)*.

There is little comfort to be derived here, however, if it is true (as it surely is) that a great many psychological generalisations relate to *particular* contents or types of content. Consider the claim that there exist various kinds of incest taboo, for example. If I say that people have an aversion to the thought of intercourse between mother and son, then I have expressed a generalisation in relation to a thought which no one else but myself can share, if holism is true. Since no one else can have an aversion to *that* thought (a thought individuated by the totality of the epistemic liaisons which it has, for me), then my attempted generalisation fails. And it would seem that, whatever (non-content-involving) direction it is that scientific psychology should head in, in order to be able to state and explain the existence of such phenomena as the incest taboo, would almost certainly obviate the need for psychological generalisations *over* contents as well.

So I conclude that premise (3) of Fodor's argument from realism about propositional attitudes to the thesis that the language of thought is Mentalese is very plausibly true: scientific psychology will not employ a notion of (cognitive) content which is holistic (in Fodor's strong sense of 'holism', at least). Moreover, as noted above, the step from the first three premises to the conclusion in (4) – that content-holism should be rejected

– is almost certainly sound. If realism about the attitudes means believing that common sense will need to be vindicated by future scientific psychology – as premise (2) maintains – then we had better also believe that content can be specified *non-holistically*.

4.4   Between holism and atomism

So far no real weaknesses in Fodor's argument have emerged. But in fact such a weakness is not far to seek. What Fodor overlooks is that there may be non-atomistic forms of semantics which would, nevertheless, fail to entail holism in his strong version of it. For example, functional-role semantics maintains that propositional attitudes are individuated in terms of their *potential* causal interactions with one another (see Block, 1986; see also Stich, 1983). These potential causal interactions can remain the same across subjects whose *actual* propositional attitudes may differ. So different thinkers, despite their differences of belief, and despite the differences in the epistemic liaisons of any given belief, may nevertheless entertain many of the same beliefs. For the same *conditionals* can be true of them.

For example, it can be true of me *both* before *and* after my formative experience with the reporter from the *Guardian*, that I believe Mrs Thatcher to be the longest serving UK prime minister of the twentieth century. For although the epistemic liaisons of that belief have changed, it will be true of me on both occasions that *if* I believe the *Guardian* to be reliable, *then* I shall regard, 'the *Guardian* says so', as a reason for holding my belief about Mrs Thatcher. And, presumably, all the other conditional truths about the role of that belief within my cognition would remain unaltered also. In which case, if content is individuated by functional role, then the content of my belief will be the same in each case.

Something similar will be true of the two people, one of whom believes the *Guardian* to be reliable whereas the other does not. While the *actual* causal antecedents and consequences of their belief in the length of Mrs Thatcher's term of office may differ from one another, the *causal role* of that belief can be the very same, if causal role is individuated by conditional truths about causal antecedents and consequences. It can be equally true of each of them, for example, that they would reply, 'So what?' in response to the claim, 'the *Guardian* says so', *if* they were to believe that the *Guardian* is not really reliable.

Notice that functional-role semantics is still, in a sense, holistic – but not in a way which fits Fodor's definition. For an account of the functional role of any given belief may require mention of many other contentful mental states (so the account is certainly not *atomistic*). But the states mentioned will not necessarily be other *actual* beliefs and desires of the agent, as in the form of account which specifies content in terms of the notion of an *epistemic liaison*. Rather, it is the way in which a given thought-content *would* interact with other *hypothetical* beliefs and desires which determines its content, on this account.

It may be objected that *some* of the actual epistemic liaisons of a belief, at any rate, must be determinative of its content. For some beliefs are apt to give rise to, or to be caused by, others immediately, not mediated by any further premise. And it seems essential to their content that they *should* so cause or be caused. Indeed, it might plausibly be maintained that all of the unmediated epistemic liaisons of a belief are partially determinative of its content. In particular, it seems clear that any *immediate and obvious* implications of a given belief will be partly determinative of the latter's content. This much, at any rate, seems to follow from the intuitive criterion of difference as a condition of thought-identity – see section 2.6 above.

Thus, if one is prepared to infer from, 'It is a whale', to, 'It is a mammal', without relying on any further premise (not even the premise, 'All whales are mammals'), then this epistemic liaison is partially determinative of the content of the former. (In contrast, in the example above I was only prepared to infer from, 'the *Guardian* says so', to, 'It is so', in conjunction with the further premiss, 'the *Guardian* is reliable.') Then someone's concept of a whale will change when they learn, for the first time, that whales are mammals and not fish, thus acquiring a new unmediated epistemic liaison. Similarly, two people who are inclined to assent to the sentence, 'Whales are endangered', will express different beliefs by that sentence if one of them is inclined to accept the inference, '*whale → mammal*', while the other still accepts, '*whale → fish*'. These consequences seem intuitively correct.

But now we have a problem. For if the identity of a belief P is partly determined by the beliefs with which it is immediately inferentially connected; and those beliefs, in turn, have their contents partly determined by the beliefs with which *they* are immediately connected; then it could turn out, after all (by the transitivity of identity), that the content of any given belief is partly determined by a great many of the person's other beliefs.

Suppose, for example, that person A accepts the unmediated inferences $P → Q$, $Q → R$, and $R → S$. Person B, on the other hand, only accepts $P → Q$ and $Q → R$ (perhaps because they lack some of the concepts necessary to grasp the thought that S). Then the functional role of R, for A and for B, must be different. But then the functional role of Q, too, must be different (because it is connected, in each case, to states which differ in functional role); and also, by the same token, the functional role of P must be different. So it turns out that A and B do not share the same belief when each accepts the sentence 'P', after all.

This is, in fact, a version of Fodor's *Ur-argument* from his 1987 (p. 60) – *some* epistemic liaisons are determinative of belief; and there is no principled way of distinguishing between those epistemic liaisons which are determinative of content and those which are not; so *all* epistemic liaisons are determinative of belief. Now, the main point to be made about this argument is that it is not a problem specific to functional-role semantics, but arises for functional individuation quite generally. So unless there is no scientifically respectable notion of a *functional state* (which is absurd), there must be something amiss with the argument against the sort of weakly holistic individuation of belief which is distinctive of functional-role semantics.

For example, the function of the heart is to pump blood around the body. And the function of the blood is to collect nutrients from the digestive system, and oxygen from the lungs, distributing them to the various organs and tissues. Now consider the change which took place with the atrophy of the second stomach to form what is now the human appendix. This was a change in the functioning of the digestive system. Was it also a change in the function of the heart? Surely not. The function of the heart remained the same throughout. Yet it is possible to construct an argument exactly parallel to the one given above for belief, thus: since the functioning of the elements of the digestive system was different, the function of the blood must have been different; and if the function of the blood was different, the function of the heart must also have been different.

One possible suggestion is that, where functional identity is partly determined by immediate – one-step – interactions with surrounding states, the latter are to be individuated by *role-bearers*, not by role (provided the overall powers of the system remain roughly the same). Then the function of the heart is to pump *blood*, where the latter is individuated by its intrinsic characteristics (red, haemoglobin-containing), rather than by its functional role (oxygen-carrying, nutrient-transmitting). Applied to the case of belief, we could then say that provided the sentence 'R' expresses *some* belief for both A and B, and a belief with the same worldly truth-condition, then the belief that Q is individuated by its connection with the *sentence* 'R' (that is, by its causal role in interacting with the surrounding *role-bearers*), even though the causal role of *that* state may be different.

Roughly speaking, the idea is that, provided an element of a functional system continues to interact with its surroundings in the same way (where those surroundings are *not* themselves individuated functionally), then it can continue to retain the same function. But, whether or not this particular solution works, the main point is that *this is a problem for functional individuation generally, not a problem for functional-role semantics in particular.* So, unless we were prepared to accept that there really exist *no* functionally individuated entities, we have as yet been given no reason for rejecting functional individuation of thoughts, either.

I conclude, then, that the step from premise (4) to premise (5) of Fodor's argument outlined in section 4.1 above is unsound. We can grant that we ought to reject holistic accounts of content, in Fodor's strong sense of 'holism', if we believe that common-sense psychology should provide a secure basis for a scientific, content-based, psychology. Yet it does not follow from this – nor is it particularly plausible to claim on the basis of this – that we should then embrace some atomistic account of intentional content instead. For there remains the possibility of endorsing what I shall call a *weakly holistic* account of meaning, such as would be provided by functional-role semantics.

4.5   Arguments for holism

It is astonishing that Fodor should have missed such an obvious possibility. Perhaps I have somehow misinterpreted him? The best way to show that I have not, and also the best way to drive home his error, is to consider the various arguments which are supposed to support holistic accounts of intentional content. These are considered in some detail in Fodor, 1987, ch. 3 (see also Fodor and Lepore, 1992). In each case I shall show, either that the argument contains a simple fallacy, or else that it does not support holism in Fodor's strong sense, but only in its weaker form.

Confirmation holism

There are a pair of arguments for content holism (in its strong form) from what might be called *confirmation holism* – though Fodor himself only considers one of them explicitly in his 1987. But both are equally, and obviously, invalid. The first takes as its premise confirmation holism with respect to our beliefs *about the world* (see Fodor, 1987, pp. 62–7). It is said to be *the total set* of our beliefs about the world which faces the tribunal of experience together, and that we cannot verify those beliefs on an individual basis. From this it is deduced that our beliefs do not have their contents on an individual basis, either.

Now the premise of this argument may well be true, but the conclusion only follows, plainly, if we accept some kind of verificationism about meaning. But why should we? For the weaknesses of verificationist theories of meaning have long been manifest. Rather, while accepting confirmation holism, we can, for example, conjoin a referential (causal co-variance) account of meaning with in-the-head functional role to get a theory which will be both realist and only weakly holistic. (Note that once weak holism is allowed as a possibility, we shall be free to offer solutions to the *misrepresentation* and *all Ss* problems which differ from Fodor's problematic proposals discussed in the last chapter.)

The second argument from a form of confirmation holism takes its start from the fact that any theory of an individual thinker's psychology must be holistically related to the evidence – that is, to the thinker's circumstances and behaviour. (See Fodor and Lepore, 1992, ch. 3.) For there is no way of directly verifying ascriptions of beliefs and desires to an individual. Rather, ascribing to someone any given belief must depend upon all the other beliefs and desires we are prepared to attribute to them. What we have to do, in fact, is try to find the best *overall* explanation of their behaviour. (This is the element of truth in Davidson's interpretationalism; see section 1.5 above.) From this it is deduced that the individual states we ascribe depend, holistically, upon all the other intentional states of the thinker.

But again the reply to this argument is obvious. It is, that how we *verify* ascriptions of content to any given individual is one thing, how we *individuate* the states so ascribed may be quite another. Indeed, there is surely no reason to think that 'believes that P' is a theoretical predicate peculiar to our theory of the individual in question. In order for strong content-holism to be plausible, our answer to the question, 'What *is* the belief that P, ascribed to A on the basis of total evidence?', would have to be, 'It is the state which is apt to interact with *A's* other states in such a way that . . .'. But why should we give such an answer? Why should not our answer, rather, delete all references to the person A, giving, in effect, an answer which commits us only to functional-role semantics?

Functional-role semantics

This now brings us to the other main pair of arguments which are supposed, by Fodor, to support content holism. These are arguments for, and from, functional-role semantics. In each case I shall claim that the arguments support only a conditionalised and restricted form of functional role, which would then be only weakly holistic. The first is an argument from functionalism about mental states *in general* (see Fodor, 1987, pp. 67–71).

The majority of philosophers now think that the way to avoid Cartesian dualism about the mental, and to understand the relationship between mind and brain, is by accepting that mental states are individuated by their causal role, conceptualised at some level of abstraction from the physical mechanisms in the brain which instantiate those roles. The argument is then, that when we extend this approach to states like *the belief that P* we get functional-role semantics, and so holism. Fodor's own response is that we should accept functionalist accounts of general categories of state such as *belief*, *desire*, and *intention*, while rejecting them for states with particular contents, such as *the belief that P* and *the desire that Q*.

Fodor's position may be a possible one. But it is obvious that he does not *need* to take any such line. For it is plain that the argument does not, in any case, support semantic holism in Fodor's strong sense of it. To see this, notice that functionalism about the mind claims to individuate mental states in terms of their *potential* causal interactions with bodily stimuli, with other mental states, and with behaviour. Causal relations with other *actual* states of the subject do not always play a defining role. For example, no functionalist would claim that my pain must be a distinct kind of mental state from yours, merely because I happen to have a desire to appear brave whereas you do not. On the contrary, functionalists will insist that our states are the same, provided that they *would* have the same effects *if* all our other mental states were similar.

In the same way, although functionalists should accept that *some* causal connections with other actual mental states (namely, the unmediated connections) play a defining role in individuating some types of mental state, they should deny that mental state identity is transitive across chains of such connections. Surely no functionalist would want to deny that blind people have desires, for example (that is, action-determining states of the same type that sighted people have), merely because of the differences in the remote causal connections of those states! (Standing-state desires tend to be activated by the belief that the thing desired is now available, and such beliefs are often caused, in the normal case, by visual experience of the desired object.)

When the argument is extended to *the belief that P*, then, it is obvious that it will not be all of the causal connections between that state and the agent's other actual beliefs and desires which individuate it, but rather the potential connections. It will not be the epistemic liaisons of a belief which constitute its content, but rather the set of conditionals about what the subject *would* think or do in the presence of various other – hypothetical – beliefs and desires. Then since these hypotheticals can remain true of a variety of individuals, with various different actual beliefs and desires, there is no threat, here, to a content-based science of psychology. And although some of the (immediate) causal connections between the belief that P and other actual beliefs or desires may be partly individuative of it, there is no reason to think that the individuation conditions will extend across chains of such connections.

The second argument for functional-role semantics is a kind of 'what else?' argument from those working on the semantics of beliefs and statements (see Fodor 1987, pp. 71–92). It is generally maintained that we cannot individuate (cognitive) contents purely in terms of reference, since this will slice them *too thick* – that is, it will fail to distinguish from one another thought-contents which are, intuitively, distinct. For example, Oedipus' belief *that Jocasta is more than 40 years old* differs in content from his belief *that his mother is more than 40 years old*, even though Jocasta is, in fact, his mother. For, not knowing that Jocasta is his mother, it would be possible for him to have the one belief without the other. Yet if the reference is the same, what *else* can distinguish these beliefs except their differences of causal role? For example, Oedipus' belief that he is 30 years old will tend to cause him to have the second of the above beliefs in the presence only of the belief that a girl of 10 cannot have a child, whereas the first of the above beliefs will only be caused if he *also* believes that Jocasta is his mother.

Fodor's own response to such examples (in his 1987) is to develop a purely referential semantics in more detail, postulating a distinct property in the world wherever we have intentional contents which are intuitively distinct. This leads to a wildly profligate and implausible ontology of properties, and one that I would have thought a scientific realist like Fodor would have taken all pains to avoid. But the important point, again, is that he does not *need* to adopt any such line. For the argument plainly only supports the conditional version of functional-role semantics, not one that leads to content holism.

For example, when Oedipus does come to believe that Jocasta is his mother, this surely does not suddenly make the two contents *Jocasta is over 40* and *my mother is over 40* one and the same, despite the fact that their epistemic liaisons would then be identical. Rather, anyone approaching semantic theory from this perspective would insist that the contents remain distinct because they *would* behave differently from one another *if* Oedipus' other beliefs and desires were different. Once again, Fodor has been sent chasing a red herring. Since functional-role semantics is only weakly holistic it does not threaten realism about the mental, and so no reason has yet been provided for us to endorse semantic atomism.

It is worth also considering a slightly more elaborate example, lest Fodor should try to respond (as he does; see his 1994, ch. 2) by appeal to compositionality, pointing out that *Jocasta* and *my mother* can be distinguished by virtue of the fact that the latter contains the concept *mother*, whereas the former does not. The example is as follows. Imagine that I have learned to use colour-terms normally, by sight, but have also learned to use a hand-held machine which *in fact* (unknown to me) responds to colour – perhaps vibrating in the hand with an intensity proportional to the dominant wavelengths it receives. And suppose that I have been trained, ostensively, to use a set of terms, 'der', 'neerg', and so on; where these terms are *in fact* co-extensive with the colour-terms, 'red', 'green', and so on. Then, plainly, there are circumstances in which I might believe that the tomato is red without also believing that it is der, or vice versa. And this despite the fact that it is the very same worldly property, surely, which my thought concerns.

Here, as before, the argument is: what *else* can distinguish the contents of the beliefs *that the tomato is red* and *that the tomato is der*, except their functional roles? For there is, by hypothesis, no overt compositional or syntactic difference between them. What makes the two beliefs different, in fact, are such things as that, for example, (unless I *also* believe that anything der is red) it is only the former which will cause me to point to the tomato if asked to exhibit something red; and if I want to check on the truth of the former I shall open my eyes, whereas if I want to check on the truth of the latter I shall pick up my vibrating-machine.

From his most recent discussion of these matters (1994), it looks as if Fodor would now wish to respond to this example by claiming that 'red' and 'der' *are* syntactically distinct, but at the level of underlying Mentalese representation. Indeed, he would now wish to say that the contents of the beliefs *that the tomato is red* and *that the tomato is der* are the very same (because concerning the same worldly referents), but that they differ in what he calls 'mode of presentation', functioning differently from one another in cognition in virtue of having distinct Mentalese representations. But this is to pitch the explanation at the wrong level. It provides an explanation only at the level of sub-personal processing, rather than at the level of personal thought. The intuition it fails to capture, in fact, is that there is a difference of *content* between the belief that the tomato is red and the belief that the tomato is der – these are, we think, two different thoughts *with different contents*, rather than thoughts with the same contents which happen to interact differently in cognition. But then the only remaining option for what distinguishes them as thoughts, is their distinct functional roles – which means accepting that content is partly individuated by functional role.

The case of Mrs T

There is one other argument that Fodor considers, which really would support content holism, if it were successful. This is the argument provided by Stephen Stich's now-famous example of Mrs T, who was afflicted by progressive memory loss (see Stich 1983, pp. 54–6. For Fodor's discussion, see his 1987, pp. 60–2 and 92–3). In her youth Mrs T knew a good deal about politics, including the fact that President McKinley was assassinated. But in old age she has lost all other memories about politics and about McKinley (she is no longer even prepared to assert that he is dead), while still being prepared to assert that he was assassinated. We are invited to share the intuition that Mrs T no longer has the same belief, *that McKinley was assassinated*. In which case the content of that belief must have been, at least partly, individuated by its epistemic liaisons. For what has changed, with Mrs T, are not the conditionals which may be true of her (or so Stich asserts). Rather, it is that she has lost others of her earlier *actual* beliefs.

Fodor's response to this example is to allow it to be true that Mrs T ceases to believe that McKinley was assassinated. But he points out that Stich needs to claim, in addition, that she still has *a* belief which she expresses in the words, 'McKinley was assassinated', only not *that* one. For Stich's claim is that content *changes* through changes in her other beliefs – his picture is that her belief undergoes a *metamorphosis* of content through losing its epistemic liaisons. But it is much more plausible to claim that she ceases to have *any* belief. Fodor's response to the example, in fact, is to claim that Mrs T ceases to have any concept of assassination – although she says the *words*, 'McKinley was assassinated', they have ceased to express any content for her. Such a reply is very plausible, I think. But it is not the only reply available. And that Fodor fails to see that it is not, is again indicative of his failure to notice the difference between strong and weak forms of content holism, as I shall now explain.

Not only does Stich need to claim that Mrs T retains a belief, he also needs to maintain that the same conditionals remain true in connection with that belief. For the example is supposed to show that belief-content varies with changes in other *actual* beliefs, not only with changes in (conditional) functional role – that is, the example is supposed to support strong as against weak holism. But it does not do so. For the causal potential of a belief does not just consist in its dispositions to *interact with* other actual beliefs, if they exist. It also consists in dispositions to *give rise to* other beliefs, and dispositions to interact with *desires* in practical reasoning. But neither of these sorts of disposition are present in the case of Mrs T. In which case the functional role of her belief is *not* constant through cognitive change, and we can then explain why the content of her belief should change without endorsing strong holism.

For example, on any account, surely, part of the functional role of the belief *that McKinley was assassinated* is that it should dispose one to believe *that McKinley is dead*. But Mrs T has no such disposition. And another aspect of the functional role of that belief would be to interact with a *desire* to list all dead Presidents of the United States by saying, 'McKinley is dead'. But again, Mrs T has no such disposition. So we do not, with Fodor, *have* to insist that Mrs T ceases to have any belief at all. We can explain how the content of her belief should have changed without commitment to strong holism, by pointing out that the functional role of her belief – the set of conditional statements which are true of her – has changed as a result of her dementia.

4.6   The need for a language-based semantics

Let us take stock of our position. Over the course of this and the previous chapter I have been arguing for three distinct claims, in fact.

First, I have argued that a semantics for natural language in terms of a prior notion of thought (in the tradition of Grice, as amended by Searle) is possible, but in some respects unattractive. Among other things, such an account forces us to give up our common-sense belief that we often think aloud *in* natural language. Rather, the account will claim that these cases are misdescribed, and that what really happens is that we *express* in natural-language thoughts which were antecedently given. This difficulty would not, I think, provide sufficient reason for us to reject the proposed semantics unless there were some other approach which is otherwise almost equally plausible. So we need at this point to consider whether it is possible to give a semantics for natural language which does not prioritise thought, and so which does not imply (when combined with the thesis that propositional attitudes are relations to sentences) that the language of thinking is Mentalese.

Second, I have argued that Fodor's proposed causal co-variance semantics for thought, in terms of asymmetric causal dependence, faces a number of difficulties. While these problems may not be sufficient to *refute* a causal co-variance approach to semantics – since it is hard to prove that there cannot be adjustments which would avoid them – what they do mean is that we are not, as yet, *forced* to accept that thoughts are the basic bearers of semantic content. So, again, we are not yet forced to accept that the language of thinking is Mentalese. But, as before, much may depend upon our success in sketching a plausible alternative semantics for thought which would be equally applicable to the sentences of natural language.

Third, I have tried to show the unsoundness of Fodor's argument which moves from realism about common-sense propositional attitude psychology to the conclusion that some form of causal co-variance semantics *must* be correct, on the grounds that the latter is the only form of semantic theory which stands any chance of being genuinely atomistic. In particular, there is a false assumption made in the step from rejection of content holism (in Fodor's strong sense of 'holism') to acceptance of atomism. The false assumption is that there is no room for a form of semantics which would be only *weakly* holistic. But the only way of showing this convincingly, is to sketch and defend some such semantic theory.

Taking all these points together, then, what I have to do in the remainder of this chapter is outline a form of semantic theory which should have the following three properties:

(1) It should be applicable to the sentences of natural language without prioritising or taking for granted a separate semantics for thought.

(2) It should nevertheless be applicable to thought, in such a way that the theory can be formulated equally for private as for public thinkings (where the public thinkings, at least, take place in natural language).

(3) The theory in question should be, at most, only weakly holistic.

In fact I shall sketch, not just one, but two such theories. The first is functional-role semantics, which will be familiar, in outline, from the discussion of sections 4.4 and 4.5 above. The second is a theory of canonical acceptance conditions, due to Christopher Peacocke. I should emphasise that my main purpose will not be to demonstrate the adequacy of either of these theories, but rather to indicate that they constitute viable research programmes, well worth further exploration. For all that I really need, for my purposes, is that there should be no good reason, as yet, to embrace an atomistic semantics (and so no good reason to believe that the language of all thinking is Mentalese).

But why, it may be asked, is it really necessary to my project that some form of language-based semantics should be viable? Since the thesis to be defended in this book is only that *conscious* thinking essentially involves natural language, why can I not concede an account of the semantics of language along the lines of the Fodor/Searle hybrid discussed in section 3.5, by insisting merely that the thoughts which are used to impose content on natural language sentences are *non-conscious* ones? Indeed, I have already had occasion to remark that we are not generally aware of the meaning-imposing intentions postulated by Grice and Searle – which then implies, if any account of consciousness along the lines to be defended in Chapter 7 is correct, that the intentions in question are non-conscious ones.

The resulting picture of the relationship between language and thought would be something like this. We express our thoughts in language – whether publicly or privately – in order for those thoughts to be reflexively available to further thought, and so in order for those thoughts to become conscious ones (at least, if the theory of consciousness to be defended in Chapter 7 is correct). But in each case the *content* of the conscious thought is inherited from the contents of thoughts which we were already capable of entertaining (and did actually entertain) non-consciously. If such a picture were correct, then we would, in a sense, have vindicated the view that (much of) human conscious thinking involves natural language. And we would also, in a sense, have vindicated the cognitive conception of such language. But the versions of these doctrines thus vindicated would be relatively weak.

It is one thing to maintain that thoughts (or some thoughts) can only achieve the status of consciousness through being formulated in (inner or outer) natural language. It would be another, much stronger, thing to maintain that there are some thoughts which can only exist at all through the possibility of being formulated, consciously, in such language. And it is one thing to maintain that language has a role in our cognition distinctive of conscious thinking. But it would be another, much stronger, thing to maintain that language is constitutive of the very existence of (some of) the thoughts which we actually employ in that form of thinking.

While the weaker versions of these doctrines would be of some considerable interest, it is only the stronger versions which would be sufficient to obtain for us, in full, the sorts of significant consequences for philosophy and psychology advertised in section 1.2. In particular, only if the language faculty is actually implicated in the contents (and not just the conscious status) of our conscious thoughts, will the scientific study of the structure of that faculty be at the same time an investigation into the structure and functioning of a great deal of our central cognition.

In any case, I certainly want to hold open the possibility of endorsing the stronger version of the thesis that language is implicated in thought, according to which language is implicated in our capacity to entertain certain thought-types, whether consciously *or* non-consciously. I therefore need to be prepared to defend the viability of a strong version of the cognitive conception of language, which necessitates, in turn, the viability of a semantic theory with each of the three properties outlined above. Remember that according to the cognitive conception, when a speaker utters a sentence their utterance will express a thought by *constituting* it, not by encoding or signalling it. And a hearer who is a competent user of the same language will then understand that utterance in virtue of it constitutively expressing, for them, the very same (or a sufficiently similar) thought.

(The cognitive conception of language needs to be made somewhat more complex than this, of course, if it is to accommodate such communicative phenomena as metaphor and irony. But there is surely little doubt that this can be done – perhaps marrying the account to elements of Sperber and Wilson's relevance theory (1986). For there is nothing to prevent a speaker from uttering a sentence which constitutively expresses one thought in order to communicate something different. That is, instead of combining inferential conceptions of language with code-breaking ones, as Sperber and Wilson do, we might augment a cognitive conception of language with some inferential auxiliaries. Alternatively, and perhaps better, there need be nothing to require that the sentence which constitutively expresses someone's thought should give a *literal* expression to it – perhaps it is possible to think as well as speak metaphorically. Such matters may safely be left to one side, for present purposes.)

4.7 Language-based semantics 1: functional-role semantics

A good deal has already been said about functional-role semantics in sections 4.4 and 4.5 above. In particular, I have tried to respond to the claim that functional-role semantics must be strongly holistic, arguing that not every connection with everything that I actually believe need be an element in functional role. Recall, too, that one argument for functional-role semantics is provided by the functionalist characterisation of mental states in general, which arguably underpins our common-sense theory of the mind. And another argument demands to know what else, besides functional role, might individuate contents finely enough, in accordance with our common-sense mode of categorisation (in accordance, namely, with the *intuitive criterion of difference* – see section 2.6). These arguments seem to me to be powerful ones.

In addition, it can be said that the general moral of our discussion of Fodor's causal co-variance semantics in sections 3.7 and 3.8 above, is that some or other form of functional-role semantics *must* be correct. In section 3.7, I made the point that our actual practice in attributing meanings to people seems to involve looking at their surrounding beliefs and inferences. And in section 3.8 it emerged, in a variety of ways, that the identity of a concept may depend upon a number of background beliefs and purposes. So if Fodor can be allowed to have an argument for a general *type* of theory, in advance of actually presenting any instance of that type which can overcome every difficulty (such as we constructed on his behalf in section 4.1 above), then so too can I.

Now, another point to note is that functional-role theories (like causal co-variance theories) can be seen as attempting to *naturalise* content. That is, they try to spell out, in naturalistically acceptable terms, what it is for a thought or sentence to possess a given content. The content of a mental state, on such an approach, is to be individuated in terms of its causal connections with other mental states and with behaviour. And it is plain that, whatever else in the world might count as a *natural* property, the property of causation is one such. This is definitely a virtue of the functional-role account. For anyone who wishes to be a realist about propositional attitudes *should* wish to naturalise content. Whether we think that beliefs and desires should be incorporated into scientific psychology, or whether we believe, merely, that they should not be inconsistent with such a psychology, it had better be the case that propositional attitudes can be shown to be natural phenomena.

More specifically, the suggestion could be that so-called *narrow*, or in-the-head, content is to be individuated solely by causal connections amongst mental states themselves, whereas *broad*, or world-involving, content is to be individuated by this together with causal connections to the world of the sort appealed to by co-variance semanticists. (And, since we are now allowing ourselves a limited degree of holism in the account, we are free to adopt solutions to the *misrepresentation* and *all Ss* problems which differ from the problematic, and strictly atomistic, solutions proposed by Fodor.)

Many different versions of functional-role semantics have been developed (see, for example, Block, 1986, Harman, 1982, Loar, 1981, and Field, 1977), the details of which need not concern us. The important point, for our purposes, is that some of these satisfy the three main *desiderata* outlined in section 4.6 – namely, being applicable to natural-language sentences, treating public and private thinkings on a par, and being only weakly holistic. I shall say a word about each of these in turn.

First, functional-role theories can characterise the functional role of natural-language sentences in relation to perception, thought, one another, and the control of action, without taking as given a prior account of the content of thought. The assertion, 'It will rain shortly', is apt to be caused by perception of storm-clouds, and is apt to cause me to stay in or to carry an umbrella (depending upon what it is that I want). Admittedly, such an assertion will normally only be made if I believe that there is someone else present with whom I wish to communicate; and it only has its effects on action by interacting with other thoughts of mine. So there is no sense in which the functional role of natural-language utterances can be characterised independently of the functional role of private thought. But then there is also no reason why it should: my claim is certainly not that language is prior to thought! (That would be absurd. To be a language-user you have to be a thinker too.)

Second, functional-role theories can be made to apply equally to natural-language utterances or to private thoughts. In both cases content will be characterised in terms of the distinctive causal roles of the token states. By hypothesis, whether I think aloud or think privately to myself, my thoughts will consist in deployments of sentences which get their (narrow) contents in virtue of the distinctive roles that they play in my cognition. In fact inner and outer thinking can be treated on a par, as essentially similar kinds of activities.

Third, and most important, functional-role theories are only weakly holistic. For although there can be a great many other contents with which any given content might potentially interact, which might need to be mentioned in specifying the distinctive causal role of the latter, such contents will only be mentioned, in general, within the scope of conditionals. The normal form of an account of the functional role of *the belief that P*, for example, will be to say, 'It is the belief which, *if* one desires that Q, would lead one to intend that R, whereas *if* one desires that S, it will lead one to intend that T . . .', and so on. These same conditionals can be true of all the individual thinkers in a population, despite their many differences in actual beliefs and desires, and so leave the notion of *content* fit to serve in a content-based scientific psychology.

One apparent problem for functional-role semantics is this: while it is naturalistic, it leaves out the essential *normativity* of content. For it may surely be objected that our ordinary notion of meaning *is* normative. We think of concepts as *requiring* us to make certain judgements in particular circumstances, we think of beliefs as *constraining* us to have certain other beliefs, and so on. It may be said that no theory of content can be satisfactory which can find no place for normativity.

In reply, we may say that functional-role semantics can at least find a causal analogue of normativity, giving normativity a substantive *explanation* at the level of causal role. For we can appeal to the way in which some contents are apt to cause in the thinker a reflective insistence on a rule of application. For where it is part of the causal role of a sentence 'P' to give rise to the sentence 'Q', we do not *merely* have to say that 'P' disposes, or causes, me to judge 'Q'. We can also say that the sentence disposes me to regard myself as *bound* to make such a judgement, and to accept *correction* if I do not, or to impose *self-correction* if I notice that I have not, and so on. This seems to be good enough to get normativity – or, at least, a naturalised version of it – into the account.

A role for simulation

A more awkward problem for functional-role semantics might seem to be this: if content is individuated by functional role, then how would we know what to expect of someone who possesses any given belief or desire? For we surely do not have an articulate grasp of the immense network of conditionals which might characterise a particular functional role. According to functional-role semantics, the functional role of any given propositional content – for example, the proposition that there is life on Mars – will be characterised by a set of conditionals specifying how that content would interact with many other classes of content to determine further belief, intention, and action. Yet how plausible is it that we actually have *access* to these conditionals when we make a prediction of what someone will do, or offer an explanation of what they have done? Such an approach to semantics makes something which in fact comes naturally and easily to us, look like a hugely daunting task.

In reply, functional-role semantics can draw on a distinction between *how* we know, and *what* we have knowledge *of*. It can be said that we know of the role of a particular content, in any given case, not by inference from a network of conditionals, but by *simulation*. On this account, what I do when I wish to know what may be expected of someone who believes that P, is to put myself into suppositional mode, asking, 'What *else* would I think if I believed that P?'. What I do, is thus place that content into my own inferential system and see what results. Perhaps I also make suitable suppositional adjustments in my other beliefs to allow for any manifest differences from my subject. I then, as it were, stand back and let my inferential machinery run, and see what happens. The output of this process will give me my predicted further thoughts for the other. This story is quite consistent with the view that the identity-condition for the belief that P can only be characterised by a network of conditionals.

The position sketched here should be distinguished from so-called 'simulation theories' of our understanding of the mind in general, which are much more ambitious. Such theories claim that our overall understanding of what the mind is, and of the different roles that mental states play, are to be provided by simulation. (For further development of the points to be made in the following two paragraphs, see my 1996a.)

In the version defended by Robert Gordon (1986, 1992, and 1994), simulation is supposed to provide the basis for my knowledge of my own mental states, and their conceptualisation, as well as of the states of mind of others. But this is highly problematic, making it extremely difficult to see how it can be possible for us to have kind of direct, non-inferential, access to our own occurrent thoughts and feelings which we manifestly do have. In the version proposed by Alvin Goldman (1989, 1992, and 1993), in contrast, my knowledge of my own states of mind is supposed to be given by direct access to their qualitative feels. It is only my ability to *predict* and *explain* the actions and mental states of myself and other people that is to be provided by simulation, on this account. But the idea that we can arrive at something resembling common-sense psychology by generalising and inferring from a basis of our awareness of qualitative feelings is just as implausible as the view of phenomenalism (now almost universally rejected) that we can arrive at a conception of the physical world by generalising and inferring from our awareness of sense-data. Or so, at any rate, I maintain. (I shall return to this point in section 5.4 below.)

I am suggesting, on behalf of the functional-role theorist, something rather different, and more limited, namely, that simulation might be said to play a role in attributing specific mental states to others (in particular, in attributing individual propositional attitudes such as *the belief that P*), within a context provided by a set of folk-psychological beliefs about normal causal role. (This sort of view is similar to the limited form of content-simulationism defended by Jane Heal – see her 1986, 1995, and 1996.) On this account, having a concept of mind means having a folk-theoretical model of the functional structure of the mind – for example, of how belief in general is related to perception, and to desire and intention. It is only when it comes to working out the causal significance of entertaining a particular belief that we might need to engage in simulation, on the present proposal. For the set of conditionals specifying the causal role of any given belief may be too complex to be explicitly (or perhaps even implicitly) entertained.

4.8 Language-based semantics 2: canonical acceptance conditions

Christopher Peacocke has argued that the content of either thought or language may be characterised in terms of a kind of inferential, or conceptual, role (see his 1986 and 1992). The crucial idea on which the theory is built, is that of the *canonical acceptance conditions* for a thought or sentence. These are the conditions which anyone who understands the thought or sentence must regard as warranting, or as being warranted by, the acceptance of it. Acceptance conditions are thus *normative*, expressing the grounds or commitments of anyone who accepts a thought or sentence to be true.

There are two basic kinds of canonical acceptance condition. On the one hand there are canonical *commitments*, or implications, of a thought or sentence. These are the thoughts or sentences which the thinker/speaker must accept as true by virtue of accepting the thought or sentence in question. Then on the other hand there are the canonical *grounds*, or evidence, for a thought or sentence. These are the thoughts or sentences whose acceptance by the thinker/speaker must be regarded as providing a reason for accepting the thought or sentence in question. Some kinds of thought or sentence have canonical commitments, some have canonical grounds, and some have both.

For example, conjunctive thoughts and sentences are said to possess both sorts of canonical acceptance condition. Anyone who understands a sentence of the form, 'P & Q', must accept that the inference: $P, Q \rightarrow (P \& Q)$, provides a canonical ground for forming the belief *that P & Q*. That is, they must see their acceptance of P and of Q as a canonical ground for accepting that P & Q. Equally, they must accept that it is a canonical commitment of their belief *that P & Q*, that they should accept each of the following inferences: $(P \& Q) \rightarrow P$, and, $(P \& Q) \rightarrow Q$. These canonical commitments are to be realised, note, in the fact that the thinker/speaker finds the inferences in question *primitively compelling*. That is, the thinker/speaker must be disposed to accept those inferences, but *not* because of something else that they believe, or in virtue of some other form of inference which they accept.

We have, here, a kind of *use-theory* of meaning, in so far as content is characterised in terms of manifestable features of a thinker/speaker's use. People can show their endorsement of a given canonical acceptance condition by the pattern of things they are prepared to say and do. The circumstances in which someone is prepared to assert a sentence can warrant counterfactuals about the further circumstances in which they would, or would not, be prepared to assert it, and this in turn can show their acceptance of a given canonical ground. Similarly, the assertions that someone is prepared to make on the basis of a given sentence can warrant counterfactuals about the assertions that they would or would not be prepared to make in a variety of circumstances, and these in turn can show their acceptance of a given canonical commitment. But although he provides us with a sort of use-theory of meaning, Peacocke maintains that the theory is not a form of verificationism, and nor does it entail any other kind of anti-realist semantics. On the contrary, he maintains that canonical acceptance conditions, when properly understood, can be seen to yield a set of realistic truth-conditions.

Let me further illustrate Peacocke's ideas in relation to one particular class of contents, dealing with observational properties like *round* or *cubic*. The canonical commitment of someone who thinks, or asserts, '*That* (perceived) object is cubic', is supposed to be something like the following:

> For any position from which the object were perceived, now, in normal external conditions, and with perceptual mechanisms functioning normally, the object would be experienced from that position *as* cubic.

This account determines the correct intuitive truth-condition for the sentence, 'The object is cubic', because if something will normally appear cubic from any angle then, surely, it *is* cubic; and if something *is* cubic then, surely, it will normally appear cubic from any angle. Other observational contents can be handled similarly. There are, of course, many other classes of content, including contents that are universal or existential in form, which will need to be handled somewhat differently. See Peacocke 1986 and 1992 for details.

Notice that on the above account, the term 'cubic' reappears *within* the clause specifying the canonical commitments (and hence the content) of someone who accepts, 'The object is cubic.' Does this make the account circular? It might seem so. For it might seem that we have then explained the concept *cubic* in terms of that very concept itself. In fact, however, there need be no circularity here, provided that the phrase 'experienced *as* cubic' picks out a type of experience whose content need not be *conceptualised*. And surely there are such experiences. We can certainly discriminate shapes on the basis of experiences for which we lack any concept. In which case, the idea of experiencing something *as* cubic need not presuppose or involve the concept of *being cubic*. (I shall have more to say about unconceptualised experience in sections 5.7 and 5.8 below.)

The above account has many attractive features for me, besides being consistent with a general realism. In particular, it meets the three *desiderata* outlined in section 4.6. Thus, it is a form of theory which can, in the first place, be applied directly to natural-language without presupposing a prior account of thought. For the basic idea of an acceptance condition can apply to sentences as well as to thoughts. A canonical ground for a natural-language sentence can mean the condition for *asserting*, or accepting as true, that sentence. And a canonical commitment for a natural-language sentence can mean a sentence which a speaker should be prepared to assert who asserts the sentence in question.

Secondly, while the account can be applied directly to sentences of natural language, it does not prioritise language over thought, either. Rather, it can be applied equally to acceptance conditions for assertions *or* thoughts, as was clear from my initial explanations, in which I spoke, throughout, of thoughts *or* sentences, and of thinker/speakers. So the account seems tailor-made for the view that we think *in* natural language, whether publicly or privately. (In fact Peacocke himself is doubtful whether thought involves language – see his 1992. I mean only that his actual semantic theory leaves this open.)

Finally, while the theory is holistic in form, it is only weakly so. It is true that many other contents may figure in an account of the canonical acceptance conditions of a given content, which must be presupposed as already possessed by the thinker or speaker in question. Yet not *all* thoughts help to determine the content of any given thought, but only those with which it is canonically, or normatively, connected. Certainly the theory provides us with no grounds for denying that any two thinkers will ever be able to entertain the very same thought-content.

While Peacocke's account is a normative one it does not, in itself, attempt to naturalise content. But there is little reason to doubt that it can be made naturalistically acceptable (see Peacocke, 1992, ch. 5). Indeed, if functional-role theories can be extended to explain the existence of norms in causal terms, as I suggested in section 4.7 that they can, then by the same token one would expect that a normative system could be *realised in* some such causal network. One might, indeed, come to regard functional-role semantics and the theory of canonical acceptance conditions as complementary accounts, operating at different theoretical levels of explanation. Certainly Peacocke's idea that contents are to be characterised in terms of the inferences which thinkers find *primitively compelling* seems to line up neatly with the idea canvassed in section 4.4 above, that the content-individuating aspects of overall functional role should be restricted to *immediate* causal connections. But it would take us too far out of the way to develop this parallel here.

The analyticity objection

A canonical acceptance condition is a commitment of meaning – a conceptual commitment – and statements of such conditions will thus have the status of analytic truths. So one objection to Peacocke's theory will come from those who follow Quine (1951) in rejecting altogether the distinction between the analytic and the synthetic. In which case, if we were to mount a full defence of Peacocke's semantic programme as being equally, or more plausible than, that of Grice and Searle, we should be required to defend the notion of analyticity against the attacks of Quine and his followers. Here I have only the space to make one or two brief remarks.

Many have found Quine's arguments against the notion of analyticity unconvincing (see, for example, Grice and Strawson, 1956, and Wright, 1980, pp. 358–63 and 415–20). Certainly, the fact that the notions of *analyticity, synonymy,* and *meaning* cannot be non-circularly defined (except one in terms of the others) does not show that those notions are in any way illegitimate or ill-understood. For such circles of conceptual dependence are familiar from other areas of discourse, including those that are unremarkable by Quine's own lights, particularly in connection with scientific theories. It is a familiar fact that the concepts of a scientific theory can often only be explained in terms of other concepts internal to the same theory. Then the only way of coming to understand those concepts is by immersion in the theory as a whole. But no one thinks that, for this reason, scientific concepts are therefore illegitimate. Indeed, as Grice and Strawson emphasise, the extent of the intersubjective agreement that exists, concerning which statements are analytic and which are not, is a reliable sign that we have, here, a concept which is well understood.

Nor does the fact that we cannot distinguish between thoughts or statements that are analytic and those that are synthetic on the basis of behavioural evidence alone show that there is, really, no such distinction. For if we reject behaviourism, and anti-realism about the mind generally, then we can allow that thinkers may have introspective access to their own norms of thought, and hence to the thoughts which are, for them, analytic. Not *direct* introspective access, admittedly, such as we have to our own states of feeling or experience. But rather access through the standard philosophical thought-experiments in which we represent to ourselves some counterfactual state of affairs, and ask whether we should be *bound* – that is, whether we should regard ourselves as bound – to judge in a certain way in those circumstances. Why should this sort of evidence not be allowed as an appropriate basis on which to determine the distinction between analytic and synthetic thoughts?

Perhaps the most important point, however, is the one made by Paul Horwich (1992). This is that the notion of analyticity to which Quine was objecting had a particular epistemological role to play in the logical positivism of Carnap and his followers. On this view, our system of knowledge is to be erected on a foundation of experience by means of analytically valid inferences which are fixed and objective, and which we can know for sure (and a priori) to be genuinely valid. We can surely agree in rejecting *this* notion of analyticity while retaining a place for concepts and for analytical connections amongst concepts, as Horwich points out.

There is room for us to maintain, in fact, that the existence of concepts, and the existence of analytical connections between concepts, may be known about relatively unproblematically, by means of an inference to the best explanation of the cognitive and linguistic data. We certainly do not have to believe that we have any sort of sure and transparent access to our own concepts and the connections between them. Rather, we can view concepts and conceptual connections partly as theoretical posits, postulated to explain our own patterns of thought, and judgement, and intuition. We can then see the standard sorts of philosophical thought-experiments as ways of gathering further data to be explained.

In any case, Quine's attack on the notion of analyticity is by no means overwhelming. So one major line of criticism of the account of meaning in terms of canonical acceptance conditions can be rebuffed. I think we can, then, allow that Peacocke's semantic programme is just as plausible – or at any rate, just as well worth pursuing – as that of Grice and Searle. And so we have, as yet, no semantic argument favouring Mentalese over natural language as the language with which we think.

Here, then, we have another plausible semantic theory, or theory-programme, to set against the programme of causal co-variance semantics. Like functional-role semantics, this programme favours – or, at any rate, is consistent with – the view that thought essentially involves natural language, in just the sort of way that causal co-variance semantics favours Mentalese. Then since each of these programmes seems to be just as plausible as that of causal co-variance semantics, with just as rich promise of further exploration and development, we have been given no reason, as yet, for believing that the language of thought is Mentalese.

Summary

Fodor is mistaken – there is no argument from realism to atomism, and so no argument, as yet, for believing that the language of thinking is Mentalese. We can remain realists about propositional attitudes, holding that they will find a place in a content-based science of the mind, while holding that such attitudes are only *weakly* holistic – their individuation requires mention of other contentful states, but not in such a way as to entail that no two people are ever in the same such state. I have, moreover, sketched two forms of semantic theory, each of which can treat private and public thought on a par with one another, and each of which will be only weakly holistic. What we have, in the end, are non-atomistic approaches to semantics that are plausible and promising enough to undermine Fodor's remaining semantic arguments for the thesis that the language of all thought is Mentalese.

5   First steps towards a theory of consciousness

This chapter will set the scene for the remainder of the book, reviewing the *desiderata* for a theory of consciousness, and setting aside some false starts. After a brief retrospect, I shall begin by explaining and defending the distinction between conscious and non-conscious mental states, before criticising two theories of the nature of this distinction which I regard as being overly simple – the Cartesian conception of consciousness, and a minimalist theory due to Robert Kirk. In the final two sections I shall defend the view that consciousness is best understood in terms of higher-order thought. This idea will then be explored much more thoroughly in Chapters 6 and 7.

5.1   Retrospect: the need for a theory of consciousness

Over the last two chapters we have considered, and found wanting, Fodor's various semantic arguments for the view that the language of all thinking is Mentalese. (Further arguments were responded to directly in the latter part of Chapter 2.) The most important of these began as the argument from foreign believers, but rapidly merged into consideration of Gricean approaches to the semantics of natural language. If some version of these latter had proved acceptable, then Fodor's position would have been vindicated (at least when combined with the view that propositional attitudes are best understood as relations to sentences). But we saw that such accounts of natural-language semantics are by no means mandatory, and that they have considerable drawbacks – indeed, in the case of Grice, if not of Searle, that they are demonstrably incorrect.

We also considered the argument that began with realism about propositional attitudes, proceeded through rejection of semantic holism, to endorsement of semantic atomism, to the conclusion that the only plausible candidates as bearers of semantic content are lexical items of Mentalese. But this argument, too, fails, at the step from rejection of semantic holism to endorsement of semantic atomism. There are a variety of possible – indeed, plausible – positions which would be to some degree holistic without conflicting with realism about propositional attitudes, and yet without being atomistic.

Let me stress that I do not regard myself as having provided, in Chapter 3, any sort of knock-down argument against Fodor's atomistic causal co-variance semantics. All I claim to have shown is that his account faces difficulties. Nor do I take myself to have demonstrated conclusively, in Chapter 4, that a semantic theory in terms of either canonical acceptance conditions or functional role is definitely superior to Fodor's – only that such theories are very plausible, and just as much worth pursuing. But then I do not think that I *need* to show anything so strong. For we still have in place the argument from introspection developed in Chapter 2, for the conclusion that our conscious thoughts are entertained in natural language, and not Mentalese. So all I really need is a stand-off. All I need to show is that Fodor has no definitely convincing argument for the thesis that the language of all thinking is Mentalese, in order for the introspective thesis to win by default. And this I do take myself to have done, at least in respect of the semantic arguments.

There only remains Fodor's argument from the thoughts of animals and infants, outlined in section 2.7. Since I want to concede that animals and infants *do* have thoughts which are genuinely propositional, I cannot maintain that *all* such thoughts involve natural language. Roughly speaking, what I shall claim is that all and only *conscious* propositional thoughts involve natural language, arguing that there is a major functional difference between thoughts which are conscious and those which are not. I shall also claim that the thoughts of animals and pre-linguistic infants (as well, of course, as computations within sub-personal cognitive systems, such as vision) are all of the non-conscious variety. So here is one reason why I need to provide a theory of consciousness – to substantiate just these claims. For if substantiated, they would be sufficient to undermine Fodor's final argument. We should then be able to allow that many types of thought are expressed in Mentalese, while denying that conscious ones are.

The second reason why I need to consider a variety of theories of consciousness, is to see whether an acceptable theory might actually undermine the argument from introspection developed in the early part of Chapter 2, and appealed to again above. I claimed, there, that we are conscious of thinking in natural-language sentences (often combined with mental images). But it may be that the nature of the introspective process systematically misleads us in this respect – either misleading us about the very existence of inner speech or, more plausibly, misleading us about its functional role. At any rate, so Fodor must claim. We therefore need to consider whether any plausible theory of consciousness could substantiate some such fallibilist position. Only if we can find such a theory will the introspective thesis fail to win by default. Given that there are no overwhelming reasons for preferring semantic theories which would support Mentalese as against natural language as the language of thought (or vice versa), the claim that we entertain our conscious thoughts in natural language will stand as firmly established if, but only if, we have reason to believe that introspection will be reliable in this regard.

The final reason why I shall need to provide a theory of consciousness, brings us back to the main project of this book – namely, to argue that it is naturally necessary that language is involved in our conscious thinking. Or, more exactly, it is to argue that the architecture of human cognition is such that human conscious thinking involves natural language, out of natural necessity. This will require us to move beyond a theory of consciousness in general, to postulate the psychological mechanisms which might underlie its human instantiation, and the evolutionary forces which may have shaped them. This will be the subject-matter of the final chapter of this book.

5.2 Conscious versus non-conscious mental states

First, we need to present some data that a good theory of consciousness should explain. The main such datum, I believe, is that all types of mental state admit of both conscious and non-conscious varieties. In the present section I shall mount a defence of this general claim, beginning with the case of perceptual states.

Conscious versus non-conscious perception

Consider routine activities, such as driving, walking, or washing-up, which we can conduct with our conscious attention elsewhere. When driving home over a route I know well, for example, I will often pay no conscious heed to what I am doing on the road. Instead, I will be thinking hard about some problem at work, or fantasising about my summer holiday. In such cases it is common that I should then – somewhat unnervingly – 'come to', with a sudden realisation that I have not the slightest idea what I have been seeing or physically doing for some minutes past. Yet I surely must have been seeing, or I should have crashed the car. Indeed, my passenger sitting next to me may correctly report that I *saw* the vehicle double-parked at the side of the road, since I deftly turned the wheel to avoid it. Yet I was not conscious of seeing it, either at the time or later in memory. My perception of that vehicle was not a conscious one.

This example is at one end of a spectrum of familiar phenomena, all of which deserve to be classed as examples of non-conscious perception. For there are, in addition, many cases in which, while continuing to enjoy conscious experience, I also display sensitivity to features of my environment of which I am *not* consciously aware. For example, while walking along a country track, and having conscious perceptions of many aspects of my surroundings, I may also step over tree roots and make adjustments for various irregularities and obstacles in my path of which I have no conscious awareness. Since all the phenomena along this spectrum involve sensitivity to changing features of the environment, and since – most importantly – they fit neatly into the practical reasoning model of explanation, they deserve to be described as perceptual experiences that are non-conscious. For it may truly be said of me that I stepped over the root in my path because I *wanted* to avoid falling, *saw* that the root was there, and *believed* that by stepping higher I should avoid tripping. So this is a case of genuine *seeing* which is non-conscious.

Consider, also, the phenomenon of blindsight, which leaves us with little option but to speak in similar terms. It has been known for some time that patients who have had certain areas of the striate cortex damaged will apparently become blind in a portion of their visual field. They sincerely declare that they are aware of seeing nothing in that region. It was then discovered that some such patients nevertheless prove remarkably good at guessing the position of a light source, or the orientation of a line, on their 'blind' side. When their high rate of success is pointed out to them, these patients are genuinely surprised – they really thought they were guessing randomly. But the data show convincingly that they are capable of at least simple kinds of non-conscious perceptual discrimination – see Weiskrantz (1986) for details. Indeed, it has been shown that some patients are capable of reaching out and grasping objects on their blind sides with something like 80 or 90 per cent of normal accuracy, and of catching a ball thrown towards them from their blind side, again without conscious awareness (Tony Marcel, Cambridge MRC Unit, personal communication).

Think how sophisticated the perceptual processing must be in these cases. When such blindsight patients reach out for a cup placed at a certain distance on the desk beside them, they have to be able to estimate the size and orientation of the object, as well as its distance from them. But all this is done, remember, while the patients think they are guessing randomly. Yet here, as before, their actions are subject to the practical reasoning model of explanation. We can say that a patient reached out her arm as she did because she *wanted* to comply with the experimenter's request to pick up the object on the desk, *saw* that the object was an upright cylinder in such-and-such a position to her right, and so moved her arm accordingly.

In addition to absent-minded activity and blindsight, there are also such phenomena as sleep-walking, where subjects must plainly be perceiving, to some degree, but apparently without consciousness. And Ned Block (1995) describes cases of epileptics who continue their activities when undergoing a fit, but who do so without conscious awareness. So we have a number of strikingly convincing examples of non-conscious perception. (For yet further examples, experimentally established, see Marcel, 1983.) One thing that a good theory of consciousness needs to do, then, is to provide a satisfying explanation of the distinction between conscious and non-conscious perception, explaining why the various phenomena in question should fall on one or other side of the divide.

Conscious versus non-conscious propositional attitudes

It seems highly likely that the distinction between conscious and non-conscious mental processes can apply to all categories of mental state, including beliefs, desires, and intentions, as well as to perceptions. But to see this, we need to recall the distinction between beliefs and desires which are *activated* (engaged in current mental processes) and those which are *dormant* (stored in memory, but not engaged). This was explained briefly in section 2.3. These cases will need to be considered separately.

First, it seems highly likely that beliefs and desires can be activated without emerging in conscious thought processes. Consider, for example, a chess-player's beliefs about the rules of chess. While playing, those beliefs must be activated – organising and helping to explain the moves made, and the pattern of the player's reasoning. But they are not consciously rehearsed. Chess-players will not consciously think of the rules constraining their play, except when required to explain them to a beginner, or when there is some question about the legality of a move. Of course the beliefs in question will remain *accessible* to consciousness – a player can, at will, recall and rehearse the rules of the game. So considered as standing states (as dormant beliefs), the beliefs in question are still conscious ones. We have nevertheless shown that beliefs can be non-consciously activated. The same will hold for desires, such as the desire to avoid obstacles which guides my movements while I drive absent-mindedly. So thoughts as events, or mental episodes, certainly do not have to be conscious.

Essentially the same point can be established from a slightly different perspective, by considering the phenomenon of non-conscious problem-solving. Many creative thinkers and writers report that their best ideas appear to come to them 'out of the blue', without conscious reflection (see Ghiselin, 1952). Consider, also, some more mundane examples. I might go to bed unable to solve some problem I had been thinking about consciously during the day, and then wake up the next morning with a solution. Or while writing an article I might be unable to see quite how to construct an argument for the particular conclusion I want, and so might turn my conscious attention to other things. But when I come back to it after an interval, everything then seems to fall smoothly into place. In such cases I must surely have been thinking – deploying and activating the relevant beliefs and desires – but not consciously.

Second, it seems highly likely that standing state, dormant, beliefs and desires, too, can be non-conscious. Of course many psychological theories, including those of Sigmund Freud, have supposed that there can be propositional attitudes which are not available to consciousness at all, except on the basis of theoretical inference. But we do not have to consider anything so controversial in order to make the point. For consider the familiar, every-day, phenomenon of *self-discovery*. We often have occasion to discover what we believe or what we want on the basis of observations of our own behaviour. It is stock-in-trade amongst novelists, for example, that the heroine (say) is behaving in a way that we, the readers, can see patently displays love for the hero. But the heroine is unaware that she loves him. Indeed, she may be inclined stoutly to deny it, until some event or self-observation makes her realise that it is true. Here, prior to self-discovery, there was a mental state which was not only non-consciously activated, but which was not even accessible to consciousness *qua* standing state.

Our task, then, must be this: not only to explain the distinction between conscious and non-conscious perception, but also to explain how the distinction comes to apply to all other categories of mental state. (In this I agree with Baars, 1988. See especially ch. 2 of that work for details of a wide range of phenomena which emphasise still further the ubiquity of the contrast between conscious and non-conscious mental states.) In fact a good theory of consciousness needs to explain what it is for a mental state, as such, to be conscious rather than non-conscious.

The absent-minded driver reconsidered

Before embarking on the task of considering theories, however, let us return briefly to the case of the absent-minded driver. Some people might be tempted to claim that this can be explained, not as an instance of non-conscious perception, but rather as an example of instantaneous – or near-instantaneous – memory loss (see Dennett, 1991, p. 137, and Kirk, 1992, p. 35). Perhaps what happens is that I *do* have conscious visual perceptions throughout the episode, but that, because I am concentrating so intensely upon other things, no space is devoted to those perceptions in memory, even in the short term. Hence the phenomenon of 'coming to', without memory of prior experience even a moment later. This explanation is surely consistent with the data, but does not force us to recognise the distinction between conscious and non-conscious visual perception.

The first thing to say about this proposal is that it does *not* apply to the phenomenon of blindsight. (Nor, of course, does the proposal apply to the distinction between conscious and non-conscious activated or dormant beliefs and desires.) For in such cases subjects will sincerely deny that they are conscious of any experience on their blind sides at the very moment when they are, nevertheless, acting appropriately. So we do, in any case, have to recognise the category of non-conscious perception. Since this is so, and since there then are, plainly, structures in the brain which can transmit perceptual information so as to guide action without that information ever becoming conscious, it is reasonable to suppose that these same, or similar, structures may be implicated in the everyday examples of routine activity. Rather than appealing to two disparate explanations to account for the phenomena – non-conscious perception *and* instantaneous memory loss – the simplest proposal is that non-conscious perceptions are involved throughout.

The second point to be made about the above suggestion, is that the two conflicting explanations are empirically testable, and that so far the evidence – albeit anecdotal – counts against the theory of instantaneous memory loss. For notice that short-term memory is necessary for perception of gradual change. If something is moving too slowly for the movement to be perceived at an instant, then you can only notice that the position of the object has altered if you can remember where it was a moment ago. Moreover, even where some change in an object *can* be perceived at an instant, memory will often be necessary if you are to notice that the *rate* of change has altered. Yet these phenomena are, surely, amongst those to which it is possible to respond absent-mindedly, without conscious awareness or decision.

As an example where perception of a changing rate of change requires memory, suppose that I am idly doodling at the piano, to the time of a slowly ticking metronome. The metronome, being clockwork, is gradually slowing down, but I nevertheless – effortlessly and absent-mindedly – keep time with it. Yet it is only possible to recognise that the present period is slightly longer than the last, and to predict the extent to which the next will be longer still, if I can *remember* the last period, and compare it (non-consciously, of course) with the present one. So it seems best to say that I non-consciously perceive the changing rate at which the metronome is ticking.

It might be replied against these considerations that in the case of routine or absent-minded activity one sometimes *can* recall at least fragments of momentarily prior experience when one eventually 'comes to', or when one is prompted to attend to what one is doing. A nice example of this is that I may only notice the striking of the town clock when it reaches the third stroke, and yet be able to recall, then, the previous two strokes. Does this not count in favour of the suggestion that the perceptions are conscious throughout? I do not believe so. For non-conscious perceptions would, in any case, have to be held in a buffer memory store for at least long enough for them to be integrated into intentional action. And the effect of prompting may be to make the information remaining in this store *become* available to consciousness. It does not follow that it was *already* so available.

It is noteworthy, too, that these examples of recovered experience tend to be ones where the experiences which subjects are able to recall are the very ones which induced them to 'come to' in the first place – it was, after all, the striking of the clock (a change in my environment which was just salient enough to demand attention) which brought me out of my reverie and made me conscious of the third stroke. Since the first and second strokes were processed and (at least) non-consciously perceived; and since it was my perception of the first and second strokes which caused me to become conscious of the third, it is perhaps not surprising that one should be able to recall those first strokes *even though they were never conscious*. Perhaps what happens in such cases is that any salient perceptual information in the non-conscious memory store is reported to whatever system subserves consciousness, attracting conscious awareness of similar stimuli. In which case, it would not be entirely surprising if one should sometimes be able to report what one had never consciously perceived.

5.3   Cartesian consciousness

The distinction between conscious and non-conscious mental states is a real one. How, then, are we to characterise the difference? Notice that non-conscious perceptions have no *feel*, no *phenomenology*. It does not *feel like anything* to have a non-conscious perception of a vehicle double-parked at the side of the road, or for a blindsight patient to have a non-conscious perception of a cup on the desk. Some people might be tempted to use this as a reason for denying that the events in question are really perceptions at all. They may be inclined to insist that a perception, by definition, is a mental event with a characteristic phenomenological aspect to it.

This would be a mistake. For, as we saw earlier, these events fit neatly into the practical reasoning model of explanation, in just the same way that conscious perceptions do. Indeed, we have just the same sorts of reasons for insisting that there are non-conscious perceptions as we have for allowing that animals and infants have beliefs and desires – namely, that the behaviours in question may be successfully explained using the practical reasoning model. But nothing of much significance turns on the terminological issue. For suppose we allow that the events in question, because lacking any phenomenology, are not true perceptions, but only *quasi*-perceptions. Essentially the same issues will still arise, since we shall need a theory of the difference between the two types of event, and since we can still enquire after the necessary conditions for an organism to enjoy genuine (that is, conscious) perceptions.

Other people may be tempted to rely upon the notion of feel, or phenomenology, in drawing the very distinction between conscious and non-conscious states which is our target. They may say that conscious mental states are simply those which do have a characteristic phenomenology, whereas non-conscious mental states are those which do not. Such people are, in fact, endorsing an aspect of the Cartesian theory of the mind (named after the seventeenth-century French philosopher, René Descartes) but adapted, now, to provide an account of the *conscious* mind by those prepared to allow – as Descartes was not – that there are non-conscious mental states.

It is important to see that this suggestion can plausibly be separated from other aspects of Cartesianism, lest it be dismissed too swiftly. In fact, the Cartesian theory of consciousness can be divided into three sorts of claim, as follows:

> *Ontological* – conscious mental states are autonomously non-physical; they are not physical states, and they can vary independently of such states.

> *Epistemological* – introspection is an infallible source of knowledge of conscious mental states; the human mind is transparently available to itself.

> *Semantic* – conscious mental states are simple, non-relational, properties, which can only be recognised, not defined; our concepts of them are mere introspective recognitional capacities.

I shall shortly try to show that the semantic thesis can be held independently of the other two. But first, each of the three elements requires some brief comment. (For further discussion, see my 1986, chs. 1–6.)

Anyone who is a fully-fledged Cartesian about the mind is also a dualist, believing that the mind is distinct from the body and brain. Some are substance dualists, believing that minds are non-physical, non-spatial, substances. But all are at least property dualists, maintaining that mental properties, even if they are properties *of* a physical thing, can vary independently of the physical properties of that thing. This is the ontological thesis. Hardly anyone, today, endorses such a view. Most are physicalists, believing, as I do, that mental states and events are, in fact, states and events within the human brain. Almost everyone else believes at least that mental events supervene upon physical ones, so that there could be no difference in the mental properties of two people without there also being some underlying physical difference.

Hardly anyone, today, endorses the epistemological thesis, either. Few believe that introspection gives us infallible knowledge of our own conscious states of mind. Many would allow that introspection gives us a kind of privileged access to our own mental states, in such a way that our claims about our own states should be granted a special authority. But they would reject the idea that we literally cannot make mistakes, or be in error, in this domain.

It is important to see that neither of these first two Cartesian theses is (at least apparently) presupposed by the third. The third, semantic, strand in Cartesianism maintains that conscious mental states are *simple* properties of the subject, in no way constituted by their causal relations to one another or to the world. Correspondingly, our concepts of the mental are simple recognitional capacities, in such a way that mental states are distinguished from one another, and recognised, purely by feel, or phenomenology.

A comparison with our grasp of the concept *red* will make this position clear. This, too, has a substantial recognitional component. A large part of our grasp of the concept *red* consists in being able to recognise the colour red when confronted with it. But the concept arguably contains much else besides. In particular, to grasp a colour-concept you have to know about normal lighting conditions, and normal observers, so that you will withdraw or emend your judgements if either of these should turn out to be unusual. The Cartesian view of the semantics of such concepts as *pain*, *experience as of red*, *belief*, and *desire*, in contrast, denies that there is anything required for grasp of these concepts besides a recognitional capacity. They are *simple* recognitional capacities. It might seem obvious that this thesis could be held independently of the other two. (I shall, in fact, challenge this claim shortly.)

Now the upshot of these considerations is that someone might, apparently, endorse only the semantic thesis of the classical Cartesian conception of the (conscious) mind, thus avoiding all the implausibility which attaches to the first two theses. Their answer to the question of what distinguishes conscious from non-conscious mental states, then, can be simply this: that conscious states are simple properties of the agent which are available to immediate introspective recognition. Conscious states *are* the states that have a phenomenology, or feel. There is nothing more to being a conscious mental state than possessing a phenomenal feel.

5.4   Why Cartesianism won't do

There are a number of reasons why the Cartesian solution to the problem of consciousness should be unacceptable. The first is, that we can have concepts of mental states which we have never enjoyed; in which case it is hard to believe that our conception of such states can consist in a bare recognitional capacity. For example, I have concepts of beliefs and desires which I have never had – indeed, I have unlimitedly many such concepts, since I have the concepts *belief that P, belief that P and Q, belief that P and Q and R,* and so on. The combinatorial powers of my language put me in position to understand unlimitedly many that-clauses, each one of which can form a component in a distinct belief-concept. Yet it is hard to see how I could have bare recognitional capacities for unlimitedly many such states. For how can I have a bare capacity to recognise a state that I have never enjoyed, let alone have unlimitedly many such capacities?

The only way forward that I can see for Cartesianism, here, is to borrow the claim to be defended in this book, that conscious propositional episodes of judging, wondering whether, and so on, consist in deployments of imaged sentences; and to couple this with the claim that we can immediately recognise such images in virtue of the way they feel to us. This enables the account to harness the creative powers of language to explain our capacity to recognise in ourselves an unlimited number of propositional episodes, and makes it seem plausible that there will, indeed, be a feeling distinctive of judging that today is Tuesday – namely the distinctive feel of *imaging the sentence,* 'Today is Tuesday.' Thus I can, on this account, recognise in myself the new act of wondering whether there is a dragon on the roof (never before encountered), because this action consists in the formation of an image of the sentence, 'Is there a dragon on the roof?' (which is a state *a bit like hearing* that sentence), and because I can recognise this image in myself in virtue of being capable of recognising the distinctive feels of its component parts.

While such a view can avoid the standard objections to Cartesianism, there remain, I believe, a great many difficulties with it. Notice, to begin with, that I should have to do a good deal of inductive learning from my own case before I could be capable of explaining and predicting any behaviour, on this account. I should have to learn, in particular, that whenever I am aware of the distinctive feel of an intention, where the feel is similar to that of hearing an utterance of the form of words 'P', that I thereafter generally find myself performing actions describable as 'P'. And since these feelings do not wear their causal efficacy on their sleeves, I should also have to reason to the best explanation, having discovered reliable correlations between feelings of various types, to arrive at a theory of the causal sequences involved.

Notice, too, just how *opaque* an explanation of action would seem at this early stage. It would have the normal form: '*This* feel and *that* feel caused *that* feel. [This belief and that desire caused that intention.] And *that* latter feel caused me to do P. [That intention caused my action.]' The suggestion that one could get from here to anything recognisable as belief-desire psychology is about as plausible (that is, immensely *im*plausible) as the claim that we can get from descriptions of sequences of sense-data to full-blown descriptions of physical reality.

Philosophers and psychologists alike have long since given up believing that children learn to construct the world of three-dimensional physical objects, and then arrive at something resembling common-sense physics, by establishing inductive correlations amongst sense-data and reasoning to the best explanation thereof. The idea that children have to construct folk-psychology from their first-person acquaintance with their own feelings should seem equally indefensible. For in both domains, note, the classifications made by the folk have to reflect, and respect, a rich causal structure. Even if we agree that all conscious mental states have introspectively accessible feels, fit to be subjects of immediate recognition, it still remains the case that such feelings are useless for purposes of explanation until supplemented by much additional causal knowledge. And such knowledge cannot plausibly be arrived at from such a meagre initial basis. (This is, in effect, a variant on the argument for innateness again, first canvassed in section 1.7.)

A further reason why the Cartesian account of the distinction between conscious and non-conscious mental states should be thought inadequate, is that it appears to occupy an unstable position, in danger of collapsing back into one which is incapable of recognising the very distinction between conscious and non-conscious mental states which we are trying to explain. For if our whole grasp of a conscious-mental-state-concept consists in a bare recognitional capacity, as the semantic thesis above maintains, then we seem forced to say that it is actually *ambiguous* – a mere lexical accident – that we employ that same term in connection with non-conscious states as well. For these are not introspectively recognisable. If the very concept *conscious perception*, for example, consists in an introspective recognitional capacity for the distinctive sort of feel which such experiences have, then the very idea of a *non*-conscious perception (a perception, remember, without any phenomenology) should be unintelligible.

Thus it is, in fact, a presupposition of the thesis argued for in the earlier parts of this chapter – namely, that all mental states admit of both conscious and non-conscious varieties – that the semantic strand in Cartesianism should be rejected. In which case, we have no option but to seek some substantive account of the basis of the distinction between conscious and non-conscious mental states, which should explain why (some) conscious mental states have distinctive feels to them.

I have rejected the Cartesian semantic thesis that our conception of each different kind of mental state consists in a bare recognitional capacity – a capacity, namely, to recognise the distinctive feel of that kind. There remains, however, the weaker thesis, that the distinction between conscious and non-conscious mental states *in general* is simply the distinction between those mental states which have phenomenal feels and those which do not. Such a Cartesian might allow that there is a great deal more to say, of a non-phenomenal sort, about what distinguishes one type of conscious mental state from another, while insisting that it is phenomenal feel, and only phenomenal feel, which marks the conscious/non-conscious divide.

While this weaker view has at least some plausibility with respect to the distinction between conscious and non-conscious perception, it is much less plausible as an account of the distinction between conscious and non-conscious propositional attitudes. Many people believe that it need not *feel like anything* to entertain a conscious thought about my sister's birthday – in the way that it feels like something to experience pain, or the colour red – and that such a thought may not be a fit subject for introspective recognition. Such people maintain that they are subject to conscious thoughts which are purely propositional – they claim to be aware of thinking *that* Ann's birthday is the 4th of July, say, without being aware of any event figuring in consciousness with phenomenal properties, such as a mental image (see Hurlburt, 1990 and 1993).

The point here needs stating with some care. For the thesis to be defended in this book is that all conscious occurrent thinkings consist, in fact, in the manipulation of images and imaged sentences. And I shall consequently argue that those people who make claims about purely propositional thinking are subject to an illusion. So I am committed to the claim that all our occurrent conscious states do in fact have a distinctive phenomenology. But this will be a contingent fact about the structure of human cognition. I think it is clear that there is nothing in the *concept* of a conscious thought, as such, to require that it necessarily feels like anything to entertain that thought (in a way that it *does* seem to be part of the concept of a conscious perception, that it must feel like something to be the subject of such an experience). This is why many people who are doubtful whether robots could ever have conscious perceptions may be quite happy to allow that they could have conscious thoughts. This is because, as we shall see more fully in section 7.3, there is nothing in the idea of conscious thought to require that such thinking should have a feel to it; and such people are doubtful only of the possibility that a robot could have feelings. So the weakened Cartesian position has, at best, picked on what is just a contingent mark of consciousness in the case of human beings.

I have a good deal of sympathy with some aspects of the Cartesian semantic thesis, despite my criticisms. For I believe that we do, indeed, have recognitional concepts for at least some kinds of mental state, specifically those states which are conscious experiences. But, as will be seen in section 7.6, I think that these concepts are best explained and understood as embedded within a network of relational beliefs about the causal structure of the mind. Moreover, and more importantly, the Cartesian who claims to have no need of a theory of consciousness, beyond the minimal thesis that conscious states are those with distinctive feels, is making at least two further mistakes.

First, even if conscious states (or, more narrowly and more plausibly, conscious experiences) *were* simple properties of the agent, having no inner structure, we could still enquire after the conditions that are *naturally* necessary and sufficient for possessing such properties. We could ask what has to be true of thinkers in order for them to be capable of possessing such properties, and under what natural conditions the capacity for possessing such properties is guaranteed. The result would be, not a theory of consciousness as such, but a theory of the natural precursors, causes, and conditions of consciousness. But still the result might be strong enough to yield the conclusion that only a language-user can enjoy conscious experiences, for example. So even if we were to endorse the Cartesian semantic thesis in its entirety, we could still seek something closely resembling a natural theory of consciousness.

Second, Cartesians are mistaken in deducing, from the simplicity of our recognitional concepts of the mental, the simplicity of the properties recognised. This mistake then turns out to be internal to the semantic thesis itself, requiring us to pull apart simplicity of concept from simplicity of property. Even if we were to grant that our concepts of the mental (or, more narrowly and more plausibly, our concepts of experience) are bare recognitional ones, having no relational component, it would not follow that experiences themselves, in their inner nature, are similarly simple. It is a fallacy to infer simplicity of worldly property from simplicity of concept. How we *think of* conscious experiences is one thing, what conscious experiences really are may be quite another.

(The only thing which might warrant such a move would be the discredited Cartesian thesis of the transparency of the mental – the epistemological thesis discussed above. Only if mental properties are transparent to the mind will it follow from the fact that we conceptualise them as simple, that they really are simple. So it turns out that the semantic strand in Cartesianism does, after all, presuppose the epistemological one.)

Thus even if the conceptual component in the Cartesian semantic thesis were granted, we could still seek a substantive theory of the nature of conscious experience, which might be relational in form. Even if our *concepts* of conscious mental states were simple, there would be nothing to prevent us from providing a theory of the *property* of consciousness. The result would genuinely deserve the title 'theory of consciousness as such'. And we could, of course, still enquire after the conditions which may be naturally necessary and sufficient for an organism to enjoy conscious experiences. These are the questions that I shall shortly begin to approach, and will continue to discuss over the next two chapters.

5.5 What kind of theory do we want?

What sort of thing is a theory of consciousness? What should a theory of consciousness look like? It is implicit in the points that I have just made, that a theory of consciousness need not be either analytic or a priori, consisting only of an analysis or elucidation of our common-sense concept of consciousness. It is true that there may be some analytic elements in a theory of consciousness – indeed, I shall defend one such element in section 5.7 below. But that is not *all* which such a theory should provide. For a theory of consciousness is not, primarily, a theory of the *concept* of consciousness. It is, rather, a theory of the worldly *property* which mental states possess when they are conscious.

Our best theory of the nature of this property may contain much besides mere analysis of concepts. It can include a metaphysical theory about what that property really is, which confers on it a causal and relational structure, for example. It may also include hypotheses about the cognitive mechanisms that are either naturally necessary or sufficient for an organism to enjoy conscious mental states, together with plausible accounts of the functions performed by these mechanisms in our overall mental economy, and of the course of their evolution.

Moreover, even if our main concern were to elucidate the *concept* of consciousness, it is by no means clear that we should need to confine ourselves to analytic truths. For recall from Chapter 1 that I subscribe to a version of the current orthodoxy in the philosophy of mind, according to which our concepts of the mental are theoretical ones, getting their life and meaning from their position within a complex and highly sophisticated implicit theory of the mind, embodied in our common-sense, or 'folk', psychology. As I pointed out, this need not mean that our folk-psychology is intended as a scientific theory of the mind. Indeed, I suspect that it is not *intended as* anything, but is rather innately given, as I argued briefly in section 1.7. But what it does mean, is that folk-psychology consists of substantive claims and generalisations about the functional structure and distinctive causal processes operative within the mind. Elucidating a psychological concept will then involve articulating some relevant aspect of the theory. This may be as true of the concept of consciousness as of any other.

One final – but vital – clarification is necessary before I can begin to consider some substantive proposals concerning the nature of consciousness. The clarification is this: what I shall understand by the phrase, 'a theory of consciousness', is a theory of what it is for *mental states* to be conscious as opposed to non-conscious. The kind of theory I am in search of is a theory of conscious, as opposed to non-conscious, mental phenomena. That is, I am looking for a theory of what Dretske (1993) calls 'state-consciousness'.

I am not looking for an account of what it is for an organism as a whole to be conscious rather than unconscious (that is, for it to be awake rather than asleep or comatose). Nor am I looking for a theory of what it is for an organism to be conscious rather than unconscious *of events in its environment* or its own body (that is, a theory of what it is for it to be aware as opposed to being unaware of – to be perceiving rather than failing to perceive – those events). For I think that there can be conscious mental states during sleep (I believe that dreams fall into this category), when the organism as a whole is unconscious (that is, asleep). And absent-minded drivers and blindsight patients are surely conscious *of* objects in their environment (at least in the sense that they see them; they display awareness of them), without their perceptions being conscious ones.

So when I deny consciousness to animals – as I shall in section 7.8, concluding my endorsement of the reflexive thinking theory of consciousness in Chapter 7 – I should not be understood as denying that animals are ever conscious. Of course animals are often conscious in the sense of being awake as opposed to asleep. And of course animals are often conscious, also, *of* events in the world or in their own bodies. But it is another matter to claim that these states of awareness are themselves conscious ones. This is what I shall deny. Animals are aware of – they see, hear, taste, smell, and touch – objects in their environment, and have pains and other states of bodily awareness. What they lack is *conscious* awareness of these things. Animals have mental states (or so, at any rate, I shall allow). What they lack are *conscious* mental states.

It might be objected that it is highly implausible to maintain that consciousness should have appeared so suddenly in the course of evolution – it is, surely, much more plausible to believe that consciousness emerges *gradually* as one moves up the phylogenetic scale. But there is, in fact, a clear sense in which this can be allowed to be true, consistent with my account. For as the cognition of animals becomes increasingly sophisticated, and the concepts (and hence thoughts) available to them become increasingly diverse, so there is much more that animals can be conscious *of*. It is entirely consistent with this to claim, as I shall, that human beings are the only creatures capable of perceptions and thoughts which are conscious. And I shall hope to make it seem plausible that this capacity should, indeed, have been a late arrival on the evolutionary scene.

It would not be very far from the truth, in fact, to say that what I am looking for is a theory of *self*-consciousness – except that this seems to suggest a developed conception of *self*, as an enduring agent with a determinate past and an open-ended future. I think that there might be organisms capable of conscious mental states which have only the most tenuous and attenuated of conceptions of *themselves* as continuing subjects of thought and experience. So they would have conscious mental states without being self-conscious. But still, a conscious mental state is one *of which* the agent is aware (or so I shall argue later), and so to this extent, at least, it involves self-consciousness.

I have said that I am *not* concerned to provide a theory of organism-consciousness. This would be a theory of the difference between waking and sleeping. Nor am I concerned to say what it is for an organism to be conscious *of* events in its environment, or its own body. This would be a theory of perception in general. I *shall*, however, be concerned to provide an account of phenomenal consciousness. An important part of my task will be to explain what it is for a mental state to have a phenomenal feel to it, and to give an account of how this can occur. I have merely claimed that the concept of phenomenal consciousness is not the same as the concept of mental state consciousness, since one can consistently believe that there are conscious mental states which lack phenomenal feels. But I do allow that it is a constraint on the adequacy of a theory of mental state consciousness, of the sort that I seek, that it should be capable of explaining why (some) conscious mental states have phenomenal properties.

Many writers have claimed that the concept of consciousness is a hybrid, or mongrel, one, embracing a number of quite distinct notions (see, for example, Dretske, 1993, and Block, 1995). And I agree that we need to be careful to distinguish the central notion of *mental state consciousness*, which is my target, from a number related phenomena, including *organism consciousness* (is awake versus asleep), *transitive* or *access consciousness* (is perceiving that P, is aware that Q), *self-consciousness* (is aware of self as a continuing entity), and *phenomenal consciousness* (has mental states with phenomenal feels to them, states which it is *like something* to have). But I do not think that it can plausibly be maintained that the notion of mental state consciousness is itself a mongrel one.

There is, surely, little attractiveness in maintaining that what makes my perception of a red apple conscious, rather than non-conscious, is something very different from what makes my act of thinking about what to have for lunch to be conscious rather than non-conscious. This is why quite a lot of the discussion of consciousness which follows in this and the succeeding chapters, concerns conscious perceptual states as well as conscious occurrent thinkings. Although the thesis which I need to establish, for the purposes of this book, only directly concerns the latter, I believe that any story about conscious thinkings needs to be tested out for plausibility in connection with conscious perceivings as well.

5.6   Kirk: presence to central decision-making

Let us now return to the question: how are we to explain the non-conscious status of the perceptions involved in absent-minded activity, or in blindsight? Robert Kirk suggests that this may be done quite simply, by supposing that the distinctive feature of conscious perceptions is that they are made available to, or are 'present to', the organism's central decision-making processes (see his 1992 and 1994; see also my 1992b for some further criticisms, in addition to the one detailed below). So the reason why neither the experiences of the absent-minded driver, nor of the blind-sighted patient, count as conscious, is because it may plausibly be assumed that the central decision-making mechanism in human beings is the one responsible for issuing verbal reports. Then since the subjects in both of the above cases lack any disposition to report their experiences, those experiences cannot have been present to their central decision-making processes, and so will not, on Kirk's account, have been conscious.

Kirk can easily extend his account to explain how the conscious/non-conscious distinction applies in the case of other categories of mental state. A conscious standing-state propositional attitude, such as a dormant belief or desire, can be said to be one which is *apt to be activated as* a propositional episode within the organism's decision-making processes. My belief that my sister was born on the 4th of July, for example, can be said to be conscious in virtue of it being disposed to emerge in an occurrent conscious thought with the same content, such as, 'Ann was born on the 4th of July.' And then a conscious act of thinking or imagining, in turn, can be said simply *to be* an appropriate episode within central decision-making.

(In fact Kirk himself resists such an extension of his account of conscious experience, and opts for a version of higher-order thought theory to explain the conscious status of conscious thinkings and reasonings. Such a combination of views seems to me unmotivated, and of doubtful coherence. It is certainly true that if such a combination *were* possible, then the task of this book would be a good deal easier. For all that I shall really need, to underpin the arguments of Chapter 8, is that conscious *thinking* should be a matter of thoughts being made available to be thought about further. I do not *need* to make any parallel claim for conscious experience. But as I indicated at the end of the previous section, it is highly counter-intuitive to claim that what makes a conscious experience to be conscious is quite different from what makes a conscious thought to be conscious. I accept, in fact, that it is a legitimate constraint on accounts of mental state consciousness that they should be univocal across different categories of mental state.)

While Kirk's account is simple and elegant, and can accommodate a good deal of the data, it is hardly very compelling. The main problem is that it fails to make any connection between the conscious status of conscious perceptions and the various features generally attributed to such experiences, particularly that they have distinctive subjective feels to them – that they possess *phenomenology*. There is something that it feels like to be the subject of a conscious perception. On this much, at least, there is widespread agreement. Where there is very considerable disagreement, concerns the ontological and epistemological status of such phenomenal feelings. What follows is a brief digression.

Some have argued that the *what it is like*ness of an experience can find no place within a physicalist ontology (see Nagel, 1974 and 1986, and Jackson, 1982). Others have maintained (rightly, in my view) that phenomenal feels raise no real threat to physicalism, arguing that to know what an experience is like is merely to have a certain set of abilities with respect to it – to recognise, remember, and imagine it, for example (see Lewis, 1988, and my 1986, ch. 5). Some people have argued that phenomenal consciousness is irredeemably mysterious, and that we shall never be able to understand how a physical system like the human brain can support states which have phenomenal properties (see Nagel, 1974, and McGinn, 1991). Others (again rightly, in my view), while accepting that there is something that a conscious experience is like, have denied that phenomenal feels have any of the mysterious properties, such as ineffability, which philosophers commonly attribute to them, and that the phenomenology of experience must surely be explicable (see Dennett, 1988 and 1991, and Flanagan, 1992). There is also dispute about whether or not conscious experiences possess any non-representative properties – that is, whether there are any features of our experiences which do not represent anything beyond themselves (see Tye, 1994).

Many of these disputes need not concern us directly, though I shall return to them briefly in Chapter 7. For what is agreed on all hands is that there *is* something that experiences are like. But what I do have to insist on here, is that there is no good reason to give up on attempts to provide a substantive explanation of phenomenal consciousness. Indeed, I have already indicated that I take it to be a constraint on a theory of mental state consciousness that it should do just this. And Kirk accepts this too. He claims, indeed, that his theory *succeeds* in explaining the phenomenology of experience. Digression over.

Yet it is, in fact, left wholly unclear on Kirk's account why it should necessarily feel like *anything* to be an organism with perceptual information present to its central decision-making processes. I believe, indeed, that this is demonstrably *not* necessary. I propose to argue, in the next section, that the subjective feel of experience presupposes a capacity for higher-order awareness which is omitted from Kirk's account. And I shall be arguing, moreover, that such self-awareness is a conceptually necessary condition for an organism to be a subject of phenomenal feelings, or for there to be anything that its experiences are like. Before embarking on that argument, however, I shall spend the remainder of this section explaining how Kirk *thinks* he can accommodate the feel of experience, and showing that his argument fails.

According to Kirk, conscious experience occurs whenever there is perceptual information present to, or acting directly upon, a system's central decision-making processes. The information in question will be carried by events which have their effects upon the system in virtue of their intrinsic, non-relational, properties. Kirk describes this by saying that those events will have *characters for* the system. And for a perceptual event to have character for the perceiving system *is* for it to have feel, he thinks; for the feel *is* the intrinsic, non-relational, character of the perceptual event.

But this is a muddle. In particular, it conflates together the thought that a perceptual event should have its effects within the system in virtue of its non-relational properties (which is just a version of the idea that all causation is 'local'), with the thought that these properties will be *for* the system, constituting the subjective aspect of the event in question. For to say that a property has effects *within* a system is not at all to say that it is *for* the system, in the sense of being available to it or represented by it.

It is plain that there could be – indeed, that there are – cognitive systems in which information about the environment, in analogue form, acts on the decision-making mechanism, but where that information is presented entirely 'transparently'. That is to say, in such systems the decision-making mechanism can respond to the events in the system which carry information about the world, but *only* on the basis of the information that they carry. These events will have *characters for* the system, but only in the sense that their causal roles will be dependent upon their intrinsic properties. For the system itself will not represent those properties. Nor will it have any means of classifying or distinguishing between its perceptual states as such. Yet in order for there to be a subjective feel to experience, I shall argue, it is necessary that the system should contain, not only representations of the information carried by its perceptual states, but also representations of the states which carry that information.

Let me present an argument by example to make just this point. Suppose that blindsighted patients could become so familiar with their condition that they no longer have to guess what is where on their blind sides. Rather, with practice they can reach a point where, by a kind of regular 'self-cueing', they automatically form beliefs about the distribution of objects on their blind sides, and they automatically respond to the presence or absence of those objects in the course of their actions. (It is permissible that this example is only imaginary, since I want to claim that the necessity here, that the subjective aspect of experience requires a capacity for discrimination between experiences as such, is a *conceptual*, and not just a natural, one.)

In such a case we would want to say, I think, that the blind-side perceptual information was present to the subject's decision-making processes – being regularly and reliably made available to enter into the subjects' practical reasonings, as well as into the control of their actions. And the events carrying that information would have characters for the subject, in one of Kirk's senses, in that their effects on the system would depend upon their intrinsic properties. Yet it seems plain that these changes are consistent with the subjects in question remaining blindsighted – that is, it is consistent with their blind-side perceptions remaining non-conscious ones, lacking any qualitative feel.

Now, what could be missing here *except* a capacity for reflective awareness of their blind-side perceptions as such? If the subjects can be aware of what is where on their blind sides without their perceptions being *like* anything for them, then this must be because they have no access to the states on whose basis they acquire their knowledge – that is, because they have no awareness of their blind-side perceptions, as and when they occur. For such people, perceptual information about their blind sides would be made available to them *transparently*, in the sense characterised earlier. They would have perceptual information about the world available to their main decision making processes, but would have no access to, or awareness of, the states which carry that information. And for that reason their blind-side perceptual states would not be *like* anything for them, and would be non-conscious.

5.7   Higher-order discrimination and feel

In this section I shall present a general argument for the conclusion that the feel of experience presupposes a capacity for discrimination between experiences as such. That is to say, any system capable of conscious perception must be able to discriminate the events within it that carry perceptual information *as* events carrying such information, where those events are available to be recognised and distinguished from one another immediately, not known by inference or relational description. The argument arises out of reflection on the thesis which I have claimed to be uncontroversial – namely, that for there to be conscious experience there must be something that the experience is *like*.

What is clear is that an organism could not *know* what its experiences were like unless it had reflective awareness of the states within it that carry perceptual information. You cannot *know* what it is like to experience red, or to be in pain, unless you are capable of knowing *that* you are experiencing red, or are in pain. (Note that I am not saying that in order to know what an experience is like, in the intended sense, an organism has to be aware *that* the experience is like some other thing *X*. The state of awareness in question need not be explicitly relational or comparative. But self-awareness there must certainly be.)

Even if knowing what an experience is *like* is a special sort of practical capacity, rather than an item of propositional knowledge (as Lewis and others have argued – see his 1988), still it is a capacity which will involve the ability to *recognise*, to *imagine*, and to *remember* a given type of experience, all of which presuppose a capacity for reflective self-awareness. In order to be able to *recognise* a pain, you have to be capable of knowing *that* you are in pain, when you are; and similarly for imagination and memory. So the conclusion is established: in order to know what an experience is like, you have to be capable of higher-order awareness of the occurrence of that experience.

It might be wondered, however, whether the organism has to *know* what an experience is like in order for there to *be* something that it is like. Why must the qualitative feel of experience – its phenomenology – presuppose any kind of reflective self-awareness? To see why there must be such self-awareness (though not necessarily, as yet, self-awareness which is conceptualised, or available to thought), consider the following.

Talk of what an experience is *like*, or of its phenomenal feel, is an attempt to characterise those aspects of experience which are *subjective*. For there will, of course, be any number of respects in which one experience is like another, and any number of intrinsic properties of experience, which are not relevant in the context of this debate. There will, for example, be physical resemblances between, or physical properties of, the events in question. Since these aspects of experience are not available to their subjects (except, in our own case perhaps, by inference or relational description) they cannot be what is meant by the *what it is likeness* of experience. The subjective aspect of experience must therefore be an aspect which is *available to the subject*. In which case, if any organism has experiences that are *like* anything, in the intended sense, then those experiences must be *available to* the organism in question.

Now consider that to say that some object or property in the world – a chair, say, or its redness – is available to an organism, is just to say that the organism in question is capable of detecting resemblances and differences between that object and others within its world, or of distinguishing between the presence or absence of the appropriate property. To say that colour properties are available to chimps but not to dogs is to say that chimps, but not dogs, are capable of discriminating between colours. And to say that movement, but not stationary shape, is available to frogs is to say that frogs are capable of detecting various forms of motion, but cannot discriminate between the shapes of stationary objects.

In the same way, then, to say that the *what it is likeness* of an organism's experience is available to the organism is to say that the organism in question must be capable of detecting resemblances and differences amongst its experiences. But then this is just to say that an organism whose experiences are *like* anything, in the relevant sense, must be capable of representing, and of distinguishing between, its experiences as such. Which is to say: any organism whose experiences are *like* anything must be capable of a degree of self-awareness. Or again: any organism with phenomenal feels must be capable of discriminating (and so representing) its own experiences, in addition to discriminating the states of the world (or of its own body) which those experiences are experiences *of*.

Many will, no doubt, wish to resist this conclusion. They will concede that the phenomenal feel of an experience is its subjective aspect, but wish to deny that this aspect must be *discriminable by* the organism to which it belongs. Rather, they will say, a phenomenal feel is just a sort of 'inner glow' which perceptual states have when they are conscious. But it is hard to see how this can really help. For how could there be any sort of 'inner glow' which was genuinely subjective, if the organism in question were incapable of telling the difference between the presence or absence of that glow? If the organism cannot discriminate that glow from its absence, then how could it possibly be a *subjective* property of the experience? The answer, surely, is that it could not. And so the point is again established: the subjective feel of experience presupposes a capacity for discriminations of experience.

Note that the argument developed here will survive translation into Thomas Nagel's preferred mode of expression, in which one speaks, not of what an experience is like, but of what it is like *to be the subject of* that experience (see his 1974). For, since the likeness in question is subjective, it must still be one that is available *to the subject*, which means that the organism in question must be capable of representing, and of distinguishing between, its own states of experience. In general, the idea that there might be a feel to experience, or a feel to being the subject of that experience, which is *un*available to the subject is surely incoherent.

Note, also, that it has not yet been shown that the subjective aspect of experience requires an ability to *conceptualise*, or *think about*, one's own experiences. For it can plausibly be maintained that there is a level of representation and discrimination which is non-conceptual. If an organism can respond to objects in its environment without necessarily conceptualising them into types, then it is open for someone to claim that an organism might similarly be able to represent its own experiences without conceptualising them. (Consider pigeons which learn to peck at triangles, but not circles or squares, to obtain food – they can plainly *discriminate* triangles from squares, but do they really have a *concept* of a triangle? Arguably not – see my 1992a, ch. 7.) In the next section the argument will be given for claiming that a capacity for discrimination of one's own experiences presupposes, in turn, a capacity for thought about them.

It is important to stress that the *what it is likeness*, or subjective aspect, of experience is not the same thing as occupying a point of view. These two ideas are conflated by Nagel in his 1974 and 1986. I would concede that any organism which satisfies Kirk's model occupies a point of view on the world, characterised by its spatial position and orientation, and by the distinctive modes of perceptual information which are available to it. But it is quite another matter to claim that it is *like* anything to *occupy* that point of view. For this surely requires that the *likeness* in question should itself be available to the organism which occupies the point of view, and this is non-trivial. It requires the further capacity to effect discriminations between its experiences on the basis of their distinctive characters.

I conclude, then, that Kirk's conditions are by no means sufficient for experiences to have qualitative feel, or for there to be anything that those experiences are *like*. On the contrary, conscious perception requires that the subject be capable of discriminating between its experiences as such – conscious perceptions are states of the subject *of which the subject is aware*. Consciousness must thus involve a degree of higher-order awareness, on the part of the subject, of its own mental states. This is a suggestion which will be pursued in some detail in the next two chapters, when we consider various forms of higher-order thought theory.

5.8 The case for higher-order thought theory

In this section I shall argue that the availability of experiences to a faculty of higher-order thought, in which thinkings are themselves sometimes available to further thought, is a naturally necessary condition for those experiences to enjoy a subjective, qualitative, feel. I propose to argue, in fact, that the higher-order thought theory of consciousness articulates the sort of cognitive structure which must, of natural necessity, be in place if a creature is to be a subject of phenomenal feels. I shall approach this conclusion in a number of stages, as follows:

1. Conscious experiences are those which have subjective, qualitative, feels to them (phenomenal feels) – that is, there is something they are *like*.
2. It is a conceptually necessary condition for there to be a subjective feel to experience, that the subject should be capable of discriminating between its experiences, as such.
3. It is a naturally necessary condition for discriminations between experience, that the subject should be capable of thinking about (and so conceptualising) its own experiences.
4. It is a naturally necessary condition for thinking about its own experiences, that the subject should be capable of distinguishing between appearance and reality.
5. It is a naturally necessary condition for distinguishing between appearance and reality, that the subject should be capable of thinking about its own thoughts.

The first premise of this argument is intended as an uncontroversial characterisation of what conscious experiences *are*, which should be available to all the participants in this debate. Premise (2) has just now been defended, in the previous section, where I argued that in order for there to be a feel to experience the subject must be aware of, and be capable of discriminating, its states of experience as such. I shall now bring evolutionary considerations to bear in defending the remaining steps of the argument.

In defence of premise (3)

Does it follow from the fact that a creature can discriminate between its experiences, that it must also be capable of reflective, conceptualised, awareness of those experiences? From the fact that it can discriminate between its experiences, does it also follow that it can *think about* them? Granted, this does not *follow* – there is no entailment from the one to the other (remember the pigeon: there can surely be discriminations without conceptualisation). But how could the structures which enable discrimination between experiences have evolved, unless those discriminations were also typically capable of conceptualisation? For of what *use* would discriminations of experience be otherwise?

In the case of discriminations between *objects* (or between states of the organism's own body) there is plainly scope for them to occur independently of conceptualisation, as in the case of the pigeon. This is because those discriminations can be fed into the control of behaviour, even if that behaviour is only governed by thoughts which are highly indexicalised, involving a minimum of conceptualisation. But what, in the case of discriminations between experiences, would be the analogue of *behaviour with respect to an object*? I have no idea what it would be to *behave with respect to an experience* except by engaging in behaviour guided by *thoughts about* that experience. In which case the point is established: to be capable of discriminating between its experiences, as such, an organism would also have to be capable of thinking about, and hence conceptualising, its own states of experience. In which case it follows that only a creature which has a theory of mind (or, at least, a concept of experience, or of types of experience) is capable of enjoying conscious experiences, or of having phenomenal feels.

Since this argument has the form, 'I can't think what else', I can only try to substantiate it by considering some alternative suggestions, concerning the role of discriminations between experience, and by showing that they are unsuccessful. First, it might be said that such discriminations can aid learning, underpinning appropriate approach or avoidance-behaviour. Thus by discriminating between pains and tickles, for example, an organism can learn to avoid events and substances which are harmful to it, but without necessarily having to conceptualise, or *think about*, its pains.

But all that is really necessary for such learning is that the organism should be capable of distinguishing between painful *events*, or painful *stimuli*, and tickling ones. That is, provided that the organism contains information-bearing states differentially caused by tissue damage in the one case, and stroking or tickling in the other, then it can learn to avoid the one but not the other. There is no necessity that it should be capable of discriminating between these information-bearing states as such, and nothing that it would stand to gain by so doing, in the absence of higher-order thought.

Again, it might be said that unless the organism could discriminate the feel of pain, it could not find its own pains intrinsically irksome. But this is not true. All that is required, is that the information-bearing states caused by tissue damage should be wired into the organism's motivational system in the right sort of way. And indeed, if Dennett (1978b) is to be believed, the feel of pain is in fact separable from its normal motivational effects in human beings. He relates how certain types of morphine lead patients to report that their pains *feel* exactly the same, but that they no longer care – they no longer particularly want to be rid of those feelings. So it is not the feel of pain which underpins its motivational role, in any case.

The only other suggestion that I can think of, is that discriminations between experience might actually aid the process of perception itself, by providing the subject with a kind of top–down fine-tuning of perceptual processing. Perhaps by noticing features of my experience I can alter (and improve) its perceptual content. But in fact, all the examples which I know of for this sort of fine-tuning are ones where what I notice or discriminate are further features *of the world*, not of my experience of the world as such. Thus by watching the movements of the cellists in the orchestra I can come to hear the sound of the cellos for the first time. But here what does the work are discriminations of movement in the world, not discriminations between my states of experience of the world.

In defence of premise (4)

I have argued that any creature with phenomenal feels would have to be capable of thinking about its own states of experience. That is, I have got as far as premise (3). I now want to get from here to the conclusion in (5), that such a system would also have to be capable of thinking, reflexively, about its own thoughts. The intermediate step is premise (4), that in order for a cognitive system to have reflective self-awareness of the events within it that carry perceptual information, it must be capable of deploying a distinction between appearance and reality. That is, it must be able to distinguish between how things seem to the system and how they really are. For what, otherwise, would be the point of the system enjoying such self-awareness?

It is surely naturally necessary – because a condition for it to have evolved in the first place – that a cognitive system capable of responding to and thinking about its own perceptual information-bearing states as being intrinsically distinct from one another, in addition to being able to respond to the conditions in the world (or in the organism) which they represent, should also be capable of distinguishing between the way things seem to the system and the way they really are. It is very hard indeed to see what possible value in survival would accrue to a cognitive system which had self-awareness of its own states of experience, unless the system could make use of that awareness to begin to learn that in some circumstances certain of its information-bearing states are *not* reliable bearers of information. But to do that, it has to be able to make a distinction between appearance and reality. (Colin McGinn makes essentially this point in his 1989, pp. 90–4.)

It might be objected that a cognitive system's self-awareness of its own experiences could have value for survival through self-reporting. For it might be useful to the individual, in a variety of ways, that others should be able to learn of the system's experiences. This may be so, but it does not affect the argument given above. For the most basic way in which knowledge of another's experiences may prove useful, lies in its contribution to practices of justifying, and seeking justification for, beliefs and actions. The usefulness of my knowing how things *seem* to you lies in its role in your attempts to justify claims about how things *are*, and in helping to reconcile the conflicting claims each of us may make about how things are. But this presupposes, of course, what we are already masters of the distinction between appearance and reality, just as was claimed above.

Someone may also object that there can be no natural necessity attaching to my account, since evolution operates by random gene mutation. But this is not to the point. My claim is not that there could never have been an *individual* creature having self-awareness of its own perceptual states without the capacity to distinguish between appearance and reality. It is rather, that such an individual would have had no advantages over other members of its species, in which case its capacity for self-awareness could not have become general to the species as a whole.

More challengingly, someone may object that a property can become general to a species without possessing survival-value of its own, by virtue of being an epiphenomenon of some genetically determined property which *does* have survival-value. So all members of a species might come to have self-awareness of the appropriate sort while lacking an appearance/reality distinction, yet without such self-awareness having any distinct survival-value. The difficulty with this suggestion, however, is to give it flesh. For there are simply no plausible candidates in the offing, for the property of which self-awareness might be an epiphenomenon. It is more reasonable to believe that a capacity for self-awareness of one's own experiences can only appear as part of a basic package of capacities which carries value in survival – especially since this capacity is, plainly, of such complexity that it would had to have evolved incrementally, rather than through a single mutation. Incremental evolution of any property surely requires selection for the presence of that property *as such*.

The move to the conclusion

My final claim is that in order to deploy a distinction between appearance and reality, in turn, it is naturally necessary – again because it is a condition for such cognitive structures to have evolved – that a system should be capable of thinking about its own thinkings on a regular basis. For of what use would be the distinction between appearance and reality, unless the system could also employ the concepts of truth and falsity? What would be the point of being able to distinguish between the way things appear and the way they are, unless the subject were able to put this distinction to work in practical reasoning, judging, for example, that beliefs formed under certain perceptual conditions are less likely to be *true* than those formed in other circumstances?

But the concepts of truth and falsity, in turn, are only possible for a system which is capable of recognising certain objects as *bearers* of truth and falsity. That is to say, only a system which can think, of a belief or occurrent thought, that it is true or false, can properly be said to possess the concepts of truth and falsity. But in order to think such things, the system's beliefs and occurrent thoughts must sometimes be available to thought – which is just the reflexive structure which I claim to be a necessary condition (at least) of conscious experience.

This final claim – that a grasp of the appearance/reality distinction presupposes a capacity to think about thoughts – receives some additional support from the developmental literature. For the evidence is that children do not acquire the ability to distinguish between appearance and reality until they also understand the notion of belief (see, for example, Wellman, 1990, ch. 9). And where an understanding of belief is lacking, as it is in the case of many autistic children, then so, too, is the ability to draw the appearance/reality distinction (see Baron-Cohen, 1989). So at the stage when young children still fail the false-belief tasks, they will also fail deceptive-appearance tasks – for example, if shown a sponge which looks like a rock, they will say it is a rock; on being allowed to handle it and discover that it is really a sponge, then they will say, both that it *is* a sponge, *and* (incorrectly) that it *looks like* a sponge; and they will also predict (incorrectly) that another person will think that it looks like a sponge.

However, it is also possible to raise an *objection* from the developmental literature, as well. I have been arguing that a capacity to effect discriminations amongst one's own perceptual states presupposes a capacity to think about one's own thoughts. But it may be objected that young children seem to possess a simple desire-perception psychology *before* they acquire the notion of belief, or of propositional thought (see Wellman, 1990). At this stage they understand that people often have goals which they will try to reach, and that the manner in which they will act will often depend upon what they can or cannot *see*; but they have no understanding of *belief* or of the possibility of false belief. This may well recapitulate an intermediate stage in the course of human theory-of-mind evolution. But anyway it suggests that there could possibly be organisms which lack any capacity to think about their own thoughts, but which are nevertheless capable of thinking about their own and others' *perceptions*. In which case, it would seem, their perceptual states may well have *feel*, contrary to what I have been arguing in this section.

In reply, I say that it is one thing to have some sort of general notion of perception, and a capacity to apply that notion to oneself and others in a theoretical (interpretative) way, and quite another thing to have the capacity to *recognise* one's own subjective perceptual states as and when they occur. Only the latter would be sufficient for one's perceptual states to have *feel*, if the argument of this section is sound. But it is only the former which is displayed by three-year-old, pre-appearance-reality, children. Indeed, the evidence is that young children have no understanding of perception as a *subjective* state of the perceiver. Rather, they think of perception purely relationally, in terms of the perceiver being attached to, or being in contact with, an object or state of affairs (see Wellman, 1990, and Perner, 1991). If I am right, then a capacity to apply perceptual concepts to oneself in a recognitional way (within any particular species, at least,) would have to wait on the evolution of a capacity to entertain thoughts about thoughts. (For a possible qualification to this claim in relation to young human children, see section 7.8 below.)

My hypothesis is thus that it was the evolution of a system capable of thinking about its own thoughts on a regular basis which provided a necessary condition for the remainder. What a capacity to think about your own thinkings gets you, is an indefinitely improvable problem solving capability. As we shall see in Chapter 7, this plainly has survival-value in its own right. Such a capacity must involve, at a minimum, the distinction between true and false thought. With these structures in place (and only if they are in place), then there would be further survival-value for the organism if it were to evolve a capacity for reflective awareness of its own perceptual states, becoming capable, in particular, of distinguishing between appearance and reality.

I have been concerned, in these last two sections, to motivate some form of higher-order thought theory of consciousness, by arguing that a capacity for higher-order thought is a *necessary* condition for having perceptual states with phenomenal feels. A stronger argument in favour of higher-order thought theories, however, is that they can *explain* phenomenal consciousness, as I shall try to show in connection with my own reflexive thinking theory in section 7.6 below. It is rarely the case that one can succeed in showing that the data (in this case, the existence of phenomenal feelings) *could not exist* unless some theory (in this case, higher-order thought theory) were also true – although this is what I have tried to do here. The more usual ground for believing a theory is that it *explains* – that is to say, it provides a sufficient rather than a necessary condition for – the data. But I believe that we do have this ground, too, for accepting some form of higher-order thought theory, as we shall see in due course.

Summary

In this chapter I have argued that all types of mental state admit of both conscious and non-conscious varieties, and that a theory of consciousness should aim to provide an adequate explanation of this distinction. I have also argued that the Cartesian theory – that conscious states are simple properties of the agent with a distinctive feel, or phenomenology – is inadequate. And I have argued that a theory of consciousness must postulate a capacity for higher-order discriminations of perceptual states, if it is to stand any chance of accommodating the subjective aspect of conscious experience. Not only this, but I have argued that capacities for such discrimination would not have evolved, except in organisms capable of higher-order thought.

6 Second (-order) steps towards a theory of consciousness

In the present chapter I shall outline, and criticise in turn, a number of higher-order thought theories of consciousness, due to David Armstrong, David Rosenthal, Daniel Dennett, and others. Elements of these theories will then be incorporated into my own reflexive thinking theory, to be presented in the next chapter. Remember that one important strategic aim of this discussion is to see whether there is any plausible theory of consciousness which might undermine the introspective argument of Chapter 2. This point will be taken up in the final section of the chapter.

6.1 Theory 1: actual and conscious

Armstrong and others have argued that conscious states are those which cause, or are apt to cause, a belief in their own existence – claiming that conscious experiences are those which cause (or are apt to cause) a belief that there is such an experience taking place; that conscious beliefs are those which cause (or are apt to cause) a belief that one has that belief; and so on (see Armstrong, 1968 and 1984, Mellor, 1977 and 1980, and Rosenthal, 1986, 1991 and 1993). Such accounts are *higher-order* because the conscious status of any given conscious state is explained in terms of mental states (specifically beliefs or thoughts) which are *about* it, which contain a reference to it embedded in their content. I have just now argued, in section 5.8, that some version of higher-order thought theory must be correct; our immediate task is to consider a number of more precisely specified variants on the approach.

Note that such accounts may be able to accommodate much of the data, at least. For it might plausibly be claimed that the distinctive feature of the experiences of the absent-minded driver, or of someone who is blindsighted, is that those experiences do *not* cause a belief in their own existence. Yet these accounts satisfy, in addition, the condition omitted by Kirk. For what makes an experience to be conscious, on such an account, is the way in which it causes the subject to believe that there is such an experience occurring. In which case conscious experiences will certainly

164

be *available to* the subject whose experiences they are, and may therefore have a subjective aspect. I shall return to this point, and develop it much more fully, in section 7.6.

Higher-order theories can vary along two different dimensions, in general. First, the higher-order theorist must decide whether or not to say that the higher-order beliefs in question are *actual* ones (that is, actually represented in the brain; and not as standing states, but in the form of activated, occurrent, events), or whether they are merely dispositional (that is, are merely *apt to be caused* or activated by the conscious mental state, if circumstances demand). And second, the theorist must decide whether or not to say that the higher-order beliefs are themselves conscious ones (that is, whether or not they themselves must cause, or be apt to cause, higher-order beliefs in their own existence), or whether they can be allowed to be non-conscious.

Combining these possibilities yields four different types of higher-order thought theory of consciousness. I shall consider these in turn, devoting a section to each. Theory 1 combines *actual* with *conscious* higher-order belief, as follows.

> Any mental state M, of mine, is conscious = M is actually causing an activated conscious belief that I have M.

This is easily the least plausible of the four suggestions, for a number of reasons. We might be tempted to wonder, in the first place, whether the account may actually be viciously circular. For in the course of saying what it is for a mental state to be conscious, the term 'conscious' is itself used on the right-hand side of the definition – thus seeming to presuppose precisely what we were trying to explain. But this need not be a problem, in fact. For the account can, rather, be *recursive*, the conscious status of a mental state at any given level being explained in terms of that of the next level up. Set out rather more strictly, then, Theory 1 would work as follows.

> Any mental state M, of mine, is conscious = M (level 1) causes the belief (level 2) that I have M, which in turn causes the belief (level 3) that I believe that I have M, and so on; *and every state in this series, of level n, causes a higher-order belief of level n + 1.*

So the level-2 belief in virtue of which M is conscious is itself conscious, because it, too, satisfies the definition – for that belief, too, causes a series of higher-order beliefs about itself. And note that in this fuller version of the account, the term 'conscious' does *not* figure on the right hand side; so there is no actual vicious circularity. Although Theory 1 can be stated most briefly and conveniently by using the term 'conscious' again on the right-hand side of the definition, as we did at first, this is by no means really necessary.

Although there may be no vicious circularity in the account, it is surely obvious that we do have an infinite regress. For if a belief *that P* is only conscious if it is actually causing me to believe, consciously, *that I believe that P*, then this in turn must be causing me to believe, consciously, *that I believe that I believe that P*, and so on. Note that each of these beliefs is distinct in content. So any given conscious belief would require me to have, at the same time, infinitely many other distinct beliefs. Even if this is not strictly incoherent, there plainly could not be room in my head for them all. Since this first theory requires *actual* higher-order beliefs to constitute the conscious status of a first-order belief, each level in this infinite series must be supposed to be explicitly encoded in the brain (and separately so, since each of the beliefs in question is distinct) – which is plainly impossible.

A second objection to the account is slightly more subtle, but equally devastating. It is that the theory gets the phenomenology of conscious experience and thought quite wrong. For when I entertain a conscious thought – for example, the thought that the Earth is getting warmer – I do not normally, at the same time, entertain the conscious thought that I am having such a thought. The sum total of what I may be consciously thinking about, is the Earth and its likely future temperature, not myself and my own states of belief. Similarly when I have a conscious perception – for example, an experience of an empty glass on my desk – I do not normally, at the same time, have a conscious thought *about* that perception. All of my actual conscious thoughts (if any) may relate to the object perceived, not to myself and my own states of experience. Any theory, such as this one, which requires me to be actually thinking, consciously, about my own states of mind whenever I have a conscious mental state must plainly be wrong.

6.2   Theory 2: actual and non-conscious

The second theory to be considered combines *actual* with *non-conscious* higher-order belief, as follows:

Any mental state M, of mine, is conscious = M is actually causing an activated belief (possibly non-conscious) that I have M.

This account avoids all the difficulties inherent in the previous one. Since there is no requirement that the higher-order belief in question be conscious, there need be no regress of higher-order beliefs attending each conscious state. And for the same reason, there can be no objection to the account arising out of phenomenology. For the thought about my own belief or experience which constitutes it as conscious, on this account, need not itself be a conscious one. So it is no objection to the account that

I am rarely aware of having such self-directed thoughts. There is, nevertheless, a major problem with this version of the theory, relating to the huge number of beliefs which would have to be caused by any given experience.

Recall just how rich and detailed an experience can be. There can be an immense amount of which we can be consciously aware at any one time. For example, imagine looking down on a city from a window high up in a tower block (as I am while I write this, in fact). In this case I am consciously perceiving the complex distribution of trees, roads, and buildings; the colours on the ground and in the sky above; the moving cars and pedestrians; and so on. And I am conscious of all of this simultaneously. According to Theory 2 above, I would have to have a distinct activated higher-order belief for each distinct aspect of my experience – either that, or just a few such beliefs with immensely complex contents. Either way, the objection is the same. It is, surely, hugely implausible to suppose that all of this higher-order activity should be taking place (albeit non-consciously) every time someone is the subject of a complex conscious experience. For what would be the point? And think of the amount of cognitive space that these beliefs would take up!

Let me stress that this is *not* an objection from phenomenology. It is an objection from *cognitive* overload, not an objection from *phenomenological* overload. The point is not that we are never *aware* of enough higher-order thoughts to explain the conscious status of each facet of our conscious experience. For I am granting that the higher-order thoughts in question are generally non-conscious ones. The point relates rather to the implausibility of supposing that so much of our cognition should be occupied with formulating and processing the vast array of higher-order thoughts necessary to render our experience conscious at each moment of our waking lives. (So Rosenthal, in responding only to the phenomenological overload problem in his 1993, pp. 209–10, has failed to address the real issue.)

There is a question as to whether Theory 2 is even coherent, in fact, if perceptual information is *analogue* (that is, 'filled in' and continuous). For belief-contents are *digital*, or chunked. How, then, could all of the indefinitely complex information contained in perception be captured in a finite set of beliefs? This problem can be avoided, however, provided that perceptual information is actually chunked as well (as it plainly must be), but below the level of personal discrimination. For then the higher-order beliefs which render experience conscious can make reference to this digitalised information.

But even if the problem of analogue perceptual content can be overcome, it remains empirically very implausible that alongside our rich and detailed perceptual contents there should, whenever those contents are conscious, be an equally rich and detailed collection of higher-order beliefs. For what sort of cognitive system could possibly make use of this vast array of beliefs? And why would such a cognitive architecture have evolved? It is hard to discern any explanation here which could support the claim that we regularly have an extensive set of non-conscious higher-order beliefs. As we saw briefly in section 5.8, and will see further in the next chapter, higher-order beliefs do have an evolutionary purpose, helping us to draw the distinction between illusion and reality, and helping us to reflect upon and improve our own patterns of reasoning. But so far as I can see, these are not activities that people engage in non-consciously.

It might be replied against these objections that the hypothesis of a rich network of higher-order beliefs accompanying every conscious experience can be avoided, if we suppose, rather, that there is always a single higher-order belief whose content is *imagistic*, mirroring the content of the experience which it concerns. But there is no real gain in this proposal. For the image in question would have to be at least as complex as the experience which it is about, in such a way that every conscious aspect of the experience is mirrored in the content of the image. For remember, the higher-order (in this case, imagistic) thought is to *explain* the difference between my conscious perception of the motion of a car, say, and my non-conscious perception of the sound of its motor. Indeed, for this reason the proposal is of doubtful coherence as well. For any image must, of its very nature, be schematic in relation to the richness of experience. It seems, in fact, that there *could not be* any image which is just as rich and detailed as the content of a conscious experience. In which case, it cannot be the presence of any image which accounts for the conscious status of the latter.

An alternative proposal might be, that there need only be a single higher-order belief accompanying any given conscious experience, provided that the belief in question is an *indexical* one, always taking the form '*That* experience is now occurring' (see Rosenthal, 1993, p. 210). According to this proposal we can, as it were, re-use the content of the conscious experience within the content of the higher-order thought which makes it conscious, without the need for any separate representation. The trouble with this proposal, however, is this: taken in one way, it is viciously circular; taken in another, and it would allow blindsighted experience to be conscious.

The first horn of this dilemma arises because indexical thoughts standardly presuppose *awareness of their objects*. In order for me to be capable of thinking, of an item in the world, '*That* object is F', the object in question must normally be perceptually presented to me. That is to say, I must be aware of it. Similarly, then, if I am to be capable of entertaining an indexical thought about my own experience, I must, on this model, already be aware of the latter. But to be *aware* of an experience just is to have a *conscious* experience, according to the higher-order thought account. In which case indexical thought about experience cannot be used to analyse the idea of conscious experience without circularity.

Another way to develop essentially this point, is to ask exactly *how* the indexical element manages to carve out, from the total set of my current perceptual contents, just those which are to be made conscious, distinguishing them from those which are to be left non-conscious. How can the indexical, by itself, manage to pick out just the former sub-set, unless it relies on my *awareness* of the members of that sub-set? For example, when I use an indexical to pick out a sub-set of people in a crowd – e.g. thinking, '*Those* men look aggressive' – I must either be directing my attention at them in particular, or be aware of some property which distinguishes them from the rest. So, too, then, in the case of indexical thought about a sub-set of my perceptual states: this must presuppose, either that I am directing my attention at the members of that sub-set, or that I am aware of something which distinguishes them. And either way, consciousness is presupposed.

The other horn of the dilemma arises if we model the account on those indexical thoughts which can be grounded in descriptive knowledge of an object. For example, on hearing that someone new has moved into the house next door, I might think, 'I hope *that* person likes children.' But now this sort of indexical thought is available to anyone who is blind-sighted, who has inferential knowledge that they are undergoing a particular (non-conscious) experience – they, too, can think, '*That* experience is occurring.' But plainly this is not sufficient to render their experience conscious.

So far as I can see, the only way out of these difficulties available to a defender of Theory 2, is to claim that the supposed richness of conscious perceptual experience is an illusion. Just such a position is apparently defended by Dennett, 1991, who points to the fact that the contents of the periphery of the visual field are in fact highly indeterminate, despite subjects' intuitions to the contrary, and to the fact that even gross changes in the perceptual environment will remain undetected if the changes are timed to coincide with saccadic eye movements. He thinks this shows that the content of conscious experience is in fact highly fragmentary, but that we do not notice because wherever we direct our conscious attention, there we obtain a (new) conscious experience.

In fact we can grant Dennett the point that the visual field, especially in the periphery, is a good deal less contentful than we are intuitively inclined to think. For the argument from cognitive overload can be constructed with respect to focused, or foveal, vision alone. If I focus on a particular object – say the palm of my own hand – then there is an immense amount of detail which can be present in the centre of my visual field. I am aware, simultaneously, of a network of fine lines and wrinkles, and of subtle texture and colour gradients. Even to begin to describe all this detail with any accuracy would occupy many thousands of words. So, even granting the poverty of peripheral vision, we can still claim that there is an immensely complex manifold of conscious perception, whose status as conscious is not plausibly accounted for by the presence of an equal complexity of higher-order belief.

Notice, moreover, that our commitment to the existence of an integrated, conscious, perceptual manifold need not mean that we have to claim that the contents of the manifold are veridical, or are continually being updated in a way which always reflects changes in the perceived environment. It may be that the manifold is only updated and changed when our perceptual systems *detect* changes in the environment. Changes which are timed to occur during saccadic eye movements, in particular, will be unnoticed and ignored. Hence the fact that subjects wearing eyetrackers (a computer device trained on the eyes which can initiate change on a TV screen during saccades) do not notice major changes in the perceived scene does *not* show that there is no manifold of experience. All it shows is that in such circumstances the manifold has not been updated. Roughly speaking, you will continue to see (have conscious experiences of) what you remember to have been there, unless something indicates a change to you. There is, therefore, no good reason here for refusing to go along with the common-sense view of the richness of conscious perceptual experience.

I conclude that the objection from 'cognitive overload' may be allowed to stand. Theory 2 requires an implausible amount of cognitive space to be taken up with higher-order beliefs, in order for any given experience to be conscious. Moreover, Theory 2 is, in fact, subject to just the same range of counter-examples which will cause problems for Theory 3.

6.3   Theory 3: potential and non-conscious

The third theory combines *potential* with *non-conscious* higher-order belief, as follows:

> Any mental state M, of mine, is conscious = M is disposed to
> cause an activated belief (possibly non-conscious) that I have M.

This account avoids all the difficulties previously mentioned as being inherent in the earlier two. As with Theory 2, there is no requirement that the higher-order beliefs be conscious ones. So there is no regress of higher-order beliefs attending each conscious state, and there can be no objection from the phenomenology of consciousness. But, in contrast to Theory 2, those higher-order beliefs are not actual but potential. So the objection now disappears, that an unbelievable amount of cognitive space would have to be taken up with every conscious experience.

More needs to be said, of course, about the kind of disposition in question. Otherwise we can make the following objection: that the perceptions of an absent-minded driver, too, or of someone who is blindsighted, are similarly disposed to cause the subject to believe that they are having such an experience. For the absent-minded driver is disposed to acquire such a belief if prompted. And someone who is blindsighted, but who also knows the details of their condition, may also be disposed to have beliefs about their (non-conscious) perceptions, in many cases – without, of course, those perceptions thereby becoming conscious ones.

These difficulties are best dealt with as follows. We can propose that conscious experience occurs when perceptual information is fed into a special short-term buffer memory store, whose function is to make that information available to cause higher-order beliefs about any aspect of its contents, where the causation in question will be direct, not mediated by any form of (consciously accessible) inference. This proposal is represented diagrammatically in Figure 1.

On this account, perceptual information is regularly passed to two or more short-term memory stores, C (conscious) and N (non-conscious), to be integrated with the subject's goals in the control of action; where C itself is defined by its relation to higher-order thought – any of the contents of C being *apt* to give rise to a higher-order thought about itself, should circumstances (and what is going on elsewhere in the system) demand. This gives us the idea of the richness of conscious experience in relation to the relative paucity of higher-order beliefs. It also solves the problem raised by the fact that absent-minded car drivers and blindsight subjects may be disposed to have beliefs about their non-conscious experiences on the basis of inference from other beliefs about their circumstances or actions. For we can insist that the formation of the higher-order beliefs should be non-inferential, if the contents of C are thereby to be conscious.

Also represented in Figure 1, is Theory 3's account of what makes a belief or thought to be conscious. (The box labelled 'belief' is intended to be ambiguous between standing-state and occurrent thoughts.) A conscious standing-state belief is one which is apt to cause the higher-order occurrent belief that one has that belief; a conscious occurrent thought is

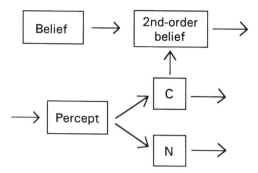

Figure 1 Potential and non-conscious 2nd-order belief

one which is apt to cause the higher-order belief that one is now enter-taining that thought; and so on. (Not represented, however, are the distinctive further effects of conscious experience and higher-order thought in cognition.)

It might be questioned whether this account is even of the right *form* to serve as a theory of consciousness. For consciousness is, surely, something categorical. When I am subject to a conscious experience, there is something actually taking place in me which constitutes my state of consciousness. How, then, can the conscious status of my experience consist merely in the fact that I am *disposed* to have an appropriate higher-order thought about it if circumstances should demand? For this is not something which is actually happening, but merely something which *would* happen if certain other things happened (see Rosenthal, 1993, p. 208). But the reply to this is easy. For there *is* something categorical taking place in me whenever I have a conscious experience, on the above account – the perceptual information is actually there in the short-term memory store C, which is defined by its relation to higher-order thought.

Compare the following: the motion of a piston in an automobile engine is a categorical event, but what constitutes that movement as the motion *of a piston* is its functional – dispositional – relation to the other parts of the engine. It is only because it is apt to be caused by the ignition of petrol from the carburettor, and is apt (when the gears are engaged) to be connected in the right way to the crank-shaft, that this particular physical movement constitutes the motion of a piston. Similarly in connection with conscious experience, it may be said: the perceptual information in the short-term memory store C is actually, categorically, there. But what defines that store, as opposed to any other, and constitutes the information contained within it as conscious, is its functional relationship with higher-order thought.

Major difficulties remain, however. One is that the account of consciousness provided by Theory 3 is subject to decisive counter-example. For there are cases in which I may believe that P, and believe, non-consciously, that I believe that P, without *consciously* believing that P. In which case Theory 3 cannot provide a sufficient condition for conscious belief. What follows is an example I owe to Tim Williamson.

Suppose that I am disposed to make judgements on utilitarian grounds whenever practical considerations of morality arise. I therefore believe that the morally correct thing to do is whatever will cause the greatest happiness to the greatest number. But I am not aware of having this belief. Indeed, if challenged, I may be inclined to deny it. (I may have heard that there are all kinds of objection to utilitarianism as a moral theory.) Yet in the course of a discussion of the merits and demerits of judging actions in terms of what will cause the greatest happiness to the greatest number, I may find myself speaking of the people who maintain such a view as 'we', and becoming angry when their views are criticised, thus manifesting the higher-order belief, that I believe myself to believe utilitarianism to be true. But this may strike me with the force of self-discovery. In which case, a disposition to have an activated higher-order belief that I have a given belief cannot be sufficient for conscious believing.

Another (closely related) difficulty with the account is this. Theory 3 does not require the higher-order beliefs, which render a given mental state conscious, to be conscious in their turn. But as a matter of fact it does seem to be the case that whenever I have a conscious experience or thought it is always *available* to *conscious* thought. It may be objected that this cannot be known to be the case, since if the thought were a non-conscious one, I would not know that I had it. This is true. But the point is that we have no reason to believe that we have such non-conscious higher-order thoughts on a regular basis, since the only cases where higher-order thoughts seem to make a difference in behaviour (barring rare cases like that of the previous paragraph) are where they are conscious ones.

It may be replied that it is, in any case, just an accident that the higher-order thoughts to which conscious states are available are always themselves conscious, having no bearing on the conscious status of the states in question, as such. But it is certainly worth exploring the possibility that there may be a deeper necessity underlying the surface phenomena here. There is an important methodological principle at issue, indeed – namely, to minimise accidents. If we have to choose between two accounts, one of which leaves accidental what the other does not, then the latter should be preferred, other things being equal.

6.4   Theory 4: potential and conscious

The fourth theory combines *potential* with *conscious* higher-order beliefs, as follows:

> Any mental state M, of mine, is conscious = M is disposed to cause an activated conscious belief that I have M.

More long-windedly and recursively, so as to eliminate the occurrence of the word 'conscious' from the right hand side of the definition, the account is as follows:

> Any mental state M, of mine, is conscious = M (level 1) is disposed to cause an activated belief that I have M (level 2), which in turn is disposed to cause the belief that I have such a belief (level 3), and so on; and every state in this series, of level n, is disposed to cause a higher-order belief of level n + 1.

This account avoids all the problems attending the other three. It solves the difficulty raised by the utilitarianism example against Theory 3, since in that example I did not *consciously* believe myself to believe that actions should be judged in terms of the greatest happiness to the greatest number. Any belief which I *consciously* believe myself to have, of course, cannot be subject to surprising self-discovery. And Theory 4 meshes nicely with the point just made, that whenever we have conscious experiences and beliefs, which are therefore available to thought, it always seems to be conscious thoughts to which they are available.

Yet since, like Theory 3, the account is dispositional, it avoids the problem of cognitive overload which attends Theory 2. And although, like Theory 1, consciousness is defined in terms of its relation to *conscious* higher-order beliefs, there need be no infinite regress since these are only dispositional. (Nor, of course, need the account be viciously circular if it is, rather, *recursive*.) In order for my belief *that P* to be conscious, it is necessary, on this account, that I should be disposed to believe consciously *that I believe that P*, which in turn requires that I should be disposed to believe consciously *that I believe that I believe that P*, and so on. I can have all of these dispositions consistent with my finite cognitive capacities.

This account is now quite close to the reflexive thinking theory of consciousness which I shall propose, and defend, in the next chapter. But two problems remain. First, it needs to be explained why is it not just a miracle that I should have all of the above dispositions in any given case. If I believe that P, and am also disposed to believe that I believe that P, then what ensures that I am also disposed to have the whole hierarchy of higher-order beliefs necessary to constitute the latter as conscious? What explains why I should have them all? Why should not the hierarchy of dispositions just break off arbitrarily at some point? Until this is explained, Theory 4 cannot be regarded as satisfactory.

The second problem relates to the characterisation of conscious (standing-state) belief, in particular. According to Theory 4, a belief gets to be conscious in virtue of its disposition to cause me to think, consciously, that I have that belief. Thus, my belief in the date of my sister's birthday is conscious, on this account, in virtue of my disposition to think consciously to myself, in appropriate circumstances, 'I believe that Ann was born on the 4th of July'. But how plausible is it that the conscious status of a standing-state belief should consist in anything higher-order, in the first instance, rather than in a disposition to issue in a conscious act of thinking with the *same* content?

On the latter sort of account, what would make my belief conscious is that I should simply be disposed to think consciously to myself, 'Ann was born on the 4th of July.' The important thing is that I should be disposed to think that thought assertorically, and deliberately act on it, not that I should be disposed to think *of* myself that I have it. On this alternative account, what constitutes the conscious status of the standing-state belief that P, is that it is apt to emerge in a conscious assertoric judgement *that P,* not in the assertoric judgement *that I believe that P.* So in this respect, too, Theory 4 is unsatisfactory as it stands, if we have reason accept the alternative characterisation of conscious belief.

What reason is there for preferring this alternative account, against the account of Theory 4? I have two arguments. The first is that it is surely possible that some people, who do nevertheless have conscious beliefs, might be extremely cautious in *ascribing* beliefs to themselves. If asked whether or not they believe that P, they may say, 'Well, I'm not sure that I really *believe* it.' They may be inclined to insist, indeed, that they have *no* beliefs. Yet this need not prevent them from having any conscious beliefs, surely, if they are nevertheless prepared to think to themselves 'P', consciously and in assertoric mode, and to act deliberately on their judgement. Provided that a standing-state belief is apt to issue in conscious judgements with the same content, it need not matter, to its status as conscious, that the subject is also apt to disavow the higher-order belief that they have such a belief.

My second argument derives from the epistemology of higher-order believing. Many writers have noted that what we actually do, when we wish to know whether or not we believe that P, is use an *answer-check procedure*, followed by a routine of *semantic ascent* (see Evans, 1982, p. 225, and Gordon, 1995). If I wish to know whether or not I believe that the Earth is getting warmer what I do, in the first instance, is ask myself the first-order question, 'Is the Earth getting warmer?' If I find myself inclined to answer 'Yes' then I ascend one level, using my preparedness to think or assert that the Earth is getting warmer as the ground on which to ascribe to myself the *belief* that the Earth is getting warmer. This certainly suggests that the aptness of a standing-state belief to issue in a first-order conscious judgement with the *same* content is prior to, and more basic than, its aptness to cause the higher-order belief that one has such a belief. In which case it is the former which should be made constitutive of consciousness, contrary to what is claimed by Theory 4.

I shall return to consider how a variant of Theory 4 can overcome these problems, when I present and discuss my own reflexive thinking theory of consciousness in Chapter 7. For the remainder of this chapter I shall be discussing two slightly different accounts of the nature of consciousness due to Daniel Dennett, and especially considering their bearing on the question of the place of natural language in conscious thinking.

6.5   Dennett 1978: availability to print-out

Dennett once suggested that conscious states are those that are available for reporting in speech – suggesting that consciousness is like the public-relations department of a major company, or like the print-out facility of a computer program. (See his 1978a; though I shall shortly argue that many of the essentials of the view seem to survive, in more complex form, into his 1991.) As with theories 3 and 4 above, he proposes that there is a special short-term buffer memory store whose function, in this case, is to make perceptual and other information available to linguistic report. So a conscious experience will consist of perceptual information which is held in this store, available for the subject to make reports on. (What seems to be distinctively different about the 1991 account, is that it is held to be radically indeterminate whether or not perceptual information is contained in the memory store in question.)

This account can explain the initial data, since neither the absent-minded driver nor the blindsighted person have any disposition to make spontaneous reports on their experiences, except on the basis of inference. It also satisfies the condition omitted by Kirk – that conscious experiences should be *available to* the subject – since it is crucial to the account that the subject should be capable of reporting on their experiences as such, and not just on the states of the world experienced. The account also shares the best features of the Armstrong-type Theory 4. Since it is formulated in terms *availability* to report, or *aptness to cause* dispositions to make reports, the account avoids all the problems of cognitive overload which attended theories 1 and 2 above. Yet there is nothing to stop Dennett insisting, too, that the dispositions to make reports must themselves be conscious ones, if the experiences or beliefs in question are to count as conscious. Moreover, I believe that Dennett's model is capable of avoiding the remaining problems with Theory 4 above, as I shall now try to explain.

In order to avoid the appearance of accident attaching to the hierarchy of potential states within the account, all we have to suppose is that the dispositions to make reports are, on a regular basis, *themselves* made available for report, and are thus conscious. For this, we need only hypothesise a sort of 'feed-back loop', whose function is to pass back information concerning the subject's dispositions to make reports to the very short-term memory store which will then make them available for reporting on in turn. On this account, then, there need be nothing accidental in the fact that conscious experiences or beliefs will be available (that is, be disposed) to cause dispositions to make reports which are, if they are actualised, themselves made available to report, and so on.

The final problem with Theory 4 can also be solved, if we suppose that my disposition to make a report, the aptness to cause which constitutes the conscious status of my standing-state belief in the date of my sister's birthday, is a disposition to report *on my sister's birthday*, and not *on my belief about my sister's birthday*. That is, what makes it the case that a standing-state belief is conscious, on this account, can be dispositions to make reports *with the very same content* as that belief. And these dispositions, in turn, will be conscious because I shall be apt to make reports on them, and so on. At no point in the account do we need to appeal to a higher-order belief about my belief – only to higher-order beliefs about my dispositions to make reports.

The main problem for Dennett, however, is that consciousness now seems to be *definitionally* tied to possession of a natural language, since only creatures with a language can have dispositions to make reports on their own states. But recall Stalnaker's intelligent Martians, discussed in section 1.4. Given the complexity and flexibility of their behaviour, we would surely wish to say, not only that they have thoughts, but also that they have *conscious* thoughts, despite their lack of natural language. So it is surely conceivable that there should be creatures with conscious mental states which nevertheless lack any disposition to make reports on their mental states.

Even if Dennett should reply that his account is not intended as an *analysis* of consciousness, but rather as a substantive theory of what consciousness *is* (in the way that I shall claim of my own account in the next chapter), the problem remains. For there seems no difficulty in supposing that the Stalnaker Martians could have evolved, either. I believe that we do in fact perform much of our thinking in natural language, and also that it may be naturally necessary that we should, given the way in which human cognition is structured. But there is, surely, little plausibility attaching to the claim that it is naturally impossible that there should exist any creatures, no matter how constituted and evolved, who entertain conscious thoughts without natural language.

A closely related difficulty for Dennett's 1978a account, is that consciousness turns out to have no evolutionary rationale apart from the usefulness of informing others about one's current mental states. (Just such a claim is made explicitly in Humphrey, 1986.) Although it is possible that this should be true, it would surely be an advantage in a theory of consciousness if it could make consciousness less epiphenomenal than this. For it *appears*, at any rate, that the status of a mental event as conscious can often make a difference to my own behaviour, quite apart from the fact that I may be inclined to report on it to other people.

Suppose that I am struck by the beauty of a particular sunset, for example, and consequently begin to paint it in oils. It is surely plausible that I *would never have acted as I did* if my experience of the sunset had not been a conscious one. Now, admittedly, in this case the action I undertake is not the kind of thing which might conduce to survival or reproduction. But, given that consciousness can make such a difference to our lives as individuals, it would surely be strange that it should not have been selected for on the grounds of at least *some* of the differences that it can make.

The reflexive thinking theory of consciousness that I shall develop in the next chapter will be modelled closely on Dennett's early view, except that any immediate connections with natural language will be broken. This will leave us able to see why the evolution of consciousness should have had value in survival in its own right.

6.6   Dennett 1991: multiple drafts and probes

Dennett's more recent view is that there is no unified, determinate, content to consciousness. Rather, at any one time there may be a number of different accounts, or drafts, of the passing scene constructed in the brain, competing with one another for canonical status, just as a contemporary academic can have a number of different drafts of an article circulating in different places round the globe through the electronic mail network. And, crucially, there is supposed to be nowhere where all these streams of processing 'come together', being routinely integrated into a conscious representation of the world.

This is the famous multiple drafts theory of cognition, according to which a number of distinct, partial, and partially conflicting accounts of reality will be constructed in different regions of the brain at any one time. On Dennett's account, there is simply no answer to the question which of these conflicting contents is conscious, until the subject is *probed* by some internal or external event. (However, this is not to say that those contents are *non*-conscious until probed, either. They are neither determinately conscious nor determinately non-conscious.) Such a probe has the effect of promoting one of the many possible accounts to the status of *determinate* consciousness.

The multiple drafts theory gains some of its initial plausibility from obvious facts about perceptual processing in the brain. Everyone now knows that information in the brain is processed largely in parallel, with specialised analysers and detectors working on different aspects of the stimulus at the same or overlapping times. Thus there are edge detectors, colour detectors, shape detectors, classifiers, face recognisers, and so on, many of which operate independently of one another. But it does not follow – nor is it known – that the same holds for *every* kind of mental state or process. In particular, it may be that the different streams of perceptual processing are pooled at some stage, and integrated into a single perceptual representation, which is then made available to central processes of thought and reasoning. For example, the thesis of modular mental organisation proposed by Fodor (1983) suggests just such a picture.

In fact, the multiple drafts theory claims much more than merely that perceptual analysis is conducted by parallel processes. It claims that *there is no stage at which* the different parallel processes are routinely integrated. So it holds that there is no manifold of conscious experience. Rather, there are many different – fragmentary and partial – streams of perceptual content being constructed simultaneously and in overlapping sequence. Which of these contents becomes determinately conscious depends on exactly when and how the subject is probed – for example, by someone asking them a question, or by some event directing their attention towards an aspect of their environment or their experience.

There are two immediate problems for such an account. The first is this: why, then, do we have such a powerful subjective impression that there is a manifold of experience? Why should we have the unshakeable feeling that we are simultaneously aware of many different aspects of our experience, if the truth is that we are conscious only of one probed content at a time? Dennett's answer is presumably this: because *wherever* we probe we do *find something*. But this doesn't explain the feeling that I don't *need* to probe, because I am *already* aware of the manifold (see section 6.2 above). Nor is it any adequate defence for Dennett to claim that since many of the probes are non-conscious ones, I am, of course, often unaware of having to do anything in order to obtain a new content.

For all this really tells us is that there will be a *sequence* of not-consciously-directed contents in consciousness, which does not begin to explain the feeling that there are many determinate contents already, simultaneously, present.

The second problem is this: is it not empirically very unlikely that the brain should only resolve differences between different drafts, and integrate different narrative fragments, when probed, or when circumstances demand? For it will then, at that stage, have to undertake the process of integration, which would involve further delay. It seems much more likely that integration should be routinely undertaken, so as to be ready to feed into different plans and projects, and so as to be available to thought, as circumstances demand. Conscious decision-making is a slow enough process as it is. One would think that there would be very great evolutionary pressure not to slow down the process still further, by requiring some degree of perceptual integration to take place in response to each sub-goal or demand of the decision-making process.

I shall consider some of Dennett's explicit arguments for the multiple drafts theory in the next section, and will return to the account in the next chapter, in connection with my own reflexive thinking theory. For the remainder of this section, I shall focus on the question of the relation between Dennett's earlier and later theories, which will then enable us to discern in his writing a further, implicit, argument for the multiple drafts account. I should say at the outset that interpreting Dennett's 1991 book is no easy matter, beautiful and stimulating though it is. For like cognition itself (on the multiple drafts view), it consists in a distributed set of partially conflicting narratives and narrative fragments, with nowhere where it all comes together for the benefit of the reader.

The relation between earlier and later Dennett

Is the only substantive change between the 1978a and 1991 accounts, that the *determinacy* of the contents of consciousness has been given up in the latter? Does Dennett still believe that a conscious state is one which is available to linguistic report? I think that he does still believe this, or at least that he should if he is to be consistent. I think that the 1991 account is this: consciousness is, as before, defined in terms of availability to report; but because Dennett no longer thinks there is any short-term memory store whose function is to make its contents available to report, he no longer thinks that there is any determinacy attaching to the question *which* contents are available to report (and so to the question which of the multiple contents are conscious ones).

Let me first focus on the question whether the notion of *availability* is the appropriate one to use in characterising Dennett's 1991 theory of consciousness. Since conscious contents (or determinately conscious contents) are said to be those which result from a *probe*, we need to ask whether consciousness is a matter of *availability* to probing, or rather whether states are only conscious which are reported in response to an *actual* probe. The answer, I think, has to be the former, otherwise there is no scope for indeterminacy. Once a probe has gone out, there must presumably be a determinate answer to the question whether it has been answered, and also to the question what the content of that answer was.

Rather, Dennett's view is that conscious contents are those which *would* constitute the answer to a probe, *if* such a probe were to be issued. But given the complexity of the brain, and the degree of parallel distributed processing contained within it, whether or not such consciousness-defining conditionals are true will depend upon the precise timing (down to micro-seconds) of the probes. If these were to vary even ever so slightly, then so might the conscious status of the contents in question. Dennett's view must be that, since the truth-values of the subjunctive and counterfactual conditionals implicit in the notion of *availability* may vary depending upon exactly when and how the subject is probed, there will generally be no determinate answer to the question which of the various drafts of experience is conscious.

Crucial to the above interpretation, of course, is the notion of a *probe*, which remains notoriously unexplained in Dennett's work. The question is: is a probe always a request to formulate a linguistic description? Certainly a probe *can* be a request for a linguistic description. But is that all? There is one passage where Dennett might be thought to commit himself to the idea that a probe can arise from motor control, without any disposition to give a linguistic report. For in discussing the absent-minded car-driver example he commits himself to the view that the perceptual information on which the driver acts is conscious throughout, only not retained in memory – perhaps, it might be suggested, because probed by the motor control unit (see his 1991, p. 137). But a careful reading of the passage yields a different interpretation, in fact. For Dennett emphasises that if the subject *had been asked* what they were seeing, they would probably have been able to report at least fragments of their experience. Now this is not, I think, a good argument – see section 5.2 above. But it does show that, even here, Dennett is still thinking of a probe as something linguistic.

Moreover, there are good reasons why he cannot allow a probe to emanate from the motor control unit, or from the demands of action generally. This is because *you don't need higher-order mental states in order to act*. A demand for action might cause fragmentary perceptual information about the world to coalesce into a determinate account, but there is no reason why it should cause higher-order awareness of this perceptual information itself. Yet Dennett himself is eulogistic about higher-order analyses (except that he thinks it unnecessary to insert any higher-order *belief* between the conscious mental state and its verbal report; see his 1991, ch. 10). And he is right to be so, or else he will have to count blindsighted and sleep-walking perceptual states as conscious (because acted on), or, like Kirk, he will lose any connection between the conscious status of a perception and the question of what that experience is *like*.

I conclude, then, that the multiple drafts theory is essentially similar to Dennett's earlier (1978a) account of consciousness, in that conscious perception is defined in terms of the availability of perceptual information to linguistic report. What has changed is that he has dropped the idea of a special-purpose short-term memory store, whose function is to make perceptual and other information about the system available to linguistic report. He no longer believes that there is any single such store, with determinate contents. In its place, there are multiple streams of perceptual information and other forms of cognitive processing in the brain, some of which may be in conflict with one another. But the idea is still that which of these streams is conscious depends upon it being accessible to linguistic report. Only now, on Dennett's present account, there is supposed to be no determinate answer to the question what someone is consciously experiencing or thinking at any given time, since different fragments from the variety of perceptual streams may become (determinately) conscious depending upon the precise nature and timing of the probe.

Dennett against the Cartesian Theatre

One argument for the multiple drafts theory of consciousness, then, goes like this: start with the idea that consciousness consists in availability to linguistic report; then deny that there is any short-term memory store whose function is to make its contents available to report – insisting, rather, that cognitive processing is conducted in parallel streams in spatially distributed regions of the brain; and then point out that *which* of these contents emerges in response to a request for a report may depend upon the precise timing and nature of the probe (just as the results of a questionnaire or opinion-poll may depend upon its timing, and on the precise way in which the questions are formulated). In which case subjunctive conditionals which are unspecific as to timing and nature (such as the consciousness-defining conditional, 'M is a state which *would* be reported on *if* circumstances were to demand') will lack any determinate truth-values. So consciousness, too, must be indeterminate, if it consists in availability to report.

Everything turns, then, on Dennett's grounds for rejecting the special-purpose short-term memory store, postulated in his 1978a. Why does he no longer believe in it? The answer is that he now thinks that it committed him to an unacceptable form of 'Cartesian Theatre' conception of consciousness. But this is where the argument starts to get murky. For there are three separable strands in Dennett's idea of a Cartesian Theatre, only two of which are definitely objectionable, in my view. One (closest to the surface of Dennett's writing) is that there is a single *place* in the brain where 'everything comes together', reaching which is definitive of conscious status. This idea is almost certainly false, and Dennett is right to insist, on the contrary, that cognition is spatially distributed.

The second strand in the idea of a 'Cartesian Theatre', is that there is a *level of functional organisation* in the brain where everything comes together – that there is a *functionally* defined memory store whose contents are the contents of consciousness. Dennett tends to run this together with the first strand, assuming that both are undermined by the fact of spatially distributed processing. But this is to miss the point that a functionally defined memory system might itself be spread out over a number of different areas of the brain. I shall return to this point in section 7.7, when defending my reflexive thinking theory against Dennettian objections.

The third strand in the idea of a 'Cartesian Theatre' has to do with the representation and experience of *time*. The idea, here, is that time of conscious experience is given simply by time of arrival in the Theatre. So time is not *represented* in the brain, but is rather carried by the times of the representing events. This picture, too, is almost certainly false, and seems inconsistent with a variety of experimental phenomena (see Dennett and Kinsbourne, 1992). But as I shall show in section 7.7, it is separable from either of the above strands. So one can continue to believe in a special-purpose short-term memory store with determinate contents (which are therefore determinately conscious) while allowing that time, like everything else, is represented in the brain. In fact, Dennett really has no argument at all against a functionally defined version of 'Cartesian Theatre', as we shall see more fully in sections 6.7 and 7.7 below.

6.7   Time and indeterminacy

What of Dennett's more explicit arguments for the indeterminacy of the multiple drafts theory? The main one arises out of a variety of puzzling temporal phenomena, some only recently experimentally established.

Consider the *colour phi phenomenon*, for example, which is the best well known. If a pair of small coloured spots, one red, one green, separated by four degrees of visual angle, are briefly illuminated (for 150 micro-seconds) in rapid succession (with a 50 microsecond interval), a single spot will seem to the observer to travel from the one place to the other, changing colour while it moves. The motion is illusory, of course, pro-duced by the visual system as its way of making the best sense that it can of the data. Now notice that in order to construct the intervening colour change from red to green (say), the visual system must *already* know that the second spot is to be green. For how, otherwise, would it know what colour to change the first spot *into*? But how can this happen without any-thing as mysterious as precognition or backwards causation? Dennett considers two types of hypothesis.

The Orwellian hypothesis (so-named after the example of the rewriting of history in George Orwell's novel, *Nineteen Eighty-Four)* is that the cogni-tive system changes its record of its own past conscious states. What happens, according to this hypothesis, is that the subject is first conscious of a stationary red light, and then very briefly conscious of a stationary green light, before an experience of a moving light which changes colour from red to green is constructed, all memory of the previous experience being erased. Since the time intervals are so short, there is no way to elicit from the subject their conscious experience of a stationary green light – by the time the question has been processed and an answer formulated, that experience has already been forgotten.

The Stalinesque hypothesis, by contrast, (so-named after the fabrication of evidence in the Soviet show-trials of the Stalin era) is that the cognitive system holds back from consciousness the information about the station-ary red light for long enough for the later green light to be processed, and for a representation of the intervening motion to be constructed. The resulting motion of a light which changes colour from red to green is then displayed in the subject's consciousness. So the subject never was con-scious of a stationary green light – by the time the green light was con-sciously experienced, it was experienced as moving. Again, since the time intervals are so short, we cannot test this hypothesis by asking the subject.

Dennett argues that it is *indeterminate* whether it is the Orwellian, or rather the Stalinesque, hypothesis which is correct. Since we cannot test these hypotheses by asking the subject (and neither, of course, can the subject test them by introspection), there is no fact of the matter waiting to be discovered. This is certainly not an intuitive conclusion to draw from the data, and it seems to presuppose Dennett's own anti-realist (instru-mentalist or quasi-verificationist) conception of the mental. For the two hypotheses certainly seem to be distinct, postulating quite different mechanisms and processes as underlying conscious experience. If we are realists about the mental we shall be inclined to think that there is some fact of the matter, which we may one day find more direct ways of testing.

Consider the Stalinesque hypothesis first, in a little more detail. This admits of two variants, in fact. The first requires that there be a delay between the time at which the first spot has been processed, until the time at which the second spot is processed, in order that those experiences should be presented to consciousness in a sequence which is both 'filled in' with motion, and also referred back in time (so there is no subjective sense of delay). Data from elsewhere suggests that this delay might have to be somewhere of the order of half a second (see Dennett and Kinsbourne, 1992). But why should the idea of such a delay be thought to be so implausible? After all, the function of consciousness (on the reflexive thinking account which I shall defend in Chapter 7, at least) is to develop flexible strategies of practical reasoning – which has to do, ultimately, with mid- and long-term action control. It would make perfectly good sense that fast-response control of current action should take place non-consciously. And, indeed, this is supported by the familiar fact that skilled activities tend to be interfered with if you try to think about them at the time, and try to bring them under conscious control at any fine-grained level of detail.

The second version of the Stalinesque hypothesis would be this: that the intervening sequence of the motion of the two spots, and the change of colour, may be constructed *while* the two stimuli are still being processed. This is made possible by the fact that the time intervals involved mean that the first spot is still being processed by the visual system at the time when the second spot begins to be, and because the temporal smear is such that the very same neurological regions of the brain are in fact processing both spots at the same – overlapping – time. (I owe this suggestion, and the temporal facts on which it is based, to personal communication from Kathleen Akins.)

Now let us briefly consider the alternative Orwellian hypothesis, that the perceptual information about the spots of light goes straight to consciousness, without any overlap or delay, and that the percept of the second stationary spot becomes conscious *before* the motion from the first to the second does. This, too, admits of two variants. In its original version, as presented by Dennett, the second spot is experienced as being stationary *before* any motion is experienced as occurring, but all memory of that experience of the second spot is supposed to be erased as soon as motion is then experienced. But this version equates the time at which the experience is felt as occurring with the actual time of its occurrence in the brain. Yet Dennett and Kinsbourne (1992) make a powerful case that time, like other phenomena, is represented by the brain, rather than given by the objective time of occurrence of a mental event. So the times of the above events will presumably be represented by the brain, as will the felt sequence of the conscious experiences – with the content of the latter representation perhaps being driven by the content of the former. But we can still ask *when* (objectively) a given conscious experience occurs, which may be different from when it is *felt as* occurring. (In my terms, this would be to ask when a given perceptual content first became available to reflexive thinking. See Chapter 7.)

As a second sort of Orwellian hypothesis, we could thus claim that the time at which an experience becomes conscious is objective, while allowing that the time at which an experience is *felt as* occurring may be different, forming part of the represented content of the experience. Of course you could not determine the former (time of conscious experience) by asking the subject – that will rather give you an answer to the latter (time as consciously experienced). Its discovery would have to be theoretically driven. On this alternative account, then, it may be that the conscious experience of the later spot occurs (objectively) *before* the motion from the first spot is filled in, but that the experience of the later spot is *felt as* occurring *after* the motion is experienced. Is this coherent? I don't see why not, and will briefly defend it in relation to reflexive thinking theory in section 7.7. Note that this would still be a version of Orwellian hypothesis, except that there need be no tampering with memory. Since the times and sequences of the conscious experiences are represented by the subject, the fact that the experience of the second spot actually occurred before the experience of motion is not something which will ever be available to the subject.

It may be difficult to see how we could ever discover which, if any, of the four hypotheses sketched above is correct. But they do seem to be distinct hypotheses. (Some of them differ over whether or not a memory system is implicated in conscious experience, for example.) So if we are realists about the mental, we should expect that there will be some fact of the matter waiting to be discovered. I shall return to discuss the multiple drafts hypothesis in the next chapter, contrasting it with my own reflexive thinking theory. For the moment just let me note that, whatever one may think about such phenomena as colour phi, or the supposed indeterminacy between the rival versions of Orwellian and Stalinesque explanations, these cannot support the much more radical indeterminacy of the multiple drafts theory.

It is one thing to claim that there are no determinate facts about what is or is not conscious for finely discriminated temporal intervals, and quite another thing to claim that there is no unified manifold of conscious experience at all – and the former cannot support the latter. It would surely be possible for someone to allow Dennett the indeterminacy between Orwellian and Stalinesque explanations of colour phi, but to insist, nevertheless, that perceptual information about less rapidly changing phenomena is routinely integrated into a single, highly complex, manifold of conscious experience – contrary to what the multiple drafts theory maintains. Moreover, Dennett's 1991 theory still faces the problem we raised for the 1978a account, that it ties the notion of consciousness too closely to natural language. So we have reason to hope for a better theory.

I shall argue in the next chapter that reflexive thinking theory is to be preferred to Dennett's account of consciousness, in either its 1978a or its 1991 versions. For the moment I shall focus on the bearing his theories have on the question of the role of natural language in *human* cognition. For we need to consider whether those theories can be recruited by the lovers of Mentalese to undermine the introspective argument of Chapter 2. Moreover, even if Dennett's views are rejected as accounts of consciousness *in general*, they can still be regarded as alternative accounts of the architecture of *human* consciousness, to be placed in competition with my own theory which will be developed in Chapter 8, on the back of my defence of the reflexive thinking theory in Chapter 7.

6.8　Dennett on the place of language in thought

Dennett's 1978a and 1991 accounts are the only ones of those canvassed over the last two chapters which might be capable of explaining how we come to be under a systematic illusion that our conscious thoughts occur in natural language, thus undermining the argument from introspection of Chapter 2. For since the dispositions to make reports on our thoughts are linguistic, it may be suggested that this would give rise to the illusion that the states reported on are also linguistic. What actually happens when we engage in a train of verbalised 'thinking', on this account, is merely that we have a sequence of dispositions to report on the *real* thinking, which takes place elsewhere in some other medium. But we naturally come to confuse our dispositions to report on our thinkings with those thinkings themselves – hence the introspective illusion.

Now one apparent problem for this suggestion, is that it ought to imply that we would have a persistent tendency to think that our conscious *experiences* are linguistic, too. For in their case Dennett's account of their status as conscious is the same – a conscious experience is one that is available to verbal report. But we don't have any such tendency. We have no inclination to think that our perceptual experiences occur in natural language. But why should this be so, if the proposal above were correct?

Supposing that neither thoughts nor experiences constitutively involve natural language, why should we have a persistent tendency to believe that *thoughts* do, but no such tendency to believe that *experiences* do? For the account of their status as conscious is the same in each case.

The defender of systematic introspective illusion has a ready reply to this objection, in fact, arising out of the analogue nature of experience as against the digitalised nature of thought. For it can be said that the reason why we feel no temptation to believe that our conscious experiences occur in natural language, although their status as conscious depends upon our disposition to express them in language, is that we are aware that there is much *more* content to them than we could ever hope to express. We are aware, that is, that our experience has a richness and a continuity in its graded contents which far outstrips our capacity for linguistic description. Our thoughts, on the other hand, are just as digitalised as the sentences which we use to express them. Indeed, since there often is, one might suppose, a one-to-one match between our thoughts and the natural language sentences which we use to express them, it is possible that we might come to confuse the thought itself with the natural language sentence, a disposition to assert which constitutes the former as conscious.

Now, to say that Dennett's account of consciousness makes a thesis of systematic introspective illusion *possible* is quite different from saying that it makes it *inevitable*. And in fact there would seem to be two quite distinct ways in which Dennett can develop his account of the conscious status of episodic, occurrent, thinkings.

First, he could claim that such thinkings just *are* dispositions to make verbal utterances. So when I consciously think to myself, 'The Earth is getting warmer, so I must use less fuel', what happens is just that I acquire a temporary disposition to *say*, 'The Earth is getting warmer, so I must use less fuel.' The distinctive feature of this first proposal would be that dispositions to make verbal reports would have, not only a public-relations, but also an executive, role in the life of the organism. Trains of conscious practical reasoning, for example, leading up to a decision or an action, would consist in sequences of dispositions to make reports (where these thoughts would have their status as conscious because they are, in their turn, available to report). On this first account, human conscious thinkings do constitutively involve natural language, and there is no introspective illusion.

Second, Dennett might claim that the real act of thinking is a process which underlies, and causes, the disposition to utter a natural-language sentence, where that process is expressed in Mentalese or some other medium of representation. This certainly fits with his tendency to speak of the language faculty in which these dispositions-to-utter are produced as being the *public-relations unit* of the system as a whole. For the public-relations office in a company or other large organisation will not normally also be charged with executive control. On the contrary, the public-relations office publishes whatever information it is told to by the executive, and often has no more access to the real deliberations and decisions of the latter than does the general public. On this account, then, the temporary disposition to say, 'The Earth is getting warmer, so I must use less fuel', would not itself be part of the cause of my subsequent choice to walk to work rather than to drive. Rather, it would itself be caused by some underlying event which partly causes me to make that choice.

The Joycean machine

Which of the above theories does Dennett himself endorse? It seems plain that his 1978a presents a version of the latter hypothesis, since the cognitive unit, dispositions to make verbal reports in which are constitutive of consciousness, outputs *only* in the form of speech and writing. In his 1991, however, the situation is more complex. For on the one hand, Dennett continues to think of our episodic verbalisations as a form of public-relations activity. But on the other hand, we are told that this stream of verbalisation constitutes a new kind of *virtual machine* in the computer which is the human brain (p. 210). It is said to be a sequential, sentence-based, program running in a connectionist, highly parallel, computer-architecture (p. 218) – a *Joycean machine*, in fact. This suggests that our internal verbalisations constitute a new form of cognition – not quite an executive system, exactly, but certainly something which plays more role in human cognition as a whole than mere public relations.

Similarly, we are told that human consciousness is created when the human brain becomes colonised, as a result of enculturation and communication, by *memes* – that is, by ideas, or concepts, acquired both with and through language (1991, pp. 210 and 219). Again the natural interpretation of this idea (which is, notice, a variant on the Standard Social Science Model, or Whorfian conception of the acquisition and function of language), is that these memes are carried by natural-language expressions, and that their role in this new form of (conscious) cognition results from the ways in which these sentences act and react in the brain.

I do not propose to pursue these interpretative issues any further. For my main aim here is not to understand and interpret Dennett's philosophy, as such, but rather to see whether we can extract from his writing a view which could be put to work in the service of Fodor. Of course it is also true that if the account just sketched of his 1991 position is correct, then Dennett presents us with an alternative, language-involving, architecture for conscious cognition, which would rule out Fodor's claim that all thinking is conducted in Mentalese, just as I myself aim to do. This would give our inner verbalisations *something like* the executive function of thought, but within the framework of multiple drafts theory, as opposed to that of the reflexive thinking theory to be developed in the next chapter. But this is not a promising strategy of argument for anyone to adopt against Fodor, since Dennett's 1991 account brings with it too much anti-realist and anti-nativist baggage to stand a chance of convincing anyone who, like Fodor, is both a realist and a nativist about much of the structure of human cognition. And since my own sympathies are with Fodor on these matters, I aim to reach a language-involving account of human conscious cognition by means of a rather different route. (Recall from the Introduction that I aim to defend a version of the cognitive conception of language *without* having to embrace any aspect of the Whorfian Standard Social Science Model.)

Another way to put the point, is that much of the argument over the next two chapters will be devoted to showing, both that the common-sense construal of the introspective data can be grounded in my reflexive thinking theory of consciousness, and that reflexive thinking theory provides us with a better framework for deliberating about consciousness than does Dennett's multiple drafts theory. So I shall take it that common sense is preferable to Dennett's competing explanation of the Joycean machine. Moreover, as a dialectical point in my debate with Fodor, if he is forced to choose between the two he should prefer the reflexive thinking architecture to Dennett's Joycean machine, since a great deal more of common-sense psychology is preserved in the former, and since the former sits better with his modularist and nativist assumptions.

In fact Dennett himself is no friend of Mentalese. But my question is whether the lovers of Mentalese can take over just enough of Dennett's theories to undermine the argument from introspection of Chapter 2, and to defend the view that all thinking occurs in Mentalese. (I thus propose to marry Fodor to Dennett, just as in Chapter 3 I married Fodor to Searle. Luckily there is no such thing as intellectual bigamy.) The main task here, as I see it, is to explain why, if our episodic verbalisations are the activity of a mere public relations unit, that unit *continues to function* when there are no public reports to be issued. What would be the point? Why should it continually be producing reports which are never issued (and in circumstances in which it is known that they *cannot* be issued, indeed, since much of our inner verbalisation goes on when we know ourselves to be alone)? Why would such a system have evolved to operate in the way that it does?

The Dennett/Fodor hybrid

We can find in Dennett's 1991 the following proposal. This is that inner verbalisation evolved from overt verbalisation, as a way of broadcasting information to different – previously unconnected – parts of the cognitive system. (So the public relations unit of the company *also* has the function of keeping different company departments informed about one another.) Dennett supposes that the cognition of pre-verbal hominids would have consisted of a great many more-or-less discrete dedicated processors, each charged with the execution of particular tasks (1991, p. 188). Some of these processors would have been connected to one another, so as to enable them to pool information, and to co-operate in solving novel or particularly demanding problems. But many of them would have been inaccessible to one another, closed off to the operations of the others, and having no direct access to each other's outputs.

Dennett then proposes that when these hominids began to acquire language, they would have swiftly discovered that by asking themselves overt questions, they could elicit by way of an answer information which they did not know that they had. That is, two (or more) mutually inaccessible sub-systems would have learned to exchange information extra-cranially, provided that each had independent access to the input/output systems of speech and hearing (1991, p. 196). These hominids would then have swiftly discovered that the very same 'good trick' could be executed intra-cranially, by means of inner, imagined, vocalisation. And this continues to be its function today. The role of inner vocalisation is not an executive one, as such (indeed, there is no central executive, on Dennett's story); rather, it enables otherwise unconnected parts of the brain to communicate with one another. The stream of inner verbalisation serves somewhat like a central bulletin board, in something like Baars' (1988) sense – messages broadcast there by any of the many different cognitive sub-systems can thereby reach other sub-systems which would otherwise be inaccessible to them.

This is, I believe, the only proposal to be found in Dennett's work which gives inner verbalisation an important intra-cognitive function (sufficiently important to explain why we do so much of it, that is) without yet according those verbalisations the (executive) role of thought. Here inner verbalisation serves, not as any sort of central executive, but rather as an inner bulletin board, enabling the various sub-systems charged with the control of different aspects of our cognition to communicate with one another. And these sub-systems might then do their thinking in Mentalese, just as Fodor has maintained.

It seems to me that the dialectical situation favours my own position, to be developed over the next two chapters. For the Dennett/Fodor hybrid we have constructed on the latter's behalf would involve giving up many of his cherished beliefs about the mind. In particular, it would involve giving up the belief that there is really such a thing as the central executive. And it would, moreover, involve Fodor in having to accept that there is little or no innate cognitive structure corresponding to what we mistakenly think of as central cognitive processes. (For remember, the proposal is that inner verbalisation acts merely as an inner bulletin board, subserving communication between specialised processors. It will be the latter which control various forms of action and cognition in their respective domains.) If Fodor is forced to choose, as I think he is, between giving up these beliefs and giving up his claim that all thinking is conducted in Mentalese, then he should surely choose the latter.

On a more detailed level, too, it can be seen that the Dennett/Fodor hypothesis is a poor one. For it makes predictions about the phenomenology of inner speech which are quite wrong. If the function of inner speech were to serve as an inner bulletin board, communicating between specialist sub-processors, then one would expect the stream of inner speech to consist of a series of question-and-answer sequences – 'Does anyone know where we are?'; 'In front of the Botanical Gardens'; 'Why are we here?'; 'It is time to go home, and this is the way home'; 'What is that sound behind me?'; 'A car approaching'; and so on. Equally, one would expect the stream of inner speech to skip around all over the place, flitting from topic to topic as one specialist processor after another competes for space on the central bulletin board.

Now sometimes, admittedly, this is what we find. Sometimes we do ask ourselves questions, and sometimes our inner speech jumps from topic to topic with no apparent direction or rationale, especially when we are mentally relaxed or day-dreaming. But sometimes, at least, it is not at all like this. Sometimes the sequence of inner speech can have the form of a piece of practical or theoretical reasoning, for example. If inner speech consisted in the attempts of different specialist sub-systems to communicate with others, then it would be little short of a miracle that it should *ever* take the form of a piece of practical reasoning, *as if* it were the broadcast of a single executive system!

Is there any refuge for the Dennett/Fodor thesis to be had in the Dennettian claim that much of the stream of consciousness need not be *determinately* conscious – only becoming so when it is itself actually probed? Perhaps many of the questions and intervening broadcast-statements remain only indeterminately conscious, and what we are actually aware of is a selection from the total stream, rendered determinately conscious in response to second-order probing? It is hard to see how this could really help. For if the second-order probe takes the form, 'What is occurring in the stream of inner speech right now?', then what we could get would still be a higgledy-piggledy selection from the wider set. And even if the second-order probes are always generated by some specialist sub-system with a particular interest in mind, so that the questions take the form, 'What is happening in the stream of inner speech right now *about X*?', it would still be a miracle that the replies should take the form of a coherent argument or coherent sequence of thought. For, by hypothesis, the stream of inner speech is itself produced by a set of sub-systems trying to communicate with, and obtain information from, one another; and rational argument is not the normal form of information-exchange.

So far, then, the common-sense construal of inner verbalisation (namely, that such verbalisation *is* a form of thinking) has survived comparison with the competition. There only remain the proposals briefly canvassed in section 3.5, that inner verbalisation serves as an aid to memory, or as an aid to self-criticism. These will be returned to and discussed at some length in section 8.3. First, I shall develop my reflexive thinking theory of consciousness in Chapter 7, and then show (in section 8.1) how it can underpin the common-sense construal of inner verbalisation.

Summary

In this chapter I have argued, on a variety of grounds, that a number of proposed higher-order thought theories of consciousness are inadequate. At the same time, many positive suggestions have emerged. These will be put to work in the chapter that follows, where I shall develop and defend my reflexive thinking theory of consciousness. Moreover, and just as importantly given the purpose of this book, I have argued that Dennett has failed to provide any viable account of the role of natural language in cognition which could undermine the introspective argument of Chapter 2.

7   A reflexive thinking theory of consciousness

In this chapter I shall present, elucidate, and defend my own proposal on the nature of consciousness, which I call the *reflexive thinking (RT) theory*. This theory will then be put to work in the chapter which follows, where I shall argue that *human* conscious thinking, at least, essentially involves public language. Since I claim that RT theory provides a better framework for considering the nature of consciousness than does Dennett's multiple drafts theory, I shall also maintain that the eventual result is a more plausible account of the role of natural language in human cognition than is Dennett's hypothesis of the 'Joycean machine'.

7.1   Reflexive thinking theory

I propose that consciousness is constituted by an accessibility-relation to occurrent thinkings, where those thinkings are conscious in turn (that is, where they are regularly made available to further occurrent thinkings, which are, if they occur, in turn made available to yet further thinkings, and so on). Conscious experiences, in particular, are those which are *available to acts of thinking which are reflexively available to further thinkings*. Conscious occurrent thinkings – conscious acts of wondering-whether, judging-that, supposing-that, and the like – are those which are *made available to further, indefinitely reflexive, thinking*. And conscious (dormant) beliefs and desires are those which are *apt to emerge as* such reflexively available thinkings. Let me now work through some examples of each of these three categories of conscious state (namely, perception, occurrent thinking, and standing-state thought), by way of illustration.

What makes my perception of a glass on the desk to be conscious, on this account, is the fact that perceptual information about the glass is held in a short-term memory store whose function is to make that information available to conscious thinkings – where those thinkings are conscious, too, in virtue of a record of each one of them being fed back, reflexively, to the same (or similar) short-term memory store to be available to be thought about in turn. When I consciously perceive the glass, my perceptual state makes it possible for me to entertain indexical thoughts about the glass (for example, '*That* glass is nearly empty'), and also thoughts about my experience of the glass (for example, 'It *seems* to me rather as if that glass were made of plastic') – where these thoughts, if they were to occur, would themselves be conscious ones.

What makes an occurrent thought (for example, my occurrent judgement that the glass is nearly empty) to be conscious, on this account, is that it is made available to further thought through the operation of a regular feed-back loop whose function is to make such thoughts available to yet further thoughts. So I can entertain a thought (for example, '*That* glass is nearly empty'), think about what I have just thought (for example, 'Why am I thinking about the glass when I should be writing?'), think about that thought in turn (for example, 'But thoughts like *that* don't actually help to *get* me writing'), and so on indefinitely, in principle. (Of course it would be rare for these reflexive embeddings to go more than one or two deep in reality; but the potential must be there, according to the RT account.)

Finally, what makes a standing-state thought (for example, my belief that my sister was born on the 4th of July) to be conscious, on this account, is that it is disposed to emerge as an act of occurrent conscious thinking with the very same content. So what constitutes my belief as a conscious one, is that I am apt to think to myself, in suitable circumstances, 'Ann was born on the 4th of July' (note, a propositional episode with the very same content as the dormant, standing-state, belief) – where this act, in turn, is available for me to think about in acts of thinking which would be made available for me to think about, in virtue of the regular, reflexive, feed-back mechanisms constitutive of conscious thinking. This is why the most basic way of discovering whether or not you believe that P is to ask yourself, 'Is it the case that P?', and to accept that you do believe it if you find yourself inclined to answer, 'Yes' (see section 6.4 above) – it is because a conscious belief that P *is* one which is apt to emerge in the conscious occurrent judgement that P.

The basic structure of the RT theory may be represented in the form of a box-diagram, as in Figure 2. On this account, perceptual information, of varying degrees of complexity and abstractness, is fed into two (or more) short-term memory stores, labelled C (*conscious*) and N (*non-conscious*), whose function is to make that information available to various kinds of thinking and practical reasoning. In the case of non-conscious perception, perceptual information *about the world* (and about the agent's own body), in N, is made available to be integrated with the agent's non-consciously activated (not presently reflexively available) beliefs and goals, so as to determine detailed, action-guiding intentions. This, I hypothesise, is

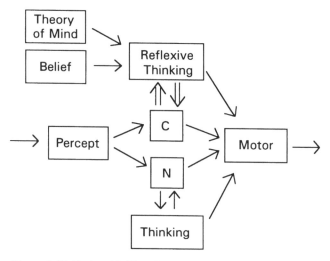

Figure 2 Reflexive thinking theory

what happens in the examples of absent-minded driving, of sleep-walking, and of blindsight.

Notice that there is an arrow back up from non-conscious thinking to N, representing that a record of each thought-content is retained in memory, to be re-employed at a later stage in the reasoning process if necessary. This is there in the model because any reasoning system of any complexity would have to keep at least a brief record of its own earlier thoughts. Drawing a conclusion from a combination of two premises, for example, *takes time*, and so the contents of those premises would have to be retained in memory long enough after their initial activation for them to achieve their effects. I shall return to this point again in section 7.3 below.

In the case of conscious experience, perceptual information, in C, is made available to reflexive thinking, and to be integrated into the control of action. This information is made available *in dual mode* (hence the double arrow up from C). That is, the perceptual information is available not only in respect of what it is a perception *of*, but also in respect of *it being* such a perception. It is not just the content of the experience, but also the fact that such an experience is occurring, which is available to reflexive thinking, when it is conscious.

The double arrow down to C is there to represent the reflexive structure of conscious thinking. I propose that a brief record of everything which we consciously think is passed to a short-term memory store (probably, but not necessarily, the same as the one involved in conscious experience) whose function is to make what we have thought, *and the fact that we have thought it*, available to be thought about in turn – and it is in virtue of this fact that those acts of thinking are conscious, according to the theory.

These double arrows up to and down from C presuppose, of course, that reflexive thinking has available to it the concepts of *perception* and *thought* (among others) which it can bring to bear on the contents of C. Since these concepts are embedded in, and presuppose, a common-sense theory of the structure and functioning of the mind (see Chapter 1), I have included in Figure 2 a box for theory of mind, with access-relations to reflexive thinking. Whether this should be conceived of as a fully-fledged and innate module (albeit a central one, operating upon conceptual rather than perceptual inputs – see Smith and Tsimpli, 1995, ch. 5), or whether it should be thought of as developing from a substantive innate basis of domain-specific constraints and attention-biases (see Karmiloff-Smith, 1992), is not something that I need to take a stand on here.

It is important to note that the double arrows up from C and down from reflexive thinking do not represent dual *channels* of informational transfer or accessibility. As will become clearer in section 7.4 below, the hypothesis is *not* that two separate sets of perceptual information are made available to conscious thinking – namely, information about the world, and information about my perception of the world. Rather, it is the reflexive thinking faculty's capacity to think about the perceptual information in C *in two ways* (in terms of its content, and in terms of its occurrence) which constitutes the dual access. Similarly, there are not two separate records of each conscious thought passed back down to C from reflexive thinking. Rather, a record of each conscious thought is mandatorily passed to C, and again it is the capacity of the reflexive thinking faculty to think about those thoughts *in two ways* (in respect of their content, and in respect of their occurrence) which constitutes the dual access upwards to reflexive thinking once again.

Consonant with the above points, indeed, I do not intend the provision of separate boxes for C and for reflexive thinking in Figure 2 to entail a commitment to the separate existence of the two systems. It may well be, that is, that reflexive thinking takes place *within* the very short-term memory store which also holds perceptual information in such a way as to make it available to such thinking. It *may* be that consciousness involves two separate memory systems – a dedicated short-term perceptual memory store, and a working-memory system which supports reflexive thinking – or it may be that there is just one memory system which performs both tasks. It would certainly be of some interest to seek empirical data to resolve the difference between these two hypotheses in the case of human beings. But the status of RT theory itself would be unaffected by the outcome.

7.2   Contrasts and advantages

The theory of consciousness embodied in Figure 2 is similar to the fourth of the higher-order thought theories considered in Chapter 6 (in section 6.4). For here, too, consciousness is defined in terms of *availability* to *conscious* thinking, where it is crucial to the account that the thinking in question can be higher-order (that is, involving thoughts *about* experience, or thoughts *about* thought). So we can still avoid the Williamson-type counter-examples to the third of the higher-order thought theories (see section 6.3). Because conscious thought is required to be available to *conscious* higher-order thought, according to RT theory, there is no problem raised by the existence of cases where someone displays *non*-conscious higher-order awareness of a first-order thought without that thought thereby being conscious. But there are two main differences from Theory 4, each of which is to the advantage of RT theory.

First, the provision of a reflexive feed-back loop down to C *explains* how a mental state can be conscious in virtue of its availability to conscious thought, where the account of the conscious status of the latter is (recursively) exactly the same. By hypothesis, each thought which is entertained by the reflexive thinking faculty is briefly held in memory in such a way as to be available to be thought about in turn; and those further thoughts, if they were to occur, would be made available in the same way to yet further thought; and so on indefinitely. There is no mystery here.

Second, on the RT account – in contrast with the account provided in Theory 4 – standing-state beliefs and desires do *not* attain their status as conscious in virtue of their disposition to produce a second-order belief in their own existence. Rather, they attain that status because (and if) they are apt to emerge in conscious occurrent judgements with the *same* contents. (This is how the arrow from belief to reflexive thinking in Figure 2 is to be interpreted.) It is only these latter events, in turn, which are conscious in virtue of being apt to cause a belief in their own occurrence, via the reflexive feed-back loop to C. RT theory only goes second-order at the second level, as it were.

The account embodied in Figure 2 is also very similar to Dennett's 1978a theory (on which, indeed, it was modelled). But there are two main differences, each of which is, again, to the advantage of RT theory. *First*, on the RT account the conscious status of an event or state is defined in terms of its accessibility to (conscious) *thinking*, rather than in terms of its accessibility to linguistic report. Indeed, nothing whatever is said about the need for language in the RT model (a point I shall shortly return to). *Second*, the thinkings in question, unlike Dennett's dispositions to make reports, are charged with some executive control in the life and cognition of the organism. Hence the arrow from reflexive thinking to the motor-control system – it is, at least sometimes, *because* of the things which we consciously think, that we go on to think and act as we do.

The diagram in Figure 2 needs to be made a good deal more complicated, of course, in various ways. To begin with, there should also be boxes for (standing-state) desire and intention, with arrows leading to reflexive thinking to represent that these states are conscious in virtue of being disposed to emerge in conscious thinkings with the same content (and in the appropriate mood, of course – a standing-state desire that P is apt to emerge in thoughts of the form, 'Would that P!', or, 'If only P!', or, 'It would be good if P'; a standing-state intention that P is apt to emerge in thoughts of the form, 'I shall make it the case that P', or, 'I am to make it true that P'). The boxes for belief, desire, and intention would also need to be provided with arrows to non-conscious thinking, if beliefs and desires which are available to consciousness can sometimes be activated non-consciously. For, as we noted in section 5.2, it is likely that beliefs and desires very often become activated without emerging in conscious thinkings at the time.

In addition to the above, there would need to be added to the model further belief and desire boxes with arrows *only* to non-conscious thinking, if there are beliefs and desires which are inaccessible to consciousness, as Freudian theories postulate, for example. We should also need to find a place in the model for emotion, and for the relations between perception, thought, and long-term memory; and so on. But these matters may safely be left to one side. (For some fruitful suggestions, see Henry Wellman's excellent flow-chart of our common-sense model of the organisation of the mind in his 1990, p. 109.) For our task is only to sketch those aspects of the structure of cognition which are directly relevant to the characterisation of consciousness.

The theory given here, like Dennett's 1978a account discussed in section 6.5 above, can explain the distinction between conscious and non-conscious phenomena while avoiding all the difficulties inherent in the various forms of Armstrong-type (higher-order thought) accounts. But, unlike Dennett's, it does not tie consciousness to natural language, either by definition or by natural necessity. So the Stalnaker Martians can come out as conscious, on the RT account, provided that their cognition is so structured that their experiences and thoughts are regularly made available to acts of thinking which are, in turn, made available to further thinking. This is, I think, to the advantage of the present proposal.

The RT account also has the further advantage over Dennett's 1978a, of allowing that the evolution of consciousness may have had value for survival independent of its use in self-reporting, by providing the organism with an indefinitely improvable problem solving capability. A faculty of reflexive thinking would get us the ability to think about, and hence modify and improve upon, our own thoughts and patterns of thinking on a regular basis. This is, surely, at the very heart of human adaptability and success, quite apart from any advantages which may accrue from communication. By thinking about what we have just thought, we are able to assess our thoughts for truth, plausibility, and appropriateness. And by thinking about the manner in which we have just been trying to think about a problem, we can sometimes see the possibility, or the need, of approaching it differently. To coin a slogan (albeit an ugly one): meta-access breeds hyper-flexibility.

This is not to deny that non-conscious thought can be flexible, of course. Indeed, all propositional thinking brings a degree of flexibility and adaptability to the organisms which enjoy it. And if the point made in section 5.2 was sound, concerning the non-conscious status of much creative thinking, then it would seem that non-conscious thinking, in the human case at least, can be genuinely innovative. I do not intend to deny these points. But a capacity for reflexive thinking gets you, in addition, the ability to reflect on, think about, and systematically assess and criticise, your own patterns of thinking and reasoning. There is, surely, every reason to think that this capacity would have brought further adaptive advantages.

Indeed, we can also begin to see *how* consciousness might have evolved, on the above account. The proposal will be elaborated for the human case in the next chapter, but basically there appear to be two necessary ingredients, in general. The first prerequisite for consciousness would have been a theory of mind, or folk-psychology (presumably innate, or having a substantial innate basis; perhaps somewhat similar to that arguably possessed by chimpanzees today – see Byrne and Whiten, 1988; but see also Povinelli, 1996). This would provide the concepts of *belief, desire, intention,* and *experience* which are to be used self-ascriptively within the model. Then, second, a kind of feed-back loop would need to be added to the relationship between experience and main decision making, so that what has just been thought or decided is then available to be thought about in turn. Each of these steps may have had independent value in survival; and we can, I shall argue, at least begin to understand what structures might instantiate them in human beings.

There is a final point of contrast to be made, this time with Dennett's 1991 theory. Since the RT theory proposes a determinate short-term memory store, C, functionally defined by its relation to reflexive thinking, it will generally be determinate whether or not a given mental state is conscious. Roughly speaking, either that state is in C, or it is not (with perhaps some scope for vagueness at the margins, particularly for finely discriminated temporal intervals). So, according to the RT theory, and in contrast with the multiple drafts theory, it will generally be determinate whether or not any given experience or thought is a conscious one. This is, I believe, to the advantage of the former. For whatever one might think about phenomena such as *colour phi*, it is very hard to believe that there are no determinate truths about my conscious experiences and thought-processes, independently of my actual dispositions to report them. However, I shall return, in section 7.7 below, to consider whether my own theory, in turn, is vulnerable to the charge of endorsing an unacceptable form of 'Cartesian Theatre' conception of consciousness.

In most of what remains of this chapter I shall attempt to defend the RT theory of consciousness against various kinds of objection. But first, in the next section, I propose to say rather more about the distinction between conscious and non-conscious thinking. For, while the account of conscious thinking gains plausibility from being embedded within a broader theory of consciousness in general, it is that account in particular which is necessary to the argument of Chapter 8 – and, indeed, to the argument of this book as a whole.

7.3 Conscious versus non-conscious thinking

Notice, to begin with, that it is not enough to constitute an occurrent thought as a conscious one that the thinker should have access to *what* they have just thought. Any reasoning system of any complexity would have to keep some record of its own earlier processes, so as to make use of an earlier premise or conclusion, or so as to conditionalise on an earlier assumption, for example. (This is the reason for the single arrow back up from non-conscious thinking to N in Figure 2 above.) Thus, any system capable of deriving the conclusion Q from the pair of premises P and $(P \supset (P \supset Q))$, must be able to hold onto the first premise for long enough to be able to re-use it in connection with the embedded conditional, following the first step of *modus ponens*, so as to derive the conclusion Q. But this need not involve any sort of meta-representation – to *remember* an earlier thought is not necessarily to *represent that* it was thought. What is distinctive of conscious thinking, on my view, is that thinkers should also have access to the fact that certain thoughts occurred in certain sequences, involving meta-representations of their own earlier occurrent thoughts.

Note also, that, while it is essential to conscious thinking that we should be capable of thinking about *what* we have just thought, and *the fact that* we have just thought it, it is not necessary that we should have access to *the way in which* we thought it. For I do not believe that it is essential to consciousness as such, that conscious thinking should involve access to, and the possibility of thought about, the *forms* as well as the contents and the occurrences of our thoughts. It may be that this is, of natural necessity, an ingredient in the structure of *human* consciousness, as I shall propose in the next chapter. But it is possible (both naturally and conceptually) that there should be kinds of conscious cognition which lack it.

I no longer believe, as I once did (1992b), that an organism's access to the forms of its own occurrent thoughts is a necessary ingredient in any kind of reflexive (conscious) thinking. For there might possibly be organisms which can have thoughts about their own recent thinkings, on a regular basis, but specified by content rather than by mode of expression. And I can see no grounds for denying that their thoughts would, in consequence, be conscious ones. We can even see how the underlying mechanisms might be constructed, I believe.

Suppose that *thinking that P* were constituted by entertaining, in appropriate mode, some sentence 'S' (of Mentalese, as it might be) which means that P. Then you could imagine a mechanism which operated by semantic ascent, so that the occurrence of 'S' in the belief mode would automatically cause the creature to be disposed to think, 'I have just thought that S' (or rather its Mentalese equivalent; where this would, by hypothesis, be the same as thinking that it has just entertained the thought that P). But this would happen without the creature having any awareness of, or mode of access to, the fact that the sentence 'S' was used in the expression of the original belief. I do not believe that this is how *we* have access to our own recent thoughts, as will emerge in the next chapter. But it is, surely, a real possibility – it might, for example, be how the Stalnaker Martians would have access to their thoughts, and I do not think we would want to deny, merely on that basis, that their thoughts were really conscious ones.

I have made the point that conscious thinking must involve *more* that mere access to the *contents* of previous thoughts; and also that it could involve *less* than full access to the *forms* in which those thoughts are entertained. Rather, conscious thinking requires us to have access to *the contents and the occurrences* of our acts of thinking, just as RT theory proposes. I shall now make the point that the kind of access required must be *non-inferential*. Or, more strictly (since it is at least arguable that any kind of cognitive access will involve sub-personal inferences of one sort or another), I shall argue that conscious thinking should *not* involve the kind of *interpretative* access to our own thoughts which we have to the thoughts of other people. It is possible that our access to our own previous conscious thoughts may involve sub-personal computations and inferences, as Alison Gopnik, for example, has argued (1993). But I claim that this access is *not* of the kind that we have to the thoughts of other people (or sometimes to the thoughts of our own past selves) when we successfully ascribe thoughts to them in such a way as to provide the best available interpretation of their actions.

As we noted in section 5.2 above, it is likely that beliefs and desires can very often become activated without emerging in conscious thinkings at the time. If so, then it will follow that attributing reasons to ourselves, even in relation to the very recent past, is often a matter of highly fallible self-interpretation. This has, to my mind, been convincingly demonstrated by a wide variety of experimental studies in which subjects offer explanations of their own recent actions which are wildly at variance with the known facts. (See Nisbett and Wilson, 1977, Nisbett and Ross, 1980, Wilson *et al.*, 1981, Wilson and Stone, 1985, and Wilson, 1985.) I will discuss some of these cases rather more fully in section 8.3 below. But, for example, if subjects are asked to choose from an array of identical items (shirts, say) identically presented, they will generally show a marked preference for items from the right-hand side of the display. But if asked to *explain* their choice, subjects will not mention position, but will rather say things like, 'It was made of better quality cloth', or, 'It was a nicer shade of colour.'

These explanations are plainly confabulated after the fact. (Remember, there was really no difference at all between the items in question.) My account of what happens in such cases will be this: lacking conscious access to the thoughts which actually determined their choice, subjects are forced to self-interpret, ascribing thoughts to themselves in such a way as to explain their action, just as they would if the action were that of another person. And it may be that many of the occurrent thoughts which people are ordinarily prepared to ascribe to themselves (normally rather more reliably than this, no doubt) are of this same non-conscious variety. Preparedness to self-ascribe an occurrent thought is thus no guarantee that the thought in question was consciously activated.

Still, my claim is that we do sometimes have access to our thinkings and reasonings which is non-inferential, at least in the sense that it is not a matter of self-*interpretation* – namely, when they take place as occurrent events within the reflexive thinking faculty. That is to say, at least sometimes our thinkings are formulated in such a way that a brief record of their occurrence is maintained in the short-term memory store C, whose function is to make them available, reflexively, to further conscious thinking. And it is only in such cases that the thoughts in question count as conscious, according to RT theory. Moreover, it is in such cases (and perhaps only in such cases) that our access to our own recent thinkings is pretty solidly reliable. When our occurrent thinkings are reflexively available (and hence conscious) we do not have to self-ascribe them on the basis of an interpretation of our own behaviour (and/or of our other mental states); rather, they are already there, in C, available to thought.

Notice that the distinction drawn here, between two very different ways in which occurrent thoughts can be self-ascribed (through self-interpretation, and through reflexive availability), gives me the materials with which to reply to one of the points made against the argument from introspection of Chapter 2. This was the point that we are often aware of our occurrent thoughts *without* being aware of any sentence figuring in imagination as the vehicle of the thought (see section 2.4). My reply is to distinguish between those cases where we are genuinely (reflexively) *aware* of what we have just thought, and those cases which are superficially similar in the sense that we are very swiftly prepared to *self-ascribe* a thought, but where the self-ascription is made on the basis of a self-interpretation. It is only in the former kind of case that the thoughts in question count as conscious, on the present account; and it is only in the former kind of case that there necessarily is, in the case of human beings, an intimate connection with public language, as I shall argue in Chapter 8.

7.4   Objections and elucidations

The RT theory faces a number of objections. First, it might be claimed that the theory must founder on a version of the cognitive overload problem, raised in relation to the second of the four second-order theories of consciousness considered in the last chapter (see 6.2). For if the perceptual information in the memory-store C has to be made available to reflexive thinking in dual mode – first in respect of the content of the perception, and second in respect of the occurrence of that perception – then does that not mean that the system would have to form a complete meta-representation of everything which is consciously experienced? When I perceive a complex scene, on this suggestion, would there not first have to be a complex representation of all the perceived details of that scene, and then an equally complex meta-representation of the fact that all of those details are experienced? And is this not, on empirical grounds, immensely implausible?

Indeed, it is implausible. But I believe that such an extra level of representational complexity is simply not needed on the RT account. For the very same perceptual states which represent the world to us (or the conditions of our own bodies) can at the same time represent the fact that those aspects of the world (or of our bodies) are being perceived. It is the fact that the faculty of reflexive thinking to which experiences are made available *can make use of them* in dual mode which turns those experiences into dual-mode representations; there do not actually have to be two physically distinct sets of representations to carry the two sets of perceptual information. This means, notice, that it is quite wrong to think of introspection on the model of external perception – for on the RT account there certainly do not have to be *inner detectors* of our conscious perceptions, acting somewhat like sense-organs to create a distinct meta-representation of the latter.

Compare the following: one and the same photograph of a portrait painting – the *Mona Lisa*, say – is a dual representation, both of the original sitter and of the portrait itself. This is so in virtue of the fact that it can be used by us in two different ways, depending on our purposes and interests. It can be used, first, as a representation of the sitter, so that we may gather from it information about that woman's appearance, wonder what she may have been thinking when in the pose captured by the artist, and so on. Then, second, the photograph can be used as a representation of the portrait itself, so that we can gather from it information about the artist's style, marvel at the deftness of his brush-strokes, and such like. The way in which it represents, on any given occasion, depends upon the use which is made of it by the viewer – that is, upon the nature and powers of the 'consumer-system', as Ruth Millikan would put it (see her 1984).

Similarly in the case of perceptual representations, in my view: it is the fact that perceptual information is present to a system which is capable of discriminating between, and making judgements about, those perceptual states *as such* which constitutes those states as second-order representations of experience, as well as first-order representations of the world (or of states of the body). To put the point in terms of RT theory: when perceptual information about the glass on the desk (say) is held in the short-term memory store C, the subject is capable of making judgements, grounded in that experience, either about the glass, or about their experience of the glass. And it is in virtue of this fact that the subject's perceptual representation is at the same time a meta-representation of its own occurrence. Put somewhat more abstractly and generally: it is because the subject's perceptual state can ground judgements like, '*That* experience may be delusory', as well as judgements like, '*That* glass is nearly empty', that the subject is aware of their own perceptual state, as well as being aware of the state of the world which it represents. So there is, I maintain, no problem of cognitive overload on the RT account.

(Notice that I have here, once again, committed myself to some form of functional-role semantics, of the sort discussed in Chapter 4. For I have claimed that the content of a representation depends, at least in part, upon the further *use* which is made of that representation within a cognitive system – what inferences it may engage in, what further judgements it may lead to, and so on. It would only be an adherence to some form of pure co-variance semantics which would warrant the claim that RT theory has to be committed to a double layer of distinct representational states, and so which would mean that the theory runs foul of the cognitive overload problem.)

Another objection parallels the one levelled against the third of the second-order theories of consciousness considered in the last chapter (see 6.3). The objection in this case is that my account analyses what is, in fact, a categorical state – a conscious experience – into dispositional terms; since I claim, namely, that perceptual information is *made available to* thinking which is regularly made available to further thinking. But my reply to this is the same as before. Whenever there is a conscious experience there *will* be a categorical state present, on the RT account. For the perceptual information is really there, active and occurrent, in the short-term memory store C. It is merely that this store is functionally defined by its availability-relations with reflexive thinking.

The next objection cannot be dealt with quite so swiftly. It is this: that there could surely be reflexive thinking which was *non*-conscious – in which case, the fact that an occurrent thought is of a type which is regularly made available to further thought cannot be a sufficient condition for it to count as a conscious one. It might be claimed, for example, that there could be all kinds of different levels within human cognition where these sorts of reflexive, feed-back, loops occur, but in which the component thoughts are not plausibly thought of as conscious ones.

In fact, I doubt very much whether such multiple feed-back loops really exist. For remember, to be of the right form the sub-system in question would have to be capable of thinking about its own component thoughts *as such,* and so would need to have a theory of mind (or at least a substantial fragment of one) in which such a concept could be embedded. But I would have to concede that *if* the appropriate sort of reflexive thinking occurs at any given level within our cognition, then the resulting thoughts would count as conscious. However, I do not see this as an objection. I do not know what *more* could plausibly be demanded of a thought, for it to count as a conscious one, other than that it is immediately available to be thought about *as* a thought – in such a way that the subject knows that they have it, and can think about the fact that they are having it.

Presumably the objector will claim that what is left out of the RT account is the distinctive phenomenology of thought – for to say that there is thinking about thinking is, as yet, to say nothing about phenomenology. Now, I do concede the force of the parallel demand in the case of experience. I agree that any account of conscious experience needs to find some place for the phenomenology – the distinctive feel – of experience; and some of the later sections of this chapter will be devoted to meeting this demand from the standpoint of the RT theory. I also concede that there is a kind of phenomenology associated with *human* conscious thinking, in so far as we are generally aware, not only of *what* we have just thought and the fact that we thought it, but also of the *way* in which we thought it – namely, the words or images which carried that content for us.

What I deny is that this is an essential feature of conscious thinking as such, in the way that phenomenal feelings *are* an essential feature of conscious experiences. For, as we saw in section 7.3 above, we should have no difficulty with the idea of modes of conscious cognition different from ours, in which thinkers *only* have access to the contents and occurrences of their thoughts, not to the forms in which those thoughts are expressed. Moreover, we surely have no temptation to believe that the words or images in which a thought is expressed are essential to the occurrence and existence of that thought, in the way that we *are* tempted to maintain that the phenomenal feel of a pain is essential to its existence. So although I agree that conscious thinking does have a kind of phenomenology, for us, this is not essential to the status of that thinking as conscious.

One further worry concerns the flow of information into and out of the various boxes in Figure 2 – for what determines it? What is it that controls *which* processed aspects of any given visual scene make it through to consciousness (to C), for example? This may be a vital question for the scientific psychologist, part of whose brief is to understand *how* cognitive processes occur. But it is less obviously an important issue for me. RT theory purports to tell us what it *is* for any given mental state to be conscious; it does not attempt to explain how or why that state *came to be* conscious. I presume, in fact, that the flow of information through cognition is partly determined by a variety of non-conscious control systems; but also partially determined by the contents of (conscious) cognition itself. What you consciously perceive in any given situation may be determined, partly non-consciously, but also partly by the direction of conscious thought and attention.

7.5   The problem of unity

Finally, the RT theory faces the following obvious objection: that the two elements of the account need not be co-instantiated. We can surely conceive, for example, of a creature which has conscious experiences but lacks the capacity to think about its own thoughts. Conversely, we can surely conceive of a creature which can think about its own thoughts while lacking the capacity for conscious experience. But I do not intend to deny either of these claims, in fact. For I am not in the business of conceptual analysis – rather, as I indicated in section 5.5, the RT model is intended as a substantive theory of what consciousness *is*, similar in form to the claim that water is H_2O. So there is no basis, here, for an objection that the RT account fails to establish a *conceptual* connection between conscious experience and conscious thought. For that is not the business it is in. Its business is rather to elucidate and flesh-out an aspect of the theory of the mind embodied in our common-sense, or 'folk', psychology.

In rejoinder it may be said that, even granting this, it is highly implausible that when ordinary people think of a conscious experience they think of one which is available to reflexive thinking. So the RT account does not even seem to be descriptively true of common-sense psychology. But there are two replies to this. The first is that the principles and generalisations of common-sense psychology are largely implicit, embodying a theory which is by no means fully articulated by its practitioners, and which will, in part, be innately given. Since much of the theory will not, in any case, be at the front of people's minds when they employ common-sense psychological concepts, it would hardly be surprising that when they think of an experience being conscious, they do not think of it in the terms characterised by the RT account.

The second reply is that the concept of consciousness which forms our target may, in fact, be a boundary-concept of common-sense psychology, setting the limits of its theoretical domain (and so almost invisible from *within* the domain). For until very recently in the history of our species most people would have – indeed, many did – regard consciousness as definitive of the mental. It has only been with the development of scientific psychology – first Freudian, now Cognitive – that the idea that there are non-conscious mental states has come to enjoy anything like general currency. Elucidating the concept of consciousness may then involve extending our common-sense theories beyond the original bounds of folk-psychology.

It is, therefore, too much to demand, as a condition on the acceptability of the RT account of consciousness, that we should be able to establish that it is either conceptually necessary or intuitively obvious that information present to a faculty of reflexive thinking will at the same time have a subjective feel to it, and conversely that any perceptual state with a subjective feel must be present to a faculty of reflexive thinking. All the same, it surely *is* a genuine requirement on the acceptability of RT theory – if it is to be a theory of what consciousness, *in general*, is – that we be able to establish that it is *naturally* necessary that any cognitive system whose perceptual states possess subjective feel will also be capable of reflexive thinking, and that any system capable of reflexive thinking will also enjoy phenomenal feelings.

I have to confess, at this point, that I am unable to demonstrate anything quite so strong. In particular, I am unable to show that any system whose perceptual states have feels must also be capable of reflexive thinking. I argued, in section 5.8 above, that any system whose perceptual states have feel must also be capable of higher-order thought, but this is not enough to establish the point. For there may possibly be systems capable of higher-order thinking (which are therefore capable of attributing thoughts to themselves and other organisms, and of assessing those thoughts for truth and falsity), but in which those thoughts are not *regularly made available to* further thinking. If may be that the perceptual states in such systems are present to a faculty of thinking which is capable of thinking about thoughts, which can distinguish between appearance and reality, and so which can recognise its own perceptual states, as such, as and when they occur. But the system may lack the sort of feed-back loop necessary for it to subject its own thinkings to further thought on a regular basis. This would then be a (naturally possible) system whose perceptual states would have phenomenal feels, but which would lack a fully-developed capacity for reflexive thinking.

Although I have had to allow that the RT theory fails to provide a complete account of what consciousness, in general, is, I do want to make the following four claims.

(1) RT theory does at least provide a full account of the nature of *human* consciousness; *our* experiences, at least, are conscious because they are present to a faculty of reflexive thinking.

(2) RT theory does at least provide an account of what conscious *thinking*, in general, essentially is; any organism whose occurrent thoughts are conscious must satisfy the relevant portions of the RT model.

(3) Any system which is capable of reflexive thinking must, of natural necessity, have its perceptual states available to such thinking *in dual mode* (as representation of the world, and as representation of experience).

(4) Any system whose perceptual states are available to reflexive

thinking in dual mode must also (and this time perhaps of *metaphysical* necessity) be a subject of phenomenal feelings. I shall shortly discuss each of these points in turn. But first let me remark that it is claims (1) and (2) which are essential (and sufficient) for the project of this book, especially as its argument will unfold in the final chapter. Claims (3) and (4) are of importance only in so far as they lend further, supplementary, support to claims (1) and (2).

(1) The claim that RT theory provides a full account of the nature of human consciousness has already been partially defended over the course of the last three chapters. It will be further defended in the remainder of this chapter, and in the chapter which follows. In fact, some of the arguments in support of RT theory, and against other forms of higher-order thought theory, turned on factors which may be specific to human consciousness. Then if they are successful, RT theory must at least have the status of a full theory of what *human* consciousness is, if not of consciousness in general. Moreover, I shall shortly be arguing that the presence of perceptual states to a faculty of reflexive thinking (in the case of human beings, at least), does provide us with an *explanation of* the felt qualities of the former.

(2) The claim that RT theory provides an account of what conscious thinking in general essentially is has already been adequately defended in the last chapter, and again in section 7.3 of the present chapter. If the arguments of Chapter 6 were sound, then no occurrent thought could be conscious without being available to further occurrent conscious thought – that is, without being available to reflexive thinking. And if the points made in section 7.3 above were sound, then the availability of an occurrent thought to reflexive thinking is sufficient for it to count as conscious.

(3) The truth of the claim that any system capable of reflexive thinking must have its perceptual states available to such thinking in dual mode follows, I believe, from the point made in section 7.4 above, that the dual availability of conscious perception to reflexive thinking arises, not through the existence of an extra informational channel between the two, but rather out of the conceptual powers of the latter. It is *because* the reflexive thinking faculty has access to a theory of mind, including concepts of perception and experience, that perceptual states present to that faculty achieve dual status, being available to thought, both in respect of their content and in respect of their occurrence. It follows, therefore, that any organism capable of reflexive thinking, in which perceptual information is made available to thought, must also be capable, in principle, of recognising the occurrence of its own perceptual states.

(Note that I am now claiming, in effect, that any extreme version of the confident blindsighted man, discussed in section 5.6, is naturally impossible. While blindsighted patients may possibly be able to train themselves to guess what is where, on a regular basis and without prompting, this is just to say that they would regularly form perceptually based *beliefs*. And this is surely consistent with their perceptual states remaining non-conscious ones. But if we imagine such a patient having access to analogue perceptual information about their environment, in such a way, for example, that they can entertain fine-grained demonstrative thoughts about that environment on a regular basis (for example, '*That* cup would fit in *that* space on *that* shelf'), then this is inconsistent with their remaining blindsighted, in my view. For they would then be in position to recognise their own perceptual states, as and when they occur – which is, on the RT account, sufficient for those states to count as conscious ones.)

I suppose it might be objected that an organism could be capable of reflexive thinking, and thus possess concepts of thought and belief, while *lacking* any concept of perception or perceptual experience. Then such an organism, while enjoying reflexive thinking, would *not* have its perceptual states available to it in dual mode, contrary to what is maintained in claim (3) above. But in fact, everything that we know about the development of common-sense psychology suggests that such an organism is naturally impossible. That is, everything we know suggests that some sort of desire-perception psychology is a *necessary* precursor of full-blown belief-desire psychology (see Wellman, 1990, and many of the contributions in Carruthers and Smith, 1996). This is because concepts of thought and belief can be of no use to an organism unless it *also* has the capacity to understand how those thoughts come to be related to the world, and to action, through perception.

(4) This claim – that any system whose perceptual states are available to reflexive thinking in dual mode must also be a subject of phenomenal feels – is the one which really matters, if RT theory is to achieve acceptance as a general theory of (human) consciousness. For it might be objected that all of the above is, in any case, to miss the point. Even if I had been successful in showing that cognitive systems which are capable, both of recognising their own perceptual states and of thinking reflexively about their own acts of thinking, constitute a basic package (inevitably evolving together), this is not yet to find a place for subjective feelings within such systems. What needs to be shown is that any such system capable of immediate recognition of its perceptual states will at the same time be a subject of phenomenal feels. What needs to be established is that such a recognitional capacity is a sufficient condition for a system to enjoy perceptual states which possess distinctive subjective feels.

Strictly speaking, I do not really need to tackle these questions, given the purposes that I want the RT theory to serve. I want to argue, in

Chapter 8, that human cognition is so structured that our capacity for conscious thinking involves (of natural necessity) the deployment of public language sentences in imagination. All that I shall need, for this, is that reflexive thinking should be a naturally *necessary* condition for the enjoyment of conscious mental states, at least in human beings. I do not also need to claim that it is sufficient. All the same, the sufficiency claim seems well worth pursuing. This is partly because it is interesting in its own right. But it is also because, if successfully defended, it may further strengthen and lend plausibility to the sort of approach to the understanding of consciousness which I have been developing in this chapter. As I remarked, at the end of Chapter 5, the most convincing ground for accepting any theory is generally that it provides the best *explanation* of the data; and in the present case the datum to be explained is that our conscious experiences have a subjective, phenomenal, aspect to them.

7.6   The problem of phenomenal feel

I now propose to argue, therefore, that phenomenal feelings will emerge, of natural (perhaps metaphysical) necessity, in any system where perceptual information is made available to thought in analogue form, and where the system is capable of recognising its own perceptual states, as well as the states of the world perceived. (The necessity here may be metaphysical, rather than merely natural, because the relation in question is one of *identity*, I shall claim. Everything will then turn on whether or not one uses the terms in question *rigidly* – see section 1.1.) For by postulating that this is so, we can explain why phenomenal feelings should be so widely thought to possess the properties of *qualia* – of being non-relationally defined, private, ineffable, and knowable with complete certainty by the subject.

I shall argue, in fact, that any subjects who instantiate such a cognitive system (that is, who instantiate the RT model depicted in Figure 2 above) will normally come to form just such beliefs about the intrinsic characteristics of their perceptual states – and they will form such beliefs, not because they have been explicitly programmed to do so, but naturally, as a by-product of the way in which their cognition is structured. I know of no better way of arguing that a regular capacity for thought about one's own mental states must be a sufficient condition for the enjoyment of experiences which possess a subjective, phenomenal, feel to them.

Non-relational definition

Let us first consider the thesis of non-relational definition for terms referring to the subjective aspects of an experience. This is a thesis which many people – philosophers and non-philosophers alike – find tempting, at least. When we reflect on what is essential for an experience to count as an experience *as of red*, for example, we are tempted to deny that it has anything directly to do with being caused by the presence of something red. We are inclined to insist that it is conceptually possible that an experience of that very type should normally have been caused by the presence of something green, say. All that is truly essential to the occurrence of an experience *as of red*, on this view, is the way such an experience feels to us when we have it – it is the distinctive feel of an experience which defines it, not its distinctive relational properties or causal role.

Now, notice that any system instantiating the RT theory of consciousness will have the capacity to classify informational states according to the manner in which they carry their information, not by inference (that is, by self-interpretation) or description, but immediately. The system will be capable of recognising the fact that it has an experience *as of red*, say, in just the same direct, non-inferential, way that it can recognise red. (This is just what it means to say that perceptual states are available to reflexive thinking, in the sense that I intend.) The system will therefore have available to it purely recognitional concepts of experience, embedded within a framework of beliefs about normal causal role. There might then be a natural tendency to 'carve off' these recognitional concepts from their surrounding beliefs, and to use them independently – especially if we find the properties which they pick out to be of intrinsic interest to us. In which case, absent and inverted subjective feelings will immediately be a conceptual possibility for someone applying these recognitional concepts. If I instantiate such a system, I shall immediately be able to think, '*This* type of experience might have had some quite other cause', for example.

I have conceded that there are (possible) concepts of experience which are purely recognitional, and so which are not definable in relational terms. (This is my concession to the semantic thesis of Cartesianism, discussed in sections 5.3 and 5.4 above.) Does this then count against the acceptability of the functionalist conceptual scheme which forms the background to my own account of consciousness? If it is conceptually possible that an experience *as of red* should regularly be caused by perception of green grass or blue sky, then does this mean that the crucial facts of consciousness must escape the functionalist net, as many have alleged? I think not. For, as was pointed out earlier, the RT account is not in the business of conceptual analysis, but of substantive theory development. So it is no objection to that account, that there are some concepts of the mental which cannot be analysed (that is, defined) in terms of functional role, but are purely recognitional – provided that the nature of those concepts, and the states which they recognise, can be adequately characterised within the theory.

According to RT theory, in fact, the properties which are picked out by any purely recognitional concepts of experience are not, themselves, similarly simple and non-relational. (This makes me a *qualia-irrealist* – I claim that there *are no* non-relational properties of experience *qua* experience.) When I recognise in myself an experience *as of red*, what I recognise is, in fact, a perceptual state whose normal cause is worldly redness, and which underpins, in turn, my capacity to recognise, and to act differentially upon, red objects. And the purely-recognitional concept, itself, is one whose normal cause is the presence of just such a perceptual state, tokenings of which then cause further characteristic changes within my cognition. There is nothing, here, which need raise any sort of threat to a functionalist theory of the mind.

With the distinction firmly drawn between our recognitional *concepts* of phenomenal feelings, on the one hand, and the *properties* which those concepts pick out, on the other, then I can claim that it is naturally (perhaps metaphysically) necessary that the subjective aspect of an experience of red should be caused, normally, by perception of red. For the RT account tells us that the subjective aspect of an experience of red just *is* analogue information about red, presented to a cognitive apparatus having the power to classify states as information carriers, as well as to classify the information carried. In which case there can be no world (where the laws of nature remain as they are, at least) in which the one exists but not the other. For there will, in fact, be no 'one' and 'other' here, but only one state differently thought of – now recognitionally, now in terms of functional role.

As we saw in section 1.1, indeed, true identities involving terms which are rigid designators are logically (metaphysically) necessary. So if it is one and the same property which is thought about – on the one hand recognitionally, on the other hand in terms of functional role – and if the terms used to refer to that property are used rigidly, then it will be logically necessary that everyone who enjoys the same capacities for colour-discrimination should be subject to the same subjective feelings.

But is it not possible – naturally and metaphysically, as well as conceptually – that there should be organisms possessing colour vision, which are sensitive to the same range of wavelengths as ourselves, but which nevertheless have their phenomenal feelings inverted from ours? I claim not, in fact. For the property of being the subjective feel of an experience of red is a functional one, identical with possession of a distinctive causal role (the causal role namely, of being a state whose normal cause is red, and which is present to a reflexive thinking faculty with the power to recognise its own perceptual states as such). In which case feeling-inversion of the type imagined will be impossible.

Privacy, ineffability, and certainty

Now, given the thesis of non-relational definition, the supposed privacy and ineffability of subjective feelings are easily accounted for, on the RT approach. For the recognition-instances of feeling-concepts cannot, of course, be exhibited to another person. Yet any attempt to describe in relational terms the character of a subjective feeling will seem to miss what is essential to the latter. When I try to describe the feel of my experience of red to you by saying, 'It is what I get when I look at a ripe tomato', it is entirely natural that I should deem myself to have failed to express my meaning. For all that I have done is to indicate the normal cause of my feeling, which has nothing to do with the way in which I myself recognise and conceptualise it.

Moreover, it is a general feature of cognitive systems to which perceptual information is presented in analogue form, that the system will be capable of discriminations which slip through its conceptual net. For example, imagine yourself watching the leaves of a tree shimmering in the breeze. You will be able to discriminate subtle changes in the pattern of movement, and will be aware of the distinctive quality of each pattern, which you are incapable of describing further. In the case of colour perception, similarly, you will be able to discriminate shades from one another where you are incapable of describing the precise difference between them, having to resort to such generalities as, 'A slightly darker shade of red.' You will also be aware of the distinctive quality of each shade without being able to describe it other than as, 'The shade of *that* object over there.'

Equivalently, then, in the case of awareness of the qualities of the experience itself – you will be able to recognise and respond to subtle distinctions, where you lack the concepts to express the precise differences in question. All you will be able to say is something like, 'It is what it is normally like to perceive *that* shade of red as opposed to *that* shade of red.' And you will be aware of the distinctive quality of each perceptual state without being able to describe it other than as, 'The way it feels to see *that* shade.' Note that this description is relational – it describes the feeling in terms of its normal cause. So anyone who thinks that subjective feelings are not relationally defined will believe that the crucial characteristic of a subjective feel must remain wholly inexpressible. All we can really do is indicate what that feeling is indirectly, by its relationships with other things.

The temptation to believe that phenomenal feels are private is mistaken, however. For 'private', here, means 'unknowable to anyone else'. But in fact there is every reason to believe that the subjective states of other humans are *not* inverted from, or radically different from, my own. (In so far as others have different discriminatory capacities from myself, of course, then to that extent one might expect some differences in felt experience too.) This is so for two reasons. First, because of the similar causal roles which the perceptual states in question manifestly occupy. And second, because of the commonalties in the physical realisations of those states within members of the same species, which further indicate that the detailed inner functional organisation of each member of the species will be the same. Given these facts, I believe I can claim to know that when another person looks at a ripe tomato then they, too, will experience the same (or a similar) subjective experience of red that I do.

The temptation to believe that phenomenal feelings are ineffable is equally mistaken. For communication is about properties and states of affairs, not about concepts and modes of presentation. What successful communication requires is only that the hearer should grasp the very same state of affairs, or the very same truth-condition, which the speaker is describing or expressing. It is not necessary that they should each of them be thinking of that state of affairs in anything like the same way. (For extensive discussion of this point, see my 1989; see also section 4.3 above.) So, provided that my relational descriptions of my subjective feelings succeed in getting across to you the properties which my recognitional concepts pick out, then I shall, in fact, have communicated them successfully. And these properties are, to repeat, relational ones, instantiated by physical properties of the brain which happen to occupy particular causal roles.

Finally, in order to explain the temptation to think that phenomenal feelings are knowable with complete certainty, we can make use of the idea that perceptual information, and the marks by which it is carried, are *present to* thinking which is available to further thinking. There might then easily seem to be no space for error in the classification of those states, other than conceptual error. If all that is involved, when one recognises a subjective state, is an act of classifying a state which is directly present to the classifier mechanisms, then provided that the classifier is in order, it can seem that there is no further room for mistake.

Although this picture is tempting, it, too, is erroneous. For there may be ways in which a classifier mechanism can cease to operate normally which are not dramatic enough for us to say that the system has thereby lost its grasp of the concepts it employs in its judgements. For example, it might prove to be the case that mood can have an effect upon colour judgements. Perhaps anger makes us literally see red, in so far as it slightly skews our colour judgements towards the red end of the spectrum. In which case, it will equally have an effect upon judgements of colour experience. Then, knowing that this is so, you may have grounds to doubt your judgements about some of your subjective states when you are angry.

Feelings explained

I have argued, then, that any system which instantiates the RT model of consciousness must necessarily be a subject of phenomenal feelings. And my argument has been, that any such system would naturally be inclined to make just the sorts of claims about its perceptual states as philosophers who believe in *qualia* have been inclined to make about their subjective feelings. Some of these claims would be true, particularly that absent and inverted feelings are *conceptually* possible. But some, although tempting, would be false. This is the case for the claims of privacy, ineffability, and introspective certainty.

I therefore claim that my RT account can *explain* the subjective feel of experience. I claim that I have, in fact, successfully explained *phenomenal consciousness* in terms of *mental state consciousness* (see section 5.5). For what it *is* for a perceptual state to have subjective feel (in our case, at least), is just for it to be present to a faculty of reflexive thinking with the power to recognise, and to entertain thoughts about, that type of perceptual state as such. (The qualification, 'in our case', is necessary because I concede that something rather less than a full faculty of reflexive thinking might be sufficient for the enjoyment of subjective feelings; see sections 7.5 above and 7.8 below.) I have therefore claimed that RT theory provides us with a naturally (perhaps metaphysically) sufficient condition for a creature to enjoy phenomenal feelings, since the 'is' in question is the 'is' of identity. These points together provide us with a further powerful reason for accepting the RT theory of consciousness.

7.7   A Cartesian Theatre?

I have argued that RT theory can find an adequate place for the subjective feel of experience – that is to say, for phenomenal feelings. But does it also commit us to a version of the 'Cartesian Theatre' conception of consciousness, which has been so vigorously attacked by Dennett (1991) and by Dennett and Kinsbourne (1992)? It might certainly seem so. For what is the short-term memory store C, if not a stage on which conscious experiences and thoughts are displayed for the benefit of the 'audience' of the reflexive thinking faculty? However, much may depend on precisely how the notion of a Cartesian Theatre is explained.

Dennett's characterisation of a Cartesian Theatre is generally this: that it is a single *place* in the brain where 'it all comes together', and at which the time of arrival of perceptual information coincides with – and determines – the time of conscious experience. Granted, there is no such place. Everything suggests that conscious cognition is spatially distributed across wide areas of the cerebral cortex. But as we saw in section 6.6, this leaves open a *functional* version of the same idea – namely, that there is a particular level of functional organisation within the brain at which a wide variety of types of information 'come together', and become conscious in virtue of such coming together. And this level of organisation might be defined by its relationship with reflexive thinking, just as RT theory suggests. (Whether or not the time at which a conscious experience is felt as occurring is determined by the time at which the perceptual information 'comes together' is then a further, separate, question, which I shall shortly answer in the negative.) Such a functional theatre might be widely spatially distributed, just as the neuropsychological evidence suggests.

It might also be suggested that indeterminacies at the margins of consciousness, concerning very brief time-intervals, are just what one might expect if the theatre were functionally defined. For to say that it is so defined, is to say that the question whether or not a particular perceptual content is already in C, at a given time, amounts to the question whether the subject *would* entertain thoughts about that content *if* a question were asked, or *if* it were relevant to the subject's present concerns to do so. But where the time interval in question is very brief, such subjunctive conditionals may have no determinate truth-values. For one way of realising the antecedent of the conditional may lead to one outcome, whereas another may lead to another.

In fact, however, things are not so easy for RT theory. For even when it is construed functionally (as it should be), it cannot avoid some commitment to neurological realisations which are at least intra-personally stable. For how, otherwise, are we to distinguish between a case where an experience was already conscious (represented in C), and was therefore successfully reported on or thought about when the subject was prompted, from a case where the experience was not yet conscious (perhaps represented in N), but *became* conscious when the subject was asked the question? (Remember the chiming of the town hall clock, from section 5.2.) For either way, the subject will provide a successful report. And so, either way, it will be equally true of the subject that they have a perceptual content represented in such a way that *if* they are prompted, *then* they will entertain a conscious thought about that content. Yet it is crucial to RT theory, as I understand it, that such matters should be determinate, at least in general.

We can provide a partial answer to this difficulty by insisting that in order to count as conscious, an experience must be contained in a short-term memory store whose *function* in cognition is to make its contents available to reflexive thinking. I think this forces us to postulate a stable physical realisation for the short-term memory store C, at least for any given individual (which may, nevertheless, still be spatially distributed across a wide area of the cortex). Then the question whether a perceptual content was already conscious, or merely apt to become conscious, will come down to the question whether it was already activated in that particular region of the brain.

Notice, however, that this – physical location – aspect of the idea of a Cartesian Theatre is quite separate from the thought that the time at which a conscious experience is felt as occurring can be equated with the time of arrival in the Theatre. I think we should concede that the latter idea is almost certainly false. A wide variety of phenomena seem to show that time and temporal sequence, like any other aspects of reality, are *represented by* events in the brain, rather than simply being carried by the times and temporal sequences of the representing events (see Dennett and Kinsbourne, 1992). There is nothing here which need be inconsistent with the RT account, however. We can claim that within the short-term memory store C there will be representations of the times of the events which are experienced, and that these representations, like the others in C, will serve a dual role – representing, also, the times at which those conscious experiences themselves occur.

Let me work through the *colour phi* phenomenon, by way of illustration. One manner in which it could happen is this. The first – red – spot would be processed, and a representation of it would arrive in C together with a representation of the time at which the red spot is seen (time t_1, say). Then the second – green – spot would be processed, and would similarly be represented in C together with an attached representation of its time of occurrence (time t_3). Then, finally, a constructed representation of motion from red to green would be inserted into C, represented as occurring *between* the times of the previous two events (at time t_2, in fact). Because these representations of the world do double duty as representations of the subject's experiences, in virtue of the conceptual powers of the reflexive thinking faculty, the subject will *experience* the motion as occurring *between* the appearance of the stationary red and green spots. The *actual* times and sequences at which percepts enter C may be one thing, the times and sequences at which those percepts are consciously experienced may be quite another.

What these points now mean, however, is that we cannot discover which regions of the brain are occupied by C by asking the subject when their conscious experience begins to occur, and plotting the regions of the brain that are then active. For all this will tell you is the time at which the conscious experience is *represented as* occurring, not the time at which it actually occurs. So our discovery of the regions of the brain occupied by C will have to be theoretically driven, and rest upon evidence which is indirect. Yet I do not see any reason, here, for denying that there is any determinate fact of the matter, unless we are already committed to a verificationist conception of meaning. If I have to rest the case for RT theory on rejection of verificationism, then I believe I am on firm ground.

7.8   Animals and infants revisited

With the RT theory of consciousness now in place, we can return to Fodor's argument from animals and infants of section 2.7. This was, you will recall, that since neither animals nor infants make use of a natural language, and yet since both animals and infants are capable of thought, it cannot be the case that thought, as such, presupposes or constitutively employs natural language. As I remarked at the time, I do not think it plausible to respond to this argument by denying that animals and infants have propositional attitudes. For – to recapitulate briefly – our practice of ascribing such thoughts to them, in order to explain and predict their behaviour, is highly successful. And although we may find ourselves forced, implausibly, to describe animal and infant thoughts using adult human concepts and categories, this is *our* problem, not theirs. It remains reasonable to believe that animals and infants will employ their own distinctive modes of conceiving the world, even if it may be difficult for us to discover what they are.

What we can do, though, is deny that animals and infants entertain *conscious* thoughts. For it is highly unlikely that either animals or pre-linguistic infants have a capacity to think about their own acts of thinking on a regular basis. In which case none of their thoughts will count as conscious ones, if the RT theory of consciousness is correct. We are then free to claim that it is conscious thoughts, and only conscious thoughts, which involve natural language. We can allow that the thoughts of animals and infants, although real enough, are expressed in some form of Mentalese, or in some other (non-sentential, imagistic or connectionist) system of representation altogether. It will only be conscious thoughts (or some subset of conscious thoughts, as I shall argue shortly) which constitutively involve natural language.

What are the grounds for denying that animals and infants are capable of conscious thinking? Well to begin with, conscious thought, on the RT account, presupposes that the thinker possesses a theory of mind. For in order to think about your own thoughts, or your own experiences, you have to possess the *concepts* of thought and experience. And these get their life and significance from being embedded in a folk-psychological theory of the structure and functioning of the mind. So in the case of any creature to whom it is implausible to attribute a theory of mind – and I assume that this includes most animals and young infants – it will be equally implausible to suppose that they engage in conscious thinking. It is true that there is now evidence that *some* animals may possess a rudimentary theory of mind, being capable, in particular, of genuine deceit (acting so as to intentionally induce a false belief in another). But this evidence is restricted to apes, especially chimpanzees (see Byrne and Whiten, 1988; for a more sceptical view, see Povinelli, 1996). There are no grounds for thinking that any other species of animal even has this (see my 1992c, ch. 6).

Possession of a theory of mind, and hence mastery of the concepts of belief and desire, is by no means sufficient for conscious thought, according to the RT account. This also requires a capacity to think about, and to have non-inferential access to, one's own occurrent thoughts on a regular basis. Is there any reason to believe that even chimpanzees have this? I think not. For they do not display the sorts of flexibility of behaviour, and sudden changes of strategy, which we would expect if they were capable of thinking about, and hence altering and improving, their own patterns of thinking.

True enough, chimpanzees are capable of arriving at sudden solutions to problems, such as stacking a number of boxes so as to be able to reach some food which was otherwise too high (see Kohler, 1925). But this is only evidence of thought, not of thinking about thought. It may be that what the chimp has to be able to do, to arrive at a sudden solution to such a problem, is *imagine* the boxes piled one on top of the other, and to visualise, and then act on, the result. Although this is intelligent and sophisticated, there is no reason to believe that the chimp must also be capable of thinking about its own sequence of images, and so no reason to believe that the chimp's own thoughts are conscious ones.

If animals (or most animals) lack higher-order thoughts, then by the same token they will lack conscious experiences. For there will be just as little reason to believe that they are capable of thinking about their own experiences, as such. If true, this conclusion may have profound implications for our moral attitudes towards animals and animal suffering (see my 1992c, ch. 8, for some tentative discussion of this). But it is important to see that the same conclusion may not be warranted in the case of apes, if it is true that apes are capable of thinking about thoughts, as indicated above, even if not of full reflexive thinking. For, as I conceded in section 7.5, the argument of sections 5.7 and 5.8 only establishes that a capacity for some higher-order thought is a necessary condition for felt (conscious) experience, not that such experience requires the possession of a full reflexive thinking faculty.

For slightly different reasons, the conclusion that human infants are not subjects of conscious experience may fail to be warranted as well. For while infants are, I suppose, incapable of conscious thought, and of thinking about their own experiences, they may nevertheless be capable of *discriminating between* their experiences. And this would be sufficient for those experiences to count as conscious ones, and to have a subjective feel.

Compare: a new-born infant is presumably incapable of conceptualising, and hence of thinking about, its surroundings. But it is still capable of making perceptual discriminations between features of its environment – it can, for example, tell a smiling face from a frowning one, and recognise the smell of milk. These discriminatory capacities form the basis on which the later conceptual structures, and hence thoughts, are built. In the same way, then, discriminations between our own states of experience must form the basis for our later conceptualisation of those states, and we might expect these discriminatory mechanisms to be in place from birth.

I argued in section 5.8 that these mechanisms would not have evolved in a particular *species* unless that species had also evolved a theory of mind and the capacity for thought about experience. It does not follow that the one cannot make its appearance before the other in the lives of individual members of a species. Indeed, the analogy with outer perception would suggest that this must be the case. So, just as a creature which can discriminate shapes in its environment without conceptualising them can count as having *awareness of* those shapes, so, too, the human infant may count as having awareness of its own experiences (and hence as having conscious experiences) while it is yet incapable of conceptualising them.

An objection to RT theory?

I have concluded that if the RT account of consciousness is correct, then animals and young infants will lack conscious thoughts, and almost all species of animal will lack conscious experiences as well. This conclusion is certainly counter-intuitive. Most of us intuitively believe that it must be *like something* to be a bat, or a cat, or a camel, and that the experiences of these creatures have subjective feels to them; which means believing that their experiences are conscious ones. So is there a problem, here, for RT theory? Do these intuitions give us grounds for rejecting my account?

In fact there is no real problem, since the common-sense beliefs in question are actually quite groundless. For how, in the first place, can we know whether it is *like* anything to be a bat, or a cat? We cannot, of course, experience the world as a bat does in order to find out. And, in the second place, the postulation of conscious experience is entirely otiose when it comes to explaining the bat's behaviour. Everything that the bat does can be explained perfectly well by attributing beliefs, desires, and perceptions to it. There is no explanatory necessity to attribute *conscious* beliefs, desires, or perceptions.

Not only are the intuitions in question without grounds, but it is easy to explain how they arise, in such a way as to *explain them away*. For, first, the distinction between conscious and non-conscious mental states is at best marginal to common-sense psychology, barely receiving any recognition in ordinary belief. (This is why the discovery of blindsight was so deeply shocking to many people, and why the data in question were, initially, so vigorously resisted by many researchers.) So when ordinary people attribute mental states to animals, as it is quite proper to do, it will never even occur to them that the states in question might be non-conscious ones. On the contrary, as we noted in section 7.5 above, it may be that for most people consciousness is more-or-less definitional of the mental.

Moreover, and secondly, one important strategy we often adopt when attributing mental states to a subject, is to try *imagining the world from the subject's point of view*, to see how things then seem. (This is one element of truth in so-called 'simulationist' theories of mental state attribution; see many of the essays in Stone and Davies, 1995, and Carruthers and Smith, 1996.) But when we do that, what we inevitably get are imaginings of *conscious* perceptions and thoughts, and of experiences with phenomenal feels to them. So, *of course* we naturally assume that the experiences of a cat will be *like* something. But this merely reflects the fact that imaginings of perceptual states are always imaginings of *conscious* perceptual states, that is all. It goes no deeper than the fact that we have no idea how to imagine a non-conscious perception.

I conclude that RT theory is not in the least threatened by its consequences for animals and infants. Although these consequences are counter-intuitive, the intuitions in question are groundless, and can easily be explained away.

Summary

In this chapter I have outlined and defended my RT theory of consciousness, building on the points which emerged from our discussion of a variety of alternative accounts in the previous two chapters. I have argued that RT theory provides a correct account of the nature of human consciousness, at least; arguing, in particular, that it can explain the phenomenal features of our conscious experience. And I have argued that RT theory gives a correct account of conscious thinking in general, unrestricted as to species. This last point has then put me in position to reply to Fodor's argument from animals and infants, leaving me free to claim that conscious thinking, which is *de facto* restricted to humans, necessarily involves public language. This will be the subject of the next chapter, beginning with the question of how the faculty of reflexive thinking comes to be instantiated in the structure of human cognition.

8 The involvement of language in conscious thinking

In the last chapter I presented, and defended, a non-species-specific account of the distinction between conscious and non-conscious mental states. I concluded that RT theory at least provides the best available account of the structure of human consciousness, and that it successfully describes the sort of cognitive architecture that any organism, of whatever variety, would have to instantiate if it is to be capable of conscious episodic thinking. In the present chapter I shall argue that there is a natural necessity attaching to the fact that such conscious thinking – in the case of human beings, at any rate – often involves natural language. I shall distinguish weaker and stronger versions of this natural necessity thesis, and argue tentatively in support of each.

8.1 An architecture for human thinking

My first task is to sketch the outline of an architecture for human cognition (or rather, of that fragment of human cognition which specifically concerns us). This outline-architecture is designed to do two things. First, it should instantiate the RT model of consciousness, already explained and defended in Chapter 7. Second, it should explain the introspective datum of Chapter 2, that much of human conscious thinking *appears* to take place in natural language. Not only should it explain that datum, indeed, but it should provide an explanation which accords with our common-sense construal of it – namely, that much of our conscious thinking *does* take place in natural language.

No one should doubt that the stream of inner verbalisation exists. Certainly, nothing in the discussion of theories of consciousness over the last three chapters has lent any support to the extreme suggestion (briefly floated in section 2.5) that the very existence of inner speech is an illusion. What remains a legitimate matter of dispute, however, is the causal, or functional, *role* of inner speech. My explanation is designed to accord it the role of *thinking*. So I shall claim that we are aware, not only of *what* we have just thought, and of *the fact that* we have just thought it (as RT theory maintains), but also of the *way in which* that thought was entertained – we are also aware of its more or less precise formulation in natural language, or in a combination of language and other images.

The components of the model

There are, in fact, five distinct components to be put into place, before I can develop my model of human cognitive architecture. Two of these have already been mentioned. The first is the introspective datum from Chapter 2, that much of human conscious thinking at least appears to take place in natural language. This is the datum which is to be explained by some suitable arrangement of the other four components. The second component is the RT theory of consciousness, which requires thinkers to have non-inferential access to their own acts of thinking, as such, if those thinkings are to be conscious ones. If I entertain a thought consciously, then I have to be capable of thinking about that thought, and the fact that I have just entertained it, without engaging in self-interpretation.

The third component is a theory of mind or common-sense psychology, which is probably innate to our species, and which is presupposed by the activity of reflexive thinking. In order to be capable of thinking about my own acts of thinking, or of thinking about my own perceptions and feelings, I have to possess the requisite concepts. That is, I must have the general concepts *thought* and *perception*, as well as their more specific variants – *believe, want, judge, wonder whether, see, feel, hear,* and so on. As was argued briefly in sections 1.6 and 1.7, these concepts get their life and significance from being embedded in a set of beliefs about the structure and functioning of the mind – common-sense psychology.

The fourth component is imagination, and will require some brief exposition before it can be put into place. Recall the thesis of modular mental organisation, outlined briefly in section 2.8 in the course of our discussion of Fodor's arguments for Mentalese. According to this thesis, the mind contains various input and output modules whose functions are, respectively, to process perceptual information before passing on the results to central cognition, and to take instructions from central cognition and transform them into detailed bodily movements (see Fodor 1983; see also Shallice 1988). The principles of operation of the various modules are, according to Fodor, mostly innately specified and extremely fast. They are also supposed to be *isolated* from central cognition, at least in the sense that they are impervious to changes in our beliefs (hence the robustness of perceptual illusions). But it is important to see that this isolation need not, and in fact does not, mean that central cognition can have no access to the structures within a module at all.

Consider mental imagery, in particular. It is now well established that imagery, of a given sensory type (visual, auditory, kinaesthetic, and so on), employs some of the same cognitive resources as does perception in the same sense-modality. For, as we noted in section 2.8, cognitive tasks which require visual imagination (such as counting the right-hand corners in an imaged 'F') will be interfered with if the results have to be indicated visually (by pointing to a number, say), but not if they can be delivered orally. Similarly, tasks which require auditory imagination (such as counting the nouns in a previously heard sentence) will be interfered with if the results have to be delivered orally, but not if they can be given visually (see Fodor, 1975, and Tye, 1991). These results are robust.

The best explanation of these and similar results is that visual imagination employs some of the same cognitive resources as does vision, auditory imagination employs some of the same cognitive resources as does hearing, and so on. The hypothesis which naturally suggests itself is that central cognition partly operates by accessing, and by activating and manipulating, some of the higher levels of representation within the input and output modules. Some of the circuits within those modules can, as it were, be run autonomously, without stimulation from the environment. This has obvious advantages for the organism, in that it can then represent to itself states of affairs which are not yet actual, and either try to avoid them or try to bring them about.

The fifth and final component is language. This, too, is very probably a distinct mental module. As we noted in section 1.7, Chomsky has presented powerful and convincing arguments for the innateness of the language faculty (see his 1988; see also Curtiss, 1989, and Pinker, 1994). And the operation of that faculty, like the operation of other modules, is both mandatory and extremely fast. But language differs from many other input and output modules in at least two respects.

First, language always takes its input *from other modules* (at least, this is so in the sense that it takes its input from the sensory transducers of other modules; in fact it may be that language can draw on this sensory information *before* the stage at which it has been processed by the sensory module in question). When an incoming sentence is processed and understood, it is always either heard (speech), seen (writing, sign-language), or felt (Braille). Other input modules, in contrast, have their own unique sensory transducers, and operate largely independently of one another. (Input modules do appear to interact, to some degree, at least at higher levels of processing. What you see is, at least sometimes, a function of what you hear or feel.)

Second, language is *both* an input *and* an output module. It not only *processes*, but also *generates*, speech (or Sign) and writing. Here, too, the language faculty may be contrasted with other output modules, in that its output always has to be routed through the operation of other motor-control modules. Roughly speaking, the language faculty can only achieve public output through movements of the larynx and hands.

The RT-based model

Let us now put all of the above components together, by means of an inference to the best explanation. What is the best explanation of the introspective datum that much of our conscious thinking appears to take place in natural language? When taken in the context of the RT theory of consciousness, the answer, I believe, is this: that human cognition comes to instantiate such a reflexive structure by accessing, and activating and manipulating, some of the higher levels of representation within our perceptual (and/or motor) faculties – specifically, in the form of images of natural-language sentences. It is then imagination, together with common-sense psychology and knowledge of language, which enables human thinking to be conscious.

The best explanation of the available introspective data is that we mostly think (when our thinking is conscious) by imaging sentences of natural language, and trains of thought consist of manipulations and sequences of such images. We have access to the forms of our thoughts because a record of each imaged sentence is briefly held in short-term memory, so that we can recall what we have just imaged. We can then think about what we have just thought because our language contains the conceptual resources to do so – in particular, because we are masters of a common-sense psychology. Having imaged the sentence (and hence thought to myself), 'The world is getting warmer', I can then image the sentence (and so think), '*That* thought may have been too hasty', and so on. Human thinking thus becomes conscious in virtue of our reflexive thinking faculty having the capacity to access knowledge of natural language, and then by deploying resources from perception so as to activate that knowledge in imagination.

Merely imagining a sentence is not yet to think the content of that sentence, of course, in at least two respects. *First*, it is possible to entertain an image of a sentence from a language one does not understand, without (of course) thereby thinking *any* content. If I have listened to a fair bit of French with only minimal understanding, for example, then it may be possible for me to entertain French sentences in inner speech, without knowing what they mean. What this shows is that the object which occupies the causal role of a thought, on the proposal being developed here, is not *only* a phonological representation of a sentence. Rather, in the normal case that representation will carry with it its syntactic structure and associated semantics. When I think, 'The world is getting warmer', by imagining that sentence, my image is immediately and non-inferentially imbued with content, just as if I had heard that sentence uttered aloud. Sentences in a language one understands are always heard under a particular interpretation, in such a way that we seem to *hear* the meaning of the utterance. The same is true of the images which constitute our thoughts – the content of the thought is *heard in* its form.

Second, it is possible to imagine a sentence without taking it to be true. When I obey the instruction, 'Imagine someone saying, "Grass is purple"', in a squeaky voice', by forming an image of the sentence in question, this is not the same as *judging* that someone has said that, let alone the same as *believing*, myself, that grass is purple. The difference in question is a difference in causal role. What constitutes an image of the sentence, 'Grass is purple', as an occurrent *judgement that* grass is purple is a battery of characteristic causes and effects – judgements are characteristically made in response to questions, whether internally or externally generated; judgements tend both to be caused by, and to further cause, long-term storage of their associated contents; and so on. What it is about any given imaged sentence which is determinative of one or other of the available causal roles – judgement, fantasy, 'idle thinking', and so on – I do not know. But, whatever it is, I doubt whether it is transparently accessible to consciousness. That is, I doubt whether we can always tell, merely by introspection – without self-interpretation – whether an imaged sentence is expressive of a judgement, or has some other cognitive role. (Thus I have to concede that even my RT-based theory must provide some limited scope for self-interpretation.)

We might, then, represent the architecture of human consciousness in the form of another box-diagram, as in Figure 3. Much of the structure here is just as it was before, the same as the general (non-species-specific) account of consciousness presented in Chapter 7. But now there is a *triple* arrow down to C, to represent that it is not just a record of *what* is thought, and of the *fact that* it has been thought, which is passed back down to C to be available to further thought, but also the *way in which* it was thought – it is not just the content and occurrence, but also the form, of our thoughts which is available to further thought. (Remember that the triple-arrow, here, does not represent three different *channels of access*. Rather, it represents that the thoughts in reflexive thinking are available to three different kinds of further thought – thoughts about their content, thoughts about their occurrence, and thoughts about their form.)

A language box has also been added, which takes input from perception and passes on its results to C, to be made available to thought. (The

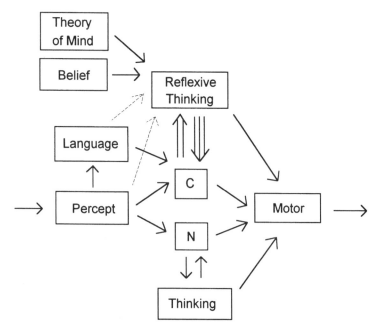

Figure 3 RT theory and language

language box will also, of course, take input from reflexive thinking and transform this into instructions for motor output, but I have left this out of the picture, for simplicity.) The dotted arrows leading from the language and percept boxes to reflexive thinking are there to represent that the latter operates by accessing structures inherent in the former two. (There should also be dotted arrows from the language box to *non*-conscious thinking, if such thinking, too, makes use of natural-language representations, but *non*-imagistically, as I shall suggest in section 8.7 that it does.) So human conscious (and properly propositional) thinkings achieve their status as such by virtue of consisting of deployments of natural-language sentences in imagination, which are then made available in short-term memory to be thought about in turn.

Note that, while I have drawn a separate box for language in the model above, there does not *have* to be any commitment in the account to the thesis that we possess a distinct, innately structured, natural language module. This is, in fact, a thesis that I believe to be true. I believe that Chomsky and others have made an overwhelmingly plausible case for the existence of an innately structured, and largely modularised, language faculty. But for present purposes it might not matter very much whether natural language is largely innate or entirely learned. That is, it might not matter whether we think of our knowledge of language as incorporated in the structure of a separate input (and output) module, or, rather, as a subset of central belief. Either way, we could still maintain that reflexive thinking makes use of that knowledge, representing natural-language sentences in imagination. In what follows, however, I shall assume that much of our knowledge of language is, in fact, innate, embodied in the structure of a specialised language faculty. Besides having a powerful claim to truth, this assumption will greatly facilitate the evolutionary story that I shall shortly begin to tell (in 8.2).

Similarly, although I have described the reflexive thinking faculty in my model as having access to an innate theory of mind (perhaps embodied in a separate module), this is not strictly necessary either. Even if commonsense psychology has to be learned or otherwise acquired in childhood, we could still maintain that reflexive thinking makes use of the concepts embedded in that theory in making judgements about its own occurrent thoughts. But I shall continue to assume, in what follows, that commonsense psychology is largely innate, both because I believe this to be true (see section 1.7 above), and because, again, it will facilitate the evolutionary story to be told in the next section.

8.2 An evolutionary story

So far in this chapter I have sketched a model of human conscious cognition in which natural language would play a central part, based on the RT theory of consciousness defended in Chapter 7. I shall now consider how the proposed cognitive architecture might have evolved. In fact it is relatively easy to see how the evolution of the structures involved in my RT-based model might have taken place, putting together, and perhaps further developing, elements which would have had independent value in survival.

Imagination would, of course, have had an important role in problem solving, as it seems to with chimpanzees today (see Kohler, 1925), and would probably have made its appearance quite early on in our ancestors' evolution. Some form of (innate) common-sense psychology, too, would have been extremely valuable to highly social creatures, such as our ancestors almost certainly were. And, of course, the arrival of natural language would then have hugely facilitated both social co-operation and the acquisition of knowledge.

In fact, as I indicated in the last section, it seems to me highly plausible that human beings have a natural-language faculty which is innately structured. (In which case the language box, in the picture of human cognition presented in Figure 3, should be thought of as a distinct input and output module, not as a subset of central belief.) Moreover, it is easy to see *why* such an innate module should have evolved, if not exactly *how* (see Bickerton, 1990, and Pinker, 1994, ch. 11, for some useful speculations on the latter). For its arrival would have made possible the detailed exchange of information, as well as the intricate but indefinitely flexible co-ordination of activity, which underlies much of the success of our species. Just how much would then have been necessary for our ancestors to begin entertaining conscious thoughts in natural language would have depended upon what sort of role was accorded to early forms of language within their cognition.

Language for thought

Suppose, first, that the public use of signs was, from the beginning, accorded a direct role in the determination of action, in such a way that those early uses of signs could quite naturally be described as a kind of 'thinking out loud'. On this model, early forms of language would have been useful, not only for purposes of communication, but would already have had some sort of executive role in cognition. This suggestion is not at all implausible. Think of the advantages which might have accrued to our ancestors if a statement like, 'If you see a snake, don't try to pick it up', (as directed from adult to child) were (other things being equal) *immediately* to have the cognitive role of a belief in its content. Equally, when early hominids debated with one another about the best way to hunt an elephant, for example, and one of them said, 'We should attack from both flanks', there would have been some advantage in this statement figuring immediately as an item in practical reasoning, to be considered, manipulated, accepted, or rejected, without having to be translated into a wholly different system of representation (Mentalese).

All that would then have been necessary was for our ancestors to start using their imaginations to represent sentences of natural language, and for a reflexive feed-back loop to be added (if it was not already present in the form of short-term memory), so that they could then make use of their folk-psychological concepts in thoughts about their own thoughts and experiences. This final step, too, would have had great survival value. For it would have enabled them to keep their thoughts to themselves, where necessary, and also to maintain a continual stream of reflexive thinking without the necessity for continuous overt verbalisation.

According to this first suggestion, then, the arrival of language was (more or less) the final condition needed to facilitate conscious – and hence indefinitely improvable – thinking. For it is reasonable to suppose that both the power to form and manipulate mental images, as well as at least the beginnings of an innate model of human psychology, would already have been in place prior to the evolution of the language faculty, just as they seem to be with chimpanzees today. On this account, in fact, it is to the evolution of an innate language faculty that we owe our distinctive status as beings with a conscious mental life.

Of course, the language faculty is unlikely to have evolved all at once, in the space of a single mutation. And it is quite possible that its emergence was interwoven with the evolution of the theory-of-mind module. It may be, for example, that the latter evolved through a series of stages, corresponding to the theory-stages postulated by developmental psychologists – for example, simple desire psychology, perception-desire psychology, and then belief-desire psychology (see Wellman, 1990, and Segal, 1996). And some psychologists have suggested that the evolution of the final stage might have presupposed some form of linguistic communication (see Harris, 1996, and Smith, 1996). So it may be more accurate to say that it is to the evolution *both* of an innate language faculty *and* of an innate theory-of-mind module that we owe our status as conscious thinkers.

(Let me stress, here, a point which has been implicit in some of the discussion of the last two chapters: namely, that the notion of modularity involved in the above speculations concerning the evolution of language and of common-sense psychology is a relatively weak one; certainly weaker than Fodor's 1983 notion. For, although the operations of these modules may be fast, mandatory, and largely innately specified, they are certainly not fully encapsulated. It is plain that we have at least partial access to the contents of our theory-of-mind module, since its concepts are consciously accessible, and since we may be capable of articulating some of its main principles, such as the practical reasoning syllogism. And if the model of human cognition represented in Figure 3 is correct, central cognition will also have access to – in the sense of being able to make use of – some of the representations of the language module. Moreover, nothing that I say here is intended to rule out the notion of modularity defended by Karmiloff-Smith, 1992, according to which knowledge of language and of theory of mind *becomes* modularised in development, starting from an innate basis of attention-biases and domain-specific learning principles.)

Language for communication

Now suppose, second, that early forms of language evolved *only* because of the role of language in communication, as many people have suggested.

On this account, language was selected for in evolution because, and only because, of its role in facilitating the acquisition of knowledge and the co-ordination of collective action. So on this model, early forms of language would *not* have had any part in the executive functions of human cognition, and a good deal more would then have had to change in order for human cognition to exemplify the cognitive architecture depicted in Figure 3.

In particular, merely using imagination to represent natural-language sentences, in such a way that those imaginings were then made available to the same imaging faculty, would not have been enough to give those imagined sentences the status of *thoughts*. In order for this to happen, those imaginings would need to have usurped (at least partly) the higher cognitive functions of planning and decision making previously undertaken at some other level of the mind, using some other mode of representation. But it is by no means implausible that such a transformation should have taken place, given the obvious evolutionary advantage which would attend the capacity for reflexive thinking. On this model, then, the acquisition of language would have been the penultimate, rather than the ultimate, step necessary for the evolution of consciousness. The final step would have been the harnessing of language to the executive functions of thought.

8.3   The argument from introspection revisited

With my RT-based model of human conscious cognition in place, let us return, now, for a final evaluation of the argument from introspection of Chapter 2. That argument took as its starting-point a datum of introspection which is not (or should not be) seriously disputed – namely, that much of the stream of human consciousness is occupied with inner speech, or with imaged sentences (spoken or heard) of natural language. These sentences mostly have the *forms* (if not necessarily the causal roles) of *thoughts* – including assertoric judgement, question, self-directed imperative, and expressions of intention and desire.

The thesis then advanced in Chapter 2, and again in section 8.1 above, was the one embodied in our common-sense psychology – that these streams of imaged sentences *are* our conscious thoughts, and have the sort of executive role in our cognition which we believe to be distinctive of conscious thinking. So it is *because* I think the words, 'The world is getting warmer', that I then go on to think, 'I must use less fuel'; and it is (in part) *because* of this that I may later be found walking rather than driving to work. I have just now (in section 8.1) sketched the sort of cognitive architecture which could enable this to happen, and have then (in section 8.2) suggested how such an architecture might have evolved.

The upshot of these recent discussions is this. When taken together with my defence of the RT theory of consciousness against Dennett's multiple drafts model (mounted in Chapters 6 and 7), and when taken also with our consideration of Dennett's alternative explanations of inner verbalisation (in section 6.8), the above discussion shows convincingly that the common-sense position survives comparison with the Dennettian alternatives. I claim, that is, that the RT-based model of the role of inner verbalisation presented in section 8.1 is certainly to be preferred, both to Dennett's hypothesis of 'the Joycean machine', and also to his hypothesis that inner verbalisation serves as an inner bulletin board, enabling different cognitive systems to communicate with one another. But what, then, are the remaining alternatives? Are there any further competing explanations of the role of inner speech, which might be consistent with Fodor's thesis that all thought is conducted in Mentalese?

Recall the Fodor/Searle account of 'thinking aloud' sketched briefly section 3.5. In answer to the question *why* we go in for this activity (of uttering sentences aloud and imposing our thought-contents on them), if those sentences are in no way constitutive of the acts of thinking in question, it was suggested that such objectification of thought may serve as an aid to memory, and also as an aid to self-reflection and self-criticism. In fact there were two distinct suggestions here, which will need to be considered separately. The point of translating our Mentalese thoughts into the public-language medium might be to enable us to remember them, and/or to think about and criticise them more easily. Plainly, each of these explanations may find an analogue in the case of private – not publicly expressed – verbalisation.

Before setting out and discussing these suggestions in some detail, let me first stress that I believe the common-sense, RT-based, explanation to be the default one. Other things being equal, we should believe what we already believe, namely that when we engage in inner verbalisation we *are* thinking. So my proposed underpinning of the cognitive conception of language – by claiming, in section 8.1, that much of our conscious thinking is conducted in natural language – gets to win by default in the absence of any stronger competitor. In effect, I claim that a draw is all that I need in order to win.

This claim is an implication of what I take to be the only really defensible, coherentist, epistemology: in forming rational, or justified, beliefs, *you should start from where you already are*. Rational epistemology does not begin from sure foundations (as foundationalists would claim) but from whatever beliefs you already find yourself possessing. You should then seek to weld those beliefs into a coherent whole: constructing explanatory theories, testing theories, seeking new data, constructing alternative theories, and so on. In the course of this process a great many of your original beliefs may come to be rejected. But, being the starting-point, they also form part of the default end-point: other things being equal, those beliefs will survive, and will continue to be rationally believed. (For further discussion of various forms of coherentism, see my 1992a, and Bonjour, 1985.)

The memory explanation

The first suggestion made in section 3.5 was that overt (publicly expressed) verbalisation of a (Mentalese) thought might help us to remember it, by fixing it more firmly before the mind as a content to interact with yet further thoughts, so serving in various ways to make our thinking more efficient. (Recall from section 7.3 above, that *all* thinking, whether conscious or non-conscious, requires memory. Since thinking takes time, thoughts must be held in memory for long enough to achieve their effects. Anything which serves to keep them in memory for longer may therefore lead to better thinking.)

This explanation seems especially plausible in connection with thoughts expressed in writing. What the written sentence does is give us a permanent, or semi-permanent, record of the thought, to which we can return attention at will, allowing it to interact with a wide variety of beliefs and other thoughts. The suggestion was then that spoken utterances may serve a similar function, somehow fixing, or helping to fix, the thoughts in question in memory. It is easy to see how this story *might* go, since a thought which is uttered, and so heard by the speaker, will be entertained twice-over – first prior to encoding in public language, and then second when the heard sentence is decoded back into a Mentalese thought again. And two exposures, or repetitions, of the thought may very well serve to make it more memorable.

The suggestion might then be that inner verbalisation would have a similar function – by translating each occurrent thought into an imaged natural language sentence, in such a way that it is then automatically decoded back into the same thought once again, we might ensure that the thought is held in memory for long enough to interact as it should with further thoughts in processes of thinking and reasoning.

Now we might wonder, to begin with, whether this can really be a convincing explanation of the stream of inner speech, since it appears to go all round the houses to achieve the desired effect. If the proposal is that memory-enhancement is achieved by *rehearsal* of the thought, then it would be a great deal simpler to *repeat* each occurrent thought – to think it twice over. Since the proposed explanation of the role of verbalisation has us thinking each thought twice over anyway, the route through public language might seem to be just an unnecessary dog-leg. In fact, however, it is a well-established fact about human memory systems that memory can be greatly enhanced by *association* (see Baddeley, 1988).

If asked to memorise a list of items, for example, it will be more efficient to associate them with something else, rather than simply repeating the names to yourself (even repeating them many times over). Thus, you might imagine walking around the rooms of your house, placing a distinct item in each room. This then gives you an independent fix on those items in memory – you can either recall them directly, or you can recall the rooms, from which you might extract the associated item. Something similar might very well take place in the case of inner verbalisation. By translating a Mentalese thought into its imaged natural-language equivalent, we get an independent fix on that thought, so making it more likely that it will be available to enter into our reasoning processes as and when the need arises.

This suggestion – that inner speech functions as an aid to memory – is then certainly a possible one. But to what extent can it really explain the data? In particular, can it explain the *extent* of inner verbalisation in our conscious lives – whether we are daydreaming, engaged in some sort of simple reasoning, or employed in a complex reasoning task? For why would we *need* to remember our thoughts if those thoughts are merely idle ones, as in day-dreaming or fantasy? And why would we bother to adopt the inner-verbalisation strategy as an aid to memory if our thoughts are simple ones, or are particularly easily memorable? Surely the prediction would be that inner verbalisation would only occur when we are engaged in complex practical or theoretical reasoning tasks that *matter*. For verbalisation takes time and energy. We surely would not do it idly.

Here my RT-based explanation can fare better. Since linguistic thinking is, by hypothesis, one of the normal modes of functioning of a special-purpose executive system (the reflexive thinking faculty), it is no surprise that inner verbalisation should continue to occur when the system is idling. For although the gains of *having* such a system only accrue when it is working seriously (flexibility, adaptability, etc.), of course it will continue to function in the same language-involving way when idling, or when taken 'off line'. (Compare: the carburettor in a car continues to inject a fuel-air mixture into the ignition-chamber even when the gears are not engaged, and the engine is idling.) According to the memory-explanation canvassed above, in contrast, inner verbalisation is just a *dodge* – a strategy exploited to make thinking more efficient by making thoughts more memorable. And it is then something of a puzzle why we would continue to exploit that (costly) strategy when thinking is easy, or done to no serious purpose.

There is some reason, then, to prefer the RT-based model (according to which inner verbalisation *is* a kind of thinking) to the suggestion that inner speech functions as a mere memory-aid for the real thought-processes which are conducted in Mentalese. The main argument which I want to stress, however, and develop at some length, is as follows:

> Given the correctness of the RT theory of consciousness defended in Chapter 7, then only if the RT-based model of section 8.1 above is correct, and inner verbalisation is a kind of thinking, do we do any conscious (propositional) thinking at all.

In fact I shall claim that it is a deep presupposition of our common-sense belief that we do sometimes engage in conscious propositional (as opposed to purely imagistic) thinking, that inner speech *is* such thinking. And note that if this argument succeeds, then it will not only rule out the memory-aid proposal currently under consideration, but will equally count against *any* theory of the role of inner speech (including Dennett's bulletin-board hypothesis) which does not accord such speech the role of thought.

According to the RT-based model developed in section 8.1, we have immediate non-inferential access to our own inner verbalisations, because a phonological representation is stored in C to be made available to further thought, just as if the sentence had been spoken or heard. And, moreover, those inner verbalisations *are* thoughts. So we have non-inferential access to some of our occurrent thoughts, which therefore count as conscious ones. For RT theory maintains that conscious thoughts are those to which we have immediate and non-inferential access.

According to the memory-aid proposal, on the other hand, the inner verbalisations to which we have non-inferential access are not our thoughts themselves, but rather events which are caused by those thoughts in order to improve memory. Our access to our own thoughts is therefore not immediate, but inferential – to know what we have thought, we have to decode back again to reach the appropriate sentence of Mentalese which is (according to this proposal) the thought itself. So the thoughts which get verbalised in inner speech are *not* conscious ones, even though they are thoughts which we may reliably know ourselves to have, much as I may reliably know of the thoughts of other people on hearing them speak.

Now, so far this is just the default-argument canvassed at the outset of this section – the RT-based model, and only the RT-based model, preserves for us our common-sense belief that conscious inner verbalisation *is* a form of conscious thinking. But when we add to this the claim that we have no *other* mode of engaging in conscious propositional thinking except through inner verbalisation, then we get the new argument, that only the RT-based model can preserve for us the belief that we engage in *any* such conscious thinking. So if we want to hang on to our common-sense belief that we do sometimes entertain conscious thoughts, and we accept the RT characterisation of consciousness, then we had better also believe that inner verbalisation is a form of thinking.

(I should stress again that by *thinking*, here, I should be understood as meaning cognitive processes which are properly propositional, or fully conceptual. Of course one can also treat manipulations of visual and other images as a form of thinking, and such manipulations can often have a serious purpose. Moreover, such images are characteristically conscious, occurring in such a way as to be available to further thought. So on any account there exists something one might call 'conscious thinking' which does not involve natural language. But a visual image does not express a proposition. In the present argument I am confining attention to those thinkings which are properly propositional.)

Against purely-propositional consciousness

In order for this new argument to work, I now need to show that we have no immediate and non-inferential access to our own propositional thoughts *except* where those thoughts are expressed in inner speech. In effect, I need to establish that there is (for us) no such phenomenon as conscious purely propositional thinking. I require an argument to show that in those cases where subjects are prepared to self-ascribe a thought while denying that they entertained that thought verbally or in the form of any visual or other image (which they sometimes do – see Hurlburt, 1990 and 1993), the thought in question was not, in fact, a conscious one. So I need to establish that human beings do not have the sort of semantic-ascent architecture that we imagined for the Stalnaker Martians in section 7.3, which might give us non-inferential access to the contents and occurrences of our Mentalese thoughts, thus rendering the latter conscious according to RT theory.

As I have already mentioned briefly in section 7.3, this has, to my mind, been convincingly demonstrated by a rich body of data coming out of the social psychology literature. Here it has been found that there are a wide variety of circumstances in which subjects will confabulate self-explanations which are manifestly false (see Nisbett and Wilson, 1977, Nisbett and Ross, 1980, Wilson *et al.*, 1981, Wilson, 1985, and Wilson and Stone, 1985). What follow are just a few salient examples:

(1) When asked to select from a range of identical items, people show a marked preference for items on the right-hand side of the array; but their explanations of their own choices never advert to position, but rather mention superior quality, appearance, and so on. And note that the explanations, here, can be offered within seconds of the original choice.

(2) People's willingness to help someone in distress is inversely correlated with the number of other observers – the more people there are present, the less willing they are to help – but subjects never mention this in explanation of their own behaviour. (This finding may now be out of date. Some of the ways in which the presence of other people can have effects upon beneficence-behaviour are now widely known, and have become absorbed into common-sense psychology. The callousness of passers-by in crowded city streets is now legendary.)

(3) People who have been paid to play with a puzzle report less intrinsic interest in it than those who do so purely voluntarily; but these reports do not correlate with the extent to which they are observed to play with it in their free time.

(4) People are very poor at knowing which factors in a situation influence their evaluations or decisions, such as which aspects of someone's behaviour influenced their evaluation of his physical characteristics (appearance, etc.), or which aspects of a job-applicant's portfolio influenced their decision to call her for interview; and interestingly, observers merely *told about* these studies make exactly the same erroneous judgements as do the subjects *in* them. Moreover, both groups (participants and observers) tend to make correct judgements when, and only when, the influential factor is recognised as such within common-sense psychology.

The best explanation of these data (and the explanation offered by Nisbett and Wilson), is that subjects in such cases lack any form of conscious access to their true thought-processes. Rather, lacking immediate access to their reasons, they engage in a swift bit of retrospective self-interpretation, attributing to themselves the thoughts and feelings which they think they *should* have in the circumstances, or in such a way as to make sense of their own behaviour.

Looking across the full range of the experimental data available, the one factor which seems to stand out as being common to all those cases where individuals confabulate false self-explanations, is simply that in such cases the true causes of the thoughts, feelings, or behaviours in question are unknown to common-sense psychology. The best explanation of the errors, then, must be that they occur in cases where individuals are actually *employing* common-sense psychology, relying on its principles and generalisations to attribute mental states to themselves. And this means that in such cases the access which they have to their own mental states is inferential and interpretative (in so far as they do have access; that is, in cases where they get it right). In particular, they do *not* have the sort of non-inferential access to the states ascribed which would be necessary for the latter to count as conscious ones, according to the RT account of consciousness.

I propose, then, that what are often described as purely propositional (non-verbal) thoughts, available to introspection (and hence conscious), are really the results of swift self-interpretation. So even where the self-interpretation happens to be correct, the thoughts in question are not conscious ones. For RT theory tells us that a conscious thought is one which must be available to the subject non-inferentially, *not* as a result of self-interpretation.

Such self-interpretations need not operate exclusively on overt behaviour, of course. Often the thoughts self-attributed may provide the best explanation of other conscious (verbalised) thoughts, or of the conscious images one was entertaining at the time, or of the way in which one was directing one's conscious attention, and so on. But I would have to predict, on this proposal, that subjects would *not* be prepared to self-ascribe purely propositional thoughts in cases where there was nothing in their behaviour, circumstances, or in their other conscious mental states which might warrant the self-ascription – that is, where there was nothing which might lead an observer who knew of the relevant behaviour and/or mental states to ascribe the very same thought by interpretation.

I believe that this prediction is borne out by (or is consistent with, at any rate) the introspection-sampling data provided by Russ Hurlburt (see his 1990 and 1993). Since many of his examples of purely propositional (or 'unsymbolised') thought are not described in any great detail, it is not always possible to determine whether or not such a thought could have been attributed by a fully knowledgeable observer. And in any case, of course, many of the relevant beliefs and intentions which might have played a part in the subject's self-interpretation may not have been conscious at the time of the consciousness-freezing beep, and so would not have been reported. For no one maintains that everything which figures in an interpretation must be conscious at the time. Nevertheless, let me work through a couple of examples by way of illustration of my approach.

In one example, the subject had been drawing a picture of her room with the radio playing, unattended, in the background just prior to the beep, but the words 'brothers in arms' had just penetrated her awareness; and at the moment of the beep, she reported that she was wondering why she had heard those particular words and not others; but this act of wondering did not involve any introspectively accessible words or other images (see Hurlburt, 1990, p. 106). It seems not at all implausible that she should really have *interpreted herself* to be so wondering, in fact. For this is just what one might, very naturally, *predict* that she would have been doing in the circumstances.

In another example, the subject was looking at a box of breakfast cereal on the shelf of a supermarket at the time of the beep. She reported that she was wondering – wordlessly – whether to buy the box; and that she was thinking – again wordlessly – that she did not normally eat breakfast, and that the cereal might therefore be wasted; and that she was also considering the expense involved (see Hurlburt, 1993, p. 94). Again, it seems reasonable that these thoughts might have been ascribed inferentially, as a result of self-interpretation, rather than occurring in such a way as to render them properly conscious. For these are just the thoughts which an observer might naturally attribute to her, who knew what she knew: namely, that she was attending to the price-label on a cereal packet; that she did not normally eat breakfast; and that she was generally careful in matters of expense.

It may be objected against my account of these examples that it does not *feel* to the subjects in question as if they are interpreting themselves. On the contrary, they report their purely propositional thoughts as having the same sort of phenomenological immediacy as any other conscious state – only without the phenomenology, as it were. But the reply to this objection is easy: nor does it *feel as if* we are interpreting *other* agents much of the time, either – rather, we just *see* much of their behaviour as intentional, and as imbued with certain thoughts. Indeed, our theory-of-mind faculty appears to have a number of the properties of a Fodorean module: besides being at least partly innately specified (see section 1.7), its operation is both mandatory and fast. We often just *cannot help* seeing the behaviour of an actor on the stage as displaying anger, or fear, or whatever, despite the fact that we know him to be acting. And much of the time we are not aware of ourselves as having to interpret his behaviour, either, as being deceitful, or conciliatory, or whatever; rather, we just *see it that way*, immediately. So it is only to be expected that when people engage in self-interpretation, this will often take place extremely swiftly, and without self-awareness of what they are doing.

(What about the puzzling data, also provided by Hurlburt, that subjects sometimes report thoughts which are definitely linguistic, and not purely propositional, but where subjects were *not* aware of any determinate words, or of any imaged sentence? How can this finding be fitted into the story I am telling in this chapter about the role of natural language in conscious thinking? For example, one subject reported that at the time of the beep she was looking at a picture of Napoleon's hat, and it was *exactly as if* she were speaking to herself (in Dutch) the words, 'What's so special about it?', except that no words were actually present in consciousness (see Hurlburt, 1990, p. 101). Here is one possible explanation, consistent with my account: perhaps inner verbalisation, like outer verbalisation, begins with some sort of conceptual representation of the message to be expressed – in LF, as it might be; see section 8.4 below – which is then used to construct a phonological representation of the sentence; and this process *takes time*. Then perhaps, in the example, the beep interrupted this process *before* a phonological representation of the sentence, 'What's so special about it?', had been constructed and placed in C, available to consciousness. But still the LF representation was in existence, already formulated; and following the beep it could have been used to generate just such a phonological representation, which would then *feel exactly right* to the subject – she would naturally have accepted it as precisely what she had been thinking at the time.)

It might be objected against the argument that I have been developing in this part of the section, that the fact that subjects *sometimes* confabulate as a result of engaging in self-interpretation, does not show that they do not *also* entertain conscious purely propositional thoughts, perhaps exploiting some form of semantic-ascent architecture. Granted, there is no entailment. But I think that there *is* a sound inference to the best explanation to be made, in the absence of any particular proposal about the range of cases in which one might entertain conscious thoughts by semantic ascent. Until that proposal is forthcoming, the most reasonable explanation is that we employ a self-interpretation strategy in *all* cases where purely propositional thoughts are self-ascribed. For we can then explain the heterogeneous range of examples in which people get themselves badly wrong – what these cases have in common is simply that the true mental causes are here unknown to common-sense psychology, and so are not available to an interpreter, self- or otherwise (see also Gopnik, 1993).

If the above explanation of the social psychology false-explanation data is allowed to stand, then we face a choice. Either we can maintain that inner verbalisation is simply an aid to memory (or functions as an inner bulletin board, or whatever), and is not itself a kind of thinking; in which case we must say that we *never* have access to our own thoughts which is non-inferential; and so we never really have thoughts which are conscious, if the RT account of consciousness is correct. Or we can allow that the inner verbalisations – to which we *do* have non-inferential access – are actually, themselves, occurrent thoughts. In which case these thoughts, at least, can count as conscious. The latter alternative is surely the more reasonable, other things being equal – preserving for us our common-sense belief that we do sometimes engage in thinking which is conscious.

The access explanation

I have argued that the memory-enhancement explanation of the stream of inner verbalisation is unsuccessful. The alternative Fodor/Searle proposal is that verbalisation of our Mentalese thoughts is designed to give us conscious *access* to the contents and occurrences of the latter. Not that those thoughts would thereby be conscious, according to RT theory, since our access to them would be inferential. But such a system would nevertheless give many of the advantages of conscious thinking, since one would thereby be able to think about one's own sequences of thinking and reasoning, gaining much of the flexibility and adaptability distinctive of RT theory.

So here is the proposal: we entertain our thoughts in Mentalese and not in natural language; these thoughts remain non-conscious, but we regularly translate them into inner-verbalised sentences to which we do have conscious access, so that we can mimic some of the advantages of conscious thinking. (Note that this proposal is, in effect, a variant on Dennett's inner-bulletin-board explanation of inner verbalisation, only embedded, now, in a more orthodox picture of mental architecture, containing some sort of central executive in which chains of practical and theoretical reasoning take place.)

This explanation can be dealt with quite swiftly, since it is subject to just the same weaknesses as the previous one. In particular, it will still force us to conclude that we do not engage in conscious (propositional) thinking *at all*. Indeed, here the counter-intuitive conclusion is forced on us even more powerfully, since it is no longer an option, even in principle, to appeal to purely propositional conscious thinking. For if we could engage in such thinking, then we would not need to engage in inner verbalisation, on the current proposal. If the whole point of inner verbalisation is to give us indirect access to our own thought-processes, then this must be because we do *not* have any other form of access to them – in particular, it must be because we do not have the sort of semantic-ascent architecture envisaged earlier. So on this proposal we really would have no option but to conclude that we *never* entertain thoughts in such a way that we have immediate and non-inferential access to their contents and occurrences. That is to say, we should have to conclude (in the presence of RT theory) that we never have any conscious thoughts at all.

The present proposal also faces similar problems to before, in explaining the range of cases where we engage in inner speech (including simple thoughts, idle thinking, day-dreaming, etc.). For why would we bother to translate our thoughts into natural-language sentences in all these cases, given that we have nothing to gain by achieving second-order access to our idle thoughts? As before, the RT-based model experiences no difficulty here, since the proposal is that our reflexive thinking faculty standardly operates by manipulating natural-language sentences in imagination – it will therefore continue to do this even when that faculty is doing no useful work. The problem for the Mentalese-based access-explanation is to find some corresponding *kind* of thinking such that all and only thoughts of that kind would routinely be translated into natural-language sentences so as to give us meta-access to their contents and occurrences, even when those thoughts are merely idle ones. I do not say that this cannot be done, but I cannot see, myself, how to do it.

I conclude this section, then, by claiming that the introspective argument of Chapter 2 may be allowed to stand. The best explanation for the stream of inner speech is that it is constitutive of conscious thinking. So, much of our conscious thinking does indeed take place in natural language, and Fodor is wrong to claim that all thinking is conducted in Mentalese.

8.4   Working memory and the central executive

In this section I shall compare the model of human cognitive architecture sketched in section 8.1 above with the account of the working-memory system developed over a number of years by Alan Baddeley (see Baddeley and Hitch, 1974, Baddeley, 1986, 1988, and 1993, and Gathercole and Baddeley, 1993). Both theories postulate special-purpose short-term memory stores intimately linked to such cognitive functions as planning, reasoning, and conscious awareness; and both assign a role to imagistic representations of language within the systems described. I shall then consider an objection to my position arising out of this comparison.

Comparison with the working-memory model

Baddeley has proposed that the working-memory system consists of a central executive and two specialised slave-systems, the *visuo-spatial sketchpad* and the *phonological loop*. The relationships between them are represented in Figure 4 (adapted from Gathercole and Baddeley, 1993,

p. 4). The central executive controls the flow of information within the system as a whole, and is charged with such functions as action-planning, retrieval of information from long-term memory, and conscious control of action. The executive also allocates inputs to the visuo-spatial sketch-pad and phonological loop, which are employed for spatial reasoning tasks and language-related tasks respectively. Since the central executive must presumably have access to linguistic knowledge, if it is to be able to generate linguistic inputs to the phonological loop, this model could easily be presented in such a way as to resemble quite closely the RT-based model of Figure 3.

One difference from my RT-based model concerns the special-purpose nature of the phonological loop. In particular, Baddeley seems to think of it as *essentially* a phonological system. (In fact, Gathercole and Baddeley consider whether the system has an articulatory rather than a phonological basis, and leave the issue unresolved. But they do appear to believe that it must be either the one or the other – see their 1993, p. 16.) In contrast, the RT-based model proposes that we can, in principle, entertain linguistically formulated thoughts through the imaginative use of any language-related sense-modality. In normal individuals, no doubt, such thinking involves auditory, or perhaps articulatory (kinaesthetic) imagination (or both). But, in the case of those whose only native language is some form of Sign, the theory predicts that their linguistic thinking will involve the manipulation of *visual* (or kinaesthetic) images. And perhaps some ordinary thinkers, too, sometimes employ visual images (in this case of written language) in their thinking.

One empirical prediction of the RT-based model, then, is that exactly the sorts of interference-effects which have been used to explore the properties of the phonological loop in normal subjects would be found in the visual (or perhaps the kinaesthetic, gestural) modality for deaf subjects whose native language is a form of Sign. Another prediction is that aphasics or other brain-damaged patients who have lost the phonological component of working memory should be able to recover their capacity for language-based thinking by employing the resources of some other form of imagination – either kinaesthetic, developing an articulatory loop, or visual, imaging written sentences. For according to the RT-based model, the exact form in which linguistic information is represented in reflexive thinking is plastic, and may vary from individual to individual, and within individuals over time.

Another difference between Baddeley's model of working-memory on the one hand, and my RT-based model of cognition on the other, concerns the *function* of the phonological loop – its causal role in the activity of the cognitive system as a whole. In Baddeley's model, as I understand

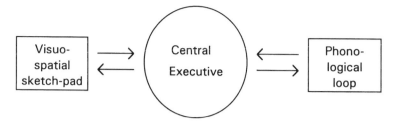

Figure 4 Working memory

it, the phonological loop is employed *only* for language-based tasks – that is, only for tasks which are explicitly *about* language, or explicitly involve language. Thus the phonological loop is said to be involved in such tasks as: memorising sequences of letters; vocabulary acquisition; reading development; and language comprehension. But there is no suggestion that it is also involved in the planning of action, or in other forms of reasoning about the world (rather than about language). These tasks are allotted, rather, to the central executive. (In fact Gathercole and Baddeley note in passing, following Hitch 1980, that the phonological loop may be implicated in mental arithmetic; see their 1993, p. 234. But nothing further is made of this point.)

In the RT-based model, in contrast, the phonological loop (and/or its equivalent in other sense-modalities) is involved in many forms of conscious thinking and reasoning about the world. My hypothesis is that it is by formulating some of our occurrent thinkings in the form of images of natural-language sentences that our cognitive system is able to gain access to (in such a way as to render conscious) its own processes of thought. The function of the phonological loop is thus much more than just to enable the system to engage in language-involving processing tasks. It is also to enable the system to gain access to its own occurrent thoughts, thus facilitating the sort of indefinite self-improvement that comes with self-awareness. And according to RT theory the sentences represented in the phonological loop often *are* the acts of thinking the thoughts which are expressed by those sentences. Thus when, in context, I entertain in auditory imagination the sentence, 'The world is getting warmer', this *is*, according to the RT-based account, my act of thinking that the world is getting warmer, and is the realiser of the latter's causal role.

Of course I do have to concede that there is also a need, within my RT-based theory, for something resembling Baddeley's central executive. For *something* must be responsible for selecting and manipulating the imaged sentences in the phonological loop, which therefore become the system's conscious occurrent thoughts (in virtue of the reflexive availability of the contents of the loop). But the contents and modes of operation of this executive will themselves be *non*-conscious. It is also true that there is a need within the RT-based theory for a visuo-spatial sketch-pad, in which spatial reasoning tasks can be undertaken in non-language-involving mode. Indeed, this has been implicit in the discussion of RT theory throughout, both here and in the previous chapter. So there are still a number of respects in which Baddeley might find my RT-based account congenial.

An objection and three replies

It may be objected that for me to concede to Baddeley the existence of a central executive charged with selecting and formulating the sentences to be imaged within the phonological loop, is for me to concede to Fodor the case against the role of language in thinking. For on standard models of sentence production, this process proceeds through a number of different stages, beginning with a conceptual representation of the message to be conveyed, and concluding with detailed instructions to the muscles in the mouth and larynx to express that message in speech (see, for example, Garrett, 1975, and Levelt, 1989). But what would 'a conceptual representation of the message' be, except a *thought* whose content is that message? Since this thought could not (on pain of vicious circularity) itself be expressed in natural language, it would presumably have to be formulated in Mentalese. And then Fodor gets his conclusion that the real thought-processes underlying inner verbalisation do not constitutively involve natural language, but rather employ Mentalese.

I have three possible replies to this objection, each one more controversial than the last. My fall-back position is to endorse at least the first. This would give me the thesis I shall later call 'NN$_w$'. I shall present arguments later in this chapter in support of the second. This would give me the thesis I shall call 'NN$_s$'. And I am strongly tempted by the third, but will not pursue it any further in this book.

(1) The least controversial reply is to concede the standard model of speech generation, and to concede that the conceptual representation of the message is expressed in Mentalese, but to claim, firstly, that this representation can only attain the status of a *conscious* thought by being expressed in natural language, in the form of inner speech; and secondly, that it is the latter imaged sentence which occupies the causal role distinctive of conscious thinking.

The first of these claims has been partially defended above, and will be returned to again in sections 8.5 and 8.6 below, in the form of thesis NN_w. I do not believe that we have the capacity for non-inferential access to our own occurrent thoughts *except* when they are formulated in inner speech (and/or other images). The second claim commits me to the truth of such counterfactuals as this: if my conceptual representation of the message, [the Earth is getting warmer] had never been realised in the imaged sentence, 'The Earth is getting warmer', then I would never have gone on to draw the conscious consequences that I did draw, nor go on to act as I did. We are warranted in believing such counterfactuals, I maintain, because the RT-based model of inner verbalisation provides a better account of the phenomena than the alternatives, as I argued in section 8.3 above.

(2) The second, more controversial, reply, again concedes the standard model of speech generation, allowing that speech processes (whether inner or outer) begin with some sort of conceptual representation of the thought to be expressed; but it denies that this representation can itself have the causal role of a thought (whether conscious or not), independent of its effects in sentence-production. Or rather, it insists that these conceptual representations are themselves natural-language ones. It may be, that is, that such representations are not central-process thoughts expressed in Mentalese, but are internal to the language faculty, having no independent causal role outside of it. I can then concede that the cognitive processes involved in the production of a sentence may include multiple levels of representation (phonological, syntactic, and – crucially – semantic), while claiming that all of these representations are themselves natural-language ones.

For example, Chomsky has maintained that there is a level of linguistic representation which he calls 'logical form' (LF), which is where the language faculty interfaces with central cognitive systems (see his 1995). I can then claim that all conceptual, propositional, thinking consists in the formation and manipulation of these LF representations. The hypothesis can be that central-process thinking operates by accessing and manipulating the representations of the language faculty. Where these representations are *only* in LF, the thoughts in question will be non-conscious ones. But where the LF representation is used to generate a full-blown phonological representation (an imaged sentence), the thought will be conscious. I shall return to this suggestion in section 8.7 below. Notice that if this proposal is to be much more than a mere variant on the access-explanation canvassed in section 8.3, then I must claim that there is a distinctive executive system which can only operate on fully represented phonological sentences; indeed, my claim is that this system is the reflexive thinking faculty.

(Philosophers and logicians should note that Chomsky's LF is very different from what they are apt to mean by 'logical form'. In particular, sentences of LF do *not* just contain logical constants and quantifiers, variables, and dummy names. Rather, they consist of lexical items drawn from the natural language in question, syntactically structured, but regimented in such a way that all scope-ambiguities and such like are resolved, and with pronouns cross-indexed to their referents and so on. And the lexical items will be semantically interpreted, linked to whatever structures in the knowledge-base secure their meanings. The important point for these purposes is that sentences of LF are *not* sentences of Mentalese – they are not central-process representations, but are rather internal to the language faculty; and they are not universal to all thinkers, but are always drawn from one or another natural language.)

What would be the motivation behind this second, more controversial, reply? It would be this: we shall need to make such a reply if we come to believe, not just that inner verbalisation is often the only way in which the system can have non-inferential access to its own occurrent thoughts (and hence render them conscious), but also that there are some thoughts which cannot be entertained independently of language. That is, if there are some thoughts (considered as types rather than tokens) which constitutively involve natural language, then we shall need to deny that any conceptual representations of those thoughts, employed in the processes which generate the sentences in question, can themselves exist independent of the language faculty. This is an issue that I shall return to in section 8.7 below, in the form of thesis NN$_s$.

(3) Thirdly, and much more controversially, I could reply to the objection by rejecting the standard models of speech-production. By way of motivation, notice that exactly the same question can be asked about the supposed conceptual representation of the message, as it might be expressed in Mentalese, as is asked about the inner verbalisation of that message in natural language – namely, 'How did it come to be formulated as it was?'. In explaining how a sentence of Mentalese is put together there are surely just the same sorts of reasons which apply in the case of natural language, for proposing that the process starts with a conceptual representation of the thought to be expressed, before proceeding to the selection of lexical items and grammatical forms to express that thought. But plainly this then would, in this case, lead to a vicious regress.

Now, if it is allowed, as it must be, that Mentalese thoughts are formulated *without* a prior conceptual representation of their content, then why should the same concession not be made for natural language? We could then adopt, for example, some variant on Dennett's 'pandemonium model' for speech production instead (see his 1991, ch. 8). According to this model, sentences are constructed in cognition out of relative chaos (and certainly without any prior representation of the message to be expressed), by multiple sub-units proposing sentence parts to a set of assessor units (presumably operating in a context-sensitive way), until the whole system settles upon a sentence which it finds acceptable.

It is sometimes objected against the hypothesis of Mentalese (for example, by Dummett, 1989), that it can bring no advantage over the hypothesis that thought is conducted in natural language, without generating a vicious regress. This is a misunderstanding if it is directed at the Mentalese-based explanation of the *content* of natural-language sentences. As we saw in Chapter 3, it may very well be possible to reduce the content of a natural-language sentence to the content of a thought, and then to offer some independent semantics for the latter (for example, in terms of causal co-variance). While I have argued that such semantic theories are by no means mandatory, and face a number of difficulties, there is no reason to think that they generate any vicious regress.

Matters may be different, however, when we turn our attention from explanations of the semantics of natural language, to explanations of the status of natural-language utterances as *intentional actions*. Here there really is a threat of a regress if we explain the intentional status of a natural-language utterance in terms of an *intentionally formulated* representation of the message to be expressed. For then we shall need yet another representation to explain the intentional status of the latter, and so on. And if we can explain how the construction of a Mentalese sentence can be intentional without appealing to any prior intention, then it is not clear why we cannot adopt just the same sort of explanation of the intentional construction of a natural-language sentence.

To put the point somewhat differently: at *some* level, plainly, sentence-based cognition (whether involving Mentalese or natural language) must be realised in processes which are *not* sentential – perhaps involving connectionist networks of various sorts. And if such processes are appealed to in the explanation of Mentalese-based thinking, then it might be possible to adopt a similar form of explanation for natural language-based thinking, cutting out Mentalese from cognition altogether. This is, at any rate, a research avenue well worth exploring.

8.5   The thesis of natural necessity (weak)

Let us now take final stock of our position. I have responded to all of Fodor's arguments attempting to show that Mentalese is the language in which all thinking is conducted. Some of these proved easy to reply to, while some – particularly the semantic ones – proved more difficult. They required a long detour to consider the semantics of natural language and of thought, conducted in Chapters 3 and 4. Then the provision of an adequate theory of consciousness, in Chapter 7, has finally put us in position to reply to the one remaining argument, from the thoughts of animals and infants. So we are now able to conclude that Fodor has given us no good reason for believing that all thinking takes place in Mentalese.

Yet we still have in place, however, the introspective argument of Chapter 2, for the conclusion that *some* thinking takes place in natural language (specifically, human conscious thinking which is genuinely propositional). Indeed, this has now been vindicated by our discussion of theories of consciousness in Chapters 5 through to the present. For although it is possible to construct theories of inner verbalisation – specifically, the Dennett/Fodor hybrid introduced in section 6.8, or the memory-enhancement explanation discussed in section 8.3 – which predict that we are systematically deceived in making the introspective claim, these theories are by no means the best available. On the contrary, the RT-based model of human conscious cognition which I have finally endorsed gives us every reason to believe that introspection is reliable on this matter.

So the conclusion is (at least tentatively) established: some thinking constitutively involves natural language. This is already enough to secure at least a weak version of the cognitive (as opposed to the communicative) conception of natural language, since we have shown that language is not just an input- and output-module of the mind, but is implicated in central processes of believing, desiring, and reasoning. However, even this conclusion is, as yet, a bare claim of fact. No modal claims are yet warranted. So this must be our final task. I propose to argue that there is a natural necessity attaching to the fact that human conscious thinking involves public or natural language. (The sense in which I intend the term 'public' will be elucidated in section 8.6 below.)

I have sketched, in outline, a model of how human conscious thinking does in fact take place, and of how such cognitive structures might have evolved. But for all that has so far been said, it might seem to remain entirely accidental that humans should ever entertain their conscious thoughts in natural language. Is there no element of necessity attaching to the model? I believe that there is. The first (weaker) version of the claim that I wish to defend is the following:

> NN_w: Some human conscious thinking (*viz.* conscious propositional thinking) is such that, of natural necessity, it involves public language, in virtue of the given architecture of human cognition together with causal laws.

In the remainder of this section I shall first comment on the scope of the above claim, and then present arguments in its defence. In the section that follows I shall then say something further about its proper interpretation.

The scope of NN_w

The claim expressed in NN_w is relatively weak in a number of different respects. First, it does not yet follow from it that there are any thought-contents (considered as types) which can only be grasped through their expression in some public language. In fact, for all that NN_w has to say, it may be that every thought which we can entertain consciously, through the medium of public language, we can also entertain non-consciously, in the medium of some sort of Mentalese. A stronger version of the thesis, which implies that there are some thought-types which can only be entertained at all in public language – NN_s – will be explored in the final two sections of this chapter.

The second way in which NN_w is relatively weak, is that it does not claim that *all* conscious human thinking involves public language. It is conceded that some conscious thinking can be purely imagistic, without involving language, as we have been allowing since near the outset of this book, in section 1.8. Admittedly (to reiterate a point from section 2.2) it may be that in many of those cases where a thought is carried by an image of an object, an embedding in a linguistic context may be necessary to confer on that image a determinate content. In which case such thoughts, too, will turn out to involve public language. So when I think, while at home, of how to arrange the furniture in my office, employing an image to express my thought, what makes that image into an image *of my office* will be an implicit or explicit sentential embedding. My full thought ought properly to be expressed thus: 'I shall arrange the furniture in my office like *this* [insert image].'

Moreover, it should also be pointed out again, that if our thoughts are to have anything like the expressive powers they actually possess, even amongst primitive peoples (setting aside thoughts about the sub-atomic particles of physics, for example), then they would have to employ some sort of symbolic language. For as we noted in section 1.8, it appears quite impossible for images, as such, to carry the content of any but the very simplest thoughts about the immediate environment. (Of course, as we noted, it would always be possible to teach someone to use images as *symbols*, somewhat like an ideographic script, and so gain all of the expressive powers of natural language. But then this would *be* a public language, in the sense that I intend. Public languages do not have to be *speakable*. An entirely visual language is still a language.) It is easy to understand how an image of a stack of perceptually presented boxes might, in context, constitute the thought of a solution to some practical problem. But it is very hard indeed to see how any image by itself, not used conventionally in the manner of an ideographic script, could carry the content of even a perfectly ordinary thought like, 'Ripe apples can be either red or green.'

Despite the above points, it has to be admitted that sometimes our conscious thoughts can consist entirely of images of objects, and not of images used as conventional symbols. As we said, the thoughts of a composer may consist entirely of auditory images, the thoughts of an engineer may sometimes consist entirely of visual images of arrangements of objects, and my thoughts as I find my way across a darkened room might consist simply in an image of its layout in egocentric space. NN_w is not intended to deny any of this.

Note, however, that a combination of the views being defended here will together entail that the status of an image *as conscious* depends upon the thinker's possession of a natural language. For if the points made in section 1.8 were sound, concerning the severe limitations on the representative powers of images, then it is almost certainly the case that no image by itself can represent, or carry a thought about, another image as such. Yet RT theory tells us that an image will only count as conscious if it is available to *conscious* thought. And if the thesis NN_w is true, these conscious thoughts will then have to be entertained linguistically. So the capacity to entertain a conscious thought *about* an image, necessary for the latter to be conscious according to RT theory, depends upon language. But this is only so *for us*. Other species (the Stalnaker Martians, and perhaps chimpanzees) may be capable of conscious thinking without employing language.

But what, then, is the intended scope of NN_w? Precisely *which* types of conscious thinking does NN_w claim (in the human case) to involve public language as a matter of natural necessity? The answer is: all those types of conscious thinking which, *as a matter of fact*, constitutively involve such language (in the manner already established in section 8.3). Wherever a conscious thought is constituted by a natural-language sentence, my hypothesis is that a thought of that type (individuated by content) *can only be* entertained consciously, by us, in its public-language form. The arguments for this view will be set out in the next part of this section, where I shall reply to a number of objections.

The argument for NN_w

In assessing the truth of NN_w, much may depend upon the correct surroundings for the model of human cognition depicted in Figure 3, and on the powers inherent in other aspects of the system. For as it stands, if we focus *only* on Figure 3, then the claim embodied in NN$_w$ is almost trivially true. For removal of the language box, or of the dotted lines of access between language and reflexive thinking, would, by hypothesis, destroy the functioning of the system as a whole. The question is whether there is any alternative way in which a (properly propositional) reflexive thinking structure could be supported in human cognition *without* employing public language. In this part of the section I shall consider four alternative possibilities. These are, so far as I can see, there are only four alternatives available. If none of them is viable, then NN$_w$ will be established as true by default.

(1) The first possibility is that some of those thought-types which are, as a matter of fact, tokened in us in the form of natural-language sentences, *could have been* tokened in the form of mental images instead. But this possibility was, in effect, ruled out in section 1.8, where I argued that purely imagistic and properly propositional thoughts constitute a *disjoint set* – that is to say, that any thought which one actually entertains in language one could not entertain purely imagistically, and vice versa.

Recall how this point was established in section 1.8, in connection with thoughts whose contents do not go beyond what can be perceptually manifest (where one might have expected there to be the strongest case for the content to be thinkable in the form of an image). We considered, in particular, the thought, [that a cat is sitting on a mat]. If this thought is tokened in the form of the English sentence, 'A cat is sitting on a mat', then according to the view defended in section 8.3, this token of that thought is constituted by the sentence in question. But might one not also entertain a token of that very thought in the form of a visual image of a cat sitting on a mat? And would this then not be an alternative manner in which the thought could be entertained consciously, provided that the image in question was itself available to reflexive thinking?

In section 1.8 I answered these questions in the negative, drawing on the claim that content is, at least partly, individuated by functional or conceptual role to make the point. Since any image always has *excess content* in comparison with a sentence, the contents of the two can never really be the same. So in entertaining an image of a cat on a mat one would not really be entertaining a thought of the very same type (*viz.* a properly propositional thought), even though it might concern the same subject matter, and might on occasion play a somewhat similar role in cognition. So the point is established: any thought-type which is in fact tokened consciously in the form of a natural-language sentence, could not have been entertained in the absence of language in the form of an image.

Of course, as we also noted in section 1.8, it is also possible to group thought-contents into types by subject matter, as well as by functional role. By this criterion, an image of a cat on a mat *can* express the same content as the sentence, 'A cat is on a mat.' And then we shall have to concede that some types of conscious thought (*viz.* thoughts whose subject-matters can be represented purely imagistically) do *not* constitutively involve public language. But it seems certain that the range of such thoughts will be extremely limited, probably being confined to representations of perceptible objects and events in our immediate spatio-temporal environment. So NN_w will still claim that conscious thoughts which concern subject-matters that are any more complex or sophisticated than this will have to involve public language.

(2) The second possible way in which someone might try to deny the thesis of natural necessity, NN_w, would be to maintain that human beings do not *need* to access knowledge of public language in order to entertain conscious propositional thoughts, because they already have an innate language – namely, Mentalese – whose forms, structures, and vocabulary they could access instead. The claim here, is that everything in the cognitive architecture depicted in Figure 3 could remain as it is, in the absence of public language, but with reflexive access to sentences of Mentalese replacing the sort of access we actually have to inner deployments of natural-language sentences.

This proposal seems plainly false, however. Even if we do possess some sort of Mentalese, we have no access, surely, to its forms and structures – we are incapable of thinking a thought in Mentalese, and then thinking (non-inferentially) about the Mentalese sentence we have just entertained. So without a public language we should be incapable of conscious (propositional) thinking, if the RT-based account depicted in Figure 3 is correct.

I suppose it might possibly be replied that we were each of us, as prelinguistic children, capable of entertaining conscious thoughts in Mentalese, but that Mentalese was later supplanted by natural language. According to this suggestion, even if we had never learned a public language we would still have been capable of thinking about our own thoughts on a regular basis, and would then have had access to their Mentalese mode of expression. But why would learning a public language *supplant* Mentalese, rather than come to exist alongside it? After all, when people learn a second natural language, and become so proficient that they can do their thinking in that language, this does not deprive them of the ability to think in their first language. Moreover, it would surely be strange indeed that not one of us should have any idea what the sentences of Mentalese might be like, if we had each of us had access to their forms and structures as young children!

(3) The third way in which someone might try to deny the thesis of

natural necessity, NN_w, would be by claiming that we do in fact have the capacity for immediate knowledge of *what* we have just thought without knowledge of *how* we have thought it, which might be underpinned by some sort of semantic-ascent mechanism in Mentalese. That is, it might be claimed that while we do employ public language in some of our conscious thinking, in the sort of way depicted in Figure 3, we *also* have the kind of 'semantic-ascent architecture' we imagined for the Stalnaker Martians in section 7.3. Support for this view might be sought in those many familiar cases where we know, immediately, why we did something, or what we were thinking or believing, *without* knowing in what form those thoughts were expressed. So, according to this suggestion, even if we lacked any public language, we might still be capable of the sort of immediate knowledge of what we have just thought which is necessary for conscious thinking.

The main problem with this suggestion was pointed out in section 8.3. It is that all the evidence suggests that our knowledge of our own recent thinkings and reasonings, where those reasons have not figured in consciousness in sentential (or imagistic) form, is not immediate, but inferential – in which case those reasonings were, in fact, *non*-conscious rather than conscious, if the RT account of consciousness is correct. I argued that this is manifest from the many cases where subjects will claim knowledge of their reasons which is wildly at variance with the facts – for example, claiming to have selected a garment for its colour, when the evidence shows that it was selected, rather, because it was on the right-hand side of an array of such garments. I claimed that what we actually do in such cases is engage in a sort of self-interpretation which is not essentially different in form from other-interpretation, but done so swiftly and smoothly that we hardly notice what we are about. In which case I am left free to claim that it is only where our reasonings occur in the form of occurrent – sententially or imagistically expressed – judgements, that we have immediate (reflexive) knowledge of them. And it is only in such cases that our reasonings should be counted as conscious, if my RT account is correct.

Notice, too, that according to this third suggested alternative to NN_w, the reflexive thinking architecture depicted in Figure 2 would have to exist alongside, and in addition to, the language-involving architecture depicted in Figure 3. For the proposal being made, is that even if we did not have the sort of reflexive access to the forms of our (public-language) thoughts, required for the functioning of the Figure 3 architecture, we could still have had reflexive access to the contents and occurrences of our occurrent thinkings. This then appears wildly extravagant. Why should we have evolved *two* such reflexive-access structures? And why would we bother to run our conscious thoughts through formulation in public language if we could think them, and know that we were thinking them, without it?

(4) Finally, the only other way in which someone could try to deny the natural necessity thesis outlined above, would be by maintaining that a human being who lacked a natural language would still be capable of entertaining conscious propositional thoughts by *inventing* a symbolic system to deploy in imagination, to whose forms the thinker would then have access. Now there are two ways of taking this proposal. And taken in one way, it seems likely to be true; but taken in the other, it seems likely to be false. Yet neither alternative genuinely threatens NN_w. Let me explain.

As we saw in section 2.1, there is evidence that our innate language faculty will seize upon any quasi-linguistic data, no matter how degenerate, to begin constructing properly linguistic representations. Thus Susan Goldin-Meadow and colleagues have found in their studies of congenitally deaf children deprived of any language experience, that the latter will pick up the gestures employed by their parents, extending, regularising, and transforming them into a simple form of natural sign-language (see Goldin-Meadow and Mylander, 1990, Butcher *et al.*, 1991, and Goldin-Meadow *et al.*, 1994). So it may be that even in the absence of linguistic exemplars, normal human beings will employ their innate language-building capacities to construct their own symbolic systems, with which they can then think, and which they could then entertain in imagination in such a way as to render their propositional thoughts conscious. But this proposal is not inconsistent with NN_w, since the resulting symbolic system would still be a natural language. So it would not be the case that the thoughts in question were ever entertained consciously in the absence of such language.

The other possible way to take this fourth suggestion, is to propose that language-deprived humans would be capable of using *central* reasoning processes to invent their own language (which would then almost certainly *not* be a natural one by Chomsky's criteria, since it would fail to satisfy the principles and parameters of the language faculty). In its literal sense, though, invention plainly requires thought – not necessarily conscious thought, perhaps, but certainly thought. For in order to invent something you have to be able to represent it to yourself – at least partially and schematically – in advance. So the question is whether our non-conscious, pre-linguistic, thoughts could have the conceptual resources and sophistication required to invent something as complex as a language. This seems highly unlikely. Is it only lack of brain-power that prevents chimpanzees from inventing a language, for example? I suggest not. It is rather that the conceptual resources available to them are simply not up to the task. Moreover, this suggestion would predict that a 'wolf-child', or a pre-signing deaf child, should be able to invent and use its own language, *even if* it suffered from some form of severe specific language-impairment. But not only is there no evidence that this happens, but it is difficult to see how it could, given the kinds of thoughts which seem available to such children.

The main point to notice, however, is that even if language-deprived children could use central reasoning processes to invent their own symbolic system to deploy in imagination, this would still not be inconsistent with NN_w. For although the resulting language would not be a *natural* one, it would, almost certainly, be a *public* one, in the sense to be discussed in the next section. That is, the thinker's conscious thoughts would still consist of images of movements, or shapes, or sounds, which could in principle be externalised in the form of *actual* movements, or shapes, or sounds. So, again, at no point would these children have been able to employ *conscious* thoughts in the absence of a public language, which is what would be necessary for this proposal to be inconsistent with NN_w.

So I conclude, then, that there are no real alternatives to the weak thesis of natural necessity, NN_w. Since human beings can neither access nor reuse the sentences of any form of Mentalese, in order to entertain thoughts about their own thoughts, nor employ some other sort of symbolic system for the same purpose, we must be dependent upon the acquisition of a public language in order to be capable of conscious propositional thinking.

8.6 Objections and elucidations

In this section I shall try to cast some further light on the thesis NN_w, first discussing the sense in which it is claimed to be naturally necessary, and then commenting on the sense in which the language employed in conscious thought has to be a *public* one (this will enable me to respond to an objection to NN_w made from a Chomskian perspective).

Natural necessity

I commented earlier on the various qualifications to the scope of NN_w. Here let me make some remarks on its status as a claim of natural necessity. One might initially think that it has an exactly parallel form and status to that of the following: 'It is naturally necessary that bodies on Earth fall with an acceleration of 32 feet per second per second.' (A restricted version of the law of gravity). This latter statement is true in virtue of the given mass of the Earth, together with the universal law of gravity. While it has to be acknowledged that the mass of the Earth is contingent, and might have been otherwise consistent with the laws of nature remaining as they are, things would had to have gone very differently in the past in order for it to be different. And if we treat the mass of the Earth as a constant, subserving a stable local sub-system of nature, then what we get is something that, given that constant, *has* to be the case.

In the same way, then, I can claim that while the architecture of human cognition is contingent (depending, as it does, on the accidents of evolution), things would had to have gone very differently in the course of our evolution in order for it to have been different. And if we treat that architecture as a constant, subserving a stable local sub-system of nature (*viz.* human psychology), then what we get is something that *has* to be the case. That is, my claim can be that human beings would had to have evolved a different cognitive architecture in order for them *not* to have entertained conscious thoughts in public language. Or equivalently: given that human beings have evolved as they have, they *cannot* now entertain conscious propositional thoughts in any other medium.

The analogy between thesis NN_w and the restricted version of the law of gravity is by no means perfect, however. For what, in the case of NN_w, corresponds to the *universal* law of gravity? What law of nature is such that, when combined with the description of human cognitive architecture depicted in Figure 3, it will yield the conclusion that human conscious thinking must involve public language? No candidates suggest themselves. While the restricted law of gravity is useful in illustrating how there can be natural necessities which nevertheless depend upon entirely contingent initial conditions, it does not provide the best model for understanding NN_w.

The model I actually prefer is this: 'You cannot make a motor-car engine out of a bicycle.' Or, more strictly and fully: 'You cannot, using only such tools as spanner and screwdriver, reassemble the parts of a bicycle into a functioning motor-car engine.' This statement is, surely, naturally necessary. Moreover, it is a necessity which, as with the previous example, depends upon the given (and contingent) facts of the respective structures of a bicycle and a car engine, and the shapes of their parts. Yet there is no single law which, when combined with descriptions of those structures, will entail the statement above. Rather, the necessity of the statement depends upon many different laws of physics and mechanics, operating at a number of distinct levels.

Similarly, then, in the case of NN_w: I suggest that the given structure and parts of human cognition (as depicted in some suitably expanded and enhanced version of Figure 3) are such that they cannot be recombined or reused in such a way as to enable conscious (reflexive) thinking to take place without employing public language, at least not if that thinking is to be genuinely propositional in nature. And then this is exactly the claim which was defended in the latter part of the previous section.

Public versus natural language

Notice that many of the claims made above have been expressed in terms of public, rather than of natural, language. This is so because, as I have already indicated, I endorse the existence of an innately structured language faculty of the sort defended by Noam Chomsky. For the term *natural language* has come to be synonymous, amongst many of Chomsky's followers, with the idea of a language *which is permitted by the innate structures – the principles and parameters – of our language faculty.* But Chomsky's thesis only predicts that the learning of an artificial language (that is, one which is non-natural in the above sense) would be very slow and laborious, not that it would be altogether impossible.

So it may remain true, consistent with the existence of an innately structured language module, that a human child could be brought up from birth, with much effort and training, to speak a non-natural language as their only language. In which case it might, in fact, be possible for an individual human being to entertain conscious thoughts by using a symbolic system that did not depend upon their prior possession of a natural language, and that failed to satisfy the innate principles and parameters of the language faculty. But this would still count as a *public* language, in at least two respects. First, it would have been learned through some public process of teaching, reward, and correction. Second, its signs, in their use in private thought, would nevertheless admit of a straightforward public expression, since they would, presumably, consist of images of patterns of shape, or sound, or movement, which could be reproduced readily in the public domain should the situation so demand.

So it might, in fact, be possible for human beings to entertain conscious thoughts without having mastery of a natural language, if they had been brought up and trained to employ some other suitably structured system of representations. But this language would still count as a *public* one, in the sense that I intend. Moreover, their use of the signs and symbols in question would still, in fact, be parasitic upon *someone's* possession and use of a *natural language.* For it would surely be impossible for in individual to invent such a system for themselves, relying only upon non-conscious, non-language-involving, thoughts. It seems highly plausible that anyone capable of inventing a non-natural language would already have to be master of some natural language. In which case, we can now claim that it is impossible for human beings *in general* to entertain conscious thoughts except through their possession of natural language. If there exist individuals who have conscious thoughts without having mastery of a natural language, then this will be parasitic upon the conscious thoughts of those who do have such mastery.

I have been claiming that human beings, both in general and as individuals, are incapable of entertaining conscious thoughts except through their mastery of some public language. Note that it is entirely consistent with this, that there should be individual human beings who do their thinking in some sort of private code, as did Samuel Pepys in his diaries. For such codes are only 'private' in the sense that, as a contingent matter of fact, no one else is in a position to interpret and understand them. The private thoughts of such people would still consist of images of potentially public symbols, which the thinker could express publicly (as Pepys in fact did, by writing them down), and which could be explained to others if the thinker should choose to do so.

True enough, such codes would only satisfy one of the two criteria for being public, set out above. For, while they would be publicly expressible, they would not have been acquired through any public process of teaching and learning. Even so, such codes would be parasitic upon some public (almost certainly natural) language for their existence, since they would have been invented through the use of the latter. Moreover, they would presumably be structurally isomorphic to some public language, at least semantically, since their invention would be largely a matter of selecting new signs to express old (publicly expressible) concepts. So I would still want to claim that such people do their conscious thinkings through the use of a public language.

One further reason for expressing thesis NN_w in terms of public, rather than of natural, language is this: I want to allow that thoughts expressed in mathematical, scientific, or musical notation, for example, should count as linguistic. For such notations are, of course, not *natural*, in the sense in which English and French are natural, but rather invented. Yet I would certainly want to allow that they make it possible for us to entertain, and are partially constitutive of, new kinds of conscious thinking. Mathematicians, scientists, and composers certainly engage in a kind of thinking, and thinking which is genuinely propositional; but this thinking need not be mediated by natural language. All the same, these are notations which have to be learned, and which have a straightforward public expression. Indeed, they are best thought of as *extensions of* natural language, rather than as wholly disjoint symbolic systems. They are therefore public, and I can thus continue to claim that it is naturally necessary that human conscious thinking should involve public language.

It is important to stress here, however, that my talk of *public* language in articulating and defending thesis NN_w, need not carry any commitment to the real existence of public languages as objects of scientific study. In particular, I do not have to accept that there really is such a language as English, in any sense other than an abstraction over a vast range (only vaguely specifiable) of slightly different individual idiolects. In fact, I do not have to be committed to what Chomsky calls E-language as opposed to I-language (see his 1986). On the contrary, I can agree with Chomsky that the proper object of scientific study is the state of the individual's language system (their I-language). I merely maintain that the mature state of that system will always be a language which is public in the sense that it is capable of public expression. In contrast with Mentalese, the languages we employ in conscious thought can always be publicly expressed, or *manifested*, in principle (abstracting from such possibilities as paralysis and motor aphasia). There is nothing here that Chomsky need object to, in my view.

I should also stress that I do not intend to be endorsing, here, any sort of rejection of *private language* in Wittgenstein's sense (see his 1953, sections 243ff.). This would be a language whose terms refer to inner private experiences. On the contrary, in section 7.6 above I conceded that it may be possible for us to deploy purely recognitional concepts of inner experience. But if these concepts are to figure in conscious propositional thoughts, then according to NN_w they will have to be expressed by terms which are public in the sense that they are images of (potentially) publicly expressible signs. The contrast I intend between public and private language is not a semantic one – it does not concern the subject-matter of the language – but rather lexical/syntactic. The intended contrast is between public language and Mentalese, in fact.

8.7   The thesis of natural necessity (strong)

I have defended the weaker version of NN, according to which our cognition is so structured that we can only entertain conscious propositional thoughts by formulating them in public (normally natural) language. But this does not yet show that such language is constitutive of the thought-types so formulated. What needs to be investigated, now, is the sort of case that can be made out in support of the stronger version of NN, as follows:

> NN_s: Some human conscious thinking is such that, of natural necessity, it involves public language (in virtue of the given architecture of human cognition, together with causal laws); and, necessarily, some of these propositional thoughts belong to types which (for us at least) constitutively involve such language.

As I noted in section 4.6, it is only if this stronger thesis can be established that it will follow that public language is constitutive of (many of) our conscious thoughts *as types* (individuated by content). And it would seem that the full significance for philosophy and psychology which we advertised in section 1.2 will only be realised if this stronger thesis can be established (I shall return to this question in section 8.8).

What NN_s implies is that many of our conscious thoughts, as tokens, constitutively involve public language, and that thoughts of those types could not have been tokened consciously in the absence of such language (this is thesis NN_w, which NN_s entails). The thesis NN_s also implies, in addition, that many of those conscious thought-tokens belong to types which constitutively involve public language, so that one could not entertain *any* token thought of that type (whether consciously *or* non-consciously) in the absence of such language.

Note that while NN_s tells us that many of our conscious thoughts, as types, must involve public language, it does not have to imply that there are any types of thought which *can only be* entertained consciously. Indeed, I can see no good reason why each of our public-language-involving thoughts should not be able to occur non-consciously as well as consciously. And in section 8.4 we saw in outline how this might be possible, in fact – propositional thinking, in us, may take place by means of the central systems accessing and deploying representations drawn from the language faculty; when these representations are in LF only, the thoughts will be non-conscious ones; but where the representations in LF are used to generate a phonological representation as well, which can then be held in the short-term memory store C in such a way as to be made available to further thought, then the thoughts in question will be conscious ones. I shall return to this proposal shortly.

The thesis NN_s, itself, therefore leaves it open whether there are some thought-types which can only be entertained consciously, or whether every thought which we can entertain consciously, in public language, we can also entertain non-consciously in the same medium. But in fact I am strongly inclined to believe the latter, on the grounds that most genuinely innovative and creative thinking appears to take place non-consciously. If it is possible to entertain non-conscious thoughts about the relativity of space-time, or about the Benzene ring, or about a chess end-game (as the evidence from both creative thinkers and ordinary experience suggests) then it seems very likely that there are no real limits on the subject-matters of our non-conscious thoughts (see Ghiselin, 1952).

How can NN_s be defended? I have two lines of argument. One is to compare NN_s directly with its Mentalese-involving competitors, arguing that the former is preferable on grounds of simplicity (among others).

The second involves returning to the arguments from developmental psychology and aphasia of section 2.1, reassessing their strength in the light of NN_w. For if we can take it as already established that public language is necessarily employed in our conscious thinking, as NN_w maintains, then the simplest explanation of the data may be that language is essentially involved in – is constitutive of – many of the types of thought which are available to us, whether those thoughts are entertained consciously or non-consciously. I shall elaborate each argument in turn.

The argument against the competition

To deny NN_s, while continuing to accept NN_w, one has to deny that *any* of the thought-types which actually involve public or natural language (when entertained consciously) *necessarily* involve such language. That is, one must maintain that it is naturally possible for us to entertain (non-consciously) the full range of thoughts which are available to us in public language, but without employing such language. There are just two conceivable ways in which this might be done, the first of which can be dismissed almost immediately.

The first way of denying NN_s is developmental. We could allow that, where our conscious thoughts involve language, all tokens of those thoughts which we ever actually entertain consciously (in the normal case) are similarly language-involving (this is NN_w). But we could maintain, nevertheless, that *if we had never acquired* public language, then thoughts of all those types would still have been available to us *non*-consciously – but in that case expressed in Mentalese rather than a public language. Such a claim would obviously be extravagant, however, and would conflict with what I have taken the lovers of Mentalese to be conceding from near the outset of this book: namely, that possession of a public language is at least a necessary condition for us to entertain many types of thought, even if it is not always thereafter *involved in* those thoughts.

The second way in which NN_s might be denied (while accepting NN_w) would be to claim that our (adult) non-conscious thinking faculty has available to it all of the conceptual resources of conscious (public-language-involving) thinking, but expressed in Mentalese rather than public language. On this account, while possession of a public language may have been a necessary condition for us to acquire certain concepts and so entertain certain thoughts; and while such language may be constitutively involved in the conscious occurrence of those thoughts (as NN_w maintains); still thoughts of those types can be activated (non-consciously) without the involvement of public language, and it would still be possible for us so to entertain them if the capacity for such language were lost.

According to NN_s, in contrast, many of our conscious language-involving thoughts belong to types which (for us at least) constitutively involve public language. So if it is possible for us to entertain tokens of those thoughts non-consciously, those thoughts, too, will be expressed in public language.

Which of these two accounts is the better? The main point to note is that the cognitive resources and structures postulated by each of them in the normal case are different, and that considerations of simplicity favour NN_s. For the Mentalese-involving explanation must suppose that conceptual resources are duplicated in normal cognition, with all our concepts being expressed *both* by public-language terms *and* by lexical items of Mentalese. (Remember, it is presupposed here that NN_w is correct, and thus that when we do entertain a thought consciously in public language, the use of those public-language signs *is* the thinking, and also that tokens of the thought in question cannot be entertained consciously in the absence of public language.) NN_s, in contrast, maintains that many of our concepts are tied to their public-language expression only.

Recall that we have been taking it for granted, since section 1.8, that propositional thoughts *are* relations to sentences. So it is not open to the opponent of NN_s to claim that there is but a single conceptual store, which may receive expression *either* in terms of Mentalese *or* in terms of public language. For, according to our sententialist assumption, concepts *are* lexical items in some or other system of signs, which are caused, stored, and processed in characteristic ways. So, in claiming that our thinking can be conducted either in Mentalese or in public language, the opponent of NN_s (who nevertheless accepts NN_w) is committed to the claim that we each of us possess two distinct, but semantically equivalent, conceptual systems. This claim appears thoroughly extravagant. Is there any way in which it might nevertheless be motivated?

I can conceive of just one possibility. It might be claimed that public-language thinking can, for some reason, *only* take place consciously. In which case it would certainly make good sense that all of our public-language concepts should be routinely copied over into Mentalese, so that we could enjoy the advantages of non-conscious as well as conscious thinking across all domains. If there exist non-conscious hypothesis-generators and problem-solving systems (as there appear to – see the remarks about creative thinking earlier in this section), then there would surely be distinct advantages in ensuring that the full range of concepts, and hence thoughts, was made available to such systems.

The trouble with this proposal lies in its initial assumption, however – namely, that language-involving thoughts can only be entertained consciously. For I can see no good reason why we should believe this. On the contrary, the hypothesis that natural language representations can be processed and manipulated non-consciously as well as consciously would appear to be well motivated. To maintain the opposite, one would have to insist that a sentence of natural language can only figure in cognition *as* a sentence with its full phonological properties represented in imagination, in such a way as to be available to reflexive thinking. But why should this be so? It is generally accepted amongst linguists working within a Chomskian framework, at least, that there is a level of language processing at which phonological properties are stripped away, leaving just syntax and semantics (this is the level of logical form, or LF). In which case, why should not those very representations be made available for use in central cognition, for purposes of non-conscious thought? Indeed, the anecdotal evidence suggests that they are. For creative non-conscious problem-solving can deal with matters which are overtly linguistic. If poets, novelists, and headline-writers can come up with their best turns of phrase, or their best language-involving ideas, in the absence of conscious reflection, as many reports suggest, then this must imply that natural-language expressions are being tokened and manipulated non-consciously.

I conclude, then, that when we compare NN_s with the Mentalese opposition, the former is seen to be much the more believable. In the end, it is more reasonable to believe that public language should be employed *both* for conscious *and* for non-conscious thinking, than it is to believe that we should employ two distinct, but semantically equivalent, representational systems.

The argument from the psychological evidence

A further set of arguments in support of NN_s can be obtained by returning to the developmental and aphasic evidence of section 2.1, but armed, now, with acceptance of NN_w. The first point to note is that the opponent of NN_s must advance a variety of explanations of different aspects of the data, as follows:

(1) The fact that cognitive and linguistic abilities normally advance together is to be explained by claiming that public language, in human beings, is the channel of communication through which we acquire many of our belief-systems, together with their embedded concepts.

(2) Ildefonso's difficulties with temporal discourse, and the fact that the play of the language-deficient twins studied by Luria and Yudovich became immensely more structured and creative within a few months of acquiring significant amounts of language, is to be explained by claiming that certain

concepts are initially tied to the deployment of public-language signs, but become available in Mentalese thereafter.

(3) The fact that global aphasics appear to have difficulties with conceptual thinking (for example, difficulties in recognising that the activities of frogs and kangaroos are alike, in that both *hop*) is to be explained by supposing that both public language and Mentalese-involving concepts are stored in the same region of the brain, almost inevitably being damaged together.

The explanation advanced by NN$_s$, in contrast, is the same in each case – namely, that the phenomena in question arise because our cognition is so structured that certain kinds of concept, and certain types of thinking, constitutively require and involve public language. Now other things being equal, one explanation which unifies a diverse range of phenomena is to be preferred to a number of distinct explanations. So there is good reason to prefer NN$_s$. Now consider the explanations (2) and (3) above in a little more detail.

(2) What the opponent of NN$_s$ has to say about the acquisition of temporal concepts, and of the logical concepts necessary for hypothetical thinking and for complex planning, is that these concepts are initially tied to the public-language expressions, through competence in whose use they are acquired; but that they are later copied onto lexical items of Mentalese, in such a way that such thoughts can thereafter be entertained in the absence of public language. But this account is difficult to understand or make sense of. If we already have one set of signs whose use constitutively expresses for us a certain range of thoughts (as NN$_w$ maintains), then what would be the purpose of copying these into another set of signs to entertain the very same range of thoughts? What would be the point? What would be the gain? Again, to make sense of this one would have to maintain that natural-language representations *cannot be deployed non-consciously*. It is surely more reasonable to believe that the capacity for entertaining those thoughts (whether consciously or non-consciously) should remain tied to their public language expressions.

(3) Consider, too, what the opponent of NN$_s$ has to say about the effects of global aphasia on conceptual thinking. Here the claim has to be that public-language lexical items and their Mentalese equivalents are stored in the same regions of the brain. This now looks much less plausible in the light of acceptance of NN$_w$. If public language had been *only* a medium of communication, then it would not have been entirely surprising, perhaps, that language should be stored in the same region of the brain as the bearers of the thoughts (in Mentalese) which it is standardly used to communicate. But if such language is also constitutive of the

occurrence of many of our conscious thoughts, as NN_w maintains, then the situation would be strange indeed. Why would the lexical items constitutive of our conscious thoughts be stored alongside, and in the same place as, the lexical items of Mentalese supposedly constitutive of our non-conscious ones, given that their overall roles in cognition would be so different? It is surely more reasonable to accept that public-language sentences are constitutive of the occurrence of many types of thought (whether consciously or non-consciously), just as NN_s maintains.

Taking together all the arguments in this section, then, I conclude that, with NN_w already established, it is much more reasonable to believe NN_s than to deny it. We should therefore accept that our cognition is so structured that many types of thought can only be entertained through the medium of public language, whether consciously or not.

8.8   The scope and significance of NN

What does seem to have been definitely established by the RT-based model of human cognition presented in this chapter (at least if that model is correct) is that much of human conscious thinking involves public language; and that this is so out of natural necessity. This is the thesis NN_w. But I have now argued that, in the light of the likely truth of NN_w, NN_s may also be taken as established. I have argued, that is, that many types of thought (individuated by content) *can only be entertained*, by us, through the medium of public language (whether consciously or non-consciously). In this final section I shall comment on the significance of these results, as well as raising, somewhat inconclusively, the question of their scope.

The significance of NN_w

The truth of NN_w is already sufficient to show, firstly, that language is not just an isolated module of the mind, but is directly implicated in the distinctively human (conscious) aspects of the central functions of believing, desiring, and conscious reasoning. This is a decisive vindication of the cognitive conception of language, as against the communicative conception. And we can claim, moreover, that it is no mere accident that our conscious propositional thoughts make use of public language. Rather, this is determined, of natural necessity, by the very structure of human cognition. So the study of natural language is the study of a faculty which is essentially implicated in the central functions of the (human) mind, just as Chomsky has sometimes maintained. However, the truth of NN_w alone is not sufficient to show that the language faculty is constitutively involved in our systems of thought and belief as such. For that, we would need NN_s.

As for the question of significance for philosophy, here, too, the truth of NN_w seems already sufficient to gain for us much of what was advertised in section 1.2. For if philosophers choose to focus their attention on the expression of thoughts in public-language, then it seems that they can be confident (in the light of NN_w) that the structure and use of the linguistic expressions will mirror the structures of the thoughts (which are, of course, the true objects of interest). For those thoughts *are* public-language sentences used and processed in characteristic ways. So the analysis of problematic concepts can proceed via consideration of their expression in language, and the 'linguistic turn' of analytical philosophy is established.

It might be argued, however, that if philosophers are concerned with the concepts and conceptual structures involved in any given thought [that P] *as such*, then there is scope for doubt about the appropriateness of the linguistic turn. For according to NN_w, this thought, as a *type*, need not involve public language, and may be thinkable, non-consciously, without it. It is only those occurrent tokens of the thought which are conscious which essentially involve public language, if NN_w is the most that can be established. So it might be wondered whether the thought as such could have an underlying structure which is only misleadingly captured by its dual modes of expression – its expression, namely, non-consciously in Mentalese, and consciously in public language.

But this is a confusion. For according to the sententialist assumption adopted in section 1.8, thoughts *are* sentences in some or other system of representation. So if one thought can be expressed by sentences from two different systems (Mentalese and natural language), then this just means that those sentences are identical in respect of their functional or conceptual role, and also in respect of their truth-conditions. There is simply no room for the possibility that the thought in question may not be *properly* expressed in one system of representation or the other. This is not to say, of course, that a sentence cannot express its own content non-perspicuously. But this just means that features of the use of the sentence cannot easily be read off from its form. It does not mean that the content is something which can exist, and which can be investigated, independently of any sentence.

The scope of NN$_s$

What is the scope of NN_s? To what thought-types does it apply? *Which* types of thought are such that they can only be entertained at all, by us (whether consciously or non-consciously) through their expression in a public (normally natural) language? Note that there is no question of us answering, here, that NN_s applies to all *propositional* thought, in the way that we did in connection with NN_w above. For public-language thinking is not now to be contrasted just with thoughts expressed in private images, as it was when it was only conscious thoughts which were in question. Rather, there may well be types of thought which can be entertained non-consciously in a form of Mentalese; and then these would count as properly propositional.

Recall that the basic argument in support of NN_s turned on the implausibility of supposing that all concepts and conceptual systems are duplicated in cognition, finding expression *both* in public language *and* in Mentalese. We suggested, rather, that public language would probably do double duty for both conscious and non-conscious thinking. But from the fact that *not all* concepts are duplicated it does not follow that *none* are. So we cannot yet conclude that all non-imagistic thought-types which are available to us in public language will be essentially public-language involving. There may well be particular domains in which, for one reason or another, our concepts are expressed both in natural language and in Mentalese. These would be domains which human beings are capable of representing, and entertaining genuinely propositional thoughts about, *before* the arrival of public language.

The most plausible general hypothesis, I think, is that public language is essentially implicated in all thoughts whose constituent concepts are dependent upon language for their acquisition. We can conclude, in fact, that all concepts which *require* public language must also *involve* public language. For if certain concepts require public language, in the sense that they can only be acquired through language-learning and/or the acquisition of information and new beliefs from other people, then by NN_w the conscious tokens of those concepts will necessarily involve public language. And then our general argument for NN_s would suggest that the *non*-conscious tokening of those concepts will also be undertaken in public language, rather than being duplicated into Mentalese. And so we get the conclusion that those concepts can only be tokened at all in public language, which means that they fall within the scope of NN_s – those concepts determine a class of thought-types which (for us) necessarily involve public language; and if we were to lose public language, then we would lose our capacity to entertain thoughts of those types.

There is surely no doubt that the class of such language-dependent concepts is very large indeed, including concepts from mathematics and the natural sciences (*prime number, gene, electron*), concepts from the social sciences (*inflation, nation-state*), as well as a whole range of perfectly ordinary concepts, including *marriage, law, permission, school, writing, story, drama, employer, wage, holiday, bus-stop, ticket, generosity,* and many, many, more. (And note, here, that to say that a concept is language-dependent is *not* necessarily to deny that it is innate – see below.) In fact, it is no exaggeration to say that *most* human concepts and thoughts will turn out to involve public language essentially, if the arguments of this chapter are sound.

Roughly speaking, then, to look for evidence of the exact scope of NN_s is to look for evidence that certain thoughts have constituent concepts which are dependent upon public language for their acquisition and/or for their continued existence. Thus if the acquisition of temporal concepts is dependent upon language, as the evidence provided by Schaller's pre-signing deaf man Ildefonso would suggest, then NN_s will imply that such concepts are necessarily language-involving. And if the sorts of general beliefs which go to make up our concepts of natural kinds (for example, 'Kangaroos hop', 'Kiwis cannot fly', and so on) are dependent upon language, as some of the evidence from global aphasia suggests, then these concepts, too, will be essentially language-involving.

Conversely, evidence that certain types of thought fall outside the scope of NN_s will be provided wherever there is evidence that the constituent concepts of those thoughts might have evolved, or might be constructable, prior to language, and so be independent of it. Thoughts about the motions and interactions of middle-sized physical objects (folk-physics), and thoughts about animal and plant kinds (folk-biology) might be plausible enough examples (see Carey, 1985). These thoughts, in going beyond what could be represented purely imagistically, would require some sort of Mentalese to be in place prior to language. But when language is then acquired, the constituent concepts would presumably be copied into the public-language medium, and the very same thoughts would then become available for expression (consciously) in public-language form. Since conscious thinking is useful, it would be easy enough to understand why such copying-across should take place.

In fact, there is now evidence that infants and pre-linguistic children have at least some understanding of a quite remarkable range of subject-matters, including causality and an intuitive mechanics, action and agency, and number (see Karmiloff-Smith, 1992, for reviews). But here we have to be careful to ensure that what is being displayed is genuinely *thought* about these subject-matters, and not merely discriminations of, or sensitivities to, them. We need to be mindful, in fact, of the distinction Annette Karmiloff-Smith draws between knowledge which is merely *implicit*, perhaps embedded in some practical procedure, and knowledge which is *explicit*, available for general use in cognition, and for interactions with centrally stored information outside of that procedure. With this distinction in place, the evidence of genuine (explicitly represented) thought about the above subject-matters, prior to language, is extremely meagre.

Even evidence that a certain body of beliefs and concepts is innate does not show that the thoughts in question are independent of language. For the evolution of those beliefs may have been closely interwoven with that of language. Our folk-psychology may serve as an example here, since I have already argued (in section 1.7) that it is probably innate. For there is also evidence, briefly cited in section 2.1, that language-ability and competence in theory of mind tasks develop together. And some researchers have begun to speculate that the crucial concepts of belief, and of false belief, can only be underpinned by language (see Harris, 1996, and Smith, 1996). Put in modular terms, the hypothesis is that a primitive form of desire-perception psychology may pre-date the arrival of language, both in evolution and in child development, but that fully intentional belief-desire psychology may have had to await the beginnings of language and linguistic communication.

It may well be, then, that the development of explicit (genuinely thoughtful) knowledge about many domains is dependent upon language – even where that knowledge is innate or has a substantial innate basis. So the evidence, cited above, that humans have domain-specific and innately constrained knowledge of such matters as folk-physics, folk-biology, and folk-psychology, does not show that it is possible for us to entertain the thoughts in question independently of language. This remains an open question. It may be, in particular, that some relevant language-experience is a crucial trigger for the innate knowledge to develop beyond the merely implicit level. Perhaps such cognitive modules can only grow and operate if they can co-opt some public signs to fill the innately determined concept slots within the module.

A research-programme for NN_s

Of course the question of the exact scope of NN_s is, ultimately, an empirical issue; and a detailed answer to it would require us to consider, and gather, a variety of kinds of developmental and neuropsychological evidence. Here just let me mention some of the kinds of evidence which appear to me to be most germane, and also say something briefly about the difficulties which stand in the way of us gathering it.

First, it would be particularly worthwhile to study congenitally deaf children who have had no exposure to conventional language, to see the range of thoughts which might nevertheless be available to them. For although, as we have seen, such children are probably not entirely languageless, we can be fairly confident that they have no language abilities beyond those that they overtly express. (Since they construct their languages for themselves, they are unlikely to be in the position of young normal children who can understand more than they can say.) So wherever we find evidence that they possess concepts which do *not* find expression in their invented sign-languages, there we may conclude that the concept in question is independent of language. It would be interesting to see what explicit knowledge such children have of the domains of folk-physics, folk-biology, and folk-psychology, in particular.

There are two main difficulties which stand in the way of such studies, however (aside from the practical problem that such children are becoming increasingly rare, as the almost total ineffectiveness of lip-reading for congenitally deaf children with no prior knowledge of language becomes generally recognised). The first is the difficulty of experimentally discriminating implicit from explicit knowledge. Only the latter will show the existence of language-independent *thought*. The second is the difficulty of devising non-linguistic tests of knowledge and understanding. As has become clear to those working in the area of theory of mind, who have been attempting to develop non-language-dependent tests of false-belief understanding for use with apes and very young children, this can be an extremely difficult thing to achieve.

Second, it would be worthwhile to study what happens to such pre-signing deaf children if they are then immersed in a signing environment, at age 6 or 7, say. Since such children would be developmentally fully ready for language, the prediction will be that they would acquire Sign extremely fast. And then it would be interesting to observe the changes which take place in their cognition as a result. If there are kinds of thought which did not appear to be available to them before, but which become available consequent upon acquisition of full-blown language, then this will be evidence that thoughts of those kinds constitutively require public language. (In effect, this would be to rerun the Luria and Yudovich twin-experiment.)

Third, we need to continue to study individuals with global aphasia, to see what kinds of thought can be spared, and which are inevitably lost with the loss of language. One problem here is that of knowing whether the aphasia is genuinely global. Perhaps in the future it may be possible to use a combination of knowledge of neural anatomy and advanced brain-imaging techniques to ascertain that *all* the language systems have been completely destroyed, and not just the input and/or output systems. Another major obstacle is, again, to develop tests for the various types of thought which are independent of language. But provided these problems can be overcome, we might discover that there are kinds of thought which can be spared in global aphasia, and so which are not necessarily language-involving, and kinds which are inevitably lost, in which case we can conclude that they *are* language-involving.

Let me stress again, however, the importance of the implicit/explicit distinction here. It is not sufficient, if we wish to establish that certain kinds of thought can be entertained non-consciously independently of language (hence restricting the scope of NN_s), to show merely that patients whose aphasia is genuinely global can engage competently in certain practical activities. For the most that this would show is that they retain an *im*plicit knowledge of the domains those activities concern – knowledge which may be embedded in their practical procedures. It would not show that they are genuinely capable of thinking (explicitly) about those domains. So once again we face the problem of distinguishing empirically between implicit and explicit knowledge.

In fact, I would predict, public language may well be required for any kinds of thought which are distinctively human, which are not available to other species of animal. Indeed, since the cognition of the average human child in its second year seems rather less sophisticated than that of many species of animal, it may be that human cognition is so structured that even relatively simple types of thought – which in other species receive expression in some form of Mentalese – require public language in the case of human beings. But I have to admit that I have no account ready to hand of the kind of complexity that marks the divide between those types of human thought which are essentially language-involving, and those which are not.

The significance of NN_s

I have argued that, in the light of the likely truth of NN_w, NN_s may also be taken as established. I have argued, that is, that many thought-types (presumably those, in particular, of the more complex and abstract variety) *can only be entertained*, by us, through the medium of public language (whether consciously or non-consciously). This would then provide philosophers with some further guarantee of the methodological soundness of the linguistic turn. Since many of the thought-types which we entertain consciously in public language are essentially language-involving, it must follow that in studying the use of the public signs we are studying the thoughts themselves. Indeed, the concepts which tend to attract the attention of philosophers, and which tend to be philosophically especially problematic, are ones which are distinctively human, and would presumably count as 'complex and sophisticated' – and so essentially language-involving – according to the above account. (Think here of concepts like *causal necessity, personal identity, objective truth*, and so on – but presumably not indexical concepts like *this*, or *here*.)

As for significance for scientific psychology, the truth of NN_s would mean that the language faculty is yet even more deeply embedded in, and partially constitutive of, central cognition. Not only would conscious propositional thinking essentially involve natural-language sentences, as NN_w maintains, but the thoughts so entertained (together with their embedded concepts) would consist in relations to natural-language expressions. Thus, not only would the language faculty be employed in central cognition, but it would bring with it many of the concepts and conceptual structures which are distinctively employed in human conscious thinking. On this picture, it really would be only an exaggeration to say that the study of language *is* the study of the mind.

Summary

In this chapter I have outlined an architecture for human conscious thinking which assigns a central role to language, and have argued that this provides a better account of the place of public language in our cognition than do the alternatives. I have also argued, on the basis of this account, for two types of natural necessity thesis. The weaker version of this thesis maintains that propositional forms of human conscious thinking necessarily involve public language. The stronger version claims that many of the thought-types so entertained are themselves essentially language-involving. I have thus suggested that it may be naturally necessary that distinctively human (complex) thinking should involve public language. But as for the exact scope of this strong form of natural necessity thesis, I have had to leave this largely undetermined.

(Note, however, that both forms of thesis NN are contingent on a creature's possession of the sort of human cognitive architecture depicted in Figure 3, and so do not extend beyond it. Thus Stalnaker's intelligent and conscious Martians remain a possibility.)

Wittgenstein famously wrote, in the preface to the only book he was to publish in his lifetime (the *Tractatus Logico-Philosophicus*, 1921), 'May others come and do it better.' I have to say, much more modestly, 'May others come and do it.' For the real work is yet to be done. I can only claim to have been pointing in the right direction.

Conclusion

In this brief concluding section of the book, I shall pull together the various threads of my discussion, reminding the reader of its starting-point, of its main lines of argument, and of its major conclusions.

Recall that the inquiry has taken place against the background of a number of assumptions, set out in Chapter 1. Most importantly, I have assumed a form of *realism* about the mind and its propositional attitudes. I have assumed that beliefs and desires are real internal states of the agent which interact with one another causally to produce other mental states and behaviour, and whose existence can be independent of our best behavioural evidence. And I have assumed that our common-sense conception of the mind not only contains an implicit theory of its structure and function, but also that the theory in question is, very likely, broadly correct. Equally significantly, I have also assumed that some or other form of *sententialism* is correct, maintaining that propositional attitudes are best understood as relations to sentences. The question then has been, 'Which sentences? – those of public language, or those of Mentalese?'

I have also made a number of *modularist* and *nativist* assumptions, although slightly less weight has been placed upon these in the argumentative structure of the book. I have assumed that the mind is (more or less) modular in structure, consisting of a number of isolable – and largely isolated – functional components, whose contents and principles of operation have a significant innate component. More specifically, I have assumed that both natural language competence and common-sense psychology are isolable features of our cognition, and that each is substantially innate.

Against this background, the argument of the book has consisted of two distinct, but interwoven, threads. On the one hand I have presented the positive case for thinking that much of our conscious thought essentially involves public language. This began as the argument from introspection in Chapter 2, developed through the discussion of a number of theories of consciousness in Chapters 5 to 7, and has just now culminated in the argument of Chapter 8, supporting thesis NN. Then on the other hand I have tried to undermine the various arguments for claiming that all think-ing must take place in Mentalese, maintaining that these are less than wholly convincing. This strand began in the final sections of Chapter 2, ran through the discussion of Fodor's various semantic arguments in Chapters 3 and 4, and concluded finally with a rejection of the argument from animals and infants in section 7.8, following the defence of my reflexive thinking theory of consciousness in that chapter.

Overall in this book I have tried to place public (normally natural) lan-guage centre-stage in the study of human cognition. For if I am right, then language is not just a very important, but nevertheless peripheral, channel of communication. It is, rather, constitutive of many of our central pro-cesses of thinking and reasoning, particularly those that are conscious. Moreover, I have tried to argue for this position from within a broadly modularist and nativist framework. Certainly I have had no truck with the Whorfian relativism of the Standard Social Science Model, according to which people's minds are more or less plastic, and are then shaped by the particular natural languages they acquire. It has been an important part of what I have tried to show, indeed, that one can deny such relativism while *still* endorsing the cognitive conception of language.

I claim, too, that the conclusions defended in my final chapters have been strong enough to warrant the methodological implications adver-tised in Chapter 1. For if language is constitutive of much of human con-scious thinking, in much the same sense that water is constituted by H_2O, then the psychological study of the forms and structures of natural lan-guage *is* the study of a crucial, and central, aspect of the human mind. And if it is necessary that our conscious thoughts should character-istically be formulated in public language, as I have maintained, then it must be legitimate and useful for philosophers to study the problematic concepts which particularly concern them by investigating the linguistic expression of those concepts.

However, let me emphasise at the close of the book, as I did at the beginning, the non-demonstrative nature of its argument. For I do not claim to have *proved* my conclusion. I only claim two things: first, to have shown that my conclusion is *possible* (in the sense of worth taking seri-ously); and second, to have made it seem *plausible*, advancing it as the best explanation of a variety of phenomena. Substantive philosophy has to content itself with at least that degree of uncertainty which attaches to all science. And highly speculative substantive philosophy, such as I have been engaged in throughout much of this book, must be content with a good deal less certainty still. But this fact should not, in my view, leave us feeling dissatisfied with the result. Indeed I claim, on the contrary, that the craving for certainty and for a priori demonstration, which is distinctive of so much of philosophy, is an intellectual disease, born of professional paranoia and philosophical error. But that is a story for another occasion.

References

Appiah, Anthony, 1986 *For Truth in Semantics*, Blackwell.

Armstrong, David, 1968 *A Materialist Theory of the Mind*, Routledge.

1978 *Universals and Scientific Realism*, Cambridge University Press.

1984 'Consciousness and Causality', in D. Armstrong and N. Malcolm, *Consciousness and Causality*, Blackwell.

Astington, Janet, 1996 'What is Theoretical about the Child's Theory of Mind?: a Vygotskian view of its development', in Carruthers and Smith, 1996.

Baars, Bernard, 1988 *A Cognitive Theory of Consciousness*, Cambridge University Press.

Baddeley, Alan, 1986 *Working Memory*, Oxford University Press.

1988 *Human Memory*, Laurence Erlbaum.

1993 'Working Memory and Conscious Awareness', in *Theories of Memory*, eds. A. Collins, S. Gathercole, and M. Conway, Laurence Erlbaum.

Baddeley, Alan, and Hitch, G., 1974 'Working Memory', in *The Psychology of Learning and Motivation*, vol. 8, ed. G. Brown, Academic Press.

Baron-Cohen, Simon, 1989 'Are Autistic Children Behaviourists? An examination of their mental-physical and appearance-reality distinctions', *Journal of Autism and Developmental Disorders*, vol. 19.

1990 'Autism a Specific Cognitive Disorder of "Mind-Blindness"', *International Review of Psychiatry*, vol. 2.

Bennett, Jonathan, 1991 'How do Gestures Succeed?', in *John Searle and his Critics*, eds. E. Lepore and R. Van Gulick, Blackwell.

Bickerton, Derek, 1990 *Language and Species*, University of Chicago Press.

Blackburn, Simon, 1984 *Spreading the Word*, Oxford University Press.

Block, Ned, 1986 'Advertisement for a Semantics for Psychology', *Midwest Studies in Philosophy*, vol. 9.

1993 'Holism, Hyper-analyticity, and Hyper-compositionality', *Mind and Language*, vol. 8.

1995 'A Confusion about a Function of Consciousness', *Behavioural and Brain Sciences*, vol. 18.

Bonjour, Laurence, 1985 *The Structure of Empirical Knowledge*, Harvard University Press.

Butcher, Cynthia, Mylander, Carolyn, and Goldin-Meadow, Susan, 1991 'Displaced Communication in a Self-Styled Gesture System: pointing at the nonpresent', *Cognitive Development*, vol. 6.

Byrne, Richard, and Whiten, Andrew, eds., 1988 *Machiavellian Intelligence*, Oxford University Press.

Carey, Susan, 1985 *Conceptual Change in Childhood*, MIT Press.

Carruthers, Peter, 1986 *Introducing Persons: theories and arguments in the philosophy of mind*, Routledge.

1987 'Conceptual Pragmatism', *Synthese*, vol. 73.

1989 *Tractarian Semantics: finding sense in Wittgenstein's Tractatus*, Blackwell.

1990 *The Metaphysics of the Tractatus*, Cambridge University Press.

1992a *Human Knowledge and Human Nature*, Oxford University Press.

1992b 'Consciousness and Concepts', *Aristotelian Society Proceedings*, supp.vol. 66.

1992c *The Animals Issue: moral theory in practice*, Cambridge University Press.

1996a 'Simulation and Self-Knowledge: a defence of theory-theory', in Carruthers and Smith, 1996.

1996b 'Autism as Mind-Blindness: an elaboration and partial defence', in Carruthers and Smith, 1996.

Carruthers, Peter, and Smith, Peter K., eds., 1996 *Theories of Theories of Mind*, Cambridge University Press.

Chomsky, Noam, 1976 *Reflections on Language*, Temple Smith.

1986 *Knowledge of Language: its nature, origins and use*, Praeger.

1988 *Language and Problems of Knowledge*, MIT Press.

1995 'Language as a Natural Object', *Mind*, vol. 104.

Churchland, Paul, 1981 'Eliminative Materialism and Propositional Attitudes', *Journal of Philosophy*, vol. 78.

Clark, Andy, 1989 *Microcognition*, MIT Press.

Copeland, Jack, 1993 *Artificial Intelligence*, Blackwell.

Cummins, Robert, 1989 *Meaning and Mental Representation*, MIT Press.

Curtiss, Susan, 1977 *Genie: a psycholinguistic study of a modern-day 'wild child'*, Academic Press.

1989 'The Independence and Task-Specificity of Language', in *Interaction in Human Development*, eds. M. Bornstein and J. Bruner, Laurence Erlbaum.

Davidson, Donald, 1975 'Thought and Talk', in his *Inquiries into Truth and Interpretation*, Blackwell, 1984.

1982 'Rational Animals', in *Actions and Events*, eds. E. Lepore and B. McLaughlin, Blackwell, 1986.

Davies, Martin, 1991 'Concepts, Connectionism, and the Language of Thought', in *Philosophy and Connectionist Theory*, eds. W. Ramsey, S. Stich, and D. Rumelhart, Laurence Erlbaum.

Dennett, Daniel, 1975 'Brain Writing and Mind Reading', in his *Brainstorms*, Harvester, 1978.

1978a 'Towards a Cognitive Theory of Consciousness', in his *Brainstorms*.

1978b 'Why you can't Make a Computer that Feels Pain', in his *Brainstorms*.

1988 'Quining Qualia', in *Consciousness in Contemporary Science*, eds. A. Marcel and E. Bisiach, Oxford University Press.

1991 *Consciousness Explained*, Allen Lane.

Dennett, Daniel and Kinsbourne, Marcel, 1992 'Time and the Observer: the where and when of consciousness in the brain', *Behavioural and Brain Sciences*, vol. 15.

Devitt, Michael, 1984 *Realism and Truth*, Blackwell.

Dretske, Fred, 1981 *Knowledge and the Flow of Information*, MIT Press.

1988 *Explaining Behaviour*, MIT Press.

1993 'Conscious Experience', *Mind*, vol. 102.

Dummett, Michael, 1973 *Frege: philosophy of language*, Duckworth.

1981 *The Interpretation of Frege's Philosophy*, Duckworth.

1989 'Language and Communication', in *Reflections on Chomsky*, ed. A. George, Blackwell.

1991 *Frege and Other Philosophers*, Oxford University Press.

Evans, Gareth, 1982 *The Varieties of Reference*, Oxford University Press.

Field, Hartry, 1977 'Logic, Meaning, and Conceptual Role', *Journal of Philosophy*, vol. 74.

1978 'Mental Representation', *Erkenntnis*, vol. 13.

Flanagan, Owen, 1992 *Consciousness Reconsidered*, MIT Press.

Fodor, Jerry, 1975 'Imagistic Representation', in his *The Language of Thought*, Harvester.

1978 'Propositional Attitudes', in his *RePresentations*, Harvester, 1981.

1981 'The Present Status of the Innateness Controversy', in his *RePresentations*.

1983 *The Modularity of Mind*, MIT Press.

1987 *Psychosemantics*, MIT Press.

1989 'Why Should the Mind be Modular?', in his 1990, ch. 9.

1990 *A Theory of Content and Other Essays*, MIT Press.

1992 'A Theory of the Child's Theory of Mind', *Cognition*, vol. 44.

1994 *The Elm and the Expert: mentalese and its semantics*, MIT Press.

Fodor, Jerry, and Lepore, Ernest, 1992 *Holism*, Blackwell.

1993 'Reply to Block and Boghossian', *Mind and Language*, vol. 8.

Fodor, Jerry, and Pylyshyn, Zenon, 1988 'Connectionism and Cognitive Architecture: a critical analysis', *Cognition*, vol. 28.

Frege, Gottlob, 1884 *The Foundations of Arithmetic*, trans. Austin, Blackwell, 1968.

1892 'On Sense and Meaning', in his *Collected Papers*, Blackwell, 1984.

Garrett, M., 1975 'The Analysis of Sentence Production', in *The Psychology of Learning and Motivation*, vol. 9, ed. G. Brown, Academic Press.

Gathercole, Susan, and Baddeley, Alan, 1993 *Working Memory and Language*, Laurence Erlbaum Associates.

Ghiselin, B., 1952 *The Creative Process*, Mentor.

Goldin-Meadow, Susan, Butcher, Cynthia, Mylander, Carolyn, and Dodge, Mark, 1994 'Nouns and Verbs in a Self-Styled Gesture System: what's in a name?', *Cognitive Psychology*, vol. 27.

Goldin-Meadow, Susan, and Mylander, Carolyn, 1990 'Beyond the Input Given: the child's role in the acquisition of language', *Language*, vol. 66.

Goldman, Alvin, 1989 'Interpretation Psychologized', *Mind and Language*, vol. 4.

1992 'In Defence of the Simulation Theory', *Mind and Language*, vol. 7.

1993 'The Psychology of Folk-Psychology', *Behavioural and Brain Sciences*, vol. 16.

Gomez, Juan Carlos, 1996 'Some Issues Concerning the Development of Theory of Mind in Evolution', in Carruthers and Smith, 1996.

Gopnik, Alison, 1993 'How we Know our Minds: the illusion of first-person knowledge of intentionality', *Behavioural and Brain Sciences*, vol. 16.

Gopnik, Alison, and Melzoff, Andrew, 1993 'The Role of Imitation in

Understanding Persons and in Developing a Theory of Mind', in *Understanding Other Minds: perspectives from autism*, eds. S. Baron-Cohen, H. Tagen-Flusberg, and D. Cohen, Oxford University Press.

Gopnik, Alison, and Wellman, Henry, 1992 'Why the Child's Theory of Mind Really *is* a Theory', *Mind and Language*, vol. 7.

Gordon, Robert, 1986 'Folk Psychology as Simulation', *Mind and Language*, vol. 1.

1992 'The Simulation Theory', *Mind and Language*, vol. 7.

1995 'Simulation without Introspection or Inference from Me to You', in *Mental Simulation*, eds. T. Stone and M. Davies, Blackwell.

Grayling, Anthony, 1992 'Epistemology and Realism', *Proceedings of the Aristotelian Society*, vol. 92.

Gregory, Richard, ed., 1987 *The Oxford Companion to the Mind*, Oxford University Press.

Grice, Paul, 1957 'Meaning', *Philosophical Review*, vol. 66.

1969 'Utterer's Meaning and Intention', *Philosophical Review*, vol. 78.

Grice, Paul and Strawson, Peter, 1956 'In Defence of a Dogma', *Philosophical Review*, vol. 65.

Harman, Gilbert, 1982 'Conceptual Role Semantics', *Notre Dame Journal of Formal Logic*, vol. 23.

Harris, Paul, 1989 *Children and the Emotions*, Blackwell.

1996 'Beliefs, Desires and Language', in Carruthers and Smith, 1996.

Heal, Jane, 1986 'Replication and Functionalism', in *Language, Mind, and Logic*, ed. J. Butterfield, Cambridge University Press.

1995 'How to Think about Thinking', in *Mental Simulation*, eds. T. Stone and M. Davies, Blackwell.

1996 'Simulation, Theory, and Content', in Carruthers and Smith, eds., 1996.

Hitch, G., 1980 'Developing the Concept of Working Memory', in *Cognitive Psychology*, ed. G. Glaxton, Routledge.

Holm, J., 1988 *Pidgins and Creoles* (2 vols.), Cambridge University Press.

Horgan, Terence, and Woodward, James, 1985 'Folk Psychology is Here to Stay', *Philosophical Review*, vol. 94.

Horwich, Paul, 1992 'Chomsky versus Quine on the Analytic–Synthetic Distinction', *Proceedings of the Aristotelian Society*, vol. 92.

Hume, David, 1739 *A Treatise of Human Nature*.

Humphrey, Nicholas, 1986 *The Inner Eye*, Faber and Faber.

Hurlburt, Russell, 1990 *Sampling Normal and Schizophrenic Inner Experience*, Plenum Press.

1993 *Sampling Inner Experience with Disturbed Affect*, Plenum Press.

Jackson, Frank, 1982 'Epiphenomenal Qualia', *Philosophical Quarterly*, vol. 32.

Karmiloff-Smith, Annette, 1992 *Beyond Modularity: a developmental perspective on cognitive science*, MIT Press.

Kertesz, Andrew, 1988 'Cognitive Function in Severe Aphasia', in *Thought without Language*, ed. L. Weiskrantz, Oxford University Press.

Kirk, Robert, 1967 'Rationality without Language', *Mind*, vol. 76.

1992 'Consciousness and Concepts', *Aristotelian Society Proceedings*, supp. vol. 66.

1994 *Raw Feeling*, Oxford University Press.

Kohler, Wolfgang, 1925 *The Mentality of Apes*, Routledge and Kegan Paul.

Kripke, Saul, 1980 *Naming and Necessity*, Blackwell.

Kuhn, Thomas, 1962 *The Structure of Scientific Revolutions*, Chicago University Press.

Lebrun, Yvan, and Hoops, Richard, eds., 1974 *Intelligence in Aphasia*, Swets and Zeitlinger B.V.

Levelt, Willem, 1989 *Speaking: from intention to articulation*, MIT Press.

Lewis, David, 1969 *Convention*, Blackwell.

1973 *Counterfactuals*, Blackwell.

1988 'What Experience Teaches', in Lycan, 1990.

Loar, Brian, 1981 *Mind and Meaning*, Cambridge University Press.

Locke, John, 1690 *An Essay Concerning Human Understanding*.

Loewer, Barry and Rey, Georges, eds., 1991 *Meaning in Mind: Fodor and his critics*, Blackwell.

Luria, A. and Yudovich, F., 1956 *Speech and the Development of Mental Processes in the Child*, trans. Kovasc and Simon, Penguin Books, 1959.

Lycan, William, 1987 *Consciousness*, MIT Press.

Lycan, William, ed., 1990 *Mind and Cognition: a reader*, Blackwell.

Malson, L., 1972 *Wolf Children and the Problem of Human Nature*, Monthly Review Press.

Marcel, Anthony, 1983 'Conscious and Unconscious Perception', *Cognitive Psychology*, vol. 15.

1993 'Slippage in the Unity of Consciousness', in *Experimental and Theoretical Studies of Consciousness*, Ciba Foundation Symposium No. 174, John Wiley & Sons.

Marr, David, 1982 *Vision*, MIT Press.

May, Robert, 1985 *Logical Form*, MIT Press.

McGinn, Colin, 1989 *Mental Content*, Blackwell.

1991 *The Problem of Consciousness*, Blackwell.

Mellor, Hugh, 1977 'Conscious Belief', *Proceedings of the Aristotelian Society*, vol. 78.

1980 'Consciousness and Degrees of Belief', in his *Matters of Metaphysics*, Cambridge University Press, 1991.

Millikan, Ruth, 1984 *Language, Thought, and Other Biological Categories*, MIT Press.

Morton, Adam, 1979 *Frames of Mind*, Oxford University Press.

Nagel, Thomas, 1974 'What is it Like to be a Bat?', *Philosophical Review*, vol. 83.

1986 *The View from Nowhere*, Oxford University Press.

Nisbett, Richard, and Ross, Lee, 1980 *Human Inference*, Prentice-Hall.

Nisbett, Richard and Wilson, Timothy, 1977 'Telling More than we can Know', *Psychological Review*, vol. 84.

Peacocke, Christopher, 1986 *Thoughts*, Blackwell.

1992 *A Study of Concepts*, MIT Press.

Perner, Josef, 1991 *Understanding the Representational Mind*, MIT Press.

Pinker, Steven, 1988 'On Language and Connectionism', *Cognition*, vol. 28.

1994 *The Language Instinct: the new science of language and mind*, Penguin.

Povinelli, Daniel, 1996 'Chimpanzee Theory of Mind?: the long road to strong inference', in Carruthers and Smith, 1996.

Putnam, Hilary, 1975 'The Meaning of "Meaning"', in his *Mind, Language and Reality*, Cambridge University Press.

Quine, Willard Van, 1951 'Two Dogmas of Empiricism', in his *From a Logical Point of View*, Harvard University Press, 1953.

Rosenthal, David, 1986 'Two Concepts of Consciousness', *Philosophical Studies*, vol. 49.

1991 'The Independence of Consciousness and Sensory Quality', *Philosophical Issues*, vol. 1.

1993 'Thinking that one Thinks', in *Consciousness*, eds. M. Davies and G. Humphreys, Blackwell.

Rumelhart, D. and McClelland, J., 1986 *Parallel Distributed Processing: explorations in the microstructure of cognition*, MIT Press.

Russell, Bertrand, 1921 *The Analysis of Mind*, Allen and Unwin.

Sachs, Oliver, 1985 *The Man who Mistook his Wife for a Hat*, Picador.

1989 *Hearing Voices*, Picador.

Schaller, Susan, 1991 *A Man Without Words*, Summit Books.

Schiffer, Stephen, 1987 *Remnants of Meaning*, MIT Press.

Searle, John, 1969 *Speech Acts*, Cambridge University Press.

1980 'Minds, Brains, and Programs', *The Behavioural and Brain Sciences*, vol. 3.

1983 *Intentionality*, Cambridge University Press.

1991 'Responses to Critics', in *John Searle and his Critics*, eds. E. Lepore and R. Van Gulick, Blackwell.

1992 *The Rediscovery of the Mind*, MIT Press.

Segal, Gabriel, 1996 'The Modularity of Theory of Mind', in Carruthers and Smith, 1996.

Senor, Thomas, 1992 'Two-factor Theories, Meaning Holism, and Intentionalistic Psychology: a reply to Fodor', *Philosophical Psychology*, vol. 5.

Shallice, Tim, 1988 *From Neuropsychology to Mental Structure*, Cambridge University Press.

Smith, Neil, and Tsimpli, Ianthi-Maria, 1995 *The Mind of a Savant: language-learning and modularity*, Blackwell.

Smith, Peter K., 1996 'Language and the Evolution of Mindreading', in Carruthers and Smith, 1996.

Sperber, Dan and Wilson, Deirdre, 1986 *Relevance: communication and cognition*, Blackwell.

Stalnaker, Robert, 1984 *Inquiry*, MIT Press.

Stampe, Dennis, 1977 'Towards a Causal Theory of Linguistic Representation', *Midwest Studies in Philosophy*, vol. 2.

Stich, Stephen, 1983 *From Folk Psychology to Cognitive Science*, MIT Press.

Stone, Tony and Davies, Martin, eds., 1995 *Mental Simulation*, Blackwell.

Turing, Alan, 1950 'Computing Machinery and Intelligence', *Mind*, vol. 59.

Tye, Michael, 1991 *The Imagery Debate*, MIT Press.

1994 'Qualia, Content, and the Inverted Spectrum', *Nous*, vol. 30.

Vygotsky, Lev, 1934 *Thought and Language*, trans. Kozulin, MIT Press, 1986.

Walker, Stephen, 1983 *Animal Thought*, Routledge.

Watson, John, 1924 *Behaviourism*, Norton and Company.

Weiskrantz, Lawrence, 1986 *Blindsight*, Oxford University Press.

Wellman, Henry, 1990 *The Child's Theory of Mind*, MIT Press.

Whorf, Benjamin, 1956 *Language, Thought, and Reality*, Wiley.

Wilson, Timothy, 1985 'Strangers to Ourselves: the origins and accuracy of beliefs about one's own mental states', in *Attribution: basic issues and applications*, eds. J. Harvey and G. Weary, Academic Press.

Wilson, Timothy, Hull, J., and Johnson, J., 1981 'Awareness and Self-Perception: verbal reports on internal states', *Journal of Personality and Social Psychology*, vol. 40.

Wilson, Timothy, and Stone, Julie, 1985 'Limitations of Self-Knowledge: more on telling more than we can know', in *Self, Situations and Social Behaviour*, ed. P. Shaver, Sage.

Wittgenstein, Ludwig, 1921 *Tractatus Logico-Philosophicus*, Routledge.

1953 *Philosophical Investigations*, Blackwell.

Wright, Crispin, 1980 *Wittgenstein on the Foundations of Mathematics*, Duckworth.

1987 *Realism, Meaning and Truth*, Blackwell.

Wyke, Maria, 1988 'The Assessment of Non-verbal Abilities in Aphasic Subjects', in *Aphasia*, eds. F. Rose, R. Whurr, and M. Wyke, Whurr Publishers.

Zangwill, O., 1964 'Intelligence in Aphasia', in *Disorders of Language*, eds. A. DeReuck and M. O'Connor, Churchill.

Index